CAMPUS WARS

KENNETH J. HEINEMAN

Campus Wars

**The Peace Movement at American State
Universities in the Vietnam Era**

NEW YORK UNIVERSITY PRESS

New York and London

NEW YORK UNIVERSITY PRESS
New York and London

Library of Congress Cataloging-in-Publication Data
Heineman, Kenneth J., 1962–
Campus wars : the peace movement at American state universities in
the Vietnam era / Kenneth J. Heineman.
p. cm.
Includes bibliographical references and index.
ISBN 0-8147-3490-1
1. Vietnamese Conflict, 1961–1975—Protest movements—United
States. 2. Peace movements—United States—History—20th century.
I. Title.
DS559.62.U6H45   1993
959.704'3373—dc20   92-27044
                              CIP

New York University Press books are printed on acid-free paper,
and their binding materials are chosen for strength and durability.

Manufactured in the United States of America

c 10 9 8 7 6 5 4 3 2 1

Book design by Ken Venezio

Let the word go forth from this time and place, to friend and foe alike, that the torch has been passed to a new generation of Americans, born in this century, tempered by war, disciplined by a hard and bitter peace, proud of our ancient heritage, and unwilling to witness or permit the slow undoing of those human rights to which this nation has always been committed, and to which we are committed today at home and around the world.

—JOHN F. KENNEDY

Contents

Epilogue: "We Stand against Fear, Hate, Systems, and Structures Not in the Service of Man": Legacies of Protest   257

List of Tables

Table

Acknowledgments

I thought that this work should begin by providing the reader with some autobiographical information which might explain in part why I came to have an interest in this topic. To begin with, I was born in 1962, too young to participate in the protest movements of the Cold War-Vietnam War era. My brother, however, was a college student antiwar protestor as well as a Vietnam War combat infantry veteran. In spite of the media and academic stereotype of blue-collar Americans as hawkish morons, my own working-class, World War II veteran father was opposed to the Vietnam War and wanted my brother to go to Canada in order to evade the draft. My parents were somewhat unconventional. Every time President Richard Nixon appeared on television, my father would rebut him point by point, convincing me that "Tricky Dickie" was evil personified. Lest we sound too liberal, my antiwar parents condemned the hippies and potheads who disrupted the 1968 Democratic National Convention in Chicago and voted for George Wallace in the 1972 Michigan Democratic primary. Our family hated Nixon, the Vietnam War, and the peace movement.

My favorite memory of the period involves our hippie neighbors who constructed a snow-sculptured peace sign which they spray-painted red, white, and blue. The other neighbors, who were Nixon supporters, reported them to the local police. Apprised by the sheriff that complaints had been made regarding their atheistic Communist display, the hippies cheerfully removed *half* of the two-fingered peace sculpture. I also fondly recall Earth Day 1970 when my elementary school required the students—a number of whom wore "Woodsy Owl" decals and were clad in granny dresses—to form a circle, clasp hands, and sing, "I'd Like to Teach the World to Sing in Perfect Harmony." Two years later, all but six of these junior countercultural enthusiasts voted for Nixon in a school mock election.

In 1969, I made a personal contribution to the Movement. Having been allowed to watch far too much television, especially the CBS Evening News reports on the trial of the Chicago Seven, I absorbed a great deal of incompletely understood information. Thus it was perhaps not too surprising when I told my second grade teacher that I would establish a school SDS chapter unless she stopped yelling at me for being inattentive. (I am mildly dyslexic; she interpreted my inability to complete assignments without repeated oral instruction as signs of laziness, disobedience, and stupidity.)

So much for autobiography; and now on to more important concerns. I have encountered many people in the course of researching and writing this work who were of great assistance. In particular, I must commend the numerous individuals who consented to be interviewed and provided me with copies of their personal papers. A few people must be singled out for their kindness: Ed Powell at SUNY-Buffalo for providing me with a place to stay while I undertook archival research at the university and enabling me to meet a variety of truly unique characters who happened by; Andy Pyle for letting me sleep in his home and for introducing me to many Kent State activists; Mim Jackson for sharing with me her experiences at Kent State, directing me to her late father's papers, and allowing me to make her little boy a bona fide chocaholic; Mary Vincent who, on the basis of a research inquiry letter which I had written to the *New York Review of Books,* invited me, sight unseen, into her home in Kent to pore through her extensive papers; and Steve Badrich and George Fish who, through numerous letters and telephone conversations, gave me a detailed account of the Michigan State Students for a Democratic Society.

A few words must also be said about the enormously helpful archivists who enhanced the research base of this study. Shonnie Finnegan and Chris Densmore at SUNY-Buffalo guided me through some fifty boxes of materials and were quite patient with me as I requested ever more arcane documents. At Penn State, Peter Gottlieb and Leon Stout dug through their collections to find every relevant piece of information. Also, the staffs of the Michigan State University Special Collections and Archives deserve recognition for their enthusiasm as well as for their foresight in collecting various

1960s era antiwar leaflets as soon as they were posted. Ms. Finnegan at SUNY-Buffalo undertook a similar course of action, braving tear gas and student mobs in the 1960s in order to gather documentation of those intense years. Who would have thought that the archival profession could be so exciting and dangerous?

Many scholars have read some or all of this manuscript, greatly improving my analysis and writing: Robert Doherty, David Farber, Todd Gitlin, Van Beck Hall, Samuel Hays, William Hixson, Irwin Marcus, Curtis Miner, Robert Newman, Robert Norman, Louis Rose, Ellen Schrecker, Mel Small, Robert F. Smith, Gerald Thompson, Barbara Tischler, Kenneth Waltzer, Wilson Warren, and Lawrence Wittner. Their encouragement and consideration have meant a great deal to me. Niko Pfund of New York University Press also deserves great credit for making this book possible and David Bailey merits my thanks for planting the idea for this kind of comparative study on me several years ago.

Finally, I must sincerely thank my former students at the University of Pittsburgh, the University of Toledo, and Iowa State University, as well as Juan Lopez, Gerry Pierson, and John Zimmerman for their editorial and computing assistance. I also extend my warmest regards to Ohio University-Lancaster which provided me with financial support to complete this work.

Excerpts from " 'Look Out Kid, You're Gonna Get Hit': Kent State and the Anti-Vietnam War Movement" by Kenneth Heineman, from *Give Peace a Chance*, edited by Mel Small and William D. Hoover, are used by permission of Syracuse University Press.

Excerpts from "The Silent Majority Speaks: Antiwar Protest and Backlash in the 1960s" by Kenneth Heineman, from *Peace and Change*, are used by permission of Sage Publications.

Excerpts from " 'A Time of War and a Time of Peace': The Anti-Vietnam War Movement at Michigan State University, 1965–1970" by Kenneth Heineman, from *Peace and Change*, are used by permission of Sage Publications.

List of Abbreviations

AEC	Atomic Energy Commission
AFSC	American Friends Service Committee (Quakers)
AID	Agency for International Development
ARPA	Advanced Research Projects Agency (DoD)
BDRU	Buffalo Draft Resistance Union
BUS	Black United Students (Kent State University)
CIA	Central Intelligence Agency
CNP	Citizens for a New Politics
CORE	Congress of Racial Equality
CSR	Committee for Student Rights (Michigan State University)
DoD	Department of Defense
FBI	Federal Bureau of Investigation
GLCO	Greater Lansing Community Organization
HOPS	Homophiles of Penn State
HUAC	(popular acronym), House Committee on Un-American Activities
IDA	Institute for Defense Analysis
KCEWV	Kent Committee to End the War in Vietnam
KLF	Kent Liberation Front
LCI	Liquid Crystals Institute (Kent State University)
MSUAG	Michigan State University Advisory Group (aka MSU Vietnam Project)
NASA	National Aeronautics and Space Administration
NUC	New University Conference
ORL	Ordnance Research Laboratory (Pennsylvania State University)

PFP	Peace and Freedom Party (Black Panthers)
PL	Progressive Labor
SANE	Committee for a SANE Nuclear Policy
SCLC	Southern Christian Leadership Conference
SDS	Students for a Democratic Society
SENSE	Penn State Students for Peace
SIL	Students for Individual Liberty (Pennsylvania State University)
SMC	Student Mobilization Committee
SURE	Student Union for Racial Equality (Pennsylvania State University)
SWP	Socialist Workers' Party
SPU	Student Peace Union
UCM	University Christian Movement
US	United Students (Michigan State University)
VVAW	Vietnam Veterans Against the War
WLF	Women's Liberation Front (Pennsylvania State University)
YAF	Young Americans for Freedom
YAWF	Youth Against War and Fascism
YSA	Young Socialist Alliance

CAMPUS WARS

Introduction

In the turbulent decade of the 1960s, so scholars, political activists of the era, and contemporary journalists have written, an affluent, socially conscious generation of students flooded into the universities. This generation became inspired by the black civil rights movement, repulsed by the Vietnam War, and angered by university administrators who denied students the right to champion political causes and speak freely on campus. In the name of *in loco parentis*, university administrators also monitored sexual relations between male and female students, regardless of whether they resided in dormitories or off-campus apartments. Desiring to change the culture and politics of the nation and the university, the 1960s collegiate generation rose up to challenge U.S. Cold War foreign policy and racism, and to abolish *in loco parentis*.[1]

To some former 1960s activists like David Horowitz and Peter Collier, this generation was a destructive one which intimidated faculty and administrators who did not embrace its leftist political agenda. Additionally, through violent protest and subversive propaganda, student and faculty militants undermined America's military effort in Indochina, sentencing millions of Asians to death or enslavement in Communist concentration camps. In stark contrast to Horowitz and Collier, Tom Hayden, a founder of the 1960s New Left organization, the Students for a Democratic Society (SDS), argued that his was a redemptive, not destructive, force in American society. Student activists politically empowered blacks, brought peace to Indochina, and exorcised malevolent Cold War spirits from the soul of the Democratic party.[2]

Regardless of the current political sympathies of Hayden, Horo-

1

witz, and Collier, activists from the 1960s have exaggerated their own historical importance, creating in the process numerous myths concerning the causes with which they identified. One myth, promoted by activists and liberal scholars, is that antiwar protest, its base on the nation's campuses, compelled U.S. foreign policy makers to end our military participation in the Vietnam conflict. In reality, even though antiwar protest turned the universities into ideological, and often actual, battlefields, the U.S. withdrew from Indochina because the war could not be won militarily.[3]

Another myth is that campus activism failed to bring about any lasting social changes. Student, faculty, and campus-based clergy protestors successfully limited the intellectual and political authority of university administrators. Activists reformed the curriculum by adding courses on peace, black and women's studies, removed nearly every restriction on student dating and participation in political organizations, created preferential treatment policies for minority students, and secured academic freedom and the right of unfettered speech on the campus. University demonstrators, by their example, also changed many Americans' attitudes towards drugs, sex, and marriage. The mounting number of divorces, teenage pregnancies, abortions, narcotics addicts, and cases and varieties of social diseases recorded since the 1960s underscore the broad cultural impact rebellious youths had on society.[4]

Youthful activists by 1972 also captured control of the majority Democratic party, driving out its blue-collar and ethnic Catholic supporters. In the process, liberal-dovish and radical social reformers transformed the Democratic party into a politically diminished organization which largely represented blacks and college-educated, upper-middle-class secularized Jews and White Anglo-Saxon Protestants (WASPS). By claiming the Democratic party as their own, affluent liberals provoked a political backlash among working-class whites which made the presidencies of conservative Republicans Richard Nixon and Ronald Reagan possible.[5]

There are myths beyond the glory-claiming or blame-placing ones mentioned above which claim the attention of this work. Almost every study of campus-based anti-Vietnam War protest in the 1960s and early 1970s has argued that student disaffection blossomed at elite state and private universities such as Berkeley, Chicago, Columbia, Harvard, Michigan, and Wisconsin. The proposition is inaccurate. Student and faculty rebellion germinated throughout

America's less prestigious state universities. Contrary to scholarly and popular belief, events at Berkeley and Columbia do not provide the paradigm for understanding the campus-based antiwar movement which developed, we are to believe, belatedly at less prestigious, culturally isolated state schools. The antiwar movement was not a belated development at the less well-regarded state universities, although there were gradations in the intensity and scope of activism. One cannot simply superimpose the Berkeley or Columbia model on other universities, thereby ignoring the differing cultural and historical context of each campus community and the ways in which those differences affected antiwar protest.[6]

The factors which have led to the universal fixation on protest at elite universities are twofold. First, contemporary journalists, activists turned memoir writers, and present-day scholars were generally trained at prestigious institutions of higher education. Such writers and elite-university educated activists shared school ties and high social-class origins which have colored their perception of events in the 1960s. Consequently, reporters and academics regarded the protest of the affluent children of the Establishment as far more important than the antiwar activities of working- and lower-middle-class students who overwhelmingly attended state universities. Second, there were some visually stunning protests at the elite schools which, due to the efforts of the news media, have become our dominant cultural images of the 1960s.[7]

These striking images come readily to mind: Berkeley activists in 1964 standing on top of a police car as they demonstrated for free speech on the campus; Harvard SDSers in 1966 waylaying Secretary of Defense Robert McNamara; Columbia student radicals seizing campus buildings in 1968; and black student militants at Cornell in 1969 brandishing rifles. Yet there is one event which does not seem to belong in such refined company but became nonetheless *the* symbol of antiwar protest: the 1970 picture of a teenage girl crouching next to the dead body of a Kent State University student who had been shot by the Ohio National Guard as it dispersed a peace demonstration. The events at Kent State did not fit the Berkeley-Columbia paradigm; indeed, it was an academically average state university far from where, scholars and journalists have reported, the real campus action of the 1960s and early 1970s was to be found. Since Kent State does not belong schematically in the same company with Berkeley, the shootings must have been an aberration. If so, then no further study beyond the actual events of May 4, 1970, is required.

National opinion molders and guardians of the public record, whether journalist or academic, perceive the United States as a cultural entity defined by the West Coast and the Northeastern seaports, with points in between consisting of Ann Arbor, Chicago, and Madison. There was in the 1960s, as now, little interest in exploring the rest of the country, let alone in examining less prestigious universities and their communities. Rather, we have come to believe that state university antiwar activists took their lead from elite-educated protestors. Consequently, we ignore protest in the communities of Kent, Ohio; Buffalo, New York; State College, Pennsylvania; and East Lansing, Michigan—the respective homes of Kent State University (KSU), the State University of New York at Buffalo (SUNY-Buffalo), Pennsylvania State University (PSU), and Michigan State University (MSU). Such Northern state schools are the focus of this book.

The great increase in the number of college students and faculty which occurred after World War II took place there, rather than at more elite locales. Columbia and Michigan could not compare in physical size and student and faculty population to MSU and Ohio State University. Other important, often overlooked, developments in the post-World War II history of state universities were their transformation from agricultural and teachers colleges into academically comprehensive institutions. So transformed, their administrators and faculties had aspirations to compete academically with the elite schools. Additionally, many commentators have failed to note the evolution of the state universities into instruments of American Cold War foreign policy. Although federal grants from Cold War governmental agencies flowed into many schools by the 1960s, the state universities became particularly dependent upon, and culturally defined by, such funding.

The origins of the 1960s campus-based peace movement are partially rooted in the universities' ties to the Defense Department. In the context of the escalating Vietnam War, university-military research projects became compelling symbols of complicity with the so-called war-machine and important rallying points for peace activists. Examination of several state schools illustrates the Cold War-inspired change in educational mission and reveals the nature of campus-based anti-Vietnam War protest. The ambitions of these institutions involved both the search for funds, leading them to undertake military research and in turn making them vulnerable to campus clergy, faculty, and student criticism, and the search for better students (often liberal arts majors in order to increase their academic prestige), bringing to the campus youths sensitive to the issues of peace and social justice. Thus were the seeds of protest planted in fertile ground.

In contrast to Harvard and Wisconsin, the schools studied here did not have a national reputation, then or now, as activist universities. To understand better the dynamics of campus-based antiwar protest, it is vital to study institutions where the majority of students and faculty were either prowar or apathetic—a more perfect mirror of American society in the 1960s. Historians and the general public seem to forget that the majority of citizens supported the U.S. military effort in Vietnam right up to March 1968 when President Lyndon Johnson announced that he would negotiate an end to the war. Moreover, academics and the news media of the era invariably conveyed the erroneous image that there was a generation gap in which youths overwhelmingly opposed the war while their parents embraced it. As far as the generation gap is concerned, George Wallace, the hawkish, anti-civil rights third party candidate for president in 1968, scored best among voters under 30 years of age. Further, one in eleven university students from working- and lower-middle-class Democratic households in 1968 voted for Richard Nixon.[8]

Given the hawkish sentiments of the majority of American citizens, including youths, it would seem advisable to focus on conservative campus communities. Such universities also claimed a much greater proportion of working- and lower-middle-class and Catholic students than was the case at Berkeley, Columbia, and Wisconsin. In consequence, the former were far more culturally, as well as ideologically, representative of the nation than the latter. At the same time, there was a significant level of antiwar protest to make our focus schools more interesting places to study than is the case with relatively inactive Southern universities.

Paradoxically, even though the campuses examined here claimed an administration, faculty, and student body which was either more hawkish or more apathetic than their counterparts at the elite universities, it is also true that antiwar protestors from these less prestigious institutions exercised considerable influence in the national peace movement. Penn State contributed two students to the national leadership of the antiwar movement: Carl Davidson, vice president of SDS in 1966, and Andy Stapp, president of the American Serviceman's Union in 1967. Struggling to define the political direction of SDS, Davidson unsuccessfully fought radical students from the elite universities who rejected his populist goal of building an ideologically inclusive, nonviolent peace movement which would join working-class youths and white ethnics.[9]

Michigan State SDSers in 1966 established the first campus-based underground newspaper in American history, *The Paper*. Its reporters—Steve Badrich, Michael Kindman, and Donald Mader—moved on to help found, respectively, the Liberation News Service, the Underground Press Syndicate, and the *Kudzu*. The latter was the first countercultural newspaper published in the 1960s South. Meanwhile, MSU claimed several faculty of distinction. Political scientist Wesley Fishel had in the 1950s, as an alleged Central Intelligence Agency (CIA) operative, made Ngo Dinh Diem president of South Vietnam and in the 1960s received covert financial aid from Lyndon Johnson to shore up academic support for the war. At the same time, Bertram Garskoff, a psychologist, attempted to build in 1967 a national radical third party movement, the Citizens for a New Politics (CNP). In 1968, Garskoff and his friends at MSU and Michigan—Bill Ayers, Linda Evans, and Diana Oughton—organized a SDS faction which evolved into a student terrorist group, the Weathermen.[10]

At SUNY-Buffalo in 1967, student government president Clinton Deveaux worked with Sam Brown and dovish national Democratic party activist Allard Lowenstein to deny renomination to Johnson. More significant in terms of national political developments, forty-five faculty members in 1970 were arrested as they occupied the university president's office in protest of the city police occupation of their campus—the largest number of academic demonstrators ever arrested at one time in the U.S. Two years later, a group of Catholic college and SUNY-Buffalo students, were charged with stealing over 30,000 Selective Service files. As a result of the trial in Buffalo, the federal judge established a national legal precedent; committing felonious acts against the state could be sanctioned on moral grounds. More than a decade later, Abbie Hoffman and Amy Carter, the daughter of former President Jimmy Carter, would cite such precedent when standing trial for harassing CIA recruiters at Brown University.[11]

Kent State activists merit attention beyond the events of May 1970. In 1963, KSU activists led by Tony Walsh staged protests which resulted in the university administration granting students the right to form political organizations and to speak freely on the campus. Those demonstrations occurred a full year before the celebrated Berkeley Free Speech Movement which journalists and scholars assert marked the birth of white university student activism. Again in 1964, Kent State activists beat Berkeley activists to the punch, establishing an antiwar group and staging peace protests months before the West Coast radicals founded the famous Vietnam Day Committee. By 1968, Kent State claimed one of the larger SDS chapters in the nation and activists such as Howie Emmer, Rick Erickson, and Mark Lencl in 1969 formed the leadership core of the Weathermen. The latter development became lost in the gunfire and political recriminations of 1970.[12]

This work will examine several themes. I intend to explore the growing involvement of the state universities after World War II in the execution of American Cold War foreign policy. This will involve laying out the state universities' increased reliance upon federal defense-related funding and the impacts of that funding upon the schools' educational mission and political orientation. The cultural and political values of the state university administrators also require great attention. Their attitudes towards university-military research, student protest, and institution-building helped to set the stage for the campus-based antiwar movement and subsequently shaped its ideological evolution. Further, I will discuss the relationship of local contextual factors to campus-based antiwar protest. Towards that end, I am studying a range of communities: a small, conservative college town (Kent State); a geographically isolated university which dwarfed the town in which it is located (Penn State); a university located near a major urban-industrial center and state capital (Michigan State); and a university situated in an economically decaying city with a large anti-Communist white ethnic community (SUNY-Buffalo).

Beyond the topics listed above, I will review the influence of clergy, faculty, and student activists' religious, cultural, class, and political backgrounds in shaping their responses to university-military research and the Vietnam War. By the same token, it is necessary to look at the profiles of hawkish students and faculty and, whenever possible, focus on several important conservative academic and campus leaders. Additionally, I will analyze the interaction of religiously motivated and Marxist-oriented antiwar campus organizations and the limits of cooperation imposed by ideological and philosophical differences. In the course of that discussion, we will see how the influence of class and culture led some individuals to embrace violent, rather than nonviolent, forms of antiwar protest. Finally, the process by which the campus-based peace movement became involved in community organizing will be explained. I will also analyze why in many cases relations between the community and the campus became so hostile that the peace movement accomplished little or nothing beyond the university's grounds.

This work is divided into three parts, the first primarily analytical and the other two narrative and chronological. In Part I, three chapters explore the mentality of university administrators, faculty, and students. Chapter 1 examines the origins of military research at the state universities and the attitudes of administrators towards such research and campus protest. The cultural context of each campus and a brief overview of local and state politics as regards higher education, anti-Communism, political surveillance, and social protest is included. Chapter 2 provides an ideological characterization of anti- and prowar faculty. Chapter 3 deals with student anti- and prowar partisans, discussing their ethnic, cultural, religious, and political backgrounds and employing some quantitative analysis. The relationship between antiwar campus-based clergy and students is also detailed.

Part II of this work, comprised of two chapters, renders a chronological and event-oriented discussion of the development and evolution, in a comparative context, of the campus-based antiwar movement. Chapter 4, covering the period 1965–1967, addresses the initial attempts to build an antiwar movement in an often unsupportive and frequently hostile environment. Despite great difficulties in organizing a peace movement, by 1967 each campus had become politically engaged, at varying levels, and faced with emerging tensions between the supporters of violent and nonviolent protest. This transformation was represented on the national level by the stark differences between the nonviolent antiwar march on Washington,

D.C., in April 1965 and the assault on the Pentagon in October 1967. Chapter 5, encompassing the chaotic period 1968–1969, examines the triumphs and failures of what had become a mass movement against the Vietnam War. This was a period when the campus-based antiwar movement expanded enormously, but also became increasingly divided and enamored of violence. It was also a time of national agony and ideological and cultural polarization, beginning with the Tet Offensive, through the assassinations of Martin Luther King, Jr., and Robert Kennedy, to the Chicago Democratic National Convention, Richard Nixon's election, and the founding of the Weathermen Underground.

The final section of the book is different in presentation. Chapter 6 focuses on the divisive year of 1970, the escalating level of political violence, and the impact of the Kent State shootings on the other campuses. The epilogue, discussing the years 1971–1972, describes the final days of the antiwar movement and its differing impacts on each campus.

PART ONE

"A New Generation of Americans . . ."

"Bastions of Our Defense": Cold War University Administrators

Military-sponsored university research in the United States dramatically increased during World War II as the federal government attempted to achieve technological superiority over the Axis Powers. The advent and intensification of the Cold War, and the United States' commitment to contain Communism, especially in the Third World, firmly joined together the university and the military. By the mid-1950s the Pentagon supplied $300 million annually for university defense research and the Massachusetts Institute of Technology (MIT) and Johns Hopkins were placed on the list of the nation's top one hundred military contractors. Thirty-two percent and 11 percent of federal research funds to universities in 1961 came, respectively, from the Department of Defense (DoD) and the Atomic Energy Commission (AEC). The leading university military contractors in 1969 were MIT, the University of California system, Illinois, and Michigan, each receiving, respectively, $97 million, $15 million, $11.6 million, and $11.4 million in defense grants. The Pentagon underwrote 80 percent of MIT's budget in 1969 while Michigan in 1967 held 64 separate contracts with the DoD totaling $11.8 million. Michigan in the 1960s also had more National Aeronautics and Space Administration (NASA) contracts than any other university in America.[1]

Universities in 1968 spent $3 billion annually for research and development. Seventy percent of this money came from the federal government, of which over half originated from defense-related agencies. One of every three dollars spent on university research and development had either a military origin or purpose. The AEC, DoD, and NASA, respectively, in 1968 gave universities $110,200,000, $243,100,000 and $129,500,000 for military-related research. Over 30 percent of all academic research funds in the physical sciences in 1971 came from the DoD while the DoD and NASA provided 65 percent of all research support in academic engineering in the early 1960s.[2]

The significance of military contracting to the universities can be shown by calculating defense-related grants from the AEC, DoD, and NASA as a proportion of overall federal government obligations to institutions of higher education. (See Table 1.1.) In 1966, 43 percent and 35 percent of the federal grants given to Michigan and Illinois, respectively, were from defense-related agencies. Conversely, 25 percent and 21 percent of the federal grants given to the University of Pennsylvania and Yale, respectively, were from defense-related agencies. In terms of defense-related funds as a proportion of overall federal financial obligations to higher education, the most prominent public universities, by the 1960s, often relied just as heavily on such grants as the private universities. The public universities were sometimes more dependent on defense contracts than the private schools.[3]

Private institutions of higher education, as opposed to the state universities, had been involved in promoting national security long before the advent of the Cold War. One way to illustrate this is to undertake a comparative study of thirteen presidents of private educational institutions and twenty-five randomly selected public university presidents in 1933. (See Table 1.2.) Ninety-two percent of elite university presidents had ties to the federal government and claimed membership on the boards of directors of influential foreign policy-oriented foundations or large corporations, many of which had substantial federal defense contracts. More important, 69 percent had rendered service to the federal government in the War and State Departments or in some agency concerned with national security. The entrance of the United States into World War I and the nation's subsequent emergence as a world power had drawn academics from the elite private universities into governmental service. After World War I, such institutions and academics, notably MIT's Vannevar Bush, remained involved in promoting national security.[4]

In contrast to the presidents of elite private schools, only 20 percent of state university presidents in 1933 claimed federal gov-

Table 1.1

Defense-Related Grants as a Proportion of Overall Federal Obligations to the Largest Private and Public University Military Contractors, 1966*

School	Total Federal Obligation	Defense-Related Grants	Proportion
	Private Universities		
MIT	$63,232,000	$46,754,000	74%
Stanford	$60,621,000	$29,417,000	48%
Cornell	$35,324,000	$15,051,000	43%
Columbia	$60,041,000	$20,877,000	35%
Rochester	$23,597,000	$7,647,000	32%
Chicago	$45,286,000	$12,313,000	27%
Penn	$38,908,000	$9,808,000	25%
Yale	$29,830,000	$6,340,000	21%
NYU	$37,688,000	$7,995,000	21%
Duke	$23,693,000	$4,728,000	20%
	Public Universities		
Michigan	$66,265,000	$28,700,000	43%
UCLA	$51,298,000	$19,722,000	38%
Illinois	$58,491,000	$20,718,000	35%
Maryland	$23,425,000	$7,525,000	32%
Purdue	$26,157,000	$6,461,000	25%
Texas	$38,208,000	$9,281,000	24%
Berkeley	$50,315,000	$11,830,000	23%
Minnesota	$35,208,000	$6,585,000	18%
Florida	$25,202,000	$3,755,000	15%
Washington	$35,575,000	$5,278,000	15%

*Calculations based on data provided by James Ridgeway, *The Closed Corporation: American Universities in Crisis* (New York: Random House, 1968), 223–35.

ernment service, primarily in agencies concerned with agriculture or education. None had been involved in the promotion of national security during or after World War I. And no public university president was a member of the board of directors of a major corporation performing defense work or of a foreign policy-oriented foundation.[5]

This situation changed decisively during and immediately after the Second World War. Sixty-eight percent of state university presidents by 1950 had served the federal government in some capacity. (See Table 1.3.) Forty percent had been employed in the Defense or

Table 1.2

Comparative Profile of Private* and Public University**
Presidents, 1933

	Private	State
Employed by the federal government at one time; member of a board of directors of a corporation performing defense work; on the board of a prestigious foreign policy-oriented foundation.	92%	20%
Formerly employed in a federal government agency engaged in the promotion of national security, e.g., War or State Department.	69%	0%

*Private (N = 13): California Institute of Technology; Chicago; Columbia; Dartmouth; Harvard; Johns Hopkins; MIT; Northwestern; Pennsylvania; Princeton; Stanford; and Yale.
**Public Universities (N = 25): Arkansas; Berkeley; Colorado; Colorado State; Connecticut; Delaware; Hawaii; Idaho; Illinois; Indiana; Iowa State; Kansas State; Kentucky; Massachusetts; Michigan; Minnesota; Missouri; Nebraska; North Carolina; Ohio State; Purdue; Rutgers; Texas; Washington; and Wisconsin.
Source: Biographical information derived from appropriate reference volumes on American educators in the 1930s. See Chapter 1, note 4.

Table 1.3

Comparison of Public University Presidents,* 1933, 1950, 1970

	1933	1950	1970
Employed by the federal government at one time; member of a board of directors of a corporation performing defense work; on the board of a prestigious foreign policy-oriented foundation.	20%	68%	72%
Once employed in a federal government agency engaged in the promotion of national security, e.g., Defense (formerly War) or State Department.	0%	40%	36%

*Same public universities as in Table 1.2.
Source: Biographical information derived from apropriate reference volumes on American educators since the 1930s. See Chapter 1, notes 4, 5, 6.

Table 1.4

Members of the IDA University Consortium

Private Universities	*Public Universities*
California Institute of Technology	The University of California system
Case Institute of Technology	Michigan
Chicago	Illinois
Columbia	Penn State
MIT	
Princeton	
Stanford	
Tulane	

Source: Ridgeway, *The Closed Corporation*, 146.

State Departments during World War II. Robert Sproul of Berkeley and Frederick Hovde of Purdue had worked under Vannevar Bush in the Office of Scientific Research and Development (OSRD) during World War II. Hovde brought former OSRD scientists, as well as defense contracts, to Purdue upon becoming president in 1946. The president of Iowa State, Charles Frieley, acquired a piece of the Manhattan Project in 1942 for his school and, in 1947, an AEC research facility.[6]

Administrators and faculty, with technical expertise in weapons development and foreign policy experience obtained in World War II, and with Ivy League pedigrees, flowed into the expanding state universities: Berkeley, Michigan, Michigan State, and Penn State, to name a few. By the end of the 1950s, the larger state universities had secured the requisite scientific personnel to be able to cooperate with elite private schools in defense research. This cooperation was formalized in 1959 by James Killian, Jr., chairman of the board of MIT, who put together the Institute for Defense Analysis (IDA), a private and state university consortium originally designed to evaluate weapons systems for the federal government. (See Table 1.4.) Smaller, less prestigious state universities, for instance, the University of Delaware and the University of Hawaii, did not amass the necessary scientific personnel and acquire significant defense contracts until the late 1960s when Defense Secretary McNamara announced the creation of Project Themis. According to the DoD in 1967, Themis was aimed at providing federal grants for military

Table 1.5
Project Themis, 1967

Project Themis grants in 1967 were awarded for research in: detection, surveillance, navigation and control; energy and power; information sciences; military vehicle technology; material sciences; environmental sciences; medical sciences; and social and behavioral sciences. The DoD funding agencies involved were: the Advanced Research Projects Agency (ARPA), the air force, the army and the navy.

Schools Receiving Themis Grants in 1967*

Alaska	Hawaii	Missouri	Southern Methodist
Arizona State	Indiana	New Mexico	Stevens Institute
Auburn	Iowa State	New Mexico	SUNY-Albany
Case Institute of Technology	John Carroll	Institute M & T	
Dartmouth	Kansas	North Carolina State	SUNY-Buffalo
Delaware	Kansas State	Ohio	Tennessee
Florida	Louisiana State	Oklahoma State	Texas A & M
Florida State	Massachusetts	Oregon State	Texas Christian
Georgetown	Minnesota	Rutgers	UC-San Diego
Georgia Tech	Mississippi State	South Dakota School of Mines	University of Houston
			Utah
			Virginia

*Kent State was awarded a Themis grant in 1968. It is evident from this list that, in spite of the DoD's intentions, a number of established and important university-military research contractors, notably the Case Institute of Technology, a member of the IDA, received Themis grants.
Source: Steve Halliwell (Columbia SDS), "Project Themis: DoD Awards Contracts," *New Left Notes*, 25 September 1967. Halliwell compiled this list from official DoD publications, among other sources. This list is accurate even if Halliwell is biased.

research to the "have-not schools." (See Table 1.5.) Both Kent State and SUNY-Buffalo received Themis grants.[7]

Elite and state universities differed not only in the timing of their penetration by the defense establishment, but also in the roles they played in promoting national security. Harvard and Yale in the twentieth century have generally served as national security managerial training and recruitment centers. Applied weapons research and technical assistance field operations in the Third World have not been the forte of elite universities. Since the advent of the Cold War, it has been the state universities which have received enormous federal grants for weapons research and development and have provided specialized personnel to staff technical assistance field operations around the world. Harvard and Yale graduates formulate national policy; Michigan State and Penn State graduates execute national policy.

Institutions of higher education received federal grants not only for support of defense-related research, but also to facilitate the universities' physical plant expansion and to provide financial aid to students. There were at least three major motivating factors behind the federal government's heightened commitment to higher education after World War II: first, the nuclear arms race and Communist revolutions in the Third World required highly educated engineers and foreign-area specialists to develop new weapons systems and counterinsurgency scenarios to advance national security; second, the nation's rapid economic expansion and the desire for sustained prosperity meant that industry needed more, and better trained, technicians; and third, the postwar baby boom created an enlarged pool of potential college students. Middle-class parents viewed higher education as a means to upward social mobility and expected the federal government to ensure that their children would be able to go to college. For these reasons, the university faculty and student population advanced at a phenomenal rate. Between 1948 and 1957 the number of faculty increased from 196,000 to 250,000. By 1968, there were half a million university faculty in the United States. In 1955, 2,418,000 and 242,000 students were enrolled, respectively, in undergraduate and graduate programs. The number of students more than doubled ten years later and nearly tripled by 1970 with 6,481,000 undergraduate and 816,000 graduate students enrolled in institutions of higher education. Public four-year institutions claimed 1,072,980 students in 1960 and 2,914,000 in 1965, or 59 percent of all college students.[8]

Political conservatism characterized the administration of American universities in the years following World War II. In 1958, 102 of 165 colleges and universities surveyed reported political firings of activist faculty. The drive to discipline activist faculty, as well as students, in part emanated from the universities' boards of trustees. In general, university trustees occupied executive positions in major corporations—companies which frequently performed defense-related contracting—and held conventionalist political beliefs. Twenty percent of all American university trustees in 1968 were on the boards of directors of leading corporations and 80 percent favored the expulsion or suspension of student activists.[9]

Clark Kerr, president of the University of California system, contended in 1963 that institutions of higher education had become "multiversities," the focal points of "knowledge production," promoting technological development in the private and public sectors:

The production, distribution, and consumption of "knowledge" in all its forms is said to account for 29 percent of GNP . . . and "knowledge production" is growing at about twice the rate of the rest of the economy. Knowledge has certainly never in history been so central to the conduct of an entire society. What the railroads did for the second half of the last century and the automobile for the first half of this century may be done for the second half of this century by the knowledge industry: that is, to serve as the focal point for national growth. And the university is at the centre of the knowledge process.[10]

Beyond its vital function as a producer of knowledge, the university was also, Michigan president Harlan Hatcher observed in 1959, a key element in performing the research necessary to ensure America's economic and military superiority over the Soviet Union. No university president in the 1950s and 1960s would have publicly disagreed with Kerr's and Hatcher's conceptions of the role of higher education in American society. A few, such as Martin Meyerson of SUNY-Buffalo, had private reservations, at least regarding the role of the university in defense research. And some, like John Hannah of Michigan State, embraced the idea of the university as "knowledge factory" and anti-Communist bulwark with unshakable fervor.[11]

Michigan State University

Born in 1902 of conservative parents, pillars of the Grand Rapids, Michigan, farming community, John Hannah dedicated his life to public service. Hannah came to the Michigan Agricultural College (later renamed Michigan State University) in 1922 to study poultry science. For the next nineteen years, Hannah worked as an agricultural cooperative extension agent for the college until succeeding his father-in-law as president—a position he held from 1941 to 1969. Hannah became secretary to the Michigan Board of Agriculture in 1940. Since Michigan was a key center of agricultural production, and food would be vital to the coming American war effort, Hannah attracted the attention of Eleanor Roosevelt. Soon, other prominent national political figures, including Nelson Rockefeller and Senator Harry Truman, heard about the dedicated and efficient agricultural expert and college president from Michigan. In 1950, President Truman selected Hannah to be a member of the International Development Advisory Board which formulated policies for the Point Four program of American diplomatic, economic, military, and technical assistance to the Third World. President Dwight Eisenhower in 1953 chose Hannah to serve as assistant secretary of Defense for Manpower and Personnel and in 1957 made him chair of the newly created Civil Rights Commission. Hannah remained on the commission during the administrations of Presidents John Kennedy and Lyndon Johnson. Upon his retirement as MSU president in 1969, Hannah joined the Nixon Administration, becoming director of the Agency for International Development (AID).[12]

As a liberal Republican educator, Hannah viewed mass, affordable, federally subsidized higher education as the best way to develop human potential and improve the quality of life for all hardworking citizens, regardless of race or creed. After leaving the Nixon Administration Hannah reaffirmed his conviction that

governments exist to provide the services and opportunities that make it possible for the largest number of people to develop the potential that God gave them so that they may make the maximum useful contribution to the society of which they are a part. This is the thinking that justified public education in the first place, that created public primary schools, secondary schools, colleges and universities. Political, social and economic systems change, but the basic role of education does not.[13]

To ensure that all people could attend college, Michigan State, unlike Michigan, maintained a virtually open admissions policy and endeavored to keep in-state student tuition at reasonable rates in order to attract lower-middle- and working-class youths. Envisioning a student population of 100,000 by 1970, Hannah undertook, in the early 1960s, the construction of the world's largest on-campus residential housing complex. In the years spanning 1950 to 1965, the undergraduate population rose from 15,000 to 38,000 and the proportion of liberal arts and social science majors grew from 20 percent of the student body in 1960 to 54 percent in 1970. Finally, the number of faculty increased from 900 to 1,900 between 1950 and 1965. By 1964, MSU commanded the eleventh-largest full-time student enrollment in the United States. At the same time, federal government support of MSU expanded so that by 1966 it accounted for 69 percent of the university's overall appropriations. Of the $22,369,000 in federal grants given to MSU in 1966, 18 percent came from AID to support the university's overseas technical assistance programs while the AEC, DoD, and NASA accounted for 11 percent.[14]

In addition to providing the masses with affordable higher education, the university, according to Hannah, also served as part of democracy's arsenal poised against the "menacing cloud of Communism," which threatened "the values and virtues so precious to free people." In an address to educators and military personnel in May 1955, Hannah proclaimed:

> Our colleges and universities must be regarded as bastions of our defense, as essential to the perservation of our country and our way of life as supersonic bombers, nuclear powered submarines, and intercontinental ballistic missiles.[15]

Given Hannah's ties to the military establishment, coupled with the fact that MSU was one of the original universities involved in Truman's Point Four program, it was logical that Vice President Richard Nixon requested the university in the spring of 1955 to undertake a mammoth technical assistance program in South Vietnam. From May 1955 to June 1962, the MSU Advisory Group (MSUAG) employed over 1,000 people and received $25 million from the the Foreign Operations Administration (later renamed AID) in an effort to train Vietnamese administrators and security personnel, thus filling the vacuum at the top bureaucratic levels created by the departing French colonial officials. Specialists from the MSU School of Police Administration quickly revamped the old Sûreté, the French-inspired Vietnamese Special Police, and in its stead created the Hooveresque Vietnamese Bureau of Investigation. Wishing to upgrade the civil police's ability to quash riots and protect South Vietnamese president Ngo Dinh Diem from his legion of enemies, MSUAG in 1955 requested the university to send: five hundred 60mm mortars; 32,000 grenade launchers; 200,000 rounds of riot gun ammo; 2,678,000 .38 caliber bullets; and 8,000 tear gas canisters. The MSUAG also, from 1955 to 1959, provided cover for CIA operations in Indochina.[16]

The university's relative success in South Vietnam led Washington to entrust MSU with more AID projects. MSU contributed 10 percent of the total number of American faculty technicians abroad by 1962, and the Police School had trained security forces in Colombia, the Philippines, South Korea, and Taiwan. In 1965, AID gave MSU $1,236,357 to establish and staff research centers in Africa, Asia, and Latin America and $643,000 for agricultural education programs in Argentina and Nigeria. In addition, the Department of the Army in 1964 furnished MSU with $239,162 to support the university's security advisory project in Okinawa.[17]

MSU's Vietnam Project, and other technical assistance programs in predominantly rightist countries, represented only one aspect of Hannah's conception of higher education as an anti-Communist weapon. In East Lansing, Hannah supported compulsory Reserve Officers' Training Corps (ROTC) for all male students, even while other schools made that program optional. At a faculty senate meeting in 1961 a motion to make ROTC optional passed by a vote of 350 to 150, in spite of Vietnam Project veteran and Police School instructor Arthur Brandstatter's cries that "the Moscow-Peking Axis" was plotting ROTC's demise in order to strip the West of its defenses. Hannah rose and observed that "since 1,400 faculty members, undoubtedly in favor of compulsory ROTC, are not here, this vote cannot possibly be valid. Therefore, I'm going to ignore it."[18]

Hannah's summary dismissal of that resolution was completely in character, for he would not tolerate being told what to do by people he considered inferiors: faculty and especially students. During the 1964–1965 academic year, Hannah was faced with requests by the Committee for Student Rights (CSR) that male students no longer be required to wear ties in the dormitory cafeterias and that female students not be required to make their constant whereabouts known to the dorm housemothers. Tired of what he considered the CSR's presumptuous suggestions, Hannah suspended its leader, history graduate student Paul Schiff, and ordered the school newspaper, the *State News*, not to print a word about CSR or Schiff.[19]

This incident was not the first time Hannah had sought retribution against a politically troublesome student and censored the campus newspaper. In December 1948, Hannah expelled Jim Zarichny, leader of the leftist American Youth for Democracy (AYD), for inviting the chairman of the Michigan Communist party to speak at an off-campus AYD meeting. Hannah had refused to recognize the campus AYD chapter in 1947 and vowed to expell any student who sought to promote the organization on or off the campus. In 1950, Hannah suspended publication of the *State News* after a reporter wrote an article critical of the American Legion for its belief that Communists did not have the constitutional right to free speech.[20]

Another example, in the spring of 1965, is illustrative of Hannah's hostile attitude towards student activism. Though chair of the Civil Rights Commission and a supporter of racial integration, Hannah was also a firm believer in law and order; accordingly, he condemned the Student Non-Violent Coordinating Committee's (SNCC) Freedom Rides in the South as well as civil rights demonstrations in East Lansing. When Robert Green, education instructor and advisor to the Southern Christian Leadership Conference (SCLC), led an open housing march on East Lansing City Hall, resulting in the arrest of fifty-nine MSU students, Hannah dispatched three university buses to transport the errant youths to the county jail. One result of this incident was that East Lansing police chief Charles Pegg, in cooperation with the MSU Department of Public Safety (DPS), established a political surveillance unit which compiled files on hundreds of faculty and student activists. These files, made possible in part by infiltrating various activist groups, were shared with the Michigan state police Red Squad and the FBI.[21]

Throughout the 1950s and 1960s the MSU administration closely monitored the political activities and beliefs of faculty and students. When Duane Chapman of the Young Socialist Club applied for a position in 1961 with the Mutual Service Insurance Companies of St. Paul, Minnesota, the director of Men's Student Affairs, John Truitt, wrote to the company apprising it of the MSU student's radicalism. In 1954, Hannah had threatened to fire any MSU faculty member who pleaded the Fifth Amendment before the House Un-American Activities Committee (HUAC). His concern with weeding out subversive faculty extended to personally blocking the promotion of American folklore instructor Gene Bluestone in the early 1960s, convinced that the professor was a Communist. The MSU president had came to this conclusion based upon information he had requested from the Minnesota state police Red Squad and after conservative MSU students complained about Bluestone's teaching.

Hannah's obsession with Communist subversion at MSU was all-consuming. At a speech dedicating the erection of a new campus building in April 1965, Hannah used this occasion to warn that "Peking-brand ideologists" had selected MSU students as "choice targets for exploitation."[22]

Hannah's opposition to student and faculty activism resulted from more than a simple resentment at having his authority challenged, his judgment questioned, and his anti-Communist ideology threatened. The president of MSU had many hurdles to surmount and many people to pacify in the struggle to build an institution respected for both research and teaching. University trustee and millionaire benefactor Forest Akers, vice president of the Chrysler Corporation and former sales director of the R.E. Oldsmobile plant in Lansing, which manufactured trucks for the South Vietnamese Army, did not approve of campus protest. Hannah also had to face down opposition from conservative faculty who feared change and loss of status within the university community. Ironically, the ambitious academics Hannah recruited in the period 1953 to 1964 to assume control over MSU's departments and colleges became increasingly critical of the university president. By the mid-1960s this group of academic superstars harbored a number of grievances against Hannah. They resented Hannah's insistence on the centralization of power which meant that the MSU bureaucracy came to a standstill during his frequent absences in Washington or abroad; and his authorization of autonomous residential colleges for humanities (Justin Morrill, 1965) and social science (James Madison, 1967) which siphoned faculty and money from the established colleges and became centers of student and faculty activism. The deans, supported by state legislators critical of campus antiwar protest, led a revolt in 1969 to limit the power of Hannah's successor.[23]

During Hannah's last five years as president, letters and telegrams from alumni, Dow Chemical executives, and American Legionnaires swamped his desk. Hannah calmly assured every critical correspondent that MSU was not a seething cauldron of revolution, but he worried privately about a backlash costing MSU needed business and government grants. He also had to appease a Michigan legislature still dominated by reactionary rural interests in order to maintain the university's state appropriations. This was a state legislature, similar to many in the Midwest, which in 1950 had: banned subversives and the Communist party; established a Red Squad in

Table 1.6

State Appropriations for Construction in Institutions of Higher
Education, 1963—1964

Rank	State	Amount of State Appropriation
1	California	$131,000,000
2	New York	$131,000,000
3	Illinois	$66,000,000
4	Pennsylvania	$60,000,000
5	Indiana	$58,000,000
6	Michigan	$47,000,000
7	Texas	$41,000,000
8	Massachusetts	$39,000,000
9	Louisiana	$34,000,000
10	Wisconsin	$34,000,000

Source: Seymour E. Harris, A Statistical Portrait of Higher Education (New York: McGraw-Hill, 1972), 728.

the state police; barred radical organizations from the ballot; and
required public employees to testify before legislative investigating
committees. On the other hand, this conservative legislature in the
1950s and 1960s consistently appropriated more money to institutions of higher education than was the case in many neighboring
states. In 1963, Michigan ranked sixth in the nation in state expen-
ditures for construction in institutions of higher education. (See
Table 1.6.) And Michigan, due chiefly to generous state-sponsored
student financial aid packages, claimed, in the fall of 1967, a larger
public university enrollment (187,565) than in the comparably affluent and populous Midwest or mid-Atlantic region states of Ohio
(145,294), New York (104,268), and Pennsylvania (126,829).[24]

Pennsylvania State University

Penn State, like Michigan State, harbored an academic inferiority
complex; the former with the University of Pennsylvania and the
latter with the University of Michigan. But unlike Michigan State
University, Penn State never devoted the financial and intellectual
resources necessary to overcome the inadequacies of its undergraduate and graduate liberal arts and social science programs. Throughout the 1950s and 1960s, Penn State remained primarily an engineering and agricultural school around which jury-rigged liberal

arts and social science departments were constructed. Two exceptions were the English and philosophy departments which obtained some measure of national recognition and became a locus of faculty and student antiwar dissent.[25]

Located in the geographical center of Pennsylvania, Penn State was, in the words of its eighth president, Edwin Sparks, "equally inaccessible from all parts of the state." The university's administration was equally inaccessible and, resembling many state universities in the 1950s, placed a premium upon political conformity. During the 1950–1951 academic year, PSU discharged the mathematician Lee Lorch for subletting his Stuyvesant Town apartment in New York City to a black family. Julian Blau, a mathematics instructor who criticized Lorch's firing, was unceremoniously dismissed. The Association of American University Professors (AAUP) PSU representative, the German-born historian Francis Tschan, declined to intervene on Blau and Lorch's behalf, feeling that Jews did not belong on the university faculty. A short while later, Wendall Scott MacRae, who worked in the PSU Department of Public Information, was fired for refusing to sign the state's loyalty oath which had been enacted in 1951 at the insistence of state senator and American Legion representative, Albert Pechan. University president Milton Eisenhower, convinced that MacRae was not a Communist, requested his reinstatement.[26]

Milton Eisenhower, brother of President Eisenhower and former director of the War Relocation Authority in 1942, became university president in 1950. He left PSU in 1956 to become the president of Johns Hopkins. Eisenhower added much-needed prestige to the university which quickly translated into faculty status-consciousness. Vance Packard, a sociologist and PSU alumnus, in 1959 recalled this anecdote:

> Some time ago, while visiting Penn State University, I found myself being escorted to a party by a dean. I mentioned to him, good-humoredly, that at Michigan deans were expected to arrive last and leave first. He laughed, and said they didn't believe in that sort of fancy protocol at Penn State. He went on to say, however, that at some colleges where he had served they had simply frightful rules of etiquette regulating social intermingling. When we arrived at the party, I noted that the party was in full progress. I noted, further, that no guest arrived after we did. We had been at the party for what seemed a short time when the dean came up to me and said he was ready to leave any time I was. There were about sixty people there. We were the first to leave.[27]

Contrary to outward appearances, Milton Eisenhower was not the dominant political figure at Penn State. That distinction belonged to Eric Walker of the College of Engineering. Walker, who had been associate director of the Harvard University Underwater Sound Laboratory, accepted in 1945 the position of head of the PSU College of Engineering. When Harvard's contract with the Department of the Navy ended in 1945, the British-born, middle-class Tory convinced the federal government to establish the Ordnance Research Laboratory (ORL) at Penn State, one of five Navy Department university weapons development centers. Penn State erected the Garfield Thomas Water Tunnel in 1949, the world's largest water tunnel designed to test torpedoes and the noise level of submarine propellers. From 1945 to 1965, the navy gave the ORL $62 million in grants, underwriting research which resulted in the development of the Polaris nuclear-tipped missile and a variety of torpedo prototypes. By 1961, the navy underwrote 76 percent of the research budget of the engineering college. In 1968, the DoD awarded $10,500,000 in contracts to PSU, representing 28 percent of the total federal obligation to the university.[28]

Walker's relationship with the military establishment enabled PSU in 1955 to become the first American university with a nuclear reactor capable of criticality. Receiving generous support from the AEC, the Penn State nuclear reactor had, by 1965, trained 175 scientists and engineers from thirty-nine nations. Selected to serve as chair of the Commission on Undersea Warfare in 1955, Walker became PSU president in 1956, a position he held until 1970 when he joined ALCOA of Pittsburgh. While university president, Walker was elected chair of the National Science Board, the governing body of the National Science Foundation (NSF), served as chair of the Naval Research Advisory Commission and made PSU part of the IDA university consortium.[29]

As student and faculty opposition to the ORL and the university's affiliation with the IDA mounted in the late 1960s, Walker reminded his critics that university-military research had contributed to America's victory in World War II. However, Walker's candid discussion of ways to assess the economic value of weapons research, delivered to military and scientific personnel off campus in 1969, only served to sicken antiwar activists:

Suppose that a cosmic ray capable of destroying all life within a radius of 100 miles would be developed. How would you measure the value of this in dollars and cents? Could you say that the research on it could be worth

100 million dollars—or one million? So you see that first of all we need a set of measurements for determining the value of projects.

In industry one can approach the probable return by estimating the net profits which might be expected to accrue from a product under development. In war, however, success is not measured by so simple a yardstick. It is measured, rather, by numbers of enemy dead or incapacitated, by numbers of our people not dead or injured, or by territorial gains, and our weapons are developed in accordance with what we think those would be.[30]

In the first ten years of Walker's presidency, student enrollment increased from 13,000 to 30,000. Penn State in 1965 had eighteen branch campuses claiming 7,000 students, while the main campus in State College enrolled 23,000 students. Although president of the fourteenth-largest university in the country, Walker, unlike Hannah, opposed educating the masses. Walker posited in 1971 that the country did not "need the land grant colleges to dig down, find talent and educate it . . . we have dug down and educated all of the talent there is and even if the world did need a lot more, it would not be available anyway. One still cannot make a silk purse out of a sow's ear."[31]

If Walker expressed contempt for land grant college students, he particularly loathed activists. To the PSU president such students were "arrogant," "naive" anarchists "eager to destroy what has been built up over the years" in the name of "social justice." In a December 1964 address to PSU Philadelphia Alumni, Walker postulated that the Berkeley Free Speech Movement (FSM) was part of "an organized attempt by foreign money to disrupt the universities of America." Communist agents, posing as students and faculty, he contended, sought to destroy American higher education by using the false slogans of academic freedom and racial equality.[32]

Political conservatism and insularity permeated all levels of the PSU administration. The fact that 21 percent of Penn State's administrators had received their doctorates from the university helped to foster an academically isolated and parochial mindset. Of the nineteen chief administrators and deans in 1970, 47 percent had come to the university in the period 1937–1947, prior to Penn State's spectacular growth. Many longed for a return to the bucolic pre-World War II era when there were fewer students, faculty, automobiles, and buildings cluttering the landscape. Obversely, 55 percent of Michigan State's eighteen deans and chief administrators in 1970 had come to the university between the years 1953–1964, during the school's rapid expansion. These Ivy League-trained cosmopolitans embraced change and growth.[33]

Ernest Pollard, the chair of the biophysics department, exemplified the attitude of Penn State administrators towards campus activists. In 1968, Pollard urged the expulsion of all student demonstrators and recommended in 1967 that "something violent" be done to the campus paper antiwar editor, and national SDS member, Bill Lee. Pollard was head of MIT's radiation laboratory during World War II and, after the war, had received a number of DoD research grants.[34]

Given Penn State's extensive and profitable ties to the DoD, it is not surprising that the administration denounced, and coverty spied upon, campus activists opposed to university-military research and the Vietnam War. The university routinely posted letters to the parents of student activists, warning them that their children were involved with the subversive SDS. PSU promptly honored FBI requests for information on students. In 1968, PSU maintained an informant network of two hundred student operatives—the largest in the nation—who cooperated with the fourteen FBI agents assigned to monitor political activism at the university. Ironically, the presence of so many FBI agents and student informers at PSU angered the Centre County Police Department. Jealous of his jurisdiction, the county police chief in 1970 summoned two activists to his office. He informed them that the university had placed wire taps on their phones and that the FBI was responsible for ransacking their apartments.[35]

The Penn State board of trustees enthusiastically endorsed the administration's political surveillance activities. This is understandable since Willard F. Rockwell of the North American Rockwell Company, as well as the directors of other major defense contractors, sat on the PSU board of trustees. Few university trustees were as outspoken and publicity conscious as those serving Penn State. In an October 1969 speech to the Bellfonte, Pennsylvania, Kiwanis Club, PSU trustee and state Secretary of Mines, H. Beecher Charmbury, made this sensational announcement:

> The Communist party is carrying out a very clever well-laid plan for the youth of America. They infiltrated our schools, our churches and now our entertainment field. Our young people [are] susceptible and sympathetic to the radical causes and the destructive, disruptive forces of the Students for a Democratic Society and this organization is ... both stimulated and financed by Communism.[36]

No Michigan State trustee, not even the deeply anti-Communist Akers, would have gone on record with such an inflammatory statement. This is largely attributable to the fact that public university trustees in Michigan are elected in state-wide contests and thus speak out as little as possible on controversial issues. In Pennsylvania, public university trustees are either appointed by the governor or invited to become a board member by other trustees. Because they are unaccountable to the electorate, state university trustees in Pennsylvania feel little compulsion to remain silent and avoid appearing foolish. Warren Bennis, SUNY-Buffalo executive vice president, discovered this in 1970 while interviewing for the position of PSU president. At his interview, a PSU trustee suspiciously asked Bennis if he had a "Hebrew strain" in his blood.[37]

The State University of New York at Buffalo

Warren Bennis in 1970 was desperately seeking to escape from SUNY-Buffalo. Since arriving in Buffalo in 1967, Bennis had fought losing political battles with conservative faculty, administrators, and city council members. Bennis' uncomfortable interview with the Penn State board of trustees was just one more distasteful incident in his personal journey toward complete disillusionment. The MIT psychologist had been lured to Buffalo by president Martin Meyerson's vision of making SUNY-Buffalo "the Berkeley of the East." Skeptics with a sense of humor depicted Meyerson and Bennis as academe's "Batman and Robin," seeking to do good in a sincere, campy sort of way. Less friendly critics dismissed Meyerson as "that Jew from Berkeley."[38]

Confronted with a limited budget, and yearning to transform the private University of Buffalo (UB) from a regional engineering and medical school to a nationally prominent, academically comprehensive institution, President Clifford Furnas (1954–1966) brought his university into the SUNY system in 1962. Although a former director of the Cornell Aeronautical Laboratory in Buffalo (1946–1954), a major defense research center, and assistant secretary of Defense for Research and Development (1955–1957), Furnas did not use his connections to the defense establishment to bring enormous military research contracts to his university. To have done so, Furnas believed, would have constituted a serious conflict of interest and made the university overly dependent upon the federal government. Hannah and Walker differed with Furnas on this point.[39]

Joining the financially munificent SUNY system permitted Furnas to, "correct the [University of Buffalo's] imbalance between 'practical' and 'liberal' programs." According to this native Midwesterner and engineer, "a university education should embrace something more than just practical training." To achieve that goal, Furnas allotted more funds to the English and psychology departments, authorized the establishment of a political science department and lured to the university such notables as the literary critic Leslie Fiedler. The university offered more financial aid to needy students so that "every person who has the requisite intellectual ability and is willing to make the effort should have the opportunity to go to college." Between 1962 and 1966 the university hired an additional 399 full-time faculty (a 42 percent increase) while full-time student enrollment rose from 7,350 to 20,000.[40]

If membership in the SUNY system provided Furnas with the funds necessary to improve his university, it also interfered with the school's internal operations and infringed upon academic freedom. As a state-supported institution, SUNY-Buffalo was subject to the 1949 Feinberg Law. This legislation required public employees to sign a loyalty oath and compelled employers to investigate them for past or present membership in un-American groups. During Furnas' negotiations with the State Board of Regents to bring the University of Buffalo into the SUNY system, he had been promised that the Feinberg Law would not be enforced at Buffalo. However, SUNY chancellor Samuel Gould disregarded this agreement and in December 1964 dismissed SUNY-Buffalo English instructor Paul Sporn for hiding past radical activities from the state.[41]

To Furnas, Gould's intervention was galling. At the height of the McCarthy Era, the private University of Buffalo had resisted government pressure to fire philosophy professor William Parry for pleading the Fifth Amendment in May 1953 before HUAC in Washington. The university had conducted its own investigation and determined that Parry, past Communist party membership notwithstanding, was not indoctrinating his students. Now, as a state school, several faculty, in addition to Sporn, were being discharged and various individuals had taken it upon themselves to cleanse the university of Communists. Furnas found himself in 1963 defending the continued employment of Parry and in 1964 afffirming the right of faculty and students to picket HUAC's Buffalo hearings. Gould let it be known that Furnas would be retiring in the near future.[42]

The SUNY Board of Regents in 1966 chose Martin Meyerson to succeed Furnas as president. Meyerson was an atypical state university president. To begin with he was young, 44 years old in 1966, Jewish, and a Great Society liberal who tolerated, and at times seemed to encourage, nonviolent campus protest. Meyerson also possessed impressive academic credentials: full professor at the University of Pennsylvania at the age of 30 (1952–1956); and acting chancellor of Berkeley (1965–1966). As Berkeley chancellor, Meyerson upheld the students' right to engage in acts of civil disobedience as long as the rights of others were respected. Since Meyerson considered the Berkeley "Filthy Speech Movement," the questionable successor to the 1964 Free Speech Movement, to be offensive to the academic community, he had suspended three student activists for carrying placards which read, "Fuck!" Weary of crossing swords with an increasingly reactionary University of California Board of Regents, Meyerson resigned and headed to SUNY-Buffalo, a school which he felt had the potential to be a catalyst for regional economic development and urban renewal.[43]

Immediately upon his installation, Meyerson confronted intense opposition from reactionary faculty and administrators, notably in engineering and medicine. These conservatives had opposed joining the SUNY system in 1962 and resented the university's increased emphasis on liberal arts programs. However, they had muted their dissent because of Furnas' popularity in the Buffalo community. Since Meyerson was an outsider, with no political clout in Buffalo and Albany or, for that matter, Washington, engineering and medical faculty felt free to criticize openly the new regime and contribute to its demise. The political weakness of the Meyerson regime was underscored when a number of faculty in biophysics, engineering, and medicine, desiring to enhance their academic prestige in the scientific community, threatened to resign unless they were allowed to work on Pentagon projects. Personally opposed to university-military research, but not wishing to be held accountable for the decimation of the Medical School, the oldest and most prestigious school at the university, Meyerson agreed to accept in 1967 a $1.2 million Themis grant. This grant, from the Department of the Navy, was to support research on the physiological possibilities of building submarine servicing centers on the ocean floor. Academic politics also required Meyerson to defend Project Themis and criticize campus activists opposed to university-military research.[44]

Student and faculty protest against Themis, and efforts to prevent CIA, Dow Chemical, and military personnel from recruiting on campus in 1967, placed Meyerson in an uncomfortable position. Although opposed to the Vietnam War, Meyerson wished to maintain an academic environment which allowed all interests to be represented, including the DoD:

If we bar some recruiters, shall we bar not all? And if we impose such a bar . . . may it not be extended in the name of conscience to many academic activities as well?

I do not think that anyone . . . is unaware that on campuses today the torment to individual consciences, the ethical dilemmas, and the impulses to passion are linked to the war in Vietnam.

But, if, in the name of that torment, we tarnish the heritage of our universities—a heritage committed among other things to peaceful dissent respectful of the rights of others—we will have damaged those institutions most vulnerable to attack and which are our greatest hope for the future.[45]

Meyerson's pleas for moderation carried little weight with antiwar students and faculty, particularly since having accepted the Themis grant, he inadvertantly eased the way for further military penetration of SUNY-Buffalo. The DoD's share of sponsored research at the university advanced from $309,612 in 1965 to $649,907 in 1969, (a 48 percent increase). Funds for sponsored research in 1969 from such Cold War agencies as the AEC, AID, and NASA rose 71 percent over their 1965 share. By 1969, defense-related agencies accounted for 11 percent of all federally sponsored research at the university, and SUNY-Buffalo, in addition to Themis research, was undertaking chemical and biological warfare studies for the DoD.[46]

One of Meyerson's first decisions as SUNY-Buffalo president was to raise admissions standards so that they were on a par with the Ivy League. This shattered alumni and community support for Meyerson. A. P. Aversano, vice president of the Foster-Milburn company of Buffalo, resigned in 1968 as president of the General Alumni Board because the new admissions standards discriminated against less well-educated local youths. The influx of Jewish students from New York City, some of whom were "red diaper babies," the offspring of Old Left activists, further alienated the Buffalo community. Lower-middle-class and blue-collar Poles and Italians, the city's political power base, seeing their children denied admittance to the university, began to call SUNY-Buffalo "Tel-Aviv Tech" and "Jew B," a play upon its former, popular name, UB. Common Councilman

Gus Franczyk in April 1966 denounced campus antiwar activists as "subversives," while state senate majority leader Earl Brydges, R-Wilson, investigated SUNY-Buffalo for providing university facilities to SDS. By 1968–1969, conservatives in the faculty and administration, allied with resentful alumni and community leaders, attempted to impede many of Meyerson's academic reforms, one of which was the storefront colleges. The storefront colleges, modeled after Michigan State's residential colleges, had become centers of student and faculty activism.[47]

Riotous confrontations between the Buffalo Police Department and students and faculty in the 1960s and early 1970s were so common that the student government in 1970 began distributing bail fund service information cards. The Buffalo Police Department photographed campus antiwar protestors and then, with clubs, motorcycles, and tear gas, broke up peaceful demonstrations. In 1968, the Buffalo police commissioner, Frank Felicetta, informed HUAC that the SUNY-Buffalo Youth Against War and Fascism (YAWF), a Maoist student group, had fomented the 1967 race riot. Campus security officers and the anti-Meyerson faction in the administration cooperated with the Buffalo Police Department in wire tapping activists' telephones, photographing peace demonstrations, and tailing prominent faculty antiwar leaders.[48]

The SUNY-Buffalo activist student and faculty relationship to the FBI was no less stormy. From 1965 to 1973, the Buffalo office of the FBI compiled 17,000 pages of files on just the SDS and the Buffalo Draft Resistance Union (BDRU), and placed an agent in the former group's leadership. This agent successfully advocated violent confrontations with law enforcement officers and noncooperation with "bourgeois liberals." A FBI investigation of a conscientious objector applicant and former antiwar student activist prompted his dismissal as a Buffalo school teacher. While questioning school district officials, FBI agents implied that the activist was a sexual deviant and a drug abuser. In field reports FBI agents described one member of the SUNY-Buffalo YAWF as "a strange individual and possibly a homosexual," as well as "somewhat mentally unstable." With unintended irony the FBI concluded that this person was a "paranoid having delusions of persecution." The FBI also reported that a female member of the BDRU and YAWF was "a Negro lover," for "she always smiles very openly whenever a black man passes by her."[49]

Kent State University

Political surveillance was prevalent at nearly every American university in the 1960s. Undercover police and FBI agents were discovered or acknowledged in 1969 on at least sixteen campuses, including Berkeley, Harvard, Minnesota, Ohio State, and Kent State. At Kent State, Maggie Murvay exploited her position as a campus radio reporter to collect information for the police on antiwar activists. Kent police chief Roy Thompson, who employed Murvay and other conservative student informers, reiterated to local civic groups that "they got a lot of these people over on that campus [Kent State] who I don't suppose are plain Communists, but an awful lot of them are pinkos." One of Thompson's chief allies, student government president Frank Frisina, in 1969 distributed anti-SDS circulars on campus warning of "outside agitators," and pledged to eradicate drugs (and pot-smoking antiwar activists) from the university.[50]

Anti-Communism and an unwillingness to invest in public higher education were the hallmarks of Ohio's political establishment in the decades after World War II. Michigan, New York, and Pennsylvania in 1963–1964 ranked among the top ten states in appropriations for construction in institutions of higher education. Ohio did not. One reason for this disparity is that the Ohio legislature viewed universities as potential breeding grounds for political subversion. After Ohio State University physicist Byron Darling invoked the Fifth Amendment before HUAC in 1953, the legislature overwhelmingly passed a bill to dismiss any public employee affiliated with subversive organizations. State auditor James Rhodes in 1953 promised to withhold appropriations from Ohio State unless Byron Darling was immediately fired. Ohio State promptly dismissed Darling, as well as other faculty, expelled radical students, and banned Communist speakers from the campus. And the Ohio Un-American Activities Committee, established in 1951, held hearings across the state in the 1950s investigating Communism at the universities. Kent State avoided Rhodes' and the Ohio Un-American Activities Committee's wrath in the 1950s by not knowingly hiring potentially troublesome faculty.[51]

Kent State, unlike MSU, PSU, and SUNY-Buffalo, remained a small teaching, rather than research, oriented institution during the 1940s and 1950s. This changed in 1959 when KSU began to offer doctoral degrees, providing research-oriented faculty with a pool of inexpensive graduate student labor and attracting scientific talent. Kent State in 1965 established the Liquid Crystals Institute (LCI) with support from the air force and army and the DoD's Advanced Research Projects Agency. The LCI, a center for physical science research, received an $800,000 Themis grant in 1968 to develop liquid crystal detectors for the army. These crystals, placed along the Ho Chi Minh Trail by Navy Seals, were designed to detect the presence, speed, and direction of North Vietnamese Army tanks and trucks. When a vehicle passed a liquid crystal detector, a beacon would be relayed to an orbiting satellite and then flashed to an aircraft carrier which then launched its strike force. Prior to Project Themis, the Department of Health, Education, and Welfare had been the university's chief source of federal funding. After 1968, the DoD became KSU's major federal benefactor. The university's eagerness to obtain defense-related grants stemmed from its difficulties in extracting funds from a fiscally conservative state legislature.[52]

As Kent State's student population rose from 5,000 in 1954 to 21,308 by 1966, becoming the twenty-seventh largest university in the United States, university president Robert White (1963–1971) confronted increased campus restlessness. In May 1969, White asserted that there were two dangerous groups who threatened the universities:

First, there are the SDS and its type. With an acknowledged avowal of destruction for destruction's sake; with an acknowledged philosophical rejection of the First Amendment, with a disregard for the rights of others, with a program of revolution solely for revolution's sake and without future objectives we can and must set them aside. . . .

Secondly, there are those whom I choose to call the "bleeding hearts," the ones who while they are no destroyers themselves are always instantly and automatically sympathetic to such culprits and strive to find justification for them.[53]

A high school teacher and principal by training, White cherished order and viewed liberal and radical students as juvenile delinquents. Conservative students who physically assaulted antiwar activists were only guilty of youthful exuberance. This attitude was in evidence at an April 1969 KSU SDS anti-Themis and antiracist rally. Seven hundred conservative students, a few of them armed with motorcycle chains and baseball bats, attacked two hundred SDS members and antiwar faculty. White suspended SDS's charter and declined to take disciplinary action against the prowar student assailants. After the National Guard slayings in May 1970, White blamed antiwar students for precipitating the confrontation, characterizing them as "human debris" who did not belong at the university.[54]

Like White, Kent State's academically undistinguished deans and administrators chose to ignore students' physical assaults on antiwar activists, fostering a climate conducive to the escalation of right-wing violence on campus. During a spring 1968 antiwar rally sponsored by the Kent Committee to End the War in Vietnam (KCEWV), several students fired pellet guns from a friend's dormitory room, wounding two dovish clergymen. Administrators responsible for student affairs declined to prosecute the culprits. The university did, however, file charges against KCEWV leader Ruth Gibson for chalking a notice of the rally on the library. Kent State had prohibited the KCEWV from publicizing the rally on the campus.[55]

The political environment off the campus was no less hostile to KSU activists. Kent was a small, conservative town, politically and economically dominated by Robert C. Dix, publisher of the local Republican newspaper, the *Record-Courier*, and president of the KSU board of trustees. Community residents heaped verbal and physical abuse upon activist students while the Portage County grand jury launched annual investigations of drug abuse at the university. Invariably, those students investigated, and subsequently arrested, for drug possession were well-known antiwar leaders. In 1966, the Ohio Bureau of Criminal Investigation (BCI), with facilities provided by KSU, opened a special laboratory. Staffed by graduates of the MSU Police School, the BCI cooperated with the FBI and the Kent Police Department in monitoring KSU activism.[56]

Ohio differed significantly from Michigan, New York, and Pennsylvania in that it never claimed an enduring progressive political tradition. The state's Republican and industrial leaders had vigorously resisted the New Deal and even after World War II did not reconcile themselves to the predominant liberal sentiment in both major national parties. Conservative state politicians in the 1960s, as in the 1930s, were willing to employ the National Guard to maintain order and score a few political points with voters. This was apparent in December 1969 when Governor James Rhodes, who had entered the Republican primary race for the U.S. Senate, mobilized *seven hundred* National Guardsmen to occupy the University of Akron following a Black Power demonstration by *three* black students. When campus protest exploded in early May 1970, after President Nixon ordered the invasion of Cambodia, Rhodes anticipated that a tough stand against unpopular radical students would seal his primary victory. The governor, and Kent mayor LeRoy Satrom, did not even bother to consult with President White prior to the Ohio National Guard occupation of Kent State.[57]

Exercising no political influence off the campus, and failing to administer discipline in an even-handed manner on the campus, President White was easy prey for critics on the left and the right. He resented student activists challenging his authority, as did most university presidents, with the possible exception of Meyerson. But White acted more decisively in 1968–1969 to crush dissent than Walker and Hannah did at their respective schools. This may be because White felt greater local and state pressure to do so than was the case in Pennsylvania and Michigan. Lacking political power, White had no choice but to comply with demands for law and order on the campus. White may have also felt some satisfaction in being able to exercise control over his students, the one group which had even less political power than the Kent State president.

It would have been inconceivable that an obscure mayor and a contentious governor could have successfully ridden roughshod over John Hannah. When a man is on a first name basis with Richard Nixon and Nelson Rockefeller, he does not tolerate interference with his perogatives of power. Consequently, law enforcement agencies had to request permission from Hannah before being allowed on the campus. And, though a committed opponent of the anti-Vietnam War movement, who became particularly enraged with MSU SDS, Hannah tried to avoid summoning local and state police officers to campus to squash antiwar protest—quite unlike White and Walker.

Certainly, Hannah was an administrator obssessed with international and domestic Communist subversion, willing to tie his university to the defense establishment. Yet, he also supported mass education and strove to insure that all Americans, regardless of race, religion, or class origins, would be able to obtain a college education. Although Meyerson may have been less authoritarian and concerned with leftist political dissent than Hannah, he was much more of an elitist. Good intentions notwithstanding, Meyerson's decision to raise admissions standards, and desire to emulate the academic pretensions of the Ivy League, meant that the SUNY-Buffalo student body would be solidly middle- to upper-middle-class, white, Protestant, and Jewish. For a Great Society liberal who believed in equality of opportunity, and loathed racial and religious discrimination, Meyerson became the most discriminatory president in SUNY-Buffalo's history. While it is regrettable that Buffalo residents lashed out against Meyerson and used anti-Semitic epitaphs, it is understandable. In his own subtle way, Meyerson was saying that the children of Buffalo working-class ethnic Italian and Polish Catholics had no place in the university and would have to be content with working in the steel mills or, more likely, remaining trapped in low-paying, unskilled, service-sector jobs.

Meyerson contended that the university could not succumb to engaging in politics by taking stands against the Vietnam War, curbing free speech by banning Dow, CIA, and military recruiters, or undermining intellectual inquiry by preventing faculty from accepting Pentagon research contracts. To the activist students and faculty, Meyerson's principled defense of a democratic system which waged war in Indochina and brought military research projects such as Themis to a university dedicated to instilling humane values, appeared hypocritical. Further, every action the university took, the activists argued, whether to permit military research or Dow or CIA recruiters on the campus, was inherently political and implicated the academy in supporting the war.

The university, of course, as Hannah frequently stated, was by its very nature an instrument of national policy, whether that entailed providing mass education to the citizenry or accepting defense-related contracts. Walker rejected the former function and embraced the latter. He would not invest in liberal arts programs or in improving the quality of undergraduate education at Penn State. In many ways, PSU existed primarily to perform defense work and to train skilled engineers who would, in the best of all possible worlds, then go on to work for military contractors. Elitism and anti-Communism combined to shape Walker's attitudes towards activist students and faculty. Indeed, the PSU president was not above denouncing members of the campus chapter of the conservative Young Americans for Freedom (YAF), who advocated student rights, as dangerous radicals. Walker would not stand for intellectually mediocre land grant college students, even conservative, anti-Communist students, presuming to tell him how to run the university.

It would be difficult to find four more dissimilar personalities and educational philosophies. The communities in which these campuses were located also could not be more dissimilar. In spite of profound philosophical differences, Hannah, Meyerson, Walker, and White, either by design or succumbing to the pressures of academic politics, acquired military contracts and tied the fortunes of their universities to a defense establishment committed to containing Communism in Indochina. The public institutions of higher education grew at a phenomenal rate in the 1960s, making administrative control an often illusory goal. As the Vietnam War escalated, and campus protest mounted, American society polarized. By 1969–1970, political confrontation and reaction became the dominant features of this polarized society. Political polarization was not new to the American historical experience. But, for the first time, university presidents were unable to escape its effects. Hannah and Walker would retire, sickened of the academy, while White and Meyerson would be driven from their institutions amidst bitter recriminations.

"Those People Would Do the Damndest Things": Faculty Peace Activists

Faculty political activism did not become widespread until the 1930s when many academics drifted in and out of the Communist party and its Popular Front organizations. But it was a rare professor who publicly identified himself as a Communist. Radical faculty activism in the 1930s consisted largely of semisecret educational forums. Fearful of losing their jobs in the midst of the Great Depression, Communist faculty generally shunned publicity and, if compelled to characterize their ideological leanings, declared themselves to be progressive New Dealers. Socialist and religious-pacifist faculty were more forthright in spelling out their ideology to students and the general public. They also considered their Communist colleagues' penchant for secrecy to be anathema to the university's mission of promoting open intellectual discourse.[1]

Stalin's Non-Aggression Pact with Hitler in 1939 led liberal and socialist faculty to distance themselves from Communist academics. Religious-pacifist faculty repudiated the Communist teachers in 1941 after the organization abandoned its antiwar stance and called for American military intervention against the Axis Powers. Disillusionment in the 1939–1941 period provided many faculty with the ethical and ideological justification for Cold War-era political repression of Communists. Literary critics Leslie Fiedler and Lionel Trilling, among others, advocated the dismissal of Communist faculty. With so many prominent academics pronouncing Communism to be a great threat to democracy, university administrators felt free to fire noncomformists.[2]

While many of the faculty victims of McCarthyism were Communists, a number were Quakers or committed civil libertarians opposed to governmental loyalty oaths and political investigating committees. Paradoxically, Communist faculty often only had to conceal their activities and remain silent in order to escape political repression. Their embittered colleagues would not do this and therefore suffered. The slightly older antiwar faculty activists in the 1960s refused to forgive the Communists for defending Stalinism and complacently looking on as civil libertarian, socialist, and religious-pacifist faculty were fired. Younger activist faculty who embraced the New Left could not understand academe's ideological battles in the 1950s and, further, did not appreciate Communist duplicity. Mistakenly, they tried to reason that the Peking or Hanoi regimes were different from, or superior to, the Moscow dictatorship.[3]

Contrasting political perceptions between the younger and older generation of faculty fed into their professional rivalries and resentments. The youthful professors who flooded into the expanding state universities in the 1960s were generally products of elite graduate schools and, as SUNY-Buffalo activist and historian Michael Frisch observed, were expected to become intellectual forces within their disciplines. Senior faculty, on the other hand, Frisch argued, "were from a sleepier era" and products of "provincial schools," with "little or no scholarly presence at all, and sometimes not even much graduate training." Not surprisingly, the faculty elders became embittered as the Young Turks shunted them aside. That the Young Turks did not share their Cold War conception of American society and foreign policy added insult to injury.[4]

Also important to understanding increased political tensions among faculty in the Cold War-Vietnam War era is the changing role academics played in American society. The image of the absent-minded professor locked away in an Ivory Tower had already lost its substance by the early twentieth century. President Woodrow Wilson issued the call for academics to enlist in the war effort. Many professors responded. Fifteen years later President Franklin Roosevelt summoned Ivy League academics to Washington to formulate and supervise New Deal, and later, war mobilization, policies and agencies. Once U.S. and Soviet relations deteriorated after World War II, academics, either out of a sense of patriotism, or because they became dependent upon federal research grants, vigorously defended American foreign policy. Frequently, the social scientists rewrote history in order to diminish the centrality of class, racial, and religious conflict in America. The academy had become politicized, and politicized at that, on the side of the status quo. Younger, less sanguine faculty perceived the intellectual corruption of the university in the 1960s and threw down the gauntlet at their colleagues' feet.

A 1969–1970 Carnegie Commission survey of 60,028 faculty at 303 junior colleges and private and state colleges and universities provides a useful social and political profile of American academics. Protestants comprised 67.6 percent of faculty, while 13 percent and 10.1 percent, respectively, were Catholic and Jewish. Nearly 30 percent claimed a father who had a college education. This statistic indicates the privileged backgrounds of many faculty, as fewer than 17 percent of Americans in 1920 finished high school. In 1969, 49.7 percent of faculty were 40 years old or younger, with 14.6 percent under 30 years of age—too young to remember the Great Depression, World War II, and Stalinist terrorism. Over 55 percent of faculty had received their doctorates after 1959 and 50.3 percent did not have tenure.[5]

Only 5.1 percent of faculty surveyed in 1969–1970 described themselves as radical, compared to 41.5 percent and 27.7 percent who claimed to be, respectively, liberal and conservative. A majority, 57.3 percent, disapproved of student activism and 83 percent considered radical youths to be a threat to academic freedom. More than 79 percent approved the expulsion of activist students and 26.2 percent argued that campus-based political demonstrations were inappropriate pursuits in an academic setting. As far as the Vietnam War was concerned, 18.3 percent advocated an immediate withdrawal and 42.3 percent hoped for a reduced American commitment and a coalition South Vietnamese government which would include Communists. An additional 32 percent wanted the United States to de-escalate the war *and* defeat the Communists. Just a minority, 7.4 percent, favored escalating the war.[6]

While faculty were nearly unanimous in their discontent with American policy in Vietnam, there was in 1969 a clear polarization on the issue of university-military research. Thirty-six percent felt that defense and corporation grants morally compromised universities and faculty. Obversely, 45.2 percent viewed classified weapons research as a "legitimate activity of the university." In spite of this division, a majority of faculty, 57.2 percent, candidly admitted that university-military research was not undertaken to advance knowledge, but rather to enhance particular academics' prestige.[7]

Faculty supporting liberal politicians and civil liberties in the 1950s, and sympathetic to the antiwar movement in the 1960s, were concentrated in liberal arts and social science departments. According to various sociological studies, only 12 percent of social science faculty in 1959 and 1964 described themselves as conservatives, compared to 41 percent of engineering faculty and 50 percent of agricultural faculty. In a Seymour Lipset and Everett Ladd analysis of the 1969–1970 Carnegie Commission's report on faculty, 49.2 percent of the 24,031 social science, humanities, law school, fine arts, and education faculty surveyed were supportive of student activism. Conversely, 72 percent of the 21,978 science, engineering, and agriculture faculty examined opposed student activism. Sociologists, social workers, political scientists, psychologists, and anthropologists, in descending order, were most pronounced in their liberalism and support of campus activism. Economics and humanities instructors were less liberal and approving of campus protest. Law school faculty were nearly evenly divided between liberals and conservatives, whereas education faculty were overwhelmingly conservative and opposed to student activism.[8]

There was a clear division within and between academic disciplines on the Vietnam War. Thirty-three percent of sociologists favored an immediate withdrawal from Vietnam and an additional 50 percent advocated de-escalation and the formation of a coalition South Vietnamese government. Seventy-three percent of English faculty supported an immediate withdrawal or de-escalation and subsequent formation of a coalition government. In contrast, 56 percent and 64 percent, respectively, of business and engineering faculty called for a military escalation of the war. Lipset and Ladd concluded that there was an extremely strong "progression to the right by the applied fields with a close connection to economic enterprises—business administration, engineering and agriculture." They might have added that faculty in the biological and physical sciences and engineering are more likely to receive defense-related grants than sociologists, social workers, and anthropologists. Consequently, they would be less likely to criticize an anti-Communist foreign policy which advanced their careers.[9]

The ideological spectrum of faculty antiwar activists ranged from liberal doves and religious pacifists to radical pacifists and New Left

partisans. Liberal doves and religious-pacifists pushed for a negotiated settlement of the Vietnam War and sought to work within the
electoral system to accomplish their ends. Radical pacifists and
adherents of the New Left critique of American foreign policy demanded an immediate military withdrawal from Indochina and rejected working within the electoral system. Instead, they endeavored through community outreach to transform public consciousness,
aiming at a metamorphosis of societal attitudes towards militarism
and racism. To further this goal, Richard Flacks, Jesse Lemisch,
Staughton Lynd, and 350 radical academics from eighty-five campuses gathered in Chicago in March 1968 to found the New University Conference (NUC). By the fall of 1968 there were twenty func-
tioning campus NUC chapters and seven hundred members, localized
in the Midwest and mid-Atlantic states. Faculty established NUC
chapters at Kent State, Michigan State, and Penn State. At these
schools, and others, NUC leaders were often fired for their antiwar
activism.[10]

Antiwar faculty adopted a variety of tactics to mobilize public
opinion against the Vietnam conflict, including petitions addressed
to political leaders, educational forums, on- and off-campus demonstrations, and electoral activities. Their ability to rally campus
and community frequently depended upon the intensity of opposition radiating from prowar faculty and students, university administrators, and local and state politicians. The relative strength or
weakness of the hawkish opposition also influenced the size of the
faculty antiwar movement, as well as the scope of its activities.
Depending upon the local political context, off-campus peace work
was just as extensive as on-campus organizing. Where the surrounding community proved to be unreceptive to the antiwar message,
faculty devoted their energies to campus mobilization.

Michigan State University

Between classes Wesley Fishel haunted the political science faculty
lounge, confiding to colleagues that his Vietnamese friend, Ngo
Diem, a MSU graduate research assistant, would someday be premier of Vietnam. Often as not, Fishel received incredulous stares,
for few MSU faculty in 1951 took this brash assistant professor of
political science seriously. But they had to admire the sureness of
his conviction and wonder how he had arranged for Diem to meet

with Francis Cardinal Spellman and Senator Mike Mansfield. After Diem became premier in 1954 and appointed Fishel as his personal advisor, MSU political scientists realized they were in the presence of a kingmaker. Less impressionable faculty, such as humanities professor Thomas Greer, scrutinized Fishel and chorused derisively: CIA.[11]

As the first head of the MSU Vietnam Project, Fishel coordinated in 1955 what was then the largest Third World technical assistance undertaking in American history. The MSU political scientist was tireless in his efforts to promote a positive image of South Vietnam and Diem. He approved the publication in 1958 of an attractive MSU Vietnam Project briefing booklet featuring photographs of alluring, air-conditioned Saigon villas for faculty advisors, and offering this useful information: "It is possible to take trips throughout the countryside on weekends or holidays and find a host of interesting things to photograph."[12]

In a 1959 article, entitled, with unintended Orwellian overtones, "Vietnam's Democratic One-Man Rule," Fishel praised Diem's love for democracy:

Is Ngo Dinh Diem a "dictator" or a "democrat"? As one examines the structure of the Republic of Vietnam and the behavior of President Ngo, he learns that (a) Ngo Dinh Diem has all the authority and all the power one needs to operate a dictatorship, but (b) he isn't operating one! Here is a leader who speaks the language of democracy, who holds the powers of a dictator, and who governs a Republic in accordance with the terms of a Constitution. The Constitution was written at his request by a National Assembly which he has caused to be elected by the people of the Republic.

Of course, MSU political scientists wrote the South Vietnamese Constitution to which Fishel referred and whose guarantees of religious toleration and fair wages Diem abrogated. But to Fishel, this was quibbling. Diem, he assured a group of state legislators in Lansing in 1961, was "a combination of George Washington and Abraham Lincoln."[13]

Diem terminated the MSU technical assistance project in 1962 despite Fishel's determined public relations efforts. The South Vietnamese leader took this course of action because of friction between his corrupt relatives in the bureaucracy and critical faculty in the advisory group. Two such professors, economist Milton Taylor and English instructor Adrian Jaffe, wrote an article in 1961 disparaging of Diem's dictatorship and contributing to the MSU Advisory Group's expulsion. Shortly after the project's termination, Taylor, Diem's former fiscal advisor, bluntly observed, "What Vietnam needs right now is an efficient dictator instead of a stupid one."[14]

Taylor criticized Diem's inefficiency, but, like many economists, political scientists, and Police School advisors, did not question the Cold War rationale behind technical assistance to the Third World. In contrast, MSU anthropologists in the advisory group, who had spent considerable time in the countryside undertaking cultural research, increasingly came to the conclusion that Communism would better serve the peasantry than an American-supported regime. Part of the explanation for this perceptual disparity lies in the fact that the economists and political scientists spent their tour of duty removed from the peasant majority, dealing solely with elite English- and French-speaking Catholic Vietnamese bureaucrats. At the end of the workday faculty advisors dined in Saigon's fashionable cafés and then retired to their villas, passing the evenings in the company of fellow Americans. Police School Administration professor Ralph Turner, who trained Diem's bodyguards, could only express bewilderment after his students assassinated the South Vietnamese leader in 1963. "Those people," Turner later said in wonderment, "would do the damndest things."[15]

MSU anthropologist John Donoghue gradually evolved into a pronounced critic of American foreign policy in Indochina. From 1960 to 1962 Donoghue lived in a South Vietnamese village under Viet Cong control. Appalled at the brutal existence of the peasantry, and disgusted with Diem's extortionate tax collectors, the anthropologist wrote scathing scholarly accounts of his experiences. In 1962 he also sought to reach a broader public through the Washington *Post*:

> There are villages in the south now flying Communist flags which are administered by the Viet Cong. But that is no reason to knock out a whole village, retaliating for terror with terror. Ultimately, we've got to get the peasants on our side, and that is not the way to do it. But the Kennedy Administration has gone along with this gadgetry and military build-up as the way the problem should be solved.

By March 1965, with the escalation of American military involvement in Vietnam, Donoghue had become sharply critical of America's Vietnam policy. He accused Johnson of deliberately distorting the truth and rejected the Administration's contention that a Moscow-Hanoi Axis inspired the Viet Cong rebellion in South Vietnam. "The people of the South," he argued, "have joined in a war of national liberation from the central government in Saigon."[16]

President Johnson's decision to send the marines to DaNang on March 8, 1965, galvanized Donoghue and other MSU faculty. Donoghue, and the noted MSU psychologist Milton Rokeach, helped to organize the nation's first Vietnam teach-in at the University of Michigan on March 24, 1965, and founded the MSU Faculty Committee for Peace in Vietnam. At MSU, the Faculty Committee for Peace sponsored, on April 11, 1965, the nation's second Vietnam teach-in. Thomas Greer, humanities department chair, and Lawrence Battistini, social science professor and, like Greer, a World War II veteran, participated in the teach-in because of their conviction that they "would not be like the silent professors in Nazi Germany who did not criticize Hitler's aggressive foreign policy." The MSU Faculty Committee for Peace declined to invite Fishel and other anti-Communist veterans of the Vietnam Project to speak at the teach-in, regarding them as Johnson's representatives.[17]

Fishel, chair of the MSU American Friends of Vietnam and, in his own mind, the foremost Southeast Asian expert at the university, castigated the doves. Joined by other MSU Vietnam Project veterans, including Turner and Taylor, Fishel accused the teach-in organizers of aiding Communist aggressors in Indochina. If the United States were to withdraw from Vietnam, they contended, South Vietnam, soon followed by Thailand, India, and Japan, would fall to the Communists.[18]

For the next year an acrimonious debate raged between anti-Communist MSU Vietnam Project veterans and the Faculty Committee for Peace. Greer and Fishel squared off in public appearances as well as in the columns of the *State News*. Unfortunately for Fishel, the exposé of the MSU Vietnam Project in April 1966 by the radical California-based magazine *Ramparts* damaged his reputation in East Lansing. After April 1966, there would be no organized prowar MSU faculty group. Indeed, a number of prowar faculty leaders defected to the peace movement. Economist Chitra Smith, an erstwhile CIA analyst and faculty advisor to the MSU People to People Association which, in cooperation with the air force, sponsored student trips to South Vietnam, signed an antiwar petition in February 1967.[19]

Fishel and Greer's struggle for the hearts and minds of the campus ensued against the backdrop of a long-standing contest of wills pitting Hannah against, to him, two particularly exasperating faculty members: economist Charles Larrowe and labor relations instructor Bob Repas. From the late 1950s to Hannah's retirement in 1969, Larrowe and Repas challenged the president on the issues of compulsory ROTC, academic freedom, student rights, political surveillance, and university-military research. Their persistence, and the critical news media publicity they generated, prompted Hannah in 1965 to summon Larrowe and Repas to his office. Gestering to a map of Michigan mounted on the wall and covered with red pins, Hannah informed them that each pin represented a place from which he received hostile letters as a result of their activism. Then Hannah, his voice rising, said, "I know there are at least three Communist agents on this campus." Repas, never one to pass up the opportunity to nettle authority figures, puckishly replied that there were far more than three Communists at the last party meeting he and Larrowe had attended.[20]

Prior to America's entrance into the Second World War, Repas' high school class had gone on a field trip to heckle Norman Thomas. After listening to the socialist-pacifist minister, Repas committed himself to Thomas' cause. He later managed Norman Thomas' various presidential campaigns in Michigan and, from 1950 to 1955, served as director of the American Friends Service Committee's (Quaker) Labor-International Affairs Program. Although devoutly anti-Communist, Repas railed against government infringements upon civil liberties, a stance which led him to be dismissed in 1953 as a Philadelphia public school teacher for refusing to sign the Pechan Loyalty Oath. When the MSU Young Socialist Club in 1962 invited a Communist party representative, Robert Thompson, to lecture at the university, Hannah barred him from the campus. Repas and Larrowe assisted the Socialist Club in locating an off-campus site for Thompson's appearance. Hannah's admonition that faculty should not be involved in leftist student activities had no effect on Repas' subsequent behavior. In 1969 Repas helped to organize the MSU NUC chapter.[21]

After MSU expelled Paul Schiff, graduate student leader of the Committee for Student Rights, in the spring of 1965, Repas, as chair of the local branch of the American Civil Liberties Union (ACLU), contacted Larrowe. Based on his investigation, Larrowe came to the conclusion that Hannah was personally behind Schiff's expulsion and had ordered the alteration of his transcript, eliminating his eligibility for readmittance to the university. Larrowe, Repas, and the ACLU took the university to court and obtained Schiff's readmission. As one result of the Schiff case, Larrowe and Repas compelled Hannah to create a standing administration-faculty committee on student academic affairs. This was an important victory since, in the course of their investigation, Larrowe and Repas discovered that the administration-faculty committee which recommended Schiff's expulsion existed only on paper.[22]

A World War II Silver Star recipient, Larrowe had left the military with a disdain for arbitrary authority and a heightened appreciation for political tolerance and diversity. Consequently, he had no difficulty reconciling support for New Left and liberal political organizations. Larrowe served as MSU SDS faculty advisor and founded a campus NUC chapter while he campaigned for Senator Eugene McCarthy in the 1968 Michigan Democratic presidential primary and worked with the liberal, clergy-dominated, Greater Lansing Community Organization (GLCO), counseling MSU students on the draft. He was one of the few somewhat older faculty activists who reached out to New Left students and younger, radical academics. Most older, liberal antiwar faculty put some distance between themselves and SDS and its academic supporters. Unlike many of his colleagues, Larrowe was willing to overlook New Left faculty and students' ideological and personality quirks.[23]

Antiwar MSU faculty found common ground in their opposition to American foreign policy in Indochina but sharply differed in their analyses of the causes of the Vietnam War and appropriate tactics for halting the conflict. Although responsible for helping to organize a Vietnam teach-in extremely critical of the Johnson Administration, Greer clung to the hope that the government would see the error of its ways. After Vice President Hubert Humphrey spoke at the MSU Auditorium in June 1965, defending Johnson's Vietnam policy, Greer handed him a peace petition signed by two hundred faculty members. He then spoke warmly to Humphrey, assuring him that antiwar activists did not blame the vice president for Johnson's wrong-headed Vietnam policy. Humphrey crushed the petition between his trembling hands and sputtered that he had been a foe of Communist conspirators long before Johnson had become president. Taken aback, the disillusioned dove walked way from Humphrey.

Greer continued, however, to believe that America was a peace-loving society, in spite of its government, and campaigned in 1968 for McCarthy.[24]

James Anderson, humanities instructor and, in 1968, faculty advisor to the MSU Resistance, a group of radical-pacifist students, rejected the notion that America sought to promote peace and democracy around the world. A member of the MSU NUC, this young Quaker propounded a radical critique of American foreign policy and institutions of higher education:

> The Cold War began as a determined effort by the United States to dictate the terms of self-determination to the colonial nations as they revolted against their weakened European rulers, as well as to "roll back" or contain a Communist challenge which for political reasons was interpreted to the American people as a monolithic tide of absolute evil. . . .
>
> The United States turned the Cold War into a holy crusade for the purpose of rationalizing, and so far as possible, concealing its own unabated appetite for empire.
>
> American universities, largely by their own choice, committed their intellectual resources to the preservation and extension of American power and domination overseas, and in doing so made themselves an arm of U.S. military and diplomatic policy, as that policy was conceived and elaborated by a small elite of industrial, military, and financial interests.

Despite Anderson's rejection of Cold War liberalism and acceptance of radical-pacifist civil disobedience strategies, he enjoyed the respect and friendship of his liberal antiwar colleagues. This was not true in the case of Bert Garskoff, MSU psychologist and a national NUC founder.[25]

The spiritual leader of Michigan State's New Left faculty and students, Garskoff came to the university in 1966. A member of the University of Michigan SDS, Garskoff advised the MSU SDS and in 1968 ran for Congress from Ann Arbor as the Peace and Freedom party (Black Panthers) candidate. The assistant professor of psychology in 1966 denounced prowar MSU students as hypocrites for not dropping out and volunteering for combat in South Vietnam and in 1968 attended university ROTC courses in order to demonstrate that:

> The ROTC program manipulates the university with its system of grades and course credit to recruit and train future officers. To accomplish its goals ROTC uses classrooms with their aura of intellectual authority to indoctrinate its cadets.[26]

Garskoff alienated many fellow Jewish antiwar activists when, at the 1967 Chicago convention of the Citizens for a New Politics (CNP), he endorsed the Black Panthers' anti-Zionist resolution and stated that white radicals were "just a little tail on the end of a very powerful black panther." In the fall of 1968, his friendship with Diana Oughton and Bill Ayers led him to ally with the University of Michigan Weathermen faction and attempt to propagate Third World Communism and Black Power at MSU. After Hannah fired Garskoff in the winter of 1969, Repas examined the dismissal on behalf of the local ACLU branch. The ACLU was unable to determine whether Garskoff had been ousted for political reasons or because he annoyed his colleagues by calling them "bourgeois assholes."[27]

Antiwar faculty at MSU were concentrated in the social sciences and the liberal arts. Of the 440 faculty signing a February 1967 antiwar petition, 63 percent taught in liberal arts and social science departments. (One-fourth of MSU's teaching and research faculty endorsed this petition, a higher proportion than was typical at many private and elite, not to mention, state universities.) Tenured faculty were just as likely to sign the petition as untenured faculty. Focusing on the fifty-five core MSU antiwar academics, several salient features emerge. Over 85 percent of activists were liberal arts and social science instructors and 93 percent were Protestant and, less frequently, Catholic. Seven percent of the core antiwar faculty, and 8 percent of the 1967 petition signers, were Jewish. Nearly half of the core antiwar faculty did not have tenure and potentially risked their continued employment. Finally, 78 percent may be described as liberal doves, compared to 22 percent who identified with the New Left. Nearly 63 percent of doves had tenure, as opposed to 42 percent of radicals, indicating the greater youthfulness of the latter group. The prominence of New Left faculty in the antiwar movement is underscored by the fact that merely 2 percent of all MSU faculty in 1970 considered themselves to be radical.[28]

Although Hannah monitored the activities of antiwar faculty, and occasionally dismissed those whom he considered to be the most objectionable, he avoided dramatic political confrontations with his thorny academics. He may have wished for Larrowe and Repas to disappear from the face of the earth, but dared not fire the former, a World War II hero, and the latter, a man with influential friends in the United Automobile Workers (UAW) union. Public opinion and

organized labor, which in Michigan is the cornerstone of the Democratic party, would not stand for their removal. The Hungarian-
Jewish criminal justice professor and antiwar stalwart, Zolton Ferency, who was chair of the Michigan Democratic party, greatly
enhanced the ability of faculty doves to engage in peace organizing
on and off the campus. Since Ferency was a Democratic party leader
and 1966 gubernatorial candidate, Hannah and hawkish Democratic
state politicians would not, at least openly, cross swords with him.
Faculty doves also had as an ally MSU trustee and labor lawyer Don
Stevens.[29]

Local clergy, who were deeply involved with faculty in electoral
peace campaigns and educational forums—notably Lynn Jondahl of
the East Lansing Christian Faith and Higher Education Institute,
Keith Pohl of the Wesley Foundation, Warren Day of the University
Methodist Church, and Truman Morrisson of the Edgewood United
Church—gave added credibility to, and public respect for, the MSU
antiwar movement. Faculty activists were also blessed with a vigorous local ACLU branch which championed academic freedom, challenged Hannah's power, and worked to abolish ROTC. Further,
antiwar faculty found an unexpected friend in the liberal Republican governor of Michigan, George Romney. A close associate of
Hannah, Romney was critical of the war and, in 1967, on the verge
of declaring himself a presidential peace candidate.[30]

This nearly unique combination of local and state political factors, coupled with the absence of an organized prowar academic
opposition after the 1966 *Ramparts* exposé, meant that MSU faculty
doves had significant community, campus, and state-wide support
and confronted relatively little political resistance. It was not often
that faculty peace activists held such a strong position on and off
the campus.

Pennsylvania State University

Fearing the probable demise of the Labour government, London's
workers in 1923 paraded through the city to demonstrate their support for socialism. John Withall, the 9–year-old son of a gas-works
laborer, defiantly marched with family and neighbors, singing the
battlecry of George Lansbury, "a revered and devoted spokesman for
England's workers":

Vote, vote, vote for Mr. Lansbury,
Punch old Blairy in the eye,
If it wasn't for the law,
We would break his bleeding jaw,
So we won't vote for Blairy anymore!

The Labour party lost the general election to the Tories in a campaign famous for its vicious Tory red-baiting. Withall's family immigrated to Canada.[31]

The New World, lacking Great Britain's rigid class barriers to higher education, was kind to Withall, even if the Great Depression of the 1930s meant the dole to his family. Securing a scholarship to Bishop's University, Withall received a bachelor's degree in 1935 and became a teacher. A socialist-pacifist conscientious objector during World War II, he volunteered to serve as a firefighter in England though he was not sent overseas. After the war, Withall obtained a doctorate in education from the University of Chicago. In 1964 he became the head of PSU's secondary education department.[32]

As a socialist-pacifist, Withall was "utterly opposed to all wars" and was intently involved in organizing Penn State's April 1965 Vietnam teach-in. Afterwards, the administration urged several of the younger antiwar academics "to behave more respectfully and patriotically" in the future or else be dismissed. The majority of Withall's colleagues in the College of Education supported the war and told him that his actions were disloyal. Political science faculty particularly raised his "ire by parroting the patriotic line that the government and the press churned out, despite their alleged knowledge and scholarship." Undeterred by faculty sniping, Withall in 1966 served as chair of the Ad hoc Committee for a Vote for Peace, supporting the unsuccessful congressional campaign of PSU Wesley Foundation director, Rev. Alan Cleeton.[33]

In response to prowar faculty charges of disloyalty, Withall defined in October 1968 his conception of patriotism and vision of America:

At the last football game, when the flag was being raised and the national anthem was being played and sung, I deliberately tried to envision the fine things that the flag and the anthem represent. . . . I recalled the humanitarianism of Eleanor Roosevelt . . . and the world-benefitting efforts of a Nobel Laureate such as Martin Luther King. I felt proud.

However, I sometimes remember the shameful things this country and members of this nation have committed. . . . When these loom large in my mind . . . and they frequently do these days . . . I feel sorrow and shame.

. . . I consistently balk at and refuse to mouth the phrase in the pledge of allegiance "with liberty and justice for all." If that is a claim that this country does presently afford liberty and justice to everyone in it I cannot accept the claim. If, however, that phrase is saying that this nation aspires to afford "liberty and justice" to all I can more readily verbalize it.

Given the education professor's background and outspokenness, it is not surprising that he disliked, and frequently clashed with, Walker, "a small-minded," "arrogant," and "immovable" administrator. Throughout the 1960s, in the unlikely locale of rural Pennsylvania, the English socialist and his Tory opponent contested the issues of the Vietnam War and university-military research.[34]

Warren Smith and Marvin Rozen, professors of theatre arts and economics, respectively, played key roles in organizing the 1965 Vietnam teach-in and, along with Withall, led the liberal dovish faculty. A reverent Quaker, Smith had been promoting peace issues at Penn State, with little success, since the late 1950s. Uncomfortable with Kennedy's handling of the Cuban missile crisis in October 1962, but hesitant to rush to judgment as the Soviet Union had precipitated the confrontation, Smith and the State College Friends meeting were unable to reach a consensus on an appropriate public stance. Penn State's Quaker faculty, the chief antiwar activists in the late 1950s and early 1960s, had no such difficulty in denouncing Johnson's Vietnam policy in 1965. The United States, they believed in this instance, was clearly wrong in bombing a largely defenseless people who were unlikely to attack America in the near or distant future.[35]

An indefatigable proponent of peace, civil rights, and free speech, Rozen served as moderator of the April 1965 teach-in and founded the diminutive faculty-student Ad hoc Committee on Vietnam. Although a liberal dove, the economist advised the PSU Socialist Club in 1965 and rallied faculty in 1969 to the defense of the SDS underground campus newspaper, the *Water Tunnel*, whose editors had been arrested for publishing pornography. During the October 15, 1969, Vietnam War Moratorium, Rozen convinced over one hundred faculty to cancel their classes and in the columns of the campus newspaper, the *Daily Collegian*, challenged the Nixon Administration's contention that an American military withdrawal from South Vietnam would undermine the United States' security:

it is asserted that if we do not remain steadfast in Vietnam, our national security would be endangered because this will embolden forces hostile to us to greater and more serious encroachments on our vital interests. Our credibility will be severely compromised. The clicking fall of dominoes, elsewhere as well as in Southeast Asia, is viewed as inescapable background music. If the survival of myth is criteria for truth, this argument must take some sort of prize. Nothing, however, could be further from the actual truth. For one thing, the rest of the world has correctly read the message of our failure to accomplish our will in Vietnam, and the death throes of our policy only prolongs the agony. What country in the world now thinks that the United States would consciously again involve itself in large-scale civil wars far from its shores? Who now is not aware that such conflicts can hardly be depicted as global and monolithic conspiracies of international subversion but rather largely reflect local conditions and the extent to which an effective and responsive government is in power? Who seriously believes that whatever will now happen in Vietnam must lead by itself, quickly and inevitably, to grave setbacks elsewhere? Does anyone still place credence in the argument that we fight in Saigon to avoid the necessity of fighting in Seattle, in DaNang rather than Denver? For another thing, our obsession with Vietnam has already cost us dearly both by straining traditional alliances and diverting our attention and energies from other parts of the world which are of much greater strategic significance and by causing us to neglect serious internal divisions at home. To admit our failure can only tell the world what it already knows; to attempt to sustain the illusion of accomplishment can only do further damage.[36]

The faculty doves, while an annoyance to Walker, could not be fired wholesale since nearly half had tenure. Radical faculty activists, on the other hand, generally did not have tenure and, consequently, were fair game. Of the thirty PSU faculty NUC members in 1969, all but one, the sociologist David Westby, had either been fired or had fled to a more politically hospitable environment by 1973. The university administration singled out labor relations instructor Wells Keddie for retribution, denying him salary raises on two occasions and in 1970 vetoing his bid for tenure.[37]

Keddie had come to the university in 1965 to teach in the Department of Labor Studies. A national SDS member, the economist assisted in organizing the April 1965 teach-in as well as the Ad hoc Committee on Vietnam. He also helped to found the campus NUC chapter in 1969. In November 1965 Keddie propounded the New Left critique of U.S. foreign relations:

It is possible to regret the loss of American lives in any war; when Americans die in support of a dubious regime unrepresentative of either Vietnamese or American ideals, one must object strongly. But when Americans of good conscience not only die, but kill defenseless non-combatants and then, in terms reminiscent of hunters' campfire talk, claim to have bagged instead a quota of Viet Cong, the immorality of our position is a flaming shame.

. . . Those who comfortably—and safely—urge the escalation of the horrors in Vietnam and who so indignantly accuse their opponents of cowardice and treason seem to have but one answer . . . "We must stop Communist aggression."

But just how is aggression defined? . . . Are peasant rebellions . . . "aggression?" By now we can find evidence of military support flowing southward to the Viet Cong. But could we in 1955? Or even in 1963, when our military experts so confidently predicted a military solution to the Viet Cong rebellion? If not, what aggressive acts are being charged, and by whom?

It is inescapable that for some in America "aggression" is synonymous with "we might lose." Time and again in our recent history those who so define aggression have had their way in the world and with our nation. It would appear that their successes in the world are now numbered. Shall they have their way with us once more, to our national disgrace and disaster?[38]

In various university forums in 1969, Keddie vainly attempted to bring together radical students and members of the United Steelworkers of America. He informed the steelworkers that they were wrong "to like best those students who are clean cut and respectful" because such youths hated the working class and sought to keep them "in their place." Invariably, the steelworkers rejected Keddie's call for a student-worker alliance, due, in no small part, to SDS's antagonistic tactics and support for the Viet Cong. Similarly, dovish faculty, as well as a few radical academics, had little use for SDS. Assistant professor of political science and PSU NUC member Jim Petras, who had been involved with the Berkeley Free Speech Movement, dismissed the campus SDS chapter as "abominable and irrelevant." Petras' criticisms of SDS in 1969 elicited accusations of being a foe of the student revolution, and prompted a death threat from a PSU Weatherman.[39]

Despite contrasting attitudes among the radical faculty towards the campus New Left, as well as dovish faculty distaste for SDS, ideological and tactical disagreements within the PSU faculty antiwar movement were kept to a minimum. Confronted with an antagonistic university administration and extensive political surveillance by state and national law enforcement agencies, and claiming few numbers until 1969, antiwar faculty justifiably felt under seige. Even after 1969, when more faculty came out publicly against the Vietnam War, their ranks remained thin. The university's decision to deny tenure to Keddie in 1970 did shock 159 faculty members into protesting this politically motivated action. But a breakdown of these faculty by departmental affiliation and academic rank underlined the limited basis of this revolt. One hundred and thirty-seven of Keddie's 159 faculty supporters, 86 percent, taught in liberal arts or social science departments. Fifty-six percent did not have tenure, thus their influence with the administration was limited. Further, they were subject to dismissal if they insisted on continuing their protest.[40]

An analysis of the forty Penn State core faculty antiwar activists underscores the preponderance of young, untenured liberal arts and social science instructors. Eighty-five percent of the university's faculty peace organizers taught in liberal arts and social science departments. A little more than 57 percent did not have tenure and 82 percent were Protestant or, infrequently, Catholic. Although Penn State's administration frequently exhibited anti-Semitic attitudes (as Blau, Lorch, and Bennis discovered), seven of the forty core activists, 17 percent, were Jewish. But only one the the seven Jewish faculty activists may be described as New Left. (The university's peculiar history dictated caution.) Seventy percent of the faculty antiwar partisans were liberal doves, with nearly half not having tenure. Ten of the twelve core radical faculty, 83 percent, also did not have tenure. Forty-five percent of the antiwar faculty worked in the departments of mathematics, English, political science, and philosophy.[41]

The majority of Penn State's faculty in the 1960s and early 1970s was either politically neutral or prowar. Indeed, a number of faculty, particularly political scientists, secretly recruited students into the CIA at least as early as 1955. As a naval weapons research and development center, and a member of the IDA, Penn State had a few hundred faculty directly dependent upon the Cold War arms race and the Vietnam War for career advancement. In addition, a number of PSU faculty in engineering, management, and social science supplemented their salaries by working for various university-military spin-off companies in the State College area. HRB Singer, Inc., founded in 1946 by three PSU staff members and purchased by Singer in 1958, employed faculty consultants in analyzing weapons systems and developing war scenarios. With 80 percent of all research funds to the Engineering College coming from the DoD in the 1960s, it is understandable that engineers would be particularly hostile to anti-war academics, students, and campus clergy's efforts to sever Penn State's ties to the defense establishment. Sometimes this hostility found peculiar expression. During the May 1970 antiwar strike, Nunzio Palladino, a nuclear engineer and developer of the Nautilus Submarine reactor series, traded blows with an antiwar student who had entered his classroom to distribute leaflets. A conservative, Palladino later became chair of the Nuclear Regulatory Commission in the administration of President Ronald Reagan.[42]

Dean of the College of Engineering in 1969, Palladino elicited the support of the PSU Young Americans for Freedom in criticizing the peace movement. Anticipating the November 15, 1969 Mobilization march on Washington, he vigorously defended U.S. military intervention in Vietnam:

We went into Vietnam to help a people defend themselves following the massacre of hundreds of thousands of South Vietnamese after the withdrawal of the French. Though we may question the wisdom of getting involved and the effectiveness of our methods, we took the action in good faith.

Our withdrawal now without a peace settlement would set the stage for North Vietnam to overrun South Vietnam and could lead to another horrendous bloodletting. It would also encourage other aggressive nations to overpower their weaker neighbors.[43]

Prowar engineering faculty received the unanimous support of colleagues in the departments or colleges of agriculture, biophysics, business, and forestry. While a vocal group, they were not noted for the subtlety and sophistication of their arguments. Consequently, the anti-Communist faculty forces benefited greatly from the efforts of eloquent, hawkish liberal arts and social science instructors. The political scientists Henry Albinski and Vernon Aspaturian, and the rhetorician Robert Oliver, delivered over the campus radio in November 1965 a seemingly convincing defense of America's Vietnam policy. Noting that an American military withdrawal from Vietnam would lead to a Communist takeover "and incite Red China to a great power drive," Oliver argued for an escalation of the war. Increased military pressure on the Viet Cong, he assured the campus, would result in an American victory within a year. Albinski also supported escalating the war in order to contain Communist Chinese expansion. More cautious, Aspaturian advocated a negotiated settlement, rather than escalation, but recognized that the latter option might be necessary to prevent Chinese domination of Southeast Asia. Oliver and Albinski had close ties to the defense establishment. The former served for eighteen years as a personal advisor to the right-wing South Korean dictator Syngman Rhee, and in 1969 the latter worked as an IDA consultant.[44]

Anti-Communist ideology and a vested interest in university-military research projects ensured that the great proportion of PSU's faculty supported the Vietnam War. In spite of this, faculty and student opposition to the Vietnam conflict and military research, while initially small and ineffective, mounted over the course of the 1960s and exerted enormous moral pressure on anti-Communist and defense research-oriented faculty. By 1969, agricultural and engineering faculty increasingly came to defend university-military research projects in terms of their applicability to the civilian sector. Hence Robert Shipman, associate professor of forest ecology, emphasized to the campus in October 1969 that his herbicide research, underwritten by the Army Biological Center at Ft. Dietrich, Maryland, could be used to aid American agriculture and not just to defoliate Vietnam's jungles. This represented an important change in the tenor of academic rationalizations on behalf of university-military research. For example, in May 1966, William Gotolski, a civil engineer, announced to the campus that his research on highway stabilization enabled the military to develop Cam Ranh Bay as a principal supply depot in South Vietnam. After 1966, few faculty publicly proclaimed that their research was helping to win the war.[45]

The large prowar faculty constituency, university political surveillance and repression, and the conservative, rural environment which enveloped the university, meant that the academic peace movement would remain small. Unable to find many faculty, community resident, and legislative allies, antiwar academics inevitably turned to their students. Penn State faculty activists who transgressed against the administration by identifying too completely with student antiwar groups usually lost their jobs. And the State College branch of the ACLU and the PSU AAUP, both of which were supposed to protect academic freedom, failed miserably in the face of administration hostility. Thus, the faculty antiwar movement at PSU was entirely campus-based and isolated.

The State University of New York at Buffalo

In September 1948, Newton Garver, a Quaker philosophy student, sent a letter to President Truman informing him that, as a "carefully considered and conscious act of civil disobedience," he had failed to register for the draft as required by the 1948 Selective Service Act. Two months later, a federal judge sentenced the Quaker to a year in the Danbury, Connecticut, Federal Correctional Institute. Having served a jail sentence for his religious principles, Garver was not about to compromise himself morally in 1964 by signing the Feinberg Loyalty Oath. Threatened with dismissal from SUNY-Buffalo, he informed his superiors that

I consider . . . the Feinberg Law, and other similar laws to be both blasphemous and inimical to free society. They attempt to define or limit what sorts of actions or positions can be taken as a matter of loyalty, integrity and conscience. Loyalty, integrity and conscience have to do with the quality of a man's heart, and for them a man is answerable to God alone: in the metaphor of Mark, coin and currency are Caesar's, but integrity and conscience are God's. In attempting to define in political terms something that is essentially divine, these laws attempt to usurp what is God's in the name of Caesar, which is blasphemy. Furthermore, man must, as William Penn said, consent to be ruled by God or he will soon find himself governed by tyranny. Steps which propose to circumscribe conscience, as do these loyalty laws, would set bounds upon the rule of God, which is through the Inner Light of conscience; and hence they are also a first-step toward tyranny.[46]

A liberal dove and supporter of McCarthy in 1968, Garver opposed on-campus recruiting by the CIA and Dow. However, he felt repulsed by SDS's increasingly violent confrontations with the administration and acts of vandalism directed against the campus Themis construction site. Disgusted with the New Left, Garver moved to the right. The political excesses of the New Left convinced the philosophy professor, as well as other liberal faculty, of the existence of left-wing McCarthyism. Garver and his dovish colleagues did not realize that a SDS leader who urged violent confrontations with the administration and ridiculed dovish faculty was an undercover FBI agent. Thus, the federal government manipulated Garver, who had devoted his life to opposing what he perceived to be sacreligious state infringements upon civil liberties, into supporting political repression.[47]

While faculty such as Garver drifted to the right in response to New Left student violence, other academics, notably Leslie Fiedler, moved to the left. A member of the Trotskyist Young People's Socialist League in the 1930s, Fiedler served in World War II as a naval intelligence officer. Perceiving Stalinism as an evil nearly as menacing as Hitlerism, the literary critic supported the supression of Communism at home and abroad. In spite of his vehement anti-Communism, Fiedler harbored a traditional Jewish "outsider" resentment towards affluent WASPs who lacked a sense of social responsibility. Hired to teach in the SUNY-Buffalo English department in 1964, Fiedler described the city as

a disaster area without having had a disaster. . . . Not war or fire, plague or earthquake has afflicted it, only history: the history of a WASP ruling class that abdicated control, no longer willing to pay the price of proximity to the mills that produced its wealth and the system of courts and cops that protected it. Retired to the suburbs and beyond . . . maintaining that happy combination of anti-Semitism and anglophilia which indicates the lifestyle it despises and the one to which it aspires . . .[48]

Fiedler began to chafe against Cold War political conformity after four English instructors were fired in 1964 for refusing to sign the Feinberg Loyalty Oath. He also questioned whether the mandatory Independence Day parties for junior faculty, given by "some extreme patriot department chairs," instilled a healthy love and respect for democracy. Increasingly enamored of the counterculture, the English professor in 1967 became the faculty advisor to Legalize Marijuana (LEMAR). Gradually, Fiedler realized that his association with LEMAR had made him a subject of police surveillance:

What is remarkable is to live under "surveillance," a situation in which privacy ceases to exist and any respect for the person and his privileges yields to a desire to "get rid of" someone with dangerous ideas. Slowly, I became aware of the fact that my phone kept fading in and out because it was probably being tapped; that those cars turning around in nearby driveways or parked strategically so that their occupants could peer in my windows, though unmarked, belonged to the police; that the "bread van" haunting our neighborhood contained cops; and that at least one "friend" of my children was a spy.

The spy, a young female drug addict whom the family had taken in out of kindness, planted drugs in the professor's home during the Passover seder. At her signal, police officers raided the house and arrested Fiedler. After a lengthy legal battle, in the course of which he lost his credit rating and the support of many fair-weather friends, with the significant exception of President Meyerson, the English professor became an ardent supporter in 1969–1970 of New Left faculty activism. He also emerged as an outspoken critic of government attacks on civil liberties.[49]

It should be emphasized that Fiedler and Garver were not key antiwar faculty at SUNY-Buffalo. They are important because their disparate attitudes towards New Left student and faculty activists mirrored those of many confused liberal-dovish academics. Opposed to the war, but respectful of the concept of academic objectivity and neutrality, and uneasy with New Left ideology, some of SUNY-Buffalo's liberal faculty doves experienced a paralysis of will which prevented them from becoming too politically active. Other doves, confronting community hostility and escalating police violence, were radicalized. Consequently, among the forty-eight core SUNY-Buffalo antiwar faculty, liberals comprised a minority, 25 percent, as opposed to the 75 percent who made common cause with the New Left. Radical faculty were younger than their dovish counterparts given that 75 percent of the former did not have tenure compared to the 83 percent of the latter who held the academic rank of associate or full professor. The youth of the radical antiwar faculty is underscored by the fact that fourteen, 39 percent, were doctoral candidates with the rank of instructor or assistant professor. Overall, 90 percent taught in liberal arts and social science departments, with English, philosophy, and sociology instructors predominating. Nearly 21 percent were Jewish. The high proportion of Jews is not surprising since there were simply a large number of Jewish faculty at SUNY-Buffalo. In the 1950s and early 1960s, Jewish academics obtained employment more readily at Buffalo than at, for example, Purdue and Penn State, which discouraged the hiring of Jews.[50]

The elder statesman of the radical faculty was the well-known biophysicist Fred Snell. Born in China of medical missionary parents, Snell graduated from the Harvard Medical School and, from 1946 to 1948, served in the navy. Stationed in Japan, he was assigned to the Atomic Bomb Casualty Commission, researching and treating survivors of Hiroshima and Nagasaki. Imbued with the evangelical Protestantism of his parents, and sickened by his grim work in Japan, Snell was uncomfortable with America's confrontational Cold War foreign policy. In 1959 Furnas recruited Snell from Harvard, offering him the opportunity to establish a new Department of Biophysics.[51]

Taken with the brilliant and personable biophysicist, Meyerson convinced Snell to become Graduate School dean in 1967, a position from which he resigned a year later, frustrated with conservative Medical School faculty who opposed academic reform. He remained as master of College A, a storefront college in which many SDSers were enrolled. His relationship with Medical School colleagues rapidly deteriorated as he allied with SDS against Themis. Almost all of Snell's fellow biophysicists after 1967 refused to talk to him, or even recognize his presence. Many faculty also wrote critical letters to administrators complaining about Snell's activism.[52]

Despite Snell's association with New Left students and faculty, by 1968 he had not abandoned faith in electoral politics, serving as chair of the Democratic (McCarthy) Coalition for Western New York. He quickly became disgusted with the political system following McCarthy's rout and the bullet he received in the mail from the Buffalo Police Department with a note attached "indicating that the next one would come from the barrel of a pistol." Snell helped to found the Radical Faculty Caucus in 1969 which endorsed the U.S. military withdrawal from South Vietnam, the abolition of ROTC, and the termination of all university-military research projects. When acting president Regan summoned the Buffalo police to occupy the campus in March 1970, Snell and forty-four faculty occupied the university president's office and were arrested.[53]

The division within the SUNY-Buffalo academic community over Themis in 1967–1970 cannot be differentiated from faculty protest against the Vietnam War and conservative opposition to the Meyerson regime. In 1967, philosophy professor and Democratic hawk Marvin Zimmerman accused Meyerson of succumbing too readily to leftist student and faculty demands. In March 1969, faculty in the schools or departments of dentistry, pathology, and pharmacy unanimously passed, pro-Themis and anti-student protest resolutions. These faculty, joined by the great majority of engineering, medical, physiology and political science instructors, as well as by a few philosophy teachers, also endorsed American military policy in Indochina and resisted Meyerson's academic reforms. Robert Mates, chair of the Department of Mechanical Engineering, who had argued in 1964 that subversive professors at the university should be fired, informed Meyerson in 1969 that DoD research support was vital to his department and demanded the suppression of anti-Themis protest.[54]

Not unexpectedly, faculty who supported the Vietnam War and university-military research tended to have been the recipients of grants from federal Cold War agencies. Project Themis director Leon Fahri stoutly defended university-military research while denouncing Communist conspirators at home and abroad. Saxon Graham of the sociology department worked in 1971 on an AID project in Afghanistan under alleged CIA auspices and vigorously defended ROTC and characterized the storefront colleges as hotbeds of Communism.[55]

The political polarization of the faculty, and the subsequent alienation of the Buffalo community, began in 1964 as SUNY chancellor Samuel Gould fired academics who refused to sign the Feinberg Loyalty Oath and HUAC opened its investigation of Communism in Western New York. Johnson's order to bomb North Vietnam in February 1965 formalized the split between anti-Communist and left-liberal faculty. Sociology professors Ed Powell and Sid Willhelm, and sociology graduate student Rick Salter, seeing an advertisement in the *Nation* concerning an antiwar demonstration planned for April in Washington, began organizing a campus peace movement. Since the Washington march was being sponsored by SDS, a group then unknown to the sociologists, in February Powell, Willhelm, and Salter decided to call their campus group SUNY-Buffalo SDS.[56]

A native Texan, Willhelm had imbibed his region's historic populism and suspicion of centralized authority. His populistic antiauthoritarian views were reinforced by his reading of C. Wright Mills' critique of power elites. After teaching at San Francisco State College (University), where he became involved on a limited basis with a group of pacifists, Willhelm arrived in Buffalo in 1962. Ed Powell, like Willhelm a Texas populist and disciple of Mills, came to the University of Buffalo in 1958 following a year of postdoctoral work at the London School of Economics. While in London, Powell was attracted to the anarchist-pacifists in the Campaign for Nuclear

Disarmament (CND). In 1960, Powell and twenty other faculty and community residents held a SANE (Committee for a SANE Nuclear Policy) peace march in Buffalo. A year later Powell became chair of the university SANE chapter and attempted, unsuccessfully, to get older sociology colleagues involved in peace issues. Although by 1966 committed to the New Left, Powell and Willhelm respected and sympathized with Meyerson, an attitude not shared by younger radical faculty who viewed him as an opportunistic liberal.[57]

In April 1965, Powell and Willhelm criticized the war on moral and patriotic grounds:

> The resort to violence is not a show of strength but a demonstration of weakness. The effort to impose our will on Vietnam by force is a confession of the failure of our foreign policy and an indictment of the amoral cynicism of the American government. Every day the war continues the stature of the United States diminishes. Therefore, in the name of reason, conscience and patriotism we must demand an immediate end to the war in Vietnam.

Over the next four years, as the war escalated, and bloody confrontations between student peace activists and the police intensified, both sociologists became less assured that America was a moral, democratic, and just nation. They did not, however, forsake their belief that reason, and not violence, could bring about at least individual, if not societal, reformation.[58]

Younger radical faculty, whose participation in the civil rights movement had convinced them of the merits of confrontational tactics, were taken with the concept of morally just violence. In their minds, committing an unlawful, violent act in order to create a lawful, nonviolent society made perfect sense. Charlie Haynie, co-founder of a storefront college, and former civil rights worker in the South, expressed the moral imperative to commit violence. Defending students who sacked the campus ROTC offices in October 1969, Haynie emphasized the historical moral force behind righteous violence:

> From the Buffalo *Evening News*, Thursday, October 16: "The raiders smashed the windows and broke doors to enter the ROTC offices. They ransacked the offices, broke a trophy display case, smeared red paint on desks and overturned furniture and duplicating machines. . . . Files were carried outside, stacked together and burned. . . ."
>
> I quote from Matthew, 21:12: "And Jesus entered the temple of God and drove out all who sold and bought in the temple, and he overturned the

tables of the moneychangers and the seats of those who sold pigeons. He said to them, 'It is written, My house shall be called a house of prayer; but you make it a den of robbers.' "

Right on, Jesus![59]

Evangelical Protestant fervor, mixed with the Judaic tradition of sustained resistance to oppression, made for an energetic and passionate radical faculty movement at SUNY-Buffalo. It was a movement whose ideology was more humanistic than Marxist. But to the police, the Common Council, community residents, and the Erie County grand jury, which launched an investigation in 1970 into the storefront colleges and their faculty, these radicals were Communist subversives.[60]

The reasons behind community hostility towards radical faculty are not difficult to fathom. Buffalo was largely populated by blue-collar Southern and East European Catholics who had relatives trapped behind the Iron Curtain and children serving in Vietnam. To them, the middle-class Protestant and Jewish radical faculty were unpatriotic outsiders and embodied, Michael Frisch recounted, "a betrayal of the community's sense of what a 'professor' should be." Academics, Buffalo's residents believed, should be like former president Furnas, a scholar-athlete who delivered pleasant homilies on democracy at civic functions. A university teacher should not be a shaggy nonconformist intellectual who consumes drugs and mans the barricades.[61]

Contrasting religious and ethnocultural values and class origins combined to create an enormous, unbridgeable social gulf between the city and the university. This gulf widened throughout the 1960s in part because radical faculty activists increasingly explored various ways of defining their life-styles which were unconventional by community standards. This encompassed communal living, group sex, LSD experimentations, and advocacy of black and gay power. Mutual hostility and conflicting values between the university and community meant that the radical, as well as liberal-dovish, antiwar faculty ultimately exercised negligible influence off the campus.[62]

Kent State University

Economic upheaval, menacing German fascism, and the promise of paradise on earth, courtesy of Stalin and Roosevelt, energized New York City's Left. Communism was Americanism, proclaimed Popular Front supporters, as Washington and Lincoln joined the Marxist-Leninist pantheon. Concerned with advancing the cause of social justice, and reacting to anti-Semitism at home and abroad, large numbers of Jews joined the Communist party in the 1930s. One Jewish Columbia University student, Sidney Jackson, found his home, his wife, and his friends, Herbert Aptheker and Phil Foner, among others, in the Communist party. After the Japanese attack on Pearl Harbor, Jackson enlisted in the armed forces. Unfortunately for the historian, with the onset of the Cold War his military service mattered little since the federal government considered his political loyalties to be suspect. FBI harassment and the academic blacklist meant that he could not obtain a high school or college teaching position.[63]

Jackson remained largely politically inactive in the 1940s and 1950s so that the FBI had gradually lost interest in him. When Kent State decided to expand its library science program in 1959, and desperately needed qualified faculty, it offered Jackson a position with the university. Apparently, the Kent State administration was not aware of his past radicalism. Jackson remained a dedicated, relatively apolitical academic until he received tenure in 1964. The mild-mannered radical professor did, however, keep up a one-sided correspondence with President Kennedy:

> I learn from the press that American military personnel are now serving in combat-support capacities in South Vietnam and may even be involved in some operations further north. According to the press they are authorized to fire if fired upon.
>
> I assume that if foreign nationals appeared in the United States some Americans, recognizing military accoutrements, might fire on them, and they might fire back. I see no reason not to expect the same thing in Southeast Asia or anywhere else.
>
> If the American public has had a chance to discuss and vote on this matter I have not heard about it.
>
> Please do not imagine that another evasion of plain realities, like Truman's "police action" and by-passing of congressional voting, will be acceptable.
>
> Your actions threaten my life and my family. I reflect on Henry David Thoreau and the Massachusetts poll tax. I shall act similarly if pushed to it by your present policies.
>
> I reject the idea that a holocaust is worth risking, in the name of "saving" Vietnam; the Vietnamese have a right to organize their life as they please; just as we do.[64]

After he received tenure, Jackson organized boycotts of segregated swimming pools in Kent, coordinated civil rights protests, and worked closely with the Kent Committee to End the War in Vietnam (KCEWV). His two children, who attended Kent State in the 1960s, received a great deal of abuse from conservative faculty, with one history professor taking pains to inform his class that there were "Stalinists in our midst." As a Marxist and a Jew, the library professor cooperated with Kent's other outsiders—blacks, Catholics, and Quakers—who did not fit the town's Protestant Republican mold. His faith in the democratic electoral process earned him the scorn of the KSU SDS in 1969 which considered his politics and religious faith to be counterrevolutionary. Kent State SDSers were also annoyed with Jackson for accepting the Liquid Crystals Institute director's word that there was no military research being performed at the university. Jackson's belief that one academic would not lie to another academic seemed incredibly naive to the student radicals.[65]

Jackson was almost alone at Kent State in the early 1960s in laboring for peace and civil rights. Nearly all of Kent State's faculty in the 1960s foreswore their role as mediators between students and the administration, and viewed campus protest and the Vietnam War as unwelcome disruptions of their routines. The university's professoriat regarded with indifference the twenty-three activist core faculty who defended academic freedom and opposed the Vietnam War. This began to change by 1967 as the social science and liberal arts departments expanded and hired more, and better-qualified, faculty. And the Ohio National Guard slayings in May 1970 jolted the academic community out of its lethargy. Much of this new-found activism, however, was not concerned with American foreign policy in Indochina. Rather, it centered around saving President White's professional reputation and emphasizing to the larger public that Kent State was not an activist university and that the shootings were a tragic aberration on a campus which respected peaceful dissent. The faculty also vainly tried to prevent the slayings from becoming politicized.[66]

On the whole, Kent State faculty were simply not concerned with the issues of the Vietnam War and social justice. The escalation of the war in March 1965 initially excited little interest among academics. Two years passed before a handful of political science and English instructors began to work closely with the student peace group, the KCEWV, which had been in existence since November

1964. In March 1967, Bob Ehrlich, an English instructor as well as KCEWV member, convinced twenty-six of his colleagues, a large number of them graduate students, to sign an antiwar petition. The English instructor, with the assistance of English professor William Hildebrand, also collected thirty-five faculty signatures in April 1967 for an antiwar Open Letter to President Johnson which appeared in the Cleveland *Plain Dealer*. Academics endorsing the Open Letter were, with two exceptions, liberal arts and social science instructors and represented 4 percent of the university's faculty. Later that year, eleven political science faculty, largely graduate students, addressed a separate antiwar letter to Johnson.[67]

In October 1967, twelve KSU professors, and two clergy affiliated with the university's religious counselor's office, established the Faculty Ad hoc Committee for De-escalation of the War in Vietnam and participated in the KCEWV's November teach-in. The Ad hoc Committee's position on the war represented the liberal-dovish point of view. Peter Crossland, political scientist and Faculty Ad hoc Committee co-chair, expressed the group's concerns with an admonition that the Vietnam War demanded heightened protest because:

1) there is a grave risk of a "world" war; 2) the strains of the present situation against detente and world peace are considerable; 3) U.S. involvement in Vietnam is increasingly damaging our relations with allies as well as Communist and neutralist countries; 4) efforts toward solution of domestic problems have been put aside or greatly curtailed; 5) the present military effort involves great cost for which no return is forseeable; 6) U.S. military operations violate U.S. moral and political standards of democracy and self-determination; 7) this situation is extraordinary because all, not just one or two of the items listed 1 through 6, characterize the present situation.[68]

By April 1968, the small radical faction within the Faculty Ad hoc Committee had moved from pleas for de-escalation to calls for nonviolent resistance. Ken Calkins, historian and co-chair of the Faculty Ad hoc Committee, urged the campus to support the draft resistance movement and warned of the dangers of a passive society:

Why didn't the Germans resist the terrors of Nazism more effectively? There is no simple answer. But certainly one of the most fundamental reasons for the success of Nazism in Germany or totalitarianism anywhere is the widespread reluctance of well-meaning people to . . . "stand up and be counted . . ."

Now we are . . . called upon . . . to declare our solidarity with those of our colleagues and friends who have been placed in jeopardy by an unjust war.

Central to Calkins' appeal for resistance was a deep commitment to pacifism, a philosophy whose effectiveness the more radical members of the KCEWV questioned. Although faculty advisor to the Lake Forest College SDS in 1966, Calkins felt "increasingly alienated by the bombastic and naive rhetoric of the SDS as well as by some of the organization's tactics." When SDS superseded the KCEWV in 1968, he saw himself as incapable of influencing the radical student movement.[69]

A few faculty sought to work with the KSU SDS in the fall of 1968 and in 1969 founded a NUC chapter which they hoped would facilitate radical academic and student cooperation. In October 1968 campus NUC organizer Tom Lough, a sociology professor and former employee of the Arms Control and Disarmament Agency, lambasted YAF leader and *Daily Kent Stater* reporter Steven Shotsberger's coverage of the SDS's Free University:

> Shotsberger sees, and the *Kent Stater* headlined, "ulterior motives" behind the Free University and its course offerings. Actually the motives are quite obvious to anyone who prefers direc'ness to conspiracy: SDS members decided it would be good to have a Free University at Kent, decided on a set of 13 topics, and did the work to get it going. Judging from the turnout and the liveliness of the discussions the choices of topics were good ones. And from all appearances it is a success.
>
> Shotsberger seems disturbed that "poverty, the war, student and civil rights . . . are prime elements in SDS's opening gambits to gain wider support . . . " This is also true of the major political parties in this country. Does he see something wrong with this?

Lough's involvement with SDS and the NUC brought him to the attention of the Kent Police Department. After the May 1970 shootings, the Portage County grand jury indicted him for conspiracy to commit riot. Radical intellectual dissent was not to be tolerated at the university.[70]

Of the twenty-three core Kent State faculty antiwar activists, a little more than 91 percent were in liberal arts and social science departments, and largely concentrated in English, history, political science, and sociology. Nearly one-third were English instructors. The Kent State faculty peace movement was also quite young, as indicated by the fact that 70 percent did not have tenure. Liberal doves comprised 87 percent of the faculty antiwar movement. Just three professors could be considered New or radical Left.

As a numerically small group which generally lacked tenure, Kent State's faculty peace activists exerted negligible influence with White as well as with the student antiwar movement. They had absolutely no power in the conservative community of Kent and, concerned for their personal safety, were careful not to attract too much attention to themselves. Since administration officials, campus security officers, and the Kent Police Department photographed antiwar demonstrators and attended peace organizing meetings, faculty activists could only feel insecure about their jobs and privacy. Further, antiwar faculty had to live with an academic community which was largely indifferent or prowar. The attack which Harvey Saalberg, a journalism professor and refugee from Germany, launched against Kent State faculty and student antiwar activists in November 1969 typified the academic position on the peace movement:

Unwittingly most Moratorium marchers are strengthening the hand of those wishing to weaken our government. They are doing so by engaging in activities for which they would be shot in any hard-core Communist country.

Demonstrating against the war in Vietnam is not demonstrating for peace. It is demonstrating for a weaker United States and a stronger Communist enemy in Red China, Albania, Cuba, Russia, Poland, East Germany, Romania, Bulgaria, Czechoslovakia, Hungary, North Korea and North Vietnam.

Do you really want to strengthen the governments of these countries? Do you want to increase the number of these countries? Then demonstrate.[71]

Faced with red-baiting, concerned with political surveillance, fearful of community and university retribution, and powerless to direct students away from confrontational tactics, after 1968 Kent State faculty peace activists anxiously awaited the spark which would blow up the campus. That explosion would rock America's entire system of higher education.

A comparison of core antiwar faculty activists from 1965 to 1972 demonstrates that, as was true on the national level, academic peace organizers were overwhelmingly liberal arts and social science instructors. (See Table 2.1.) A larger percentage of MSU core antiwar faculty had tenure compared to their KSU, PSU, and SUNY-Buffalo counterparts. This indicates that the MSU faculty peace activists were somewhat older and had more job security than their antiwar

Table 2.1

Comparative Profile of Core Antiwar Faculty at KSU, MSU, PSU, and SUNY-Buffalo—1965–1972

	KSU (N = 23)	MSU (N = 55)	PSU (N = 40)	SUNY-Buffalo (N = 48)
Liberal Arts/Social Science Instructors	91%	85%	85%	90%
Tenured, e.g., Academic Rank of Associate or Full Professor	30%	53%	42%	42%
Liberal Doves	87%	78%	70%	25%
Radicals	13%	22%	30%	75%
Liberal Doves with Tenure	30%	63%	54%	83%
Radicals with Tenure	33%	42%	17%	25%

colleagues at the other three universities. The contrast between Kent State and MSU faculty antiwar activists is particularly striking, with just 30 percent of the former, compared to 53 percent of the latter, having tenure.

The proportion of liberal-dovish faculty at Kent State, Michigan State and Penn State falls at or above 70 percent, with radical faculty accounting for 13 percent, 22 percent, and 30 percent of core antiwar academics at each, respectively. These proportions are nearly reversed at SUNY-Buffalo, with only a minority of core antiwar faculty, 25 percent, who can be described as liberal doves. The battles between the Buffalo Police Department and antiwar students led many faculty to move to the left. There was no such impetus at PSU and MSU to radicalize the antiwar faculty to such a great extent. Significantly, the Ohio National Guard slayings did not radicalize the liberal-dovish faculty and the majority endeavored to prevent further mass student protest. It is also worth noting that 42 percent of core radical antiwar faculty at MSU had tenure. This meant that MSU radical faculty were somewhat older, perhaps more intellectually and emotionally mature, and also had a higher degree of job security than was the norm. Since 83 percent of PSU's core radical faculty did not have tenure, it is not surprising that so many of these vulnerable academics were fired for their activism. Penn

State's liberal-dovish faculty were not in a much stronger position than their radical allies, as 46 percent also did not have tenure.

In terms of numbers and scope of activism, MSU and SUNY-Buffalo faculty were key participants in the peace movement at their campuses. PSU had fewer and less active faculty than MSU and SUNY-Buffalo, while Kent State antiwar faculty played a small and subordinate role in what was there primarily a student movement. Antiwar MSU faculty were also heavily involved in community organizing. In contrast, SUNY-Buffalo faculty activists tended to shun off-campus organizing and immersed themselves in the counterculture. PSU activists concentrated on campus organizing as State College was distant from even medium-sized urban centers and, in any event, largely populated by students. Because so many of PSU's faculty were hawks dependent upon military research contracts, activists concentrated on organizing their students, rather than fellow academics. And the handful of Kent State antiwar teachers kept a low profile off the campus, being as ineffective in conservative Kent as they were on the campus in influencing the student movement.

"The Genius of a Nation": Student Dissenters

As late as 1940, just 16 percent of American college-aged youth could afford to attend an institution of higher education and prestigious private and public universities restricted the admission of Catholics and Jews. Liberals, from Franklin Roosevelt to Congressman Lyndon Johnson, believed that higher education, if made financially accessible and less culturally exclusive, would enable less privileged citizens, particularly the New Deal's core constituency of industrial workers and ethnic Catholics and Jews, to achieve upward social mobility. Therefore, the federal government began in the 1930s to provide students with education grants and exerted some moral, and later legal, pressure on universities to abolish religious quotas.[1]

Once the United States found itself engaged in the Cold War, liberals came up with additional reasons to educate larger numbers of youth. As Clark Kerr and Harlan Hatcher argued in the 1950s and early 1960s, the demands placed upon the nation by the emerging American-centered global economy, as well as by an escalating nuclear arms race, required the creation of a technologically proficient, college-educated, society. Additionally, Cold War liberal intellectuals such as Arthur Schlesinger, Jr., and Daniel Bell came to view higher education as a means to create a politically centrist, classless society. Ideally, educated citizens would cease to identify themselves by their class and cultural backgrounds. This loss of identity was necessary for, to a nation locked in struggle with international Communism, class and cultural consciousness served only to promote disunity and lay bare America's historic class, ethnic, religious, and racial diviseness. In any event, Cold War liberals reasoned, the end of ethnic, religious, and racial discrimination in higher education, and the fact that more youths could obtain government education aid, signaled that class and cultural distinctions among Americans were disappearing.[2]

Guided by a Cold War liberal vision of the world in which divisive class and cultural consciousness, and radical left and right political doctrines were ideologically repugnant, the federal government successfully promoted mass education. University enrollment expanded dramatically: from two million in 1950 to nearly four million in 1960 and further to seven million in 1968. By 1970, 50 percent of all college-aged youths attended an institution of higher education. With greater numbers of youths entering the universities in the 1960s, the title "student" began to take on the connotation of an occupation, albeit a temporary one. Intellectuals ranging from psychologist Kenneth Keniston to Michigan student activist Tom Hayden, ironically mirroring their Cold War counterparts, described students as part of a new social class, a class which was neither blue nor white collar and which stood apart from the larger society. Moreover, this new class had personal and political concerns which were quite different from those of workers and professionals.[3]

In many regards, students by the 1960s did represent a new social group. Escape from parental supervision, the mounting popularity among youth of vaguely anti-authoritarian rock 'n' roll music, and the increased prevalence on the campus of marijuana and psychedelics, combined to define a student life-style which was distinct from mainstream society. But despite those developments, it would be misleading to categorize students only by their life-style. Even though Cold War liberal intellectuals proclaimed the end of class and cultural differences in America, such distinctions had not disappeared. In the 1960s, students' class and cultural backgrounds helped to determine which ideas they studied and adopted and which type of life-style they embraced.[4]

Ironically, students who became involved in peace protest and the New Left in the 1960s were the beneficiaries of the expansion of higher education after World War II, an expansion ideologically justified in part by the intensifying Cold War. With the military escalation of the Vietnam War, many sons and daughters of blue-collar workers and ethnic Catholics and Jews revolted against the political system which had made possible their entrance into the universities. Antiwar student activists, particularly those from middle- and upper-middle-class secularized Protestant backgrounds, championed the notion of student power. Such activists considered American youth to represent a new community which had, as Cold War liberals predicted, become declassed. On the other hand, there were a number of antiwar students, generally working- and lower-middle-class and often Catholic, who, while accepting in part the idea of students as a new, declassed social group, acknowledged that their class and cultural heritages informed their politics.

White student activism of the 1960s owed much to the crusading reformist spirit of the New Frontier and the civil rights movement. Activism received further stimulus with the military escalation of the Vietnam War and the subsequent loss of the universities' scholarly neutrality as it became increasingly apparent to students that American institutions of higher education, through military research projects, were tied to the defense establishment. Alienation from the impersonal "multiversity," which stressed administrative form over intellectual content, and rejection of intrusive *in loco parentis*, also contributed to the political mobilization of students. Additionally, the federal government's conflicting educational policies, bound up with the draft and the war, promoted student rebellion. Citing a desperate shortage of primary and secondary school teachers and citizens schooled in the humanities, the federal government exhorted students to go into the fields of education and the arts. At the same time, the federal government awarded student draft deferments based upon a system which ranked education and humanities majors as least essential to national security and, therefore, least worthy of military service exemptions.[5]

University administrators unwittingly set the stage for student disaffection by placing an increased emphasis upon liberal arts and social science programs. Larger numbers of college students in the 1960s pursued studies in the humanities and social sciences. Significantly, liberal arts and social science majors predominated in the ranks of protestors. This may be explained by the nature of the social sciences and the humanities, which encourage critical approaches toward analyzing authority (and attract critical students), offer no specific avenues to jobs, and require sensitivity to, and reflection on, social problems. Science and business majors primarily deal with specific problems that have absolute answers and are not accustomed to dealing with social problems whose solutions are debatable. In addition, such majors often have specific jobs open to them and, since they typically work for corporations benefiting from defense contracts, are not inclined to be critical of the government.[6]

Contrary to contemporary stereotypes, students who became involved in anti-Vietnam War protest were not all middle class and privileged. Indeed, student peace activists came from a variety of class and cultural backgrounds. One reason that the stereotype of the affluent student antiwar activists arose was because of the great news media attention which privileged, secularized Protestant and Jewish, radical youths received. Such activists did exist in number at elite schools and were considered newsworthy because they represented, figuratively and literally, the children of the Establishment. Culturally secure, and the products of elite university educations, these activists operated comfortably from a position of privilege and, since economic factors did not constrict their horizons, their idealism and expectations were accordingly great. They did not have to work while in college in order to pay for tuition and, further, could afford the luxury of not being career-oriented; their parents could support them indefinitely. This privileged cultural and class background led some upper-middle-class Jewish and Protestant activists to believe that all whites were similarly advantaged and all blacks conversely disadvantaged. Convinced that they constituted the most intellectually and morally advanced segment of society, well-to-do student activists such as Bill Ayers, Diana Oughton, and Terry Robbins issued secularized jeremiads against "American imperialism" which exploited their black, brown, and yellow comrades at home and abroad. This was the class and cultural milieu which produced the most violence-prone faction of the 1960s New Left: the Weathermen.[7]

The 1960s academic and activist melting pot also included culturally insecure and less privileged groups, particularly working- and lower-middle-class Jews and Catholics. Jewish student activists, regardless of their degree of secularization and assimilation, absorbed from their backgrounds a propensity towards political awareness and liberalism. Once uprooted from Eastern Europe in the early twentieth century, Jewish immigrants confronted a culturally ambiguous environment in America. Unlike other cultural groups which, upon gaining upward social mobility, increasingly adopted more conservative politics, Jews did not tend to forsake their commitment to civil rights, civil liberties, and trade unionism. According to a 1970 Louis Harris survey, 23 percent of Jewish students termed themselves leftist, compared to 4 percent of Protestant students.[8]

One possible explanation for Jewish political exceptionalism lies in part in their persistent cultural anxiety expressed by the image of the outsider who cannot accept that he has been accepted. There was some substance to Jewish cultural anxiety, given the fact that their economic success had been achieved largely in the independent professions of law, medicine, and teaching. Up to the 1970s, Protestant corporate America closed its doors to Jews and Catholics. It also must not be forgotten that for 1960s red diaper babies, 1950s McCarthyism underscored perceptions of vulnerability as well as injustice. Red diaper babies grew up with FBI harassment, economic hardship if their parents were blacklisted, and lived in fear that their parents would be arrested and executed like Julius and Ethel Rosenberg. For these reasons, Jewish youths often only interacted with one another until entering college. Richard Flacks and Steve Max, both red diaper babies and founders of SDS, were surprised to discover the existence of Midwestern Christian radicals at the 1962 Port Huron SDS convention. Indeed, Max did not meet his first Catholic until the Port Huron convention.[9]

Catholic student activists were at once similar to, and greatly different from, Jewish student activists. Ideologically, Catholics tended to absorb from their church a reflexive distrust of Communism. However, the Catholic church also taught its followers the need for community, mutual assistance, and social justice. Culturally, the parents of Catholic activists had experienced discrimination similar to that which had confronted the parents of Jewish student activists. Catholic student activists were also just as culturally insecure and insular as their Jewish counterparts. Mary Verala, a Hispanic Catholic student activist, expressed wonderment at the 1962 Port Huron convention upon meeting "my first Communist, Steve Max . . ." In part this was because their upward mobility was largely, like that of Jews, the product of the New Deal. In addition, it is important to keep in mind that it was not until 1960 that even a Harvard-educated and wealthy Catholic could get elected president of the United States.[10]

A final group of student activists may be broadly characterized as working and lower middle class, frequently Catholic or brought up in what Vance Packard called "low-status" Protestant denominations, Methodist, Baptist, and Lutheran. Scholars of the 1960s, as well as journalists at the time, have given short shrift to this group since they overwhelmingly attended state, rather than private, schools. For example, in 1967, 34 percent of entering Penn State students identified their parents as unskilled or skilled laborers. Nationally, just 17 percent of college students in 1966 came from working- and lower-middle-class families.[11]

According to Richard Sennett and Jonathan Cobb, working- and lower-middle-class students whom they studied in the 1960s frequently developed feelings of cultural and intellectual inferiority vis à vis more economically privileged and culturally secure undergraduates. In New Left circles, these activists often found themselves condescended to and ridiculed because they were unfamiliar with the jargon employed, and authorities cited, by middle- and upper-middle-class students. Raised in a cultural milieu which placed a premium upon clear and direct discourse, less privileged activists became frustrated with the upper-middle-class students' opaque language.[12]

Working- and lower-middle-class student activists experienced enormous psychic tensions. Not infrequently, these activists' parents did not support their decision to go to college, considering it to be a wasteful endeavor and an indication that they were too lazy to work. If supportive, working- and lower-middle-class parents wanted their children to concentrate on studying, not protesting, which would alienate future employers and get them in trouble with the government. Less privileged student activists, in contrast to middle- and upper-middle-class radicals, also had to concern themselves with paying for their educations since their parents had little disposable income and often opposed their enrollment in the university in the first place. This imposed limits on their degree of activism, giving rise to feelings that they were not doing enough to stop the war.[13]

Finally, less privileged student activists, whose parents were frequently anti-Communist New Deal Democrats, found themselves choosing between their new political orientation and their upbringing. Jewish student activists, at least, had generally liberal to left-of-center parents who supported their children's activism. This was not the case for working- and lower-middle-class activists who, as Texas SDS organizer Jeff Shero bitterly noted, often had to break with their past:

If you were a New York student and became a member of SDS, it was essentially joining a political organization, which was a common experience. In Texas to join SDS meant breaking with your family, it meant being cut off—it was like in early Rome joining a Christian sect—and the break was so much more total, getting involved with something like SDS you had to be much more highly committed, and you were in a sense freed, 'cause you'd get written off. If you were from Texas, in SDS, you were a bad motherfucker, you couldn't go home for Christmas. Your mother didn't say, "Oh, isn't that nice, you're involved. We supported the republicans in the Spanish Civil War, and now you're in SDS and I'm glad to see you're socially concerned." In most of those places it meant, *"You Goddamn Communist."*

In Shero's terminology, "New York student" is to be understood as Jewish, while a "Texas student" is a stand-in for working- and lower-middle-class Catholic, Baptist, or Methodist. This quote encompasses far more cultural tensions than just those represented by regional differences.[14]

Student activists, their political values shaped by their varied class and cultural backgrounds, also dwelled in separate realities; there really never was one antiwar movement, or one New Left. Instead, there were in the 1960s many movements and any number of New Lefts, linked by their opposition to the Vietnam War or by their affiliation with SDS, a national organization only in name. After Tom Hayden, joined by Michigan and Oberlin College students, had completed the 1962 *Port Huron Statement,* SDS's manifesto, the privileged activists were able to get an audience with the historian and Kennedy Administration advisor, Arthur Schlesinger, Jr. At this meeting they proclaimed the birth of a new social reform movement. Similarly, Todd Gitlin, an early SDS president, and the Harvard peace group TOCSIN had a back channel into the White House at the beginning of the 1960s. Such access was not extended to most university activists. Indeed, state university student activists never dreamed that such access was possible. Moreover, such student radicals had their energies consumed at their own campuses in simply trying to gain the right to be politically active. Securing this basic right, one which state university administrators did not consider to be a right at all, involved a great deal of effort. The possibility of meeting with a White House representative, then, was so remote as to be ludicrous; they often could not even get an appointment with the dean of student affairs. Further, the ideological struggles within the SDS National Office in Chicago were of little concern to the rank-and-file activists; their attentions were focused on the local struggle for peace and social justice.[15]

Michigan State University

Born in the Bronx to working-class German-Polish Jewish parents, Edward Gewirts (later anglicized to Garrett) entered Michigan State College in 1937. With an uncle serving as an official in the then militant American Federation of Labor, Gewirts gravitated towards campus leftist groups. Although an associate of several East Lansing radicals, Gewirts never joined the Communist party and broke off all relations with Moscow-oriented campus organizations after the 1939 Stalin-Hitler Pact—a decision he mentioned to a dean who noted his break and which subsequently saved him from "the worse ravages of the McCarthyite inquisition of the early Fifties." Eventually, Gewirts married a Methodist school teacher who supported Henry Wallace's 1948 presidential candidacy and settled in Kalamazoo, Michigan. The Garretts became active in local Democratic party politics and were frightened by the televised Army-McCarthy hearings.[16]

The Garretts' liberalism and ties to Michigan State influenced their son's politics and led him to East Lansing in 1961. Excited by the Cuban revolution and exposed to the Cold War dissent of such liberal magazines as the *Nation* and the *New Republic*, Jan Garrett, a scholarship student, joined the university's model United Nations (UN) which attracted the most socially aware students on campus. Garrett subsequently refused to participate in compulsory ROTC, involved himself with free speech issues on the campus, and helped to revive the Young Socialist Club (YSC).[17]

At least as early as 1961, Hannah had authorized the university's Department of Public Safety (DPS) to spy upon and infiltrate activist campus organizations, sending names and photographs of student protestors to the Michigan Red Squad. One student informant infiltrated the YSC and incorrectly identified Al Meyers, a political science professor and anti-Communist social democrat, as its faculty sponsor. The university also employed as informants *State News'* reporters who provided photographs and phone tips which enabled the DPS to collect several file drawers of data on student groups by the early 1960s. Garrett's efforts to revive the YSC, and invite a

Communist, Robert Thompson, to speak at MSU in 1962–1963, elicited overt university hostility.[18]

The *State News* dramatically headlined the YSC's invitation, "Young Socialists Sponsor Red." Livid, Hannah denied university facilities to Thompson, exerted pressure on the student government president to revoke the YSC's charter, and met with, and chastised, two YSC members. At that meeting, the MSU president read to the students excerpts from HUAC's "100 Things to Know about Communism." The MSU board of trustees, belatedly informed by Hannah that he had banned Thompson from the campus, divided, with a large minority affirming the right of a Communist to speak at the university. Trustee Don Stevens, noting that his anti-Communist credentials dated from the 1930s as an activist in the Congress of Industrial Organizations (CIO), supported the YSC invitation. The Lansing ACLU and faculty activists Larrowe and Repas joined the fight to uphold free speech, as did MSU Humanist Society leader Peter Werbe, who later became an editor of the Detroit-based underground newspaper, *Fifth Estate*. Ultimately, the Delta Sigma Phi fraternity offered its backyard to Thompson and a thousand curious people gathered there, a considerable number coming to heckle his speech.[19]

While the YSC-Hannah confrontation radicalized few students, it did serve to underscore MSU's changing political environment. Larry Lack, a Goldwater supporter who grew up in a working-class Baltimore, Maryland, neighborhood, came to MSU in 1961 and participated in the university's model UN. Partly as a result of associating in the model UN with "the sons and daughters of African revolutionaries" who had been recruited to the university by the school's aggressive international affairs programs, Lack became interested in American race relations and informally affiliated with the MSU Friends of the Student Non-Violent Coordinating Committee (SNCC). After listening to Ivanhoe Donaldson speak at MSU, Lack went South with the civil rights activist to deliver textbooks to a black college. While driving through Georgia, they were arrested and Donaldson severely beaten. Appalled, Lack moved to the left and after graduating from MSU in 1963 became a reporter for the underground newspaper, the Los Angeles *Free Press*.[20]

Lack's radicalization was the product of an increasingly assertive civil rights movement, and part of a national as well as local process which swept up larger and larger numbers of students. In East

Lansing, the MSU Friends of SNCC initiated the picketing of local businesses which discriminated against the university's burgeoning African, Asian, and Latin American student population. Picketing gave way to marches on behalf of open housing in the city, culminating in the largest mass arrest in East Lansing's history in 1965. Fifty-nine students marched on city hall and wound up in the county prison. Against this backdrop of escalated protest, dozens of student volunteers took part in the Student Tutorial Education Project (STEP) and spent their summers teaching economically deprived blacks at Rust College in Holly Springs, Mississippi. In that intensely hostile and racist environment, MSU students learned how to form support networks and to sustain commitment. When such students returned to East Lansing, their experiences had prepared them to challenge the university administration and the Vietnam War.[21]

Immediately after the march on city hall, the *State News* published the names of the students who had been arrested and "tarnished" the image of the university. Although not noted by the *State News*, at least eight of the students were members of the then straitlaced campus SDS chapter. Established in 1963 by a handful of discontented history, political science, and sociology graduate students, SDS sharply criticized American Cold War foreign policy and a variety of university rules and regulations. Unlike its sister chapter in Ann Arbor, MSU SDS claimed a good share of working- and lower-middle-class students. Jack Sattel, a MSU SDS leader, came from a working-class, German immigrant family. In high school, Sattel "had some sense of being an outsider . . . since the majority of my friends were solidly middle class and college-bound." Upon graduation from high school, Sattel enlisted in the air force. Trained in electronics and the operation of nuclear weapons which "scared the hell out of" him, he began "to read seriously about politics and history" and developed a new view of the nation's foreign policy. His political consciousness was heightened as a result of witnessing Japanese student peace demonstrations and developing friendships with black soldiers who were excited by the Freedom Rides. By the time Sattel left the air force in 1961 to go to MSU, he considered himself a radical.[22]

Noticing the existence of the Young Socialist Club in the fall 1961 MSU catalogue, Sattel indicated his interest in the group on his application to the university, a fact subsequently noted in his Michigan Red Squad file. "The size and anonymity of MSU," Sattel recalled, did not disturb him "after four years in the Air Force . . . although it clearly seemed to bewilder a lot of the undergraduates and seemed to anger them." He reserved his anger "for things *outside* the university: nuclear war; racial injustice; poverty."[23]

In 1962–1963, Sattel started to attend YSC meetings which he came to view as:

> arcane and frustrating—arguments about sectarian left-political issues . . . however, the group did some support work for the Southern student movement, brought in some trade-unionists, began demonstrating against racial discrimination in off-campus housing, etc. It served as a way of connecting people and issues—it gave me a sense of purpose/direction while also pursuing my degree. At the same time, I always had one or two friends who were *not* political . . . with whom it was more fun to go out and raise hell . . . . Most of this group was too serious to have much fun with. I saw politics as a way to *transform* society in more open, satisfying ways; they tended to see politics as an end to itself.

It was the serious politicos of the YSC, Ed and Sheri Lessin, Paul Schiff, Brian Keleher, Harvey Goldman—a 15–year-old scholarship student—and Stu and Janet (Goldwasser) Dowty—frequent travelers to Ann Arbor and friends of Al Haber—who founded MSU SDS.[24]

In its early days, MSU SDS was very much a family affair, with members frequently entering into relationships which culminated in marriage. Sue Van Eyck, whose lower-middle-class parents lived in Royal Oak, Michigan, came from a conservative Republican background, offset somewhat by the influence of her neighbor and rebellious schoolmate, Tom Hayden. The prohibitive costs of attending Michigan, and realization that she would not fit in socially with the more affluent students at Ann Arbor, led her to MSU in 1961. At the university, she was exposed to activist guest speakers and met and married Jack Sattel. Both became heavily involved in the antiwar movement: Jack as president of MSU SDS and Sue as president of the East Lansing chapter of the Women's International League for Peace and Freedom.[25]

The Sattels deeply believed in nonviolent protest and identified with community and labor union organizing. Sue had no patience for those in the MSU and the national SDS who advocated "rock throwing," describing such activists as the "sons and daughters of the ruling class" who "wanted 'to win this' and to win (bring revolution) soon . . . due to their being used to getting what they wanted if they wanted it bad enough." Jack also did not care for the upper-middle-class Columbia and Michigan SDSers who came to East Lansing in the late 1960s to sow discord within MSU SDS and urge violent confrontations with the university administration. Similarly, MSU SDS member George Fish, a scholarship student from an Indianapolis, Indiana, lower-middle-class German Catholic family, railed against the elitist Michigan and National Office (Chicago) SDS travelers. Fish viewed them as "patronizing colonizers" bringing light to economically and intellectually inferior MSU SDSers. Class antagonisms between the MSU and Michigan SDS, and among MSU SDSers, mounted throughout the 1960s and contributed to the factionalism of the East Lansing chapter after upper-middle-class Columbia and Michigan SDSers seized control of the National Office in 1969.[26]

While class conflict divided MSU SDS, the East Lansing chapter was largely spared the discord resulting from overt male chauvinism. At the outset, female MSU SDSers such as Sue Sattel, Sheri Lessin, Denise Ryan, Kaye Bradley (who became a regional traveler in the South), and Carlie Tanner (later a National Office organizer), played key roles in formulating chapter policies and tactics. Initially, these women, heirs to a tradition of female subordination, had to force themselves "to speak up at meetings" and to "be taken seriously and not just get the coffee." Their efforts to influence the direction of the chapter succeeded and they received the support of "enlightened" male SDSers who were not threatened by female assertiveness. The MSU SDS's relatively egalitarian relationship between the sexes was exceptional. In general, sexism pervaded the New Left.[27]

An important religious-left alternative to the secular-left SDS, the University Christian Movement (UCM) emerged in East Lansing in the mid-1960s. The UCM, founded in September 1966, evolved from the religious, apolitical National Student Christian Federation. UCM's founders proclaimed that God acted on earth only through political modes; fundamental social change could be realized by activist humans working toward "community dialogue, diversity, freedom, and the abolition of bourgeois complacency through radical education." MSU UCM members, thirty in number by the fall of 1966, came from rural, moderate-to-conservative, white, evangelical Protestant families. Seemingly, their backgrounds precluded radical political activism, but their rooted home-grown religious convictions, most of all their belief that all human life was sacred, led them to disavow the war. Further, they argued that if Christian Americans truly believed in God and democracy, they could not fight on behalf of an undemocratic, immoral South Vietnamese government.[28]

The UCM's emphasis upon social issues, and its evangelical zeal for converting students to the cause of peace, served to bring together Catholics, Jews, Methodists, and Quakers, surmounting theological differences. This united religious front, however, had a price. UCM advisors Lynn Jondahl and Keith Pohl became the subjects of intense police surveillance and Michigan Red Squad agents broke into the University Methodist Church to copy documents pertaining to local clergy-faculty draft counseling efforts. Moreover, older hawkish faculty and residents at the University Methodist Church resented the younger Methodists' unpatriotic, morally self-righteous opposition to the war. Methodist UCM activists found the generation gap too great to bridge and proceeded to drop out of the church. In October 1966, the University Methodist Church held three services every Sunday for eight hundred students. By 1968, only fifty students showed up for the one remaining service.[29]

MSU UCM organized students on three levels. At the first level, students formed support networks and discussed their problems in adjusting to the impersonal multiversity. Students in the first level who became interested in civil rights and peace issues graduated to the second level and joined Depth Education Groups (DEGs). Those students in the DEGs who had studied a particular social issue and had become convinced that political action was required flowed into the third level, where activist cadres were spawned. These cadres organized teach-ins, rallies, and formulated strategies with SDS. It was through this intense, politicizing indoctrination in social interaction that a once conservative religion major from western Michigan, Dave Stockman (later President Reagan's director of the Office of Management and Budget), became a MSU antiwar leader.[30]

Given Stockman's subsequent, controversial political career, it is necessary to point out that he in no way later set aside his commitment to social reform. The bright and energetic child of solid, conservative farmers, whether as antiwar organizer or as Reagan's budget director, possessed an ingrained distrust of the federal government, particularly of the DoD. He also consistently championed the cause of civil rights and risked his congressional seat in the 1970s by denouncing racists in his district. Sue Sattel, who worked with Stockman on the 1967 Vietnam Summer program, praised him as a committed and enthusiastic peace worker, as did Jondahl and Pohl. When a hawkish student in April 1967 denounced MSU SDS as un-American, Stockman defended the radicals who had pledged to resist the draft as America's true patriots:

A nation is not defined by the particular policy, of a particular administration, in power at a particular point in time. Rather, the genius of a nation is expressed in those lofty ideals and broad spiritual currents which have threaded their way through the fabric of its history. In our country these ideals are embodied in concepts like: distributive justice, limited government; individual freedom of speech, assembly and worship; and the rights to life, liberty and the pursuit of happiness .... Many of us feel that American intervention in Vietnam runs contrary to the spirit of this historical tradition. Therefore, our commitment to the real core values and ideals that have made this nation great, demands that we oppose the war.

There have been many expressions of this opposition. One of them being the SDS anti-draft union .... I think the action of many of those ... is motivated by a broader courage than simple, blind obedience, and by a sense of responsibility to values higher than the shallow rhetoric of the present administration.

Stockman never repudiated the sentiments he expressed on behalf of SDS; the Methodist populist did, however, come to loathe the organization after it became committed to violence in 1969.[31]

A disproportionate number of students in the MSU SDS, the UCM, and the campus antiwar movement in general were National Merit Scholarship recipients. In 1963, in order to enhance the university's national prominence, MSU began a campaign to recruit greater numbers of scholarship students and to create special honors programs with close student-faculty interaction. Hundreds of highly motivated, sensitive, intelligent Merit Scholars flocked to East Lansing. Here they were soon disenchanted with the large, impersonal, bureaucratic nature of the university and with Hannah's insistence upon in loco parentis, which cast a shadow across every aspect of their social lives. These alienated scholars, soured by an administration promising more than it could deliver, formed mutual support groups, developed close relationships, and became reform-minded activists. In 1965, when MSU's enrollment of Merit Scholars surpassed the number attending Harvard, Look magazine profiled the university's academic superstars. Within a year, MSU's academic superstars had acquired a new collective label: "John Hannah's Worst Nightmares."[32]

Hannah's nightmares filled the ranks of the Committee for Student Rights and SDS and founded, in 1965, the first campus-based underground newspaper in the nation, *The Paper*. Merit Scholar-SDS reporters for *The Paper* honored Hannah with a comic strip, "Land Grant Man." Inspired by "Batman," scholarship student Steve Badrich, the product of a working-class, Yugoslavian immigrant family, conceived the idea of the comic strip. With dialogue by Jane Munn, the scrappy daughter of legendary MSU football coach and athletic director Clarence "Biggie" Munn, President "Palindrome" (Hannah), once he thumped a hoe on the floor and shouted the magic word "Poultry!" became the inept caped crusader, "Land Grant Man." Gleefully, the comic strip writers subjected Hannah's alter ego to acid trips, gang rape by sexually repressed coeds, and assault by his wife who did not recognize him in the "Land Grant Man" costume.[33]

The lese majesty explicit in "Land Grant Man" reflected the impact of events, chiefly the escalation of the Vietnam War, on activists' attitudes towards authority. It also signaled a transforming cultural-political style on the left. Activist students who entered the university in 1965 were prepared to act upon the philosophy Jack Sattel had embraced in 1962—the belief that humor and fun were integral to, and not mutually exclusive of, politics. One MSU SDSer, acting upon this idea, acquired legendary status following his summons to report for induction into the military. During his physical examination, the medical doctor ordered the SDSer to drop his pants and to bend over. The doctor noticed something protruding from the student's anus and, shocked, asked "what the hell" it was. Nonchalantly, the SDSer replied, "Oh, that's my pet rat." He was not drafted. Humor and politics were also deployed against the local news media. A group of MSU SDSers, living off-campus in the facetiously dubbed "Lenin House," learned that a news reporter was coming over to investigate rumors that SDS was recruiting volunteers to fight in the North Vietnamese Army. The gullible reporter subsequently witnessed students performing military drills.[34]

MSU student antiwar activists were overwhelmingly of Northern and Western European (72 percent), or Jewish (19 percent), stock, as well as male (75 percent). (See Table 3.1.) They largely majored in the liberal arts and the social sciences (76 percent) and were under-

Table 3.1
MSU Antiwar Student Activists, 1965–1972 (N = 263*)

	Northern-Western European	Southern-Eastern European	Jewish		
Ethnicity	72%	9%	19%		
	Female	Male			
Gender	25%	75%			
	Liberal Arts/ Social Science	Business/ Science			
Major	76%	24%			
	Metropolitan Area	Large City	Medium City	Small City	Small Town
Residence I	43%	5%	9%	14%	30%
	In-state	Out-of-state			
Residence II	54%	46%			
	Undergraduate	Graduate			
Status	87%	13%			
	National Merit Scholar/ Honors College	Humanities and Social Science Residential College			
Specific Academic Characteristics	12%	9%			

*Of 349 names collected, I identified 263 (75%) as to majors, residence, and status. The figures reported for ethnicity and gender are derived from the entire data base.

graduates (87 percent). A significant minority came from metropolitan areas (43 percent), and (46 percent) were not Michigan residents. Further, a disproportionate number were National Merit Scholarship-Honors College students (12 percent), and enrolled in the humanities and social science residential colleges (9 percent).[35]

The significant characteristics of the MSU student antiwar movement become evident when they are compared to those of the overall student body. In 1969, 17 percent of MSU students were from out-of-state, while 46 percent of antiwar activists were not Michigan residents; Jews were 10 percent of the student body but 19 percent of activists; National Merit Scholarship-Honors College and residential college students constituted, respectively, 2 and 3 percent of the student body, compared to 12 and 9 percent of antiwar activists. Finally, business and science majors were underrepresented in the antiwar movement; 46 percent of the student body, and just 24 percent of peace activists.[36]

Contrasts between the overall student body and members of MSU SDS are particularly striking. (See Table 3.2.) Compared to the student body at large and non-SDS antiwar students, MSU SDS had fewer Southern and Eastern European Catholics, disproportionately more Jews (24 percent), and somewhat greater numbers of females, although they were underrepresented given their campus total. By contrasting *just* liberal-dovish antiwar students to radicals, we learn that fewer SDSers (16 percent) majored in business and science than non-SDS antiwar students (29 percent), while a majority of the former (53 percent) came from metropolitan areas as opposed to a minority of the latter (35 percent). More SDSers claimed out-of-state residences (52 percent) than non-SDS activists (42 percent), and were disproportionately National Merit Scholarship-Honors College (16 percent), and residential college (10 percent), students. MSU SDS attracted to its ranks people who considered themselves culturally disfranchised from American society and the university: Jews, intellectuals, women, and urbanites transplanted into an alien environment which caused them to suffer culture shock.

To an extent, certain social characteristics of student antiwar activists and SDSers differed only slightly from those of prowar students. (See Table 3.3.) A caveat is in order. By taking a public stand in favor of military intervention in Indochina, prowar activists set themselves apart from the apathetic or anti-Communist majority on campus. If we accept the fact that liberal arts and social science

Table 3.2
MSU SDS, 1965 1970 (N = 109*)

	Northern-Western European	Southern-Eastern European	Jewish			
Ethnicity	71%	5%	24%			
	Female	Male				
Gender	29%	71%				
	Liberal Arts/ Social Science	Business/ Science				
Major	84%	16%				
	Metropolitan Area	Large City		Medium City	Small City	Small Town
Residence I	53%	4%		6%	12%	25%
	In-state	Out-of-state				
Residence II	48%	52%				
	Undergraduate	Graduate				
Status	89%	11%				
	National Merit Scholar/ Honors College	Humanities and Social Science Residential College				
Specific Academic Characteristics	16%	10%				

*Of 145 names collected, I identified 109 (75%) as to majors, residence, and status. Figures reported for ethnicity and gender are derived from the entire data base.

Table 3.3

MSU Prowar Student Activists, 1965–1972 (N = 112*)

	Northern-Western European	Southern-Eastern European	Jewish		
Ethnicity	82%	9%	9%		
	Female	Male			
Gender	15%	85%			
	Liberal Arts/ Social Science	Business/ Science			
Major	57%	43%			
	Metropolitan Area	Large City	Medium City	Small City	Small Town
Residence I	35%	6%	11%	12%	36%
	In-state	Out-of-state			
Residence II	67%	33%			
	Undergraduate	Graduate			
Status	87%	13%			
	National Merit Scholar/ Honors College	Residential College			
Specific Academic Characteristics	2%	2%			

*Of 148 names collected, I identified 112 (76%) as to majors, residence, and status. The figures reported for ethnicity and gender are derived from the entire data base.

majors are more prone to speak out and be engaged in the political process than their career-oriented business and science counterparts, then it should be no surprise that they comprise the majority of *prowar*, as well as antiwar, activists. Nonetheless, business and science majors have a greater propensity to make a prowar, rather than antiwar, stand.

Prowar activists differed slightly from the overall MSU student body, at least in terms of majors and representation in the honors and residential colleges. On the other hand, a third of MSU prowar student activists came from out-of-state, nearly twice the norm, although 9 percent were Jews, nearly their proportional representation on campus. It is when prowar students are compared to non-SDS antiwar students and SDSers, in terms of gender, residential status, and enrollment in the honors and residential colleges, that contrasts become striking. Female students, if inclined to become activists, gravitated more frequently to the left than to the anti-Communist center or right. Further, antiwar students, SDS and non-SDS alike, were more often from out-of-state than prowar students. Although there is no difference between non-SDS antiwar students and prowar students as far as metropolitan residence is concerned, there is a sharp divergence between MSU SDSers and prowar students who came from such locales: 53 percent as opposed to 35 percent. Finally, honors college and residential college students were disproportionately antiwar, rather than prowar.[37]

While the locus of student antiwar protest and organization was largely confined to the "Old Campus," where the liberal arts and social science departments were situated, gaining few business and science majors on the "New Campus" across the Red Cedar River, prowar students after 1966 exercised little negative influence in shaping antiwar protest. MSU student peace activists had momentum and went on the offensive in 1966, reasonably assured that prowar student resistance would be sporadic and of little political consequence. Antiwar activists were also aided, ironically, by the outspokenness of anti-Communist Vietnam Project veterans and President Hannah who, inadvertently, demonstrated the university's considerable role in creating the Indochinese conflict. Also, Hannah's zealous anti-Communism, as well as his strong ties to the defense establishment, made him a perfect foil for SDSers. He was their best recruiter. Consequently, antiwar activists found that the MSU student body was relatively easy to mobilize and radicalize.

Pennsylvania State University

In the midst of the Great Depression, the winds of change began to blow across the nation and even Western Pennsylvania's culturally and physically isolated "Hunkies" and Celtic Appalachians felt that breeze of liberation. The winds blew from Washington and Pittsburgh. Roosevelt promised a New Deal for "one-third of a nation ill-housed, ill-clad, ill-nourished" and, with section 7(a) of the National Recovery Act, guaranteed workers' right to join labor unions. From Pittsburgh, in the shadow of the U.S. Steel Corporation, Father Charles Owen Rice and Philip Murray exhorted industrial workers to organize. Murray backed up his words with action, dispatching Steel Worker Organizing Committee representatives to the region's river mill towns. They organized relentlessly and by World War II had secured a better life for the Mon Valley's residents.[38]

The history of the Mon Valley in the 1930s, a history of struggle and triumph, exerted enormous influence on one Aliquippa, Pennsylvania, working-class boy who acquired national stature in the 1960s antiwar movement: Carl Davidson. Born in 1943, Davidson, the son of a mechanic, found his hometown in the 1950s to be fairly prosperous but culturally limited. While his neighbors listened to country and western music, Davidson, seeking relief from Aliquippa's drabness, tuned into Pittsburgh rock 'n' roll radio stations and saw "Rebel Without a Cause" eleven times. After graduating from high school in 1961, "Aliquippa's James Dean" received a scholarship to attend Penn State, becoming the first member of his family to go to college. Penn State was particularly attractive to him since the then private University of Pittsburgh was very expensive and offered no financial assistance.[39]

At Penn State, Davidson's intellectual potential was realized, nurtured by nationally respected philosophy professors such as Joseph Flay and Alphonso Lingis. He also became politically conscious as a result of extended conversations with his Quaker roommate who gave him literature on conscientious objection and nonviolent civil disobedience. Soon, Davidson followed his friend into the campus antiwar group, SENSE-Students for Peace, a collection of "Old Left red diaper babies, Quakers and cultural rebels." Within a year, the son of blue-collar, anti-Communist, New Deal Democrats had refused to participate in the university's compulsory ROTC program. He also spent a great deal of time "hanging out with the cultural rebels" in the Hetzel Union Building (HUB), listening to Beat poetry recitations and leftist folk music. Self-conscious about their non-conformist political and cultural styles, Davidson's friends invented a new name for the HUB: "the Home for Unloved Beatniks."[40]

Although Davidson styled himself to be an outcast from society, and grew a drooping "Pancho Villa" mustache to establish his cultural revolutionary lineage, his heart always remained in conventional, working-class Aliquippa. When he protested against the escalating Vietnam War, his thoughts were filled with the memories of drafted friends and relatives who had died in Indochina. As he argued against movement violence in the late 1960s, he viewed his "upper-middle-class" opponents as "elitists" and "fanatics" with a profound "contempt for ordinary people." Unlike the movement's privileged activists, Davidson respected Aliquippa's Depression-era labor organizers and heeded their most basic tenet: in union there is strength and in strength there is power. If ordinary people in the 1930s could forge an instrument of social change by uniting disparate and bickering groups, then, he reasoned, students in the 1960s could do likewise. And he advocated such unity at the 1966 National SDS Convention in Clear Lake, Iowa, a locus of 1930s farmer-labor radicalism. It was time, Davidson argued, to build a student syndicalist movement, a movement patterned after the pre-Cold War industrial union movement. Student syndicalism, Davidson believed, could lead to the building of a coalition of ordinary people who would change the world. His vision fired the imaginations of the convention delegates who swept the elite, university-educated "Old Guard" out of the SDS National Office. Davidson became vice president of SDS and working-class Iowa State activist Greg Calvert was elected president.[41]

A year before the Clear Lake SDS convention, Davidson helped to found the Penn State Ad hoc Committee for Student Freedom, which represented nascent student syndicalism directed against the university's rigid policy of in loco parentis. Wishing to build a popular coalition movement which would span the ideological spectrum, he enlisted the support of the PSU YAF, appealing to conservative students' libertarian sensibilities. While most of the graduate student members of the Ad hoc Committee for Student Freedom, many of whom were involved in SENSE, supported Davidson's overtures to YAF, one dogmatic English graduate student, Neil Buckley, dissented sharply:

... the more I think about your suggestion for a coalition between the New Left and the libertarian right I get cramps in my brain ... simply allowing the concept of civil liberties as defined by the Constitution— which we see for what it is—to be perpetuated within our movement is detrimental, both because it allows people to take out frustrations through a system which in no way changes the basic tenets of capitalism and because it is internally inconsistent to base any of our analysis on the civil libertarian analysis which is several centuries out of date. . . . Honest to Christ, Carl, sometimes I can't figure out your politics.

Buckley's criticism of Davidson's political strategies would be echoed throughout the 1960s by numerous middle-class Marxists who could not relate to home-grown, blue-collar populism. Nor did privileged activists appreciate Davidson's notions in 1965 that "our idea of freedom is not apart from the responsibility of law" and that arbitrary, unresponsive authority, reduced "the process of law-making . . . to mockery." A law-and-order radical was an unsettling phenomenon to the movement's revolutionaries.[42]

Davidson's fellow Penn State activists were, by State College and, for that matter, national New Left standards, a curious collection of radicals. Leverett Millen, a graduate psychology student from Brookline, Massachusetts, was a member of SENSE, a civil rights worker in South Carolina, and a founder of the PSU SDS chapter. He was unusual in that few religiously observant Orthodox Jews could be found in the ranks of the New Left. To Millen, deeply rooted religious conviction represented the means by which to achieve universal moral salvation. This belief had been influenced by the example of PSU's civil rights and peace activist clergy, in particular, Baptist minister Robert Boyer and Wesley Foundation director Alan Cleeton. Admiring the activist Catholics in the campus Newman Club, Millen sought to mobilize the university's growing Jewish student population as well as to fuse Judaism and radicalism. Towards those ends, he founded the SDS-affiliate, the Hillel Liberation Front (HLF) in 1966, and identified the organization with the Old Testament prophets and other isolated revolutionaries:

The HLF does not intend to be representative of the Jewish students at Hillel. Like the prophet Jeremiah, we say, "I am in derision daily; everyone mocketh me daily." For the prophets who spoke the words: "seek justice, undo oppression; defend the fatherless, plead for the widow," were, unfortunately, not representative of the Jewish people of their time. And the few Germans like the sainted Bonhoeffer, who spoke out against the horrors of Auschwitz were, unfortunately, not representative of the German people. In our unrepresentativeness, then, we claim good company. . . .

. . . many of the more "representative" students have suggested to us that taking part in the street protests and denouncing the atrocities inflicted by Americans on innocent Vietnamese is not good public relations, and that as

Jews we cannot become involved in this matter. We say to these more "representative" students that you have an intimate moral kinship with the millions in Nazi Germany whose only moral guide was "Don't get involved!"[43]

While Millen's rhetoric tended to be strident, he was immensely amiable and full of the spirit of reconciliation, as were nearly all of PSU's radicals before the escalation of the Vietnam War. Jim Grant, a graduate chemistry student from Suffield, Connecticut, was a rare black peace activist who identified with the Old Left and developed friendships with several YAF members. Bill Lee, a friend of Davidson, gave YAF sympathetic news coverage in 1967 when he became the editor of the *Daily Collegian*. Andy Stapp, a former president of SENSE (and later a founder of the antiwar American Serviceman's Union), debated congenially with YAFers in the HUB and, to demonstrate gently American society's disturbing deference to the military, once directed traffic in State College for several hours dressed in a ROTC cadet uniform. Pam Farley, an English graduate student and product of a middle-class Boston family, had worked with Paul Potter while attending Oberlin and taught poor white children for several years in Zanesville, Ohio. Her turn towards radical feminism came about after 1965 because a number of male PSU SDSers denied women leadership roles.[44]

Antiwar activists at Penn State gravitated towards SENSE, which had been founded in 1961 and thereafter staged hunger strikes and campus demonstrations against American foreign policy. It was a small group, no more than forty members by the winter of 1965. By 1965 the organization disproportionately attracted Jews, graduate students, liberal arts and social science majors, and residents of Philadelphia and its suburbs. (See Table 3.4.) According to a 1965 study by PSU sociologist and peace activist David Westby, and his graduate student Richard Braungart, 68 percent of SENSE members were from middle- and upper-middle-class backgrounds. The sociologists concluded that SENSE was predominately an organization of the "fully 'arrived' stratum, upper-middle-class individuals" who "can afford the luxury of 'deviance' from straight-line conformist politics, especially if their position is relatively well-established, and the mobility not too recent." But another analysis of SENSE membership can be advanced using Westby and Braungart's data. The fact that 32 percent of SENSE members came from working- and lower-middle-class families is significant, for that figure is pro-

Table 3.4
PSU SENSE-Students for Peace, 1965 (N = 29*)

	Northern-Western European	Southern-Eastern European	Jewish		
Ethnicity	59%	13%	28%		
	Female	Male			
Gender	24%	76%			
	Liberal Arts/ Social Science	Business/ Science			
Major	79%	21%			
	Metropolitan Area	Large City	Medium City	Small City	Small Town
Residence I	55%	7%	0%	3%	35%
	In-state	Out-of-state			
Residence II	83%	17%			
	Philadelphia	Philadelphia and its suburbs			
Residence III	21%	38%			
	Undergraduate	Graduate			
Status	79%	21%			

*In 1965, there were approximately 40 members of PSU-SENSE; I identified 29 (72%). The figures reported above are based upon the 29.

portionate to their representation on campus. This means that less privileged students, far from representing, in the sociologists' words, a "status-threatened group" which moved towards the right in reaction to social protest and the upward mobility of blacks, were just as likely as well-off students to become peace activists. Consequently, Carl Davidson was not an aberration; working-class student activists were acting out their parents' dreams and expressing their parents' grievances against society.[45]

Penn State's radicals were culturally isolated from the majority of undergraduates who found drunken fraternity parties and football games to be far more appealing than discussing foreign policy issues. Jim Andrews, a Quaker graduate student, recalled his efforts in 1961 to interest undergraduates in American involvement in Vietnam:

> The war in Vietnam, in the very early Sixties, just didn't seem to be an issue that fired the imagination or energies of many people at Penn State. As a graduate student I was teaching an undergraduate course in public speaking. . . . I remember vividly talking with some students who wanted to give speeches on the situation in Vietnam. . . . I was constantly urging students to try to answer the question that we agreed would be foremost in the minds of their audiences: "What do events in Vietnam have to do with me?" The irony of that question became painfully apparent a few years later . . . [46]

After the Vietnam War became more relevant to students in the spring of 1965, hostility replaced indifference. James Creegan, a member of the Penn State Socialist Club in 1965 and a founder of the campus SDS chapter in 1966, experienced "culture shock" upon leaving Philadelphia for State College. The son of an Irish Catholic labor and Communist party organizer in Great Britain, who later immigrated to America, Creegan was frequently assaulted on the campus and in his dormitory by athletes. Similarly, Farley complained that hawkish students and community residents were sending signed death threats to herself as well as to her parents. She also had to contend with the hawkish students who congregated in the English department to listen to graduate student David Morrell's prowar compositions, some of which became the basis for his novel, *First Blood*. The creator of "Rambo" never volunteered to waive his Canadian citizenship in order to fight in Vietnam. However, this did not deter him from denouncing peace activists as cowards.[47]

The mental and physical abuse which peace activists endured in State College disturbed PSU YAF members who, before 1968, supported government programs for disadvantaged minorities and defended individuals' right to protest against the Vietnam War. Established in 1961, YAF's spiritual leader was Carl Thormeyer, a lower-middle-class German Catholic student who had been radicalized by the brutal Soviet suppression of the 1956 Hungarian uprising. As members of a group which was just as culturally isolated as SENSE, YAF's founders established a rapport with the radicals. In the early 1960s, Thormeyer made friends with SENSE leaders Jim Grant and Barry Clemson and the two organizations graciously heckled each other. When Davidson approached Thormeyer about joining the Ad hoc Committee for Student Freedom, he enthusiastically

Table 3.5
PSU YAF, 1965–1969 (N = 53*)

	Northern-Western European	Southern-Eastern European	Jewish		
Ethnicity	61%	15%	24%		
	Female	Male			
Gender	18%	82%			
	Liberal Arts/ Social Science	Business/ Science			
Major	57%	43%			
	Metropolitan Area	Large City	Medium City	Small City	Small Town
Residence I	58%	6%	4%	4%	28%
	In-state	Out-of-state			
Residence II	89%	11%			
	Philadelphia	Philadelphia and its suburbs			
Residence III	23%	55%			
	Undergraduate	Graduate			
Status	92%	8%			

*Of 55 YAF members noted, I identified 53 (96%). The figures reported above are based upon the 53.

enlisted in the movement and was soon criticizing the university administration for red-baiting the committee.[48]

In 1965, according to Westby and Braungart, PSU YAF was overwhelmingly an organization of small-town WASPs and German Catholics. After 1965, the conservative group attracted more urban and suburban residents and Jews. (See Table 3.5.) Nearly a quarter of PSU YAFers in the period 1965–1969 were Jewish and 55 percent came from Philadelphia and its suburbs. Tense race relations in late 1960s Philadelphia, as well as an ethnic counter mobilization led by Police Commissioner Frank Rizzo, resulted in greater numbers of

Table 3.6
PSU Prowar Student Activists, 1965–1972 (N = 193*)

	Northern-Western European	Southern-Eastern European	Jewish		
Ethnicity	71%	15%	14%		
	Female	Male			
Gender	13%	87%			
	Liberal Arts/ Social Science	Business/ Science			
Major	57%	43%			
	Metropolitan Area	Large City	Medium City	Small City	Small Town
Residence I	39%	7%	6%	5%	42%
	In-state	Out-of-state			
Residence II	83%	17%			
	Philadelphia	Philadelphia and its suburbs			
Residence III	12%	29%			
	Undergraduate	Graduate			
Status	87%	13%			

*Of 244 names collected, I identified 193 (79%) as to majors, residence, and status. The figures reported for ethnicity and gender are derived from the entire data base.

Jews moving to the right. This ethnic backlash also caught up numerous Southern and Eastern European Catholic ethnics and it is not surprising that they represented 15 percent of PSU YAF's membership in these years. Jewish students were also drawn to YAF because of New Left anti-Zionist sentiment and the campus Black Power movement's charge that Jews, all of whom were exploitative slumlord oppressors of blacks, were members of the "Kosher Konsciousness Klub—KKK."[49]

Penn State prowar students, including YAF members, claimed largely Northern and Western European ancestry and over a third came from metropolitan areas. (See Table 3.6.) Such students were mostly male undergraduates (87 percent) and Pennsylvania residents (83 percent). Over half majored in the liberal arts and social sciences and 29 percent lived in Philadelphia and its suburbs. Compared to the overall PSU student body, prowar students claimed proportionately fewer females and disproportionately more Philadelphia residents. When YAF members are segregated from prowar students in general, a few important distinctions may be made between the hard right and the moderate supporters of the Vietnam War. Nearly 59 percent of YAF members resided in metropolitan areas as opposed to 32 percent of politically unaffiliated prowar students. Further, 55 percent of YAF's membership came from Philadelphia and its suburbs, with 23 percent from Philadelphia proper. In contrast, 19 percent of non-YAF prowar students lived in Philadelphia and its suburbs and just 8 percent lived in Pennsylvania's largest city. Jewish students, if they supported the war, disproportionately affiliated with YAF; 24 percent of PSU YAFers were Jewish while 10 percent of non-YAF prowar students came from Jewish backgrounds. There is also a difference between the two groups in terms of gender. A somewhat greater proportion of females (18 percent) may be found in non-YAF ranks than in the ranks of the hard right (10 percent). There is little difference in the proportion of liberal arts and social science majors in both groups.

The student antiwar movement at Penn State attracted a heavily metropolitan population (50 percent), with a good share from Philadelphia and its suburbs (30 percent). (See Table 3.7.) Nearly a third of antiwar students were not Pennsylvania residents and 34 percent were pursuing graduate degrees. It was a movement disproportionately composed of liberal arts and social science majors (83 percent) and had a large Jewish representation (32 percent). Contrasted to the overall student body, the antiwar student movement was unrepresentative of the campus. There were negligible numbers of business and science majors (17 percent) and scarcely any females (19 percent). Non-Pennsylvania residents and graduate students were overrepresented in the peace movement. Philadelphia residents and Jews were also disproportionately represented in antiwar student ranks.

A comparison of PSU anti- and prowar students indicates that there were significant differences between the two groups in terms of academic status, ethnicity, majors, and residence. The contrasts become striking when YAF and SDS members are excluded from our tabulations. Non-SDS antiwar students embraced nearly three

Table 3.7
PSU Antiwar Student Activists, 1965–1972 (N = 423*)

	Northern-Western European	Southern-Eastern European	Jewish		
Ethnicity	60%	8%	32%		
	Female	Male			
Gender	19%	81%			
	Liberal Arts/ Social Science	Business/ Science			
Major	83%	17%			
	Metropolitan Area	Large City	Medium City	Small City	Small Town
Residence I	50%	8%	5%	4%	32%
	In-state	Out-of-state			
Residence II	68%	32%			
	Philadelphia	Philadelphia and its suburbs			
Residence III	17%	30%			
	Undergraduate	Graduate			
Status	66%	34%			

*Of 564 names collected, I identified 423 (75%) as to majors, residence, and status. The figures reported for ethnicity and gender are derived from the entire data base.

times the proportion of Jews and the share of graduate students, and 13 percent and 17 percent, respectively, more metropolitan and non-Pennsylvania residents. Further, non-SDS antiwar students had twice the proportion of females than could be found in the non-YAF prowar student ranks.

Focusing on the PSU student left, we find that SDS was a heavily Jewish (42 percent) and undergraduate (87 percent) organization whose members largely came from metropolitan areas (62 percent), notably Philadelphia and its suburbs (45 percent). (See Table 3.8.) Thirty-five percent of Jewish SDSers hailed from Philadelphia and its suburbs. If antiwar students were unrepresentative of the campus, then SDSers were more so. Merely 7 percent of the overall student body came from Philadelphia, while 31 percent of SDSers

Table 3.8
PSU SDS, 1965–1972 (N = 110*)

	Northern-Western European	Southern-Eastern European	Jewish		
Ethnicity	50%	8%	42%		
	Female	Male			
Gender	15%	85%			
	Liberal Arts/ Social Science	Business/ Science			
Major	79%	21%			
	Metropolitan Area	Large City	Medium City	Small City	Small Town
Residence I	62%	5%	7%	4%	21%
	In-state	Out-of-state			
Residence II	79%	21%			
	Philadelphia	Philadelphia and its suburbs			
Residence III	31%	45%			
	Undergraduate	Graduate			
Status	87%	13%			

*Of 130 SDS members noted, I identified 110 (85%) as to majors, residence, and status. The figures reported for ethnicity and gender are derived from the entire data base.

were residents of that cosmopolitan city. In addition, 21 percent of SDSers had out-of-state residences, compared to 12 percent of the student body. Jewish students and liberal arts and social science majors were also disproportionately represented in the PSU New Left. Finally, the preponderance of undergraduates and metropolitan Philadelphia and non-Pennsylvania residents in SDS was significantly greater than in the non-SDS antiwar student category. This generally holds true when SDSers are compared to non-YAF prowar students.[50]

Interestingly, there are more similarities than differences between the extreme campus Left and Right. Both PSU SDS and YAF drew in nearly identical proportions of males, metropolitan residents, and undergraduates. Slightly more SDSers were residents of Philadelphia and its suburbs, Jewish, and from out-of-state than PSU YAF partisans. A telling distinction between SDS and YAF may be made in that 22 percent more SDSers were liberal arts and social science majors.[51]

As the Vietnam War escalated militarily in 1965, the culturally isolated and numerically weak student Left and Right endeavored to mobilize an apathetic campus. Both extremes of the political spectrum grew as the campus polarized over the issue of the Indochinese conflict. Ultimately, SDS and YAF splintered, but not before alienating nearly everyone on campus. Politically moderate peace groups did emerge, but the university administration and residents, resentful of the influx of Philadelphia-based activists, made no distinction between radicals and moderates. Any student actively opposed to the Vietnam War could expect to be spied upon by administrators and zealous, hawkish students. It required a great deal of stamina to be an antiwar activist at PSU, for cultural and geographical isolation, coupled with opposition from the university administration, took an enormous emotional toll.

The State University of New York at Buffalo

In April 1964, HUAC came to Buffalo to investigate Communist subversion. The last time the committee had been in Buffalo, in 1957, Joyce Wike, an instructor at UB, and Arthur Bolton, a social worker at the Buffalo Jewish Center, were identified as Communists. David Kochery, UB law professor, served as legal counsel to Bolton and his wife. At the 1957 hearings, the committee had been largely concerned with the existence of Communist student groups at UB. But HUAC also devoted considerable attention to Ed Wolkenstein, a Buffalo Communist party leader who had obtained a job at Bethlehem Steel in order to organize the work force in preparation for a Marxist revolution. Wolkenstein pleaded the Fifth Amendment and the hearings proceeded without incident.[52]

HUAC's 1964 Buffalo hearings were not so tranquil. Republican congressman John R. Pillion of Buffalo, concerned that his party's wildly unpopular presidential candidate, Barry Goldwater, would also drag him down to defeat, hoped to exploit fears of domestic Communist subversion, a tried and true vote-getting tactic. Hence HUAC came to Buffalo and the Congressman sent numerous tickets to the hearings for the local United Anti-Communist Action Committee, an organization made up of Hungarians, Poles, Lithuanians, and Ukrainians. These ethnics were traditional New Deal Democrats, but Pillion believed that the specter of Communism would swing the city's dominant Polish voting bloc behind the Republicans. It was also helpful that nearly all of the individuals summoned before the committee were Jews, a cultural group which had never been beloved by Poles.[53]

The hearings commenced on a strained note when a SUNY-Buffalo instructor insisted on checking the witness table for wiretaps prior to testifying. Tension mounted after a Buffalo Communist party member revealed that he had been a FBI informant since 1942. And then Wolkenstein, once again appearing before the committee, insisted that he be allowed to make some prefatory remarks. Denied this opportunity, his upset wife was dragged from the hearings swinging at the federal marshals. Meanwhile in the streets, two hundred SUNY-Buffalo students, among them Wolkenstein's daughter, Rachel, chanted denunciations of the committee.[54]

Organized by the SUNY-Buffalo student government, the anti-HUAC protest proved enormously successful, if only because, for the first time in the university's history, a large number of students had been mobilized around a political issue. This demonstration also signaled the birth of a new campus spirit. SUNY-Buffalo's student government expanded the scope of its political activities, establishing a Civil Rights Committee in October 1964 to register blacks to vote. Over 150 students were involved in canvassing Buffalo's ghetto. Following the presidential election, these students began to investigate, and picket against, racial discrimination in the city. Further, the student government in the winter of 1965 vigorously protested the firing of several university instructors for refusing to sign the Feinberg Loyalty Oath.[55]

The newborn activist spirit on campus in 1963–1964 inspired two students who would subsequently become leaders of the early SUNY-Buffalo anti-Vietnam War movement: Clinton Deveaux and Jerry Taylor. Deveaux, one of the few black state university student government presidents in the nation, tirelessly defended campus activists. In April 1965, he orchestrated a student government resolution chastising the Buffalo *Courier-Express* for arguing that

perhaps we have many young people invading institutions of higher learning who have no business being there. It could be that through closer scrutiny and weeding out of some of the alleged students room could be found for those whose main purpose is to get an education and not to picket the White House, get carried to a paddy wagon, or disdain soap, combs and personal grooming.

After graduating from the university, Deveaux, along with Sam Brown, founded in 1967 the liberal-dovish Alternative Candidate Task Force in order to deny Johnson a second term in office.[56]

In contrast to Deveaux, Jerry Taylor identified himself with, and became a leader of, the campus New Left. Following his participation in the 1964 anti-HUAC protest, the Buffalo Police Department's Subversive Squad tapped Taylor's phone and closely monitored his subsequent political activities. Taylor's ascension in 1965 to the position of editor in chief of the campus newspaper, the *Spectrum*, resulted in an already radicalized publication, which had denounced loyalty oaths and HUAC, shifting further to the left. A pacifist deeply influenced by Quaker teachings, Taylor promoted SUNY-Buffalo SDS and argued that the New Left had a grand historical mission:

> The New Left must resist a war this nation seems committed to. It must find alternatives to ignorance and deprivation, not just here in this country, but throughout the world. It must prepare its participants, not just for a momentary flash of radicalism during the college years, but for lives of quiet, passionate service to ideals. It must surmount the hatreds and betrayals of two hundred years of exploitation and butchery. It must bring the whole world back past Kronstadt and Barcelona, Bekin and Madrid, back past Budapest and Rotterdam, Leopoldville and Cape Town. It must bring this country back past Montgomery and Haneyville, past Appomattox and the Bay of Pigs.
>
> The New Left must write a new geography, a new grammar. These are not easy things to do, but the tools to do them are at hand.[57]

As the New Left emerged at SUNY-Buffalo, it cooperated with, and competed against, an entrenched Old Left. The chief campus Old Left organization was the Youth Against War and Fascism, led by Ed Wolkenstein, who had been expelled from the Communist party in 1961 for Maoist sympathies. YAWF's anti-Vietnam War leaflets in January 1965 avoided mentioning the group's affinity for the Communist Chinese dictatorship. Rather, the Maoists argued that their intention was to oppose the escalation of the Vietnam conflict in order to avoid provoking a Third World War. YAWF presented a moderate political front to students, denounced anti-Communist extremists, and allied with other antiwar organizations, chiefly SDS. Forming alliances with other groups on the left was important to YAWF, for its disciplined cadres wished to influence and then take over their allies' organizations. Having successfully seized control of a rival left group, YAWF's members abandoned any pretense at ideological moderation and toleration.[58]

A key SUNY-Buffalo YAWF leader in the 1960s was Gerry Gross, the son of a local furrier. Gross joined the campus SDS chapter and became an organizer of the Buffalo Draft Resistance Union (BDRU). The YAWF chair received extraordinary attention from the FBI because, unbeknownst to him, one of YAWF's Buffalo founders was a police informant. Gross won his way into the hearts of the city's FBI agents in 1965 for writing an effusive letter to Communist China's representative in Canada and erroneously sending it to the Nationalist Chinese (Taiwan) consulate:

> While in Toronto during "International Days of Protest," one of my comrades had the pleasure of meeting you and of expressing his warm regards for The People's Republic of China and the Chinese People's internationalist struggle against U.S. imperialism. He suggested to me that I write to you in order to express my support for the position of The People's Republic of China on Vietnam and also to express my sincere thanks for your support for our student demonstrations against the U.S. war in Vietnam.
>
> . . . We are attempting in a sincere way to study hard the thinking of Mao Tse-Tung on philosophy so as to be better able to apply materialist dialectics to our struggle against the Johnson Administration ruling clique and to expose the hypocrisy of religious leaders and organizations that back these murderers.

Bemused, Taiwan's representative forwarded Gross's letter to the Department of Justice.[59]

Radical students who were not attracted to YAWF and SDS attempted to work with both groups while declining to embrace their ideological agendas. One such student was Larry Faulkner, the son of a notable New York City Old Left attorney. Faulkner had completed his undergraduate studies at Cornell where he had worked in the campus SANE chapter with graduate student, and later SUNY-Buffalo faculty activist, Charlie Haynie. After the Cornell SANE chapter elected to picket the Soviet embassy, as well as the White House, on behalf of an atmospheric nuclear weapons test ban treaty, Faulkner dissented: "When the United States tests atomic bombs it is for war; when the Soviet Union tests atomic bombs it is for peace." Faulkner became less dogmatic by 1965 when he entered graduate school at SUNY-Buffalo and became a draft resister as well as a draft counselor to working-class Buffalo teenagers. The activist rejected movement violence as counterproductive and tried to convince radicals that confronting the police would only antagonize an already suspicious community. He also worried about an anti-Semitic backlash in Buffalo, given the fact that many of the student advocates of violence were Jewish.[60]

An industrial center long dominated by automobile, chemical, and steel corporations, Buffalo's largely blue-collar and ethnic Catholic population had not achieved political power until the New Deal. And relative economic security was not realized until the industrial union movement, a number of whose organizers were Jewish Communist party members, overcame the open shop. After World War II, the ethnics, in reaction to the Soviet conquest of Eastern Europe, ousted their radical Jewish union officers. This was the beginning of an ethno-cultural and ideological struggle which continued into the 1960s, given new life by student-police confrontations. Exacerbating cultural tensions was an emerging race problem. Eighty thousand Southern blacks moved to Buffalo in the postwar years, creating a ghetto which encompassed forty blocks and where one-fifth of its residents received welfare payments. White university radicals, many of them Jews, felt more kinship with poor blacks than with working-class Poles and therefore gravitated towards the ghetto. Such ties made the ethnic community wary.[61]

By the time of the city's first race riot, and after black nationalists at SUNY-Buffalo in 1968 assaulted Common Councilman Raymond Lewandowski, a stout defender of the police department, ethnics' fears had been seemingly realized: white university radicals and black militants were conspiring to harm them. It was no wonder, then, that Common Councilman William Lyman sponsored a resolution requiring landlords to notify the police if they had any student tenants so that they could be monitored. Buffalo's Democratic congressman, Richard McCarthy, who had been elected in the 1964 Democratic landslide, also decried the peace movement.[62]

And yet, in spite of the Buffalo community's ingrained anti-Communism, hostility towards the student antiwar movement, and anti-Semitism, the majority of residents went on record against the Vietnam War as early as the summer of 1966. The Buffalo Common Council in 1966 canvassed voters on the war and found that 81 percent favored negotiations with North Vietnam while a strong minority, 40 percent, wanted the United States to withdraw its troops. Faulkner appreciated the ethnics' frustration with a war which was killing their sons and sought to build bridges to the community. Unfortunately, many radicals were not so discerning and answered anti-Communism and anti-Semitism with violent radicalism and anti-Catholicism. Community-student relations worsened as police agents in SDS and YAWF became prominent leaders in the movement. One SDS police agent provocateur reveled in his role as Jewish radical come to Buffalo to avenge himself upon culturally conservative Italians and Poles.[63]

Although opposition to antiwar protest was great in the city, such sentiment exercised little influence on the campus. One explanation for this development is that the two likely bastions of conservatism, the Greek system and the athletic department, were inconsequential. Merely eight hundred students were members of fraternities and sororities in 1966, giving SUNY-Buffalo one of the smallest Greek populations for a university of its size in the country. Athletics, in particular football, received minimal emphasis and inspired even less student enthusiasm. Consequently, liberal political activism became an important outlet for students' energies. In addition, the influx of radical New Yorkers, as well as Meyerson's progressive administrative style, reinforced the campus' liberal ambiance. For these reasons, by the fall of 1965, SUNY-Buffalo YAF had just twenty members, as opposed to SDS's two hundred, and thereafter went into rapid decline.[64]

The SUNY-Buffalo student antiwar movement attracted a large number of Jews (44 percent), more than twice their proportional representation on campus. (See Table 3.9.) Male students dominated the antiwar ranks. It was also an undergraduate movement. Additionally, 47 percent of the activists were residents of New York City and its suburbs, while just 29 percent came from Buffalo and the Niagara Frontier. Only a handful were not New York residents. In contrast, 58 percent of prowar student activists claimed Northern and Western European ancestry and 28 percent were Southern and Eastern European Catholics. (See Table 3.10.) Sixty-three percent came from the Niagara Frontier. Prowar, like antiwar, students were overwhelmingly males, undergraduates, and New York State residents. The crucial differences between the two groups were cultural and residential. More Jews and Catholics identified, respectively,

Table 3.9
SUNY-Buffalo Antiwar Student Activists, 1965–1972 (N = 231*)

	Northern-Western European	Southern-Eastern European	Jewish	
Ethnicity	49%	7%	44%	
	Female	Male		
Gender	23%	77%		
	Metropolitan Area	New York City and its suburbs	Niagara Frontier	
Residence I	51%	47%	29%	
	In-state	Out-of-state		
Residence II	92%	8%		
	Undergraduate	Graduate		
Status	92%	8%		

*Percentages reported for residence and status are based upon the 231 students I identified out of a total of 427 (54%). The figures reported for gender are from the entire data base, while the percentages given for ethnicity are derived from 379 of a total of 427 (86%) names. Given what appeared to be 48 anglicized surnames, I chose not to include them in the calculations. Percentages are not cited for majors in the Buffalo tables because the campus directories did not provide such information.

with the anti- and prowar positions, while contrasting residential origins underscored the historic upstate and New York City political cleavage.

Analyzing the members of the BDRU, SDS, and YAWF, we learn that the radicals were disproportionately Jewish, 62 percent, while just 3 percent came from Southern and Eastern European Catholic backgrounds. (See Table 3.11.) Radicals from Northern and Western European backgrounds accounted for 29 percent of the membership of leftist organizations. In addition, 46 percent of the radicals were New York City area residents while just a third hailed from the Niagara Frontier. Finally, 42 percent were Jewish New Yorkers.

With little opposition from prowar students, and blessed with two university presidents, Clifford Furnas and Martin Meyerson, who respected the right of students to dissent politically, the SUNY-Buffalo student antiwar movement blossomed on the campus. A

Table 3.10
SUNY-Buffalo Prowar Student Activists, 1965–1972 (N = 117*)

	Northern-Western European	Southern-Eastern European	Jewish	
Ethnicity	58%	28%	14%	
	Female	Male		
Gender	15%	85%		
	Metropolitan Area	New York City and its suburbs	Niagara Frontier	
Residence I	24%	18%	63%	
	In-state	Out-of-state		
Residence II	96%	4%		
	Undergraduate	Graduate		
Status	96%	4%		

*Of 191 names collected, I identified 117 (61%) as to majors, residence, and status. The figures reported for gender and ethnicity are derived from the entire data base.

number of students had already been mobilized by the anti-HUAC protest and community civil rights work by the time the Vietnam War escalated militarily. SUNY-Buffalo in 1965 was a liberal campus which elected activist student government representatives and endorsed the left-of-center editorials published in the *Spectrum*. At the same time, however, antiwar students, like their faculty counterparts, found themselves culturally and politically isolated from the Buffalo community. When Meyerson proclaimed his intention to make SUNY-Buffalo "the Berkeley of the East," the majority of students embraced his vision of creating an intellectually progressive, nationally respected institution of higher education. One anonymous Cassandra, though, anticipated ominous developments: "Can they hope to have that university's [Berkeley's] greatness without its scandal, strife and ugliness?"[65]

Kent State University

The lanky Kent State undergraduate entered his place of work, Sam's Pizza Shop, and greeted several friends. Dissatisfied with the

Table 3.11
SUNY-Buffalo SDS, YAWF, and BDRU, 1965–1970 (N = 69*)

	Northern-Western European	Southern-Eastern European	Jewish
Ethnicity	29%	3%	62%

	Female	Male	
Gender	17%	83%	

	New York City and its suburbs		Niagara Frontier
Residence I	46%		33%

	In-State	Out-of-state	
Residence II	90%	10%	

	Undergraduate	Graduate	
Status	75%	25%	

*The figures reported above are derived from the entire data base. Percentages reported for ethnicity do not add up to 100 because I excluded Puerto Ricans from the cultural category.

Greek system's domination of university student life and with Kent's bland cultural conformity, he and his friends had organized a racially integrated antifraternity club, "The Macedonians," which met at Sam's. Their political activities were confined to intellectual ruminations. He was the son of a South Carolina cotton farmer who had relocated his family to Akron in order to escape grinding poverty. And so his father found the American dream: unrelenting toil in an Akron tire factory. The son wanted to go to college, but his father argued that a man did not need more than a high school education to work in the factory. As the prospect of spending the rest of his life in a factory did not appeal to the son, he studied hard, won a debate scholarship to Kent State, and left home. He became the first and only member of his family to attend college. But his college education at once alienated him from routinized university life as well as expanded his intellectual horizons. After three years at Kent State he had had enough and left for New York City to become a playwright. Ten years later, Carl Oglesby was national president of SDS and, for a while, one of the most influential figures in the American Left.[66]

Oglesby's education at Kent State provided him with the intellectual tools necessary to connect the economic exploitation of poor Americans to that of Third World citizens. Further, his culturally and economically deprived background enabled him to understand the aspirations of the less privileged and to sympathize with revolutionaries seeking to free themselves from Western economic and political domination. With rhetorical flourishes reminiscent of Tom Watson and Huey Long, this Southern populist in 1965 looked to Jeffersonian defenses of revolution and considered American and global politics to be informed by the struggle between the poor and the rich.[67]

While Kent State's conventional life-style endured for the remainder of the 1950s, the forces of change had begun to overcome the university's cultural inertia by the early 1960s. The rate of expanding student enrollment, growing 48 percent from 1963 to 1964, and the construction of more dormitories, signaled Kent State's transformation from a commuter and teachers college to a residential and academically comprehensive university. As the only public institution of higher education in the area (the state universities of Akron, Cleveland, and Youngstown were not established until the mid-1960s), Kent State drew in students from the region who either could not afford to attend, or could not gain admittance to, Oberlin and Western Reserve University. Consequently, the university's student body had many sons and daughters of Akron, Cleveland, and Youngstown blue-collar workers and businessmen. The majority of students in the 1960s were, not surprisingly, from Northern and Western European backgrounds, although one-fifth claimed Southern and Eastern European Catholic ancestry. This underscored the humble class origins of many students since, nationally, the majority of Catholic ethnics were working and lower middle class. Less than 5 percent of Kent State's student body were Jewish, indicating that their proportional representation on the campus was significantly lower than was the norm at more prestigious universities.[68]

Kent State seemed to be an unlikely place to have a student movement in the early 1960s. Nonetheless, a student movement did take shape. The Kent State student movement's dynamo was Tony Walsh, the son of Irish Catholic immigrants. Placed in a Cleveland orphanage at an early age, Walsh's mother having died shortly after his birth and his father unable to support him, he was eventually taken in by an ill-tempered uncle. The uncle had been a soldier in the Irish Republican Army (IRA) but fled the Emerald Isle one step ahead of the English authorities. Settling in Cleveland, Walsh's uncle became deeply involved in the struggle in the 1930s to unionize Republic Steel's work force. Given Republic Steel's obstinacy, the uncle was more than willing to employ IRA-style tactics against the corporation's private security forces. Years later, when Walsh worked as a caddy at an exclusive Cleveland golf club, he would listen to senior executives of Republic Steel denounce labor unions in general, and one "wild Irish bastard" union organizer in particular. Walsh wisely chose not to reveal his kinship, contenting himself with a smirk.[69]

Walsh was drafted into the army in 1958, stationed for a while at Ft. Benning, Georgia, where he developed a strong distaste for Southern racial discrimination. After his military discharge in 1961, he worked at a variety of jobs, made friends with several black co-workers, and married. Having spent his formative years in an orphanage, and then with an activist uncle, Walsh had developed profound sympathies for the less fortunate, while his military experiences led him to scorn social regimentation. His desire to further the causes of social justice and cultural diversity was realized when he enrolled at Kent State as an honors student. In 1963, Walsh and several student civil rights activists founded a university chapter of the Congress of Racial Equality (CORE). Although there were no more than twenty members of the KSU CORE, the organization became controversial. The president of the KSU student government, whose father was a conservative police lieutenant, resigned in protest after his fellow representatives gave official recognition to the radical group. KSU CORE activists initiated campaigns to integrate city swimming pools and formed an Ad hoc Committee on Free Speech in the fall of 1963 which challenged the university's ban on political activities on the campus. The organization also protested against the university's policy of *in loco parentis*, as well as succeeded in electing Walsh to the student government.[70]

The university's student activists in 1963–1964 were an ideologically diverse and politically persecuted group. Walsh, not entirely facetiously, described himself as an "Irish Catholic Bolshi" whose political philosophy was summed up in this advice to protestors: "If it feels good, do it." One of Walsh's opponents in the student government saw in that statement the seeds of Communism. The orthodox Marxists in the KSU CORE gravitated towards English instructor and Young Socialist Alliance (YSA) leader Bob Ehrlich. A veteran of the Southern Freedom Rides, Ehrlich tended to be somewhat paranoid. However, his fear of political surveillance and retribution was justified. In November 1965, Ehrlich and several KSU radicals were arrested after police, on the pretext that the radicals were serving alcohol without a license, raided a Socialist Workers' party function in Cleveland. Adding to Ehrlich and the YSA's sense of vulnerability was hostile local newspaper publicity. The *Record-Courier* made it a point, beginning in 1963, to identify YSA members and contend that the group was on the U.S. attorney general's list of subversive organizations. It was not, and publisher and Kent State trustee president Robert Dix knew that it was not.[71]

Following a visit to KSU in the fall of 1964 by a State Department representative who defended Johnson's Indochina policy, Walsh and Ehrlich founded the Kent Committee to End the War in Vietnam. The KCEWV had less than a dozen members, including Joseph Jackson, the son of the group's faculty advisor, Sidney Jackson, and Bob Bresnahan, a YSA organizer whose father was an executive of the Ridgeway Express Company in Akron. In the early days of the KCEWV's existence, few faculty endorsed the peace group and many professors, mostly those lacking tenure, were anxious lest they appeared to be sympathetic to the organization. In contrast, local clergy, notably William Jacobs of the University Christian Fellowship Union, Peter Richardson of the Unitarian-Universalist Church, and Donald Miller of the Newman Center, publicly supported the KCEWV and provided facilities to the activists. Rev. Richardson even went so far as to counsel students on conscientious objection, advise student draft resisters, and open a coffeehouse in the basement of the Unitarian Church which served as a meeting place for KCEWV members. One frequent guest of the coffeehouse was a campus police officer who taped activists' conversations.[72]

University president White and the campus police were not the only parties who took an active interest in the KCEWV. The Kent Police Department and the Portage County prosecutor's office, as well as the Ohio highway patrol and the Cleveland field office of the FBI, also monitored the organization, especially after it recruited more members by the mid-1960s. Student reporters for the campus newspaper, the *Daily Kent Stater*, and the campus radio station, WKSU, enthusiastically collected information on the KCEWV for the university administration and local law enforcement agencies.

The director of WKSU, Bob Carpenter, also was not above circulating stories over the radio that KCEWV leader Ruth Gibson had been impregnated at various times by assorted militants. On the campus and off, KCEWV members generally traveled in groups in case they were set upon by hawkish students or community residents. On one occasion, at a Kent tavern in 1965, Joseph Jackson became involved in a discussion of the Vietnam War and was roughly ejected from the bar. He felt panic and isolation.[73]

Given this environment of hostility and repression, it is not surprising that a number of freshmen and sophomores who joined the KCEWV in 1966 were warped by their experiences and wound up as university and national Weathermen leaders by 1969. Initially, the KCEWV's founders opted for community dialogue, rejecting confrontational tactics which, they believed, were neither feasible nor desirable. But the next generation of KCEWV members were, in 1966–1967, beginning to access the virtues of educational outreach programs and moving tentatively towards the idea of revolutionary violence. On the side of confrontation were middle- and upper-middle-class antiwar activists: Rick Erickson, the son of a former Democratic mayor of Akron; Howie Emmer, whose parents had been Ohio Communist party organizers and victims of McCarthyism in the 1950s—though his parents still managed to live in affluent Shaker Heights; and Robin Marks, the daughter of a successful New York City writer. Pitted against these privileged radicals were working-class activists such as Jim Powrie who came to Kent State on a football scholarship. Powrie identified with his working-class Irish Catholic heritage which Emmer castigated as racist and bourgeois. He could only reply in injured tones that it made no sense to alienate Kent residents and students who were largely working class and had relatives being killed by the Viet Cong.[74]

As the seeds of ideological and class divisions in the campus antiwar movement were planted in 1966–1967, a cultural revolution had begun. The city of Kent's proximity to the Ohio Turnpike and other major highways made it a convenient way station from points East to Cleveland, Detroit, and Chicago. With the burgeoning resident student population, Kent became a youth-oriented locale. Easy access and the youth market attracted rock 'n' roll and jazz bands from Cleveland, Detroit, and Chicago, which found in Kent's remarkable number of bars a place to work on their acts before breaking into the major leagues. Joe Walsh haunted Kent's taverns

Table 3.12

KSU Antiwar Student Activists, 1965–1972 (N = 275*)

	Northern-Western European	Southern-Eastern European	Jewish
Ethnicity	72%	13%	15%
	Female	Male	
Gender	34%	66%	
	Metropolitan Area	Cleveland and its suburbs	
Residence I	31%	16%	
	In-state	Out-of-state	
Residence II	72%	28%	
	Undergraduate	Graduate	
Status	80%	20%	

*Of 413 names collected, I identified 275 (66%) as to residence. The figures reported for ethnicity, gender, and status are derived from the entire data base. Percentages are not cited for majors in the Kent State tables because the campus directories did not provide such information.

developing his sound, and one of Lou Reed's "cellophane-wrapped" dancers studied at Kent State, spending her summers with the "Velvet Underground" in New York. Consequently, an iconoclastic musical subculture developed in conservative Kent, a subculture in which KCEWV members and "Devo" founders Bob Lewis, a lower-middle-class Welsh Methodist, and Jerry Casale, a working-class Italian Catholic, sought to fuse leftist politics with rock. Throughout the 1960s, the fame of Kent's bar and music scene spread across the Midwest, making the city a magnet for revelers, drifters, and activists. Increasingly, the city's residents were torn between their desire to profit from their student tourists, and fear that law and order was cracking under the weight of pot-smoking Communists.[75]

Kent State's activists were, beyond obvious ideological and counter-cultural attributes, atypical students. To begin with, 15 percent of Kent State antiwar students were Jewish, though they represented merely 5 percent of the overall student body in 1969. (See Table 3.12.) Further, 31 percent came from metropolitan areas and 16

Table 3.13
KCEWV, 1964–1967 (N = 47*)

	Northern-Western European	Southern-Eastern European	Jewish
Ethnicity	66%	17%	17%
	Female	Male	
Gender	23%	77%	
	Metropolitan Area	Cleveland and its suburbs	
Residence I	32%	15%	
	In-state	Out-of-state	
Residence II	72%	28%	
	Undergraduate	Graduate	
Status	89%	11%	

*KCEWV constant membership from the years 1964 to 1967 probably added up to no more than 70 students, although by the spring of 1967 as many as 200 students showed up for KCEWV peace rallies. According to KCEWV presidents Tony Walsh (1964–1966) and Ruth Gibson (1966–1968), yearly membership was, on the average, as follows: 1964, 12; 1965, 12; 1966, 20; 1967, 40. Percentages reported for residence are based upon the 47 students I identified out of a total of 53. Figures cited for ethnicity, gender, and status are derived from the entire data base.

percent were residents of Cleveland and its suburbs. In contrast, just 17 percent and 9 percent, respectively, of the student body came from metropolitan areas and Cleveland and its suburbs. Additionally, 20 percent of antiwar students were graduate students, even though they represented only 7 percent of the student population. Finally, 28 percent of antiwar students claimed out-of-state residences compared to 17 percent of the student body.

Examining the student composition of the KCEWV from 1964 to 1967 we find a disproportionate number of Jews, out-of-state residents, and students from metropolitan areas. (See Table 3.13.) In comparison to the general category of antiwar students, however, we find that the KCEWV attracted fewer graduate students and more Southern and Eastern European Catholics. After the more doctrinaire activists abandoned the KCEWV in 1968 and founded a campus SDS chapter, the leftist antiwar movement became even less

Table 3.14
KSU SDS, 1968–1969 (N = 66*)

	Northern-Western European	Southern-Eastern European	Jewish
Ethnicity	63%	18%	19%
	Female	Male	
Gender	27%	73%	
	Metropolitan Area	Cleveland and its suburbs	
Residence I	51%	21%	
	In-state	Out-of-state	
Residence II	59%	41%	
	Undergraduate	Graduate	
Status	94%	6%	

*Of the 77 SDS members noted, I identified 66 (85%) as to residence and status. Figures reported for ethnicity, gender, and status are derived from the entire data base.

representative of the campus and the liberal-dovish campus antiwar movement. (See Table 3.14.) Kent State SDS was overwhelmingly an undergraduate organization, with a substantial minority of out-of-state students (41 percent) and a majority of metropolitan residents (51 percent). Jewish students were disproportionately represented in the KSU SDS (19 percent) but, in contrast to the other campus SDS chapters profiled, the group had a substantial number of Southern and Eastern European Catholics (18 percent), largely Italian ethnics. Of course, as a mainly working- and lower-middle-class school, KSU had a great number of ethnic Catholic students in general, far more than at comparable state institutions of higher education.

Prowar activists were generally male, while antiwar activists claimed a somewhat larger proportion of females. (See Table 3.15.) Few graduate students and out-of-state residents were found in prowar activist ranks. Seventy-three percent of prowar students were from Northern and Western European backgrounds, while 20 percent claimed Southern and Eastern European ancestry. Just 7 per-

Table 3.15
KSU Prowar Student Activists, 1964–1970 (N = 57*)

	Northern-Western European	Southern-Eastern European	Jewish
Ethnicity	73%	20%	7%
	Female	Male	
Gender	7%	93%	
	Metropolitan Area	Cleveland and its suburbs	
Residence I	28%	14%	
	In-state	Out-of-state	
Residence II	86%	14%	
	Undergraduate	Graduate	
Status	94%	6%	

*Of 69 names collected, I identified 57 (82%) as to residence. Figures reported for ethnicity, gender, and status are derived from the entire data base.

cent were Jewish. A disproportionate number of prowar student activists, as was true for their antiwar counterparts, came from metropolitan areas. Whether or not being raised in cosmopolitan environments, rather than in small towns like most KSU students, made prowar activists less violent than hawkish students in general, is debatable.

Kent State student peace activists operated in a profoundly hostile environment, culturally set apart from the campus and the Kent community. Only a handful of faculty supported the antiwar students, and the professors' moral and intellectual contributions to campus peace organizations were minimal. Far more important to students were the activist clergy who provided advice, facilities, and encouragement to antiwar students. The student antiwar movement had been founded by a curious mixture of working-class Catholics, upper-middle-class Protestants, and red diaper babies. In the halcyon days of 1964 and early 1965, it appeared as if the Indochinese conflict could be quickly resolved by students through petitions and nonviolent protest. Despite cultural and class differences, as well as political isolation, Kent State's antiwar student activists were members of a small, close-knit family. As the war escalated, activists experienced intensified campus and community persecution. Yet the peace movement grew. But in reacting to local hostility, class and cultural differences which had been muted in 1965 began to tear the movement apart.

The emergence of student political activism at state schools predated the 1964 uprising at Berkeley which, according to various scholars, spawned white student activism. Student activists at Kent State, Michigan State, and SUNY-Buffalo, their numbers varying from campus to campus, were involved in free speech protests several months prior to the Berkeley Free Speech Movement. In addition, student activists at Kent State, Michigan State, and Penn State had established antiwar organizations months, if not years, before the military escalation of the Vietnam War and the founding of the famous Berkeley Vietnam Day Committee.[76]

Moreover, contrary to scholars who have contended that state university student activists were less articulate, intelligent, and effective than their elite educated counterparts, the fact remains that eloquent, bright, and dynamic, as well as nationally prominent, antiwar student leaders emerged from less well-regarded universities: Carl Davidson, Clinton Deveaux, Howie Emmer, Carl Oglesby, and Andy Stapp, to list only a few. These activists contributed a moral and political approach to the peace movement, an approach shaped by their class and cultural values. Set forth by particular activists were possibilities for CIO-inspired student syndicalism and Old Testament-influenced Marxist liberation theology. However, class and cultural differences among activists, and between activists and community residents, ultimately undermined such sweeping visions, leaving in their wake political fragmentation and bitter conflict.[77]

The influence of the local environment on the development of each campus' antiwar movement was significant. Students did react to national events and the ebb and flow of the civil rights and anti-Vietnam War movements. At the same time, though, students' tactics and perceptions of American society reflected their immediate cultural and political environment. The type of relationship antiwar students had with university administrators, prowar students, law enforcement agencies, and community residents determined the mode of dissent as well as the ways in which confrontation unfolded. Each campus was quite different from the others in such regards and bore little semblance to the so-called activist schools: Berkeley, Columbia, Harvard, and Michigan.

State university student activists greatly differed from elite university protestors as far as class and cultural origins are concerned. Activists from the less prestigious universities drew upon a diverse membership of red diaper babies, upper-middle-class secularized Protestants, and working- and lower-middle-class Catholics and Protestants. At the elite schools, student activists were overwhelmingly middle and upper middle class. Moreover, even though Jewish students represented a significant part of SDS and the New Left at the state universities, their numbers, with the exception of SUNY-Buffalo, were much greater at schools such as Columbia and Michigan (anywhere from 50 to 75 percent). Finally, the state universities claimed far more Catholic student activists than the heavily WASP elite schools.[78]

PART TWO

"Tempered by War . . ."

FOUR

"Let Us Try to Succeed with Reason": 1965–1967

In response to Viet Cong attacks on U.S. military personnel in South Vietnam, Lyndon Johnson began in February 1965 to bomb North Vietnam. Opposition to his Indochina policy appeared on many campuses, coalescing once he began to dispatch large numbers of combat forces to South Vietnam in March. Initially, state university protestors were a small minority and regarded in their communities as Communist subversives. At such locales, antiwar protest from 1965 to 1967 was nonviolent and the most common types of protest against the war were teach-ins, peace petitions addressed to Johnson, and low-key picketing.

In contrast to the state universities, elite schools experienced an immediate wave of violent protest. In the fall of 1965, thirty-eight University of Michigan students were arrested for trying to close down an Ann Arbor draft board. Among those taken into custody were Diana Oughton, a Bryn Mawr graduate and the daughter of an affluent Illinois restauranteur, and Bill Ayers, the son of a multimillionaire utilities company president. Threats by Selective Service to draft Ayers and the other privileged male Michigan militants were mysteriously and rapidly withdrawn.[1]

A year later, Berkeley activists physically intimidated on-campus naval recruiters and the small minority of hawkish students; Harvard SDSers ambushed McNamara's car, refusing to allow the defense secretary to leave the campus until subjected to an extended session of jeering and cursing; and five hundred Chicago students occupied a campus building to protest university administration of

129

a Selective Service examination. By 1967, Wisconsin radicals, protesting Dow Chemical recruiters at the university, were smashing windows and brandishing clubs. The majority of the activists from these universities were upper middle and upper class, chiefly the children of lawyers, doctors, academics, and corporate executives.[2]

Interestingly, after Madison police arrested nineteen Wisconsin students at the Dow protest, the chancellor posted their bail and the state attorney general castigated the officers for excessive use of force against the children of wealthy alumni. Thus seemingly immune from serious criminal prosecution and university discipline, Berkeley, Chicago, Michigan, and Wisconsin activists subsequently adopted even more violent tactics. Wisconsin militants repaid the university for its consideration by firebombing the office of the associate dean for student academic affairs.[3]

As the elite universities witnessed violent demonstrations, and less privileged activists at state schools struggled to build a popular, nonviolent peace movement, the war escalated. At the same time, the peace movement expanded. However, opposition to the antiwar movement increased throughout 1965 and 1966, with the public directing its anger at the restive campuses. By 1967, frustration with the peace movement's inability to stop the war sparked mounting dissension within campus antiwar ranks. Moreover, ideological and cultural divisions among peace activists became difficult to ignore. As the public became disenchanted with Johnson and his failure to win the Vietnam War, and as race riots erupted across America, the campus advocates of nonviolent protest at the state universities began to lose control of the peace movement. Simultaneously, campus activists exposed the universities' ties to the defense establishment and the academy became a target, as well as a locale, of protest. Battle lines were drawn and they ran through the heart of the sprawling campuses which owed their expansion and prosperity to an increasingly discredited, divisive Cold War foreign policy.

Michigan State University

On the evening of March 4, 1965, Lawrence Battistini spoke to a small number of students in the campus YSA chapter. Battistini, a Southeast Asian specialist, informed his sparse audience that Johnson's Vietnam policy would inevitably replicate France's futile, humiliating experience in Indochina. Further, he argued, America was illegally intervening in a civil war between the Saigon government and the dissident National Liberation Front (NLF). "Neither the United Nation's charter, nor customary international law," Battistini contended, "concedes the right to help either side in a civil war." Americans who believed that the Indochinese conflict was the result of Communist aggression from North Vietnam, instead of an internal civil uprising, the professor concluded, were the victims of presidential and press duplicity.[4]

After Battistini finished his remarks, Brian Keleher, political science graduate student and vice president of the MSU YSA, announced that the MSU SDS and YSA were sponsoring a peace march on Washington for April 17 in order to protest Johnson's Vietnam policy. One thousand demonstrators, including thirty MSU students, were expected to attend the peace rally. It seemed that few MSU students and faculty, and Americans in general, were interested in Vietnam, trusting Johnson to champion democracy at home and abroad.[5]

Johnson's decision to send the U.S. Marines to DaNang on March 8, 1965, immediately generated greater interest in Vietnam. Battistini, Greer, Donoghue, and Rokeach organized the seventeen-member Ad hoc MSU Faculty Committee for Peace in Vietnam. They also arranged for a Vietnam teach-in at the university on April 11. MSU's first Vietnam teach-in attracted 2,000 students, including one hundred disruptive, hawkish Young Democrats, and was twice interrupted by bomb threats. The Young Democrats and the MSU Young Americans for Freedom repeatedly heckled the antiwar speakers. Hawkish faculty, who believed that professionals should not criticize the government, glared hostilely at their antiwar colleagues. Despite the tense, chaotic atmosphere of the teach-in, many students and faculty felt that it had a solid intellectual content that clearly defined the issues and, as the first open, campus-wide antiwar statement, lent a sense of legitimacy to its participants.[6]

Students and faculty at the teach-in passed two resolutions by acclamation: first, the U.S. must immediately negotiate an end to the war; and second, MSU should work to eliminate the potential for future international conflict by establishing a campus War and Peace Research Center. In a letter to Hannah, Donoghue expressed hope that Johnson had been observing events in East Lansing:

The President and his advisors are unaware of the deep concern and the moral distress which that policy [Vietnam] has induced among many of us. . . Our government, once aware of our moral concern, will be responsive to the citizens' quest for justice and human decency.[7]

Reinhard Mohr, political science graduate student and chair of MSU SDS, was equally optimistic about the power of the teach-in in promoting awareness, for it effectively raised hitherto indifferent students' consciousness of Vietnam. One hundred and thirty MSU students attended the April 17 rally in Washington, four times the original number who had signed up for the antiwar protest two weeks before the teach-in.[8]

Hawkish faculty, chiefly Vietnam Project veterans led by Fishel, castigated Battistini, Donoghue, and Greer. The MSU YAF and the People to People Association joined the anti-Communist faculty chorus. In scathing letters to the editor of the *State News*, hostile students and faculty accused antiwar activists of being "cowards," "Communist appeasers," "psychotics," and "traitors." President Johnson also quietly intervened on behalf of the campus hawks, giving Fishel $25,000 in private funds to establish a national prowar speakers' bureau and information center.[9]

Organizers of the MSU Faculty Committee for Peace in Vietnam challenged the prowar campus organization, the MSU Friends of Vietnam, to a series of debates. Fishel set the acrimonious tone of the debates by misquoting and insulting Battistini and Greer, while his colleagues in the audience heckled the peace activists. After Greer received a standing ovation from hundreds of students in Anthony Hall, Fishel snapped: "After that, I'm not sure whether to address you as members of the Madmen's Society, or Future Beasts of America."[10]

The first confrontation between antiwar students and the university administration occurred in October 1965 at the student union. Twenty students from MSU SDS set up booths on either side of a marine recruiting table which featured battle films of U.S. aircraft napalming various targets. Two of the activists quietly held up placards bearing the pictures of children disfigured by napalm burns. The marines threatened them with bodily harm unless they left the building. Soon, the Placement Bureau director demanded that the antiwar students vacate the premises immediately. Acting on their own initiative, five SDSers refused to obey his order. The director of the MSU Department of Public Safety subsequently charged them with trespassing and distributing commercial literature on university property. After the SDSers were released on bail, awaiting their trial in March 1966, the *State News* derisively labeled them "Vietniks" and condemned them for violating the property rights of the university.[11]

Alarmed at the growing number of antiwar activists and the mass of leftist literature flooding the campus, YAF, the Michigan branch of the American Legion, and the MSU chapter of the Delta Tau Delta fraternity, which dominated the student government, collected 15,872 student, faculty, and community residents' signatures on a petition supporting Johnson's Vietnam policy. The *State News* welcomed YAF's initiative, but argued in November that Senator Barry Goldwater's proposal for ending the war through the nonstop, intensive bombing of North Vietnam was superior to Johnson's surgical bombing strategy and use of counterinsurgency ground forces. This editorial, published a few weeks after the university had prohibited reporters from covering the activities of the Committee for Student Rights, led four of the five student editors to quit and found *The Paper*.[12]

During the interim between the *State News* walkout and the founding of *The Paper*, forty MSU antiwar students, subdued by YAF's success in rallying support for Johnson, as well as by the unabated escalation of the Vietnam War, made a second pilgrimage to Washington on November 27. At the previous spring rally the mood had been cheerful, with activists believing that once Johnson saw how many Americans objected to his Vietnam policy he would quickly seek peace. The ensuing months of increased troop commitments and draft calls rapidly deflated their optimism. With winter approaching, the 50,000 people who assembled in Washington realized that the struggle for peace would be a long, tiring process. They would have to continue to organize larger rallies, while hostile critics branded them as traitors and Communists.

That November day in 1965, however, did offer the activists some consolation and inspiration to take back to their campuses. Carl Oglesby, president of the national SDS, provided an analysis of American liberalism and foreign policy that became the cornerstone of the New Left interpretation of the Vietnam War. He compared the Communist insurrection in South Vietnam to the American Revolution. Of course the Communists committed excesses, but revolutions, including the American Revolution, were by definition bloody affairs. In this manner, he enabled antiwar activists to rationalize that they were not appeasing the Communists. Rather, they were furthering the ideals of Paine and Jefferson which had been corrupted by liberals who shamelessly denounced any social movement as Soviet-directed if it challenged American military and economic interests. Now antiwar partisans could respond to the red-baiters that they were the true patriots, defending traditional democratic American values against "corporate liberal imperialism." [13]

Shortly after Oglesby's riveting speech, Selective Service director Lewis Hershey, citing a need for more soldiers, ordered that college student draft deferments (2–S) be cut by at least 20 percent. In order to maintain 2–S status at MSU, students had to have a "C" grade average and score 70 percent on a Selective Service intelligence examination, an examination largely composed of mathematics questions which favored engineering and business majors and placed liberal arts and social science majors at a great disadvantage. Colonel John Holmes, director of Selective Service in Michigan, exhorted President Hannah to expel ever greater numbers of students, stating that only 10 percent of the MSU student body was qualified to be in school. The other 90 percent, Holmes argued, were unworthy of college educations and were shirking their patriotic duty in Vietnam. [14]

The prospect of losing 2–S status and being compelled to fight in an "unjust war" weighed heavily on the minds of students. Jim Thomas, a MSU sophomore and friend of SDSer Steve Badrich, decided in March 1966 to enlist in the marines rather than spend two more anxious years at the university while his draft board made frequent inquiries into his academic standing. Mike Kindman, Merit Scholar and editor of *The Paper*, was saddened by Thomas' decision, but recognized that university students who struggled to keep their 2–S status were only putting off the inevitable:

The war may well go on for years. We in college are like men in an overcrowded lifeboat; some have to be pushed over the side to save the rest. . . . Our time is limited; four years . . . less with upper division standing. And we all wonder, as we sit in classes and go to meetings, finding our "adventure and usefulness not so close to the bone of combat," if help will arrive in time. [15]

Perceiving that the threat of the draft had grown exponentially since November of 1965, providing larger numbers of apprehensive, potential recruits for the antiwar movement, MSU SDS accelerated its peace education offensive in East Lansing. In March 1966, SDS focused attention on the court cases of the five students who had been arrested in the union in October. Noted New York City civil liberties attorney Conrad Lynn unsuccessfully represented the five antiwar activists before a Lansing justice of the peace. Lynn appealed their convictions at the Ingham County Circuit Court on March 29. Circuit Court judge Marvin Salmon increased their fines, sentenced the activists to ten-to-thirty day jail terms, and denied them bail despite their expressed intention to appeal to the Michigan Supreme Court. The Detroit *Free Press* criticized Salmon's decison to deny the students bail, noting that "it forced them to serve the sentences he imposed before their appeals could be heard and judged, thus inflicting punishment whatever the outcome."[16]

Immediately following Salmon's ruling, twenty-eight students camped in front of Cowles House, Hannah's campus residence. For three very cold days and nights they fasted, protesting the Circuit Court's denial of due process of law. Among the campers, much to Hannah's chagrin, were Jane Munn and Louise Holmes, the daughter of Michigan Selective Service director John Holmes. Unfriendly students threw water balloons at them and Hannah refused to speak to the "martyrs." By the third day of the protest, two hundred students rallied around Beaumont Tower and the protest had become a major story for the state's leading newspaper and television stations.[17]

Although the Michigan Supreme Court upheld the convictions of the antiwar students, the campus peace movement, through the trials and related protest rallies, garnered favorable publicity from the Detroit *Free Press*, if not from the conservative Republican Lansing *State Journal*. Hannah's refusal to establish a dialogue with the campers, as well as his insistence that prosecuting attorney Donald Reisig demand maximum sentences for the activists, according to the *Free Press*, undermined his image as a champion of civil rights and due process.[18]

Just as the controversy surrounding the trials of the antiwar protestors began to subside, the radical West Coast magazine *Ramparts* published in its April issue a sensational story about MSU-CIA ties in the defunct Vietnam Project. The fallout from the *Ramparts'* bombshell blanketed MSU. The *Free Press*, the *New York Times*, and the three national television networks descended upon Cowles

House; state senator Jack Faxon, D-Detroit, announced that a special hearing of the Subcommittee on Higher Education would be held in May to investigate MSU-CIA links; MSU political scientist and former assistant to the head of the Vietnam Project, Robert Scigliano, resigned and fled to SUNY-Buffalo; and the state legislature rescinded a $10 million appropriation to MSU which was to have been used to establish a law school. Fishel called the *Ramparts* article a "silly, slimy smear" and defended the Vietnam Project: "it was necessary to build a modern police force for a modern state, which is nothing to be ashamed of." On April 14, a flustered Ralph Smuckler, former head of the Vietnam Project and now dean of International Programs, assured the *State News* that MSU did not provide cover for CIA operations in Indochina in the 1950s. A few hours later, however, he admitted to the *New York Times* that MSU and the CIA had had a special arrangement by which CIA operatives were granted faculty status at the university. Hannah contradicted Smuckler's admission of MSU-CIA cooperation and he in turn was contradicted by former CIA inspector general Lyman Kirkpatrick. Kirkpatrick observed that only an "idiot" could not have known that the CIA had used the MSU Vietnam Project as a front.[19]

On April 23, Hannah informed the news media that *Ramparts'* deceitful attack on MSU merited contemptuous silence instead of vocal defense. Nonetheless, Hannah defended MSU's role in creating the South Vietnamese state. Michigan State's primary mission, he contended, was to carry out national policy for the benefit of the free world:

When our faculty members are engaged in providing service, either within Michigan, elsewhere in the country, or overseas, we do not consider their activities as a "diversion of the university," but instead a recognition of a significant and defensible function of the university.

To say that a university should never undertake to serve the national policy is to deny the right of the public university to exist. In everything it does, the public university carries out the national policy. . . . We are not about to abandon that mission .[20]

Furthermore, Hannah argued, *Ramparts'* charge that the Vietnam Project served as a front for the CIA was a lie. "Michigan State did not have a spy operation within its Vietnam Project. It did not have CIA people operating under cover provided by the university, or in secret from the Vietnamese government." Hannah also denied *Ram-*

parts' claim that MSU made $25 million from the Vietnam Project (or nearly one-fifth of MSU's annual operating budget from 1955 to 1962), citing a significantly lower figure of $7.8 million. Finally, he assured taxpayers that "no armaments nor ammunitions were supplied through the Michigan State contract." *Ramparts'* inventory of MSU-procured weapons for Diem could only be a forgery.[21]

The MSU president's press conference did not resolve the *Ramparts* controversy. Kirkpatrick continued to insist that, until 1959, the CIA had used the Vietnam Project as a front for covert activities, and Smuckler confirmed MSU-CIA links before the state legislature. If students, faculty, or reporters wished to verify *Ramparts'* report of MSU's $25 million in profits or role in procuring armaments for Diem, they had only to go to the library and check out Robert Scigliano and Guy Fox's *Technical Assistance in Vietnam: The MSU Experience* or *The Final Report Covering Actvities of the MSU Vietnam Advisory Group*. On page four of *Technical Assistance*, Scigliano and Fox stated that the federal government gave the university $25 million for the MSU project, and the *Ramparts* inventory of MSU-procured weapons that Hannah claimed was a forgery came from *The Final Report*. A MSU student had photocopied the inventory and mailed it to *Ramparts*.[22]

Fishel redoubled his efforts to defend American policy in Vietnam, addressing a thousand curious and suspicious students in the Union Ballroom on April 20. But his praise for Johnson fell upon deaf ears. *Ramparts* had undermined his scholarly credibility as well as dealt a death blow to campus prowar organizations. SDSers Steve Badrich, Joel Schkloven, and David Hooker dedicated a song to Fishel which they performed on campus (sung to the tune of Johnny Rivers' "Secret Agent Man"):

> Sitting in his Berkey office one day,
> Saigon planning tables the next day,
> Wesley always gets his way,
> He's backed by the CIA,
> Odds are he'll be anywhere tomorrow.
> Super-Fishel man, Super-Fishel man,
> Where Wesley takes his field-trips
> Not even Bond would go.
> Saigon's first regime was his creation,
> We wondered where he went that spring vacation,
> Because in the public eye,

He's a teacher, not a spy,
A servant of the truth, and not the nation.
Super-Fishel man, Super-Fishel man,
We haven't lost a teacher,
We've gained an agent man.[23]

MSU SDS, in spite of, or because of, such entertainment, became in 1966 a magnet for larger numbers of bright, nonconformist students. Andy Pyle, a Merit Scholar and lanky, slow-talking West Virginian, joined SDS because it was an intellectual refuge from the anonymity and isolation of dormitory life. George Fish had been a nonconformist since his first day on campus when he had annoyed university officials by wearing an antiwar button during class registration. He looked to SDS as an organization in which to express unorthodox ideas as well as a sanctuary from a dormitory roommate whose one-word vocabulary, "Fuck!" offended the Merit Scholar's parochial school sensibilities. SDS at MSU attracted a variety of characters—radicalized Catholics, culturally displaced Jews, secularized Protestants, and countercultural rebels. The organization was loose enough to allow its members to engage in any number of uncoordinated political activities: writing and publishing *The Paper*; putting together antiwar teach-ins and rallies; establishing a leftist film series which largely financed the chapter's projects; and laying plans to wrest control of the student government away from the conservative fraternities. If MSU SDS had one weakness in 1966, it was, ironically, also its strength: a disproportionate share of creative academic superstars who sometimes behaved like jealous intellectual prima donnas. Jack and Sue Sattel, being a few years older than the new SDSers, increasingly functioned as the chapter's big brother and sister, soothing bruised egos and cooling down inflamed passions.[24]

As MSU SDS grew, a new student antiwar organization came into existence, the University Christian Movement. During the *Ramparts* controversy, a number of concerned students in the hitherto apolitical United Campus Christian Fellowship grappled with the issue of Vietnam and Michigan State's contribution to the establishment of the undemocratic Saigon government. The MSU Christian Fellowship came to the conclusion that a political and religious university organization was needed to oppose the war, while at the same time offering an alternative to the secularized SDS. At a stormy, marathon national meeting of the United Campus Christian Fellowship on

September 6, 1966, a member of the MSU delegation, Bill Skocpol, Merit Scholar and STEP veteran, wrote tiredly to his fiancée, Theda Barron, that a new activist University Christian Movement opposed to the Vietnam War would replace the Christian Fellowship. The UCM would work towards establishing community rapport in order to reform the university, educate the people about Vietnam and civil rights, and strive to ensure social democracy for the world.[25]

In East Lansing, an informal alliance emerged between MSU SDS and the UCM based upon a friendship network rather than upon ideological considerations. Theda Barron, also a Merit Scholar and STEP veteran who was much further to the left than her Texas-bred fiancé, was friends with the Sattels, as well as with Char Jolles and Chris Steensma, SDSers and writers for *The Paper*. MSU UCM activist Dave Stockman, like Skocpol a former Goldwater supporter and devout Methodist, attended SDS meetings, wrote for *The Paper*, and earned Sue Sattel's respect, if not the respect of other SDSers who viewed the UCM's concept of "Jesus Christ, The Revolutionary" as somewhat overdrawn. Badrich considered Stockman and the UCM to be rather "parochial" and "naive." But then, he had gotten this impression from Stockman's girlfriend whom Badrich was also dating.[26]

While MSU SDS and the UCM intensified their campaign against the war and established a nascent populist alliance, *The Paper* carried a series of dispatches from Vietnam by marine private Jim Thomas. MSU students read the terse, depressing stories and poems Thomas wrote and contemplated their own fates after graduation. One poem, addressed to an imaginary Viet Cong guerilla, revealed Thomas' frustration at having to fight an insane, futile war against a people he could not hate:

It is an affair between you and me,
This momentary madness that allows us,
who toe no party lines when we're calm,
To engage in comparing reflexes,
Winner to walk still, and see.
If behind these eyes may grow remorse,
it should be ours to hold, together with
no bit of balm,
Save knowing we shared what mattered to us.
What do we care for his so lofty tears,
He who survives, since he never was here

To gain a part of our sorrows, our cares,
Knowledge of loss of what never will be?
We died, you and I, when we might have shared
Rice and a bowl of *nuc-doc*, which is tea.

On December 20, 1966, Thomas was killed in action.[27]

With Thomas' death burned into their minds, MSU SDSers Mike Price, a graduate speech student and chapter theorist, and Harvey Goldman went to the national SDS convention at Berkeley. The national SDS, on December 28, voted to form antidraft unions in order to disrupt military recruitment and induction. SDS had committed itself to illegal confrontation with the federal government. To Goldman, moral and constitutional law made this confrontation necessary:

When a system that is malfunctioning uses its laws to repress opposition, then, in order to be effective, we must strike at the oppressive laws and expose them for what they are. The Selective Service Act is morally and constitutionally repugnant. It violates the 13th Amendment (which prohibits involuntary servitude of any kind) and is designed so that if one encourages opposition and refusal to serve, the penalties will be severe. If, in order to present genuine alternatives to the American people, it is necessary to break the "law," then the obligations of our moral law will force us to commit such a crime continually.[28]

The MSU SDS's decision to form an antidraft union, which Stockman and the UCM quickly endorsed, evidenced an awakened spirit of political activism and boldness among students. When Ken Lawless, an American thought and language instructor, was fired in the fall of 1966 for editing the leftist, pornographic student literary journal *Zeitgeist,* 1,000 students occupied Bessey Hall, home of the professor's department. This event represented the first time MSU students occupied a campus building. Out of the Bessey Hall sit-in arose United Students (US), a radical student rights group which replaced the moribund, moderate Committee for Student Rights. The chair of US, Dick Oestreicher, a Merit Scholar and New York City red diaper baby, soon joined SDS.[29]

While invigorating student activism, the Bessey Hall demonstration also revealed small ideological fissures among the university's antiwar faculty. With the welcome assistance of *Ramparts* in 1966, activist faculty had vanquished their prowar faculty opponents and discredited Hannah and hawkish sentiment on the campus. But the new student militancy divided antiwar faculty ranks. Predictably, faculty activist Larrowe had joined the students in the occupation of Bessey Hall. Though not necessarily a fan of Lawless' Beat poetry, he believed that faculty and students had the right to publish whatever incomprehensible musings came to their fertile minds. Greer, on the other hand, abhorred the potential for violence associated with sit-ins and argued for calm, rational discourse. As Larrowe increasingly identified himself with the New Left, Greer moved closer to the community's nonconfrontational dovish clergy.[30]

Greer and local clergy convened the Interfaith Convocation on War and Peace at the East Lansing People's Church in January and February of 1967. The Convocation brought together three hundred liberal-dovish MSU faculty, students, and community religious leaders. Greer warned the Convocation participants that the Vietnam War undermined America's image as a friend of peace and increased the risk of nuclear confrontation with Russia and China:

The war has severely injured our position so far as our image goes in most parts of the world . . . not *one major power* has offered us military asistance in Vietnam; even those nations which are our allies and our presumed friends show little sympathy for our military intervention in Asia. Many, in fact, have been shocked, not only by the intervention in Vietnam, but by our reckless manner of conducting the war—in such a way as to provoke, openly and persistently, military counter-actions by China, Russia, or both. Fortunately, they haven't reacted yet, but it isn't because we haven't given them an opportunity. The long-held view in the world of America as a peace-loving, moral, and humane nation has been profoundly shaken.[31]

A few weeks after the Convocation, the UCM regional headquarters of the Vietnam Strategy Committee endorsed national wars of liberation from Western domination:

We support the efforts of people of underdeveloped nations to free themselves from oppressive political systems and condemn the consistent U.S. policy of anti-revolutionism. We recognize the need for new economic, social and political structures in the emerging nations of Asia, Africa, and Latin America in order to provide for self determination and an adequate standard of living for their population.

Since the regional UCM had developed an interpretation of the Vietnam War somewhat similar to that of the national SDS, though the former was more concerned with the threat of Marxist dictatorships than the latter, MSU SDS and UCM began to coordinate their antiwar activities. Kindman, Price, Stockman, and thirty-nine other activists placed an advertisement in *The Paper* stating their intention to refuse to fight in Vietnam and to encourage others to do likewise.[32]

Stockman, as chair of the MSU UCM Peace Coordinating Committee, also helped draft a proposal for antiwar activists to capture the student government in the spring 1967 elections. If a large share of students could be educated to see the Vietnam War within the context of undemocratic, un-American imperialism and racism, Stockman believed, then the radicals would have enough votes to gain control of the student government. The newly radicalized student government could then challenge the university's defense-related research and demand that students be given more freedom and power. Upon achieving these goals, the UCM-SDS coalition could emerge as a model for a national radical third party movement.[33]

The 1967 spring student government elections were the most intense, and bizarre, that had ever occurred in East Lansing. Coordinating the radicals' campaign efforts was W. C. Blanton, a Merit Scholar from Kentucky and an editor of *The Paper*. A born politician, Blanton had to gloss over the striking ideological and cultural differences among the New Left, UCM, and liberal-dovish candidates and their organizations. For example, UCM activist Gil Peach, a sociology graduate student, defined his group as radical in philosophy, but moderate in approach: "Basically, we believe the bombing should be stopped and the U.S. should negotiate with the National Liberation Front. But there is no need to grow beards and rebel." In contrast, SDSer Brad Lang, who had been elected to the student government in 1966, and helped to establish the annual "Gentle Thursday" festivities on campus which fused antiwar dissent, rock music, and LSD, characterized the war as an imperialist-capitalist conspiracy. Lang frequently campaigned under the influence of LSD, although psychedelics, his friends noted, did seem to improve his eloquence. In spite of the incompatibility of the antiwar groups and candidates, Blanton and SDS captured control of the student government.[34]

Having gained control of the student government, antiwar MSU students attended the April National Vietnam Week Mobilization rally in New York City, along with 250,000 other concerned citizens. Stockman went to the rally, but believed marching to be of limited political value, for Vietnam policy makers were only products of an insensitive capitalist system. Consequently, he argued, it was the "System" that had to be changed:

It will take more than a leisurely stroll down Madison Avenue, or even revulsion toward war atrocities, to put this ghastly thing to an end. The real determinants of the war are built into the structure of the corporate system. Concomitantly, political indifference and moral insentiency are inter-woven in the fabric of middle-class culture. Unless people get out and start radical-izing themselves and others, LBJ and his wizards will lead us right into the "Great Society" which George Orwell prophesied in his famous novel.[35]

A week after the Mobilization rally, SANE, Clergy and Laity Concerned about Vietnam, Rev. Martin Luther King, Jr., and Carl Oglesby, among other organizations and individuals, announced that they were sponsoring Vietnam Summer, a nationwide antiwar project operated by students, workers, professionals, and clergy and aimed at educating the public about the folly of Johnson's Vietnam policy and how to effect its change. Since Johnson had ignored the Vietnam Week rallies in New York City and San Francisco, Vietnam Summer organizers hoped to establish communication among the people opposed to the war, politicize the indifferent, and convert the hostile in order to exert grass-roots pressure on Congress.[36]

In the greater Lansing area, one hundred volunteers, largely MSU students and a few community residents, worked for the Vietnam Summer Project which was headquartered at the Wesley Founda-tion. Rev. Jondahl served as chair of the ten-member steering com-mittee. Lansing Vietnam Summer cast a wide ideological net, as was evident in the composition of its steering committee and sponsors: Battistini, Greer, Larrowe, Repas, Zolton Ferency, Lang, Sue Sattel, Rev. Day, Rev. Morrison, and Stockman. Many of the MSU faculty sponsoring Lansing Vietnam Summer had previously worked to-gether on planning the winter Interfaith Convocation on War and Peace.[37]

From the beginning of June to the end of September, Lansing Vietnam Summer volunteers canvassed one voting precinct every week, urging community residents to address their concerns about the war to Congress, local newspapers, business associates, friends, and relatives. In the first three weeks of Lansing Vietnam Summer, 2,000 new people were reached. Compilations from a random sam-ple of 150 questionnaires indicated that while there was little sup-port in Lansing for the current prosecution of the war, people disagreed on how to end the carnage. Fifty percent favored a negotiated withdrawal, while another 35 percent advocated an all-out military effort to win, followed by a U.S. withdrawal. Significantly, those advocating negotiations felt powerless, ignored by the administration in Washington and resigned to the continued escalation of the war.[38]

A number of volunteers, including Stockman, recommended that community members participate in the Citizens for a New Politics, "an independent grass roots political force" working "through the electoral process for pervasive change in the domestic and foreign policy which created the Vietnam tragedy." Bert Garskoff described the CNP as an "antiwar alternative to the established parties." Republicans and Democrats, he argued, belonged to "two indistinguishable and equally corrupt political parties—the great tweedledum and tweedledee of the modern scene."[39]

To many of the SDS and UCM members involved in Lansing Vietnam Summer, the CNP seemed to be the radical coalition party of the future that could bring about fundamental social change. However, to the MSU activists' dismay, the dream of a radical coalition party died that very September as Vietnam Summer came to a close. Garskoff, along with radicals and antiwar liberals from across the nation, gathered in Chicago as a result of a call by the National Conference for New Politics to forge a national third party. Militant Black Panthers intimidated and dominated the cacophonous white convention crowd. They defeated a resolution to form a third party and issued an anti-Semitic diatribe against Israel. Garskoff, who believed blacks, not whites, represented America's revolutionary vanguard, endorsed the Panthers' actions. His acquiescence, and that of many fellow Jewish SDSers, fostered division and diverted attention from the antiwar struggle. The CNP convention foreshadowed the disintegration of SDS, as religious Jewish and Christian SDS members clashed with their secularized colleagues.[40]

Following the mixed community response to Lansing Vietnam Summer and the CNP debacle, MSU students once again marched on Washington. The spirit of the October 1967 rally, unlike the 1965 April and November marches, was confrontational; moderates' pleas for reconciliation had given way to calls for "Confronting the Warmakers." One hundred thousand protestors, frustrated with the unrelenting escalation of the war, and tired of hawks accusing them of prolonging the war through their peace activism, were determined to wage symbolic war against the Pentagon. Jeff Snoyer, a reporter for *The Paper,* described his frustration with Johnson's response to antiwar protest and subsequent radicalization as a result of the events of that violent, exciting fall day:

When I had left East Lansing, I had decided not to become directly involved in the militant aspect of the march. As a college student, I couldn't afford the time or expense of an arrest, and I believed that demonstrations for peace should be peaceful and that our mere presence in numbers was worth something. Well, I walked up a slope and somehow ended up in front of the group which made the first charge up the Pentagon steps. Soldiers by the hundreds poured out of the Pentagon doors and furiously began bashing faces with the butts of their rifles. I was sincerely for peace and non-violence, but I found myself grabbing the arm of a GI whose rifle butt was about to crush in the head of a girl in front of me; I was pushing and being hit—soldiers were rushing all around us—what was happening???? The mobilization's theme was "Confront the Warmakers." . . . This was Americans fighting Americans, pitted against each other by the System.[41]

Snoyer and his fellow protestors sat down around the Pentagon, temporarily checking the GIs' advance. In the evening, after a few hundred students burned their draft cards, U.S. marshals moved in on the activists, clubbing and arresting those sitting in their path. "The Armies of the Night" had brought the war home. At MSU, the era of petitions and teach-ins had come to a close. Contending antiwar factions, one advocating confrontation with the "System" and the other committed to community organizing, began to emerge.

Pennsylvania State University

President Walker was not in good spirits in December 1964 when he informed alumni that the Communists had launched their campaign to seize control of the nation's universities. He did assure his conservative audience, however, that subversives would not be able to operate well in State College. Penn State was blessed, Walker observed, in being "out in the sticks where students and faculty members can't fade back into the community" after stirring up trouble. But still, he continued, "such trouble . . . could come to Penn State unless we prepare some defense."[42]

Confronted with Walker's thinly veiled threats, Penn State's peace activists chose the path of polite defiance. After Johnson began bombing North Vietnam in February 1965, SENSE leaders Philip Henning, a New Jersey resident and a Quaker, and Carl Davidson organized a thirty-person march across the campus. A few days later, SENSE members, with Rev. Cleeton's support, embarked upon a three-day hunger strike for peace. Their reasons for fasting were forthright:

We believe that the government's actions in Vietnam are morally wrong, and as Americans we all feel guilt for those actions.

We now feel the necessity of fasting to show symbolically our empathy with the Vietnamese people who are suffering immeasurably as a result of U.S. supported actions and U.S. supported dictatorships in their country.

During the peace fast, Davidson expressed his personal opinion on how to end the war, quoting President Kennedy: "Never fear to negotiate—it commits us to nothing other than reason."[43]

The campus response to SENSE's peace protests was not even remotely sympathetic. Hawkish *Daily Collegian* editors endorsed Johnson's tempered Vietnam policy, characterized SENSE's call for negotiations as ludicrous, and published numerous prowar letters by faculty and students. One small-town, Western Pennsylvania student stoutly defended the war:

South Vietnam is the present battlefield of the Cold War. Korea, Laos and Cuba are former battlefields. America has never had a decisive victory over Communism on any of the battlefields because of self-restraint. . . .

It is time for the United States to show its strength to the world by turning South Vietnam into a place of victory. America is capable of winning in South Vietnam and I sincerely hope that it does not restrain itself here.

Nothing would please me more than to know that the war has been carried into North Vietnam. Even though this runs the risk of another world war, what good is living if one doesn't have something that is worth dying for?[44]

Following the first barrage of prowar *Daily Collegian* editorials and hawkish letters, Davidson criticized the advocates of military escalation:

It seems that a great many people in this country have accepted the idea that to negotiate in Vietnam is, in some way, to lose.

I think this idea is extremely dangerous because it undermines that spirit of creative dialogue, compromise and human interaction on which our democratic ideals are based.

To negotiate in Vietnam does not signify failure; it only signifies that we recognize our opponent as a human capable of reason and dialogue.

. . . Another dangerous attitude I find is the willingness of so many people to advocate, out of frustration, if nothing else, the escalation of the war. To these people I would say this: that unless you personally are willing to die right now over "the issues" in Vietnam, then you have no ground on which to make this same claim of others.

. . . Finally, the most dangerous attitude that has prevailed lately, is that war in some way solves a problem. At best, I would say that war only dissolves immediate problems while creating many more for the future. War signifies, without glory, the utter failure and complete breakdown of all that is human in men.

. . . While there is still time, let us urge our government to cease fire and negotiate in Vietnam. Let us try to succeed with reason rather than to fail with bullets.[45]

Despite Davidson's eloquent appeal, the escalating Vietnam War remained a remote concern to the majority of PSU students and faculty. Johnson's introduction of U.S. combat forces into South Vietnam, however, generated more campus interest in the war. SENSE and faculty activists Keddie, Withall, and Rozen organized a teach-in on April 8. Two hundred students attended, a small turnout compared to other campuses. Nonetheless, Rozen considered the event to have been a success since it attracted "a great many students who ordinarily don't come to these things."[46]

Following the teach-in, SENSE and the PSU Socialist Club escalated their peace offensive. Their achievements were underwhelming; just thirty-nine PSU students went to the April peace march in Washington. The editors of the *Daily Collegian* trivialized and castigated the Washington antiwar rally, describing the demonstrators as "militants" with unkempt beards and long hair. Appalled, Rev. Clecton remonstrated against the campus newspaper for emphasizing the appearances of a few activists while ignoring respected dovish speakers such as Senator Ernest Gruening.[47]

Hostility towards PSU's antiwar activists was widespread, going far beyond the *Daily Collegian's* slanted reporting. When the Socialist Club invited a Haverford College activist to come to Penn State in April to narrate a Viet Cong propaganda film, chaos ensued. Hundreds of hawkish students crowded into the Sparks Building to curse the speaker. The Pittsburgh *Press* joined the prowar chorus, condemning Walker for allowing the film to be shown at the university:

Officials of the Pennsylvania State University have a duty to explain why a Communist propaganda film on Vietnam was permitted to be shown in a classroom. . . . This shocking lack of responsibility on the part of university leaders can only be regarded as an insult to the U.S. servicemen who are dying in Vietnam.

. . . There can be no excuse for university officials allowing this type of enemy propaganda. . . . Academic freedom is distorted when it condones activity in support of a band of terrorists such as the Viet Cong who—under the pretext of "liberation"—have slaughtered hundreds of Vietnamese villagers who dared to oppose them, and many Americans who went to their aid.

Penn State owes an apology to all Pennsylvanians for this shameful and disgusting incident . . . .[48]

In complete agreement with the Pittsburgh *Press*, the PSU YAF declared, "We didn't hear anybody yell for 'academic freedom' for the Nazis during World War II." YAF also accused SENSE and other "peace mongers" of offering Americans a program of "piecemeal surrender" to the Communists. But for all of that, YAF newsletter editor and student rights activist Carl Thormeyer had kind words in April for past SENSE president and student government presidential candidate Barry Clemson. YAF's relative political tolerance was further underscored when Thormeyer became a summer *Daily Collegian* reporter, covering the activities of SENSE and campus civil rights groups. His columns were more objective than standard *Daily Collegian* fare.[49]

PSU YAF, in the months following Johnson's escalation of the Vietnam War, embraced any number of seemingly contradictory political attitudes. The organization supported SENSE's right to speak out against the war, but did not believe that the concept of academic freedom extended to arbitrarily defined Communists. Thormeyer and YAF were sympathetic to the civil rights cause and participated in campus protests against *in loco parentis*. The student conservatives considered SENSE's advocacy of a negotiated U.S. settlement with the Viet Cong to be treasonous, yet, in the same breath, described the peace activists as well-intentioned pacifists and counted Clemson and Socialist Club activist Jim Grant among their friends. Such ideological inconsistencies were born of a feeling of intellectual isolation which YAF and SENSE shared in 1965, as well as the fact that face-to-face interaction moderated the conservatives' abstract political ideals.[50]

If the campus Right appeared torn between its dual desires to support and denounce the radicals, then the campus Left in the fall of 1965 was no less of two, or several, minds. SENSE's membership, according to activist and English graduate student Paul Ennis, ranged from conservative to Communist. He also noted that "the only thing that unifies the membership is that all of them do take issue with some armed conflict that is going on around the globe. Some take issue with all, some with a particular conflict." On the issue of the Vietnam War, Ennis stated, some SENSE activists favored a military de-escalation and negotiations while others advocated an immediate American withdrawal. Max Molinaro, a freshman SENSE member who had been a Student Peace Union activist at the academically respected Philadelphia Central High School, advanced a modest view of the value of antiwar protest: "I think the most I can do is try to get rid of some of the stupidity and poor, fallacious reasoning by which people on the American scene are making their decisions." To Molinaro, the war was the result of a series of tragic mistakes which could be corrected by negotiations with North Vietnam. In contrast, James Creegan, Molinaro's high school friend and a freshman Socialist Club leader and SENSE partisan, did not believe that the war was a product of American foreign policy makers' mistaken reasoning. Rather, the war provided evidence of American capitalist plans to "maintain the entire underdeveloped world as a source of colonial exploitation." Creegan, and SENSE's hard left faction, wanted the NLF to defeat U.S. imperialism and encourage other Third World peoples to do the same.[51]

The philosophical chasm increasingly separating SENSE's radical (violent revolutionary) and conservative (pacifist to liberal dovish) factions was temporarily bridged by the issue of draft resistance which all members could, in varying degrees, support. In October, four members of the Socialist Club and SENSE burned their draft registration cards at the campus mall as one hundred students watched. Lively discussion ensued when Creegan urged the student body to "join us against the war machine of United States imperialism which is perpetuating most of the crimes of this war." Hawkish students pummeled Creegan and FBI agents from Philadelphia soon descended upon State College in search of the draft resisters.[52]

Walker warned that the draft resister limited "his employment possibilities . . . not only because his loyalty is suspected, but because his rationality also is questioned." He did not understand the activists; they were profoundly moralistic, not career-minded. Socialist Club leader and New Jersey native Jacob Heyman defended his actions as necessary to promote social justice:

> Whether an unjust law is local state or federal law [it] is still an unjust law and must be corrected. No law is sacred and irrevocable, but has to change with the times. In January 1964, with this principle in mind, I civilly disobeyed the state of Georgia's trespass law which was used as an instrument to maintain that government's policy of segregation.
>
> . . . We were arrested for breaking the trespass law. . . . In the same sense I civilly disobeyed the recent draft card law. . . . I view the draft as an instrument of the United States government for continuing its unjustified war against the Vietnamese people.
>
> . . . I would willfully serve in a war against a fascist or a reactionary government, but would object violently to being drafted to fight against the Vietnamese people in their struggle for independence.[53]

SENSE president Andy Stapp described his actions as absolutely necessary to stop the war, for "We wouldn't be fighting in Vietnam now if we didn't have the draft. The draft is not the cause but the means." After Stapp made this brief public statement he disappeared. Rumors abounded on the campus as to his whereabouts and YAF members who inquired after Stapp's fate were met with fearful looks. It later developed that Stapp, faced with the choice of prison or military induction, chose the latter. While stationed at Ft. Sill, Oklahoma, he became an organizer of the antiwar Soldiers' Union and was subsequently court-martialed in 1967.[54]

With Stapp's mysterious disappearance, and unannounced visitations by FBI agents, PSU's antiwar students in the fall of 1965 were clearly on the defensive. Worse, hawkish students continued to assault peace activists and to disrupt antiwar events. During a SENSE picket of a campus guest speaker, General Maxwell Taylor, a Vietnam policy architect, a crowd surrounded the thirty demonstrators. The prowar partisans marched in an ever-narrowing circle around the picketers, lobbing eggs and hurling obscenities at them. This continued for some time while campus police officers looked on, prepared to arrest the antiwar demonstrators if they attempted to break out of the circle. And so, the campus peace movement was under symbolic and actual siege.[55]

The *Daily Collegian*'s editors offered no quarter to SENSE activists, characterizing them as "extremist," "hysterical," and an "embarrassment" to the university. *Daily Collegian* news editor Laurie Devine, who had covered the fall draft card burnings, eagerly cooperated with the FBI, identifying all of the activists involved and expressing glee at the prospect of their imprisonment. The PSU Greek system in November sent 5,000 prowar postcards to U.S. soldiers in Vietnam, and the student government joined the Greeks in defending Johnson's foreign policy. This was not surprising since PSU's fraternities and sororities, representing the largest Greek system in the country, dominated the student government and had decisively defeated all of the radical and YAF reform candidates in the spring elections. Meanwhile in Harrisburg, the state senate overwhelmingly passed a ban on radical speakers and organizations at public universities who "exploit the youth in our country and thus plant the seeds of dissent in the minds of our college students."[56]

Despite this hostile environment, the campus peace movement at least made its presence known. In addition to picketing Taylor and burning draft cards, ten Socialist Club members in October braved residents' taunts and marched in front of a State College army recruiting office. That same month, as part of the International Days of Protest which involved peace demonstrations in one hundred American cities, SENSE, for the first time, picketed the ORL, thus publicly linking university-military research to U.S. Cold War-Vietnam War policy. Yet Rozen was able to convince just forty PSU students and faculty to participate in the November peace rally in Washington.[57]

A bitter fall gave way to a winter of discontent for campus antiwar activists. SENSE attempted to go from dormitory to dormitory provoking discussion of the war, and once again picketed the State College army recruiting office, this time being pelted with snowballs and icicles for several freezing hours. A few days after this protest, its organizer, Mark Gould, an undergraduate liberal arts major from New York City, was one of nine students arrested by sixteen undercover police officers on the campus for marijuana possession. Not coincidentally, all nine were well-known activists in SENSE and the Socialist Club. The peace activists also tried another one hundred-hour peace fast in the Hetzel Union Building (HUB) in order to raise students' political consciousness.[58]

One faction of SENSE, tiring of ineffective peace fasts and polite picketing, attempted to push the organization further to the left. In response, Molinaro advanced an amendment to the organization's policy statement placing SENSE on record against violent revolution:

SENSE, while sympathetic toward the aspirations of the Vietnamese people, must, as an organization favoring peaceful settlement of conflict, state that we cannot support military means to achieve a victory by any side in an armed conflict.

This amendment sparked intense discussion, with Creegan supporting Third World armed revolution and declaring that "the causes for war in this world are basically starvation and social degradation, and the main party responsible for it is the United States through its foreign policy." Unable to reconcile the pacifist and Marxist positions, Molinaro and ten other SENSE members resigned.[59]

With the departure from SENSE of many of its most moderate and effective members, and with Davidson's decision to pursue graduate studies at Nebraska, the organization was crippled. Believing that SENSE had outlived its usefulness, Gould moved to establish a campus SDS chapter:

The need for an SDS chapter on this campus has been shown by the recent factionalism in SENSE, which of course points out the lack of a unified radical student movement.
. . . We ask for student support insomuch as the students of this campus are the future members of our society and, if they enter our society and want to see a truly democratic society—then they can't afford to be apathetic and unconcerned, which is my impression of the Penn State student body as a whole.

Eventually, Molinaro joined SDS in hopes of exerting a moderating influence on the chapter. Writing frequently to his friends, Davidson chided them for sowing divisions within the peace movement.[60]

As the campus Left fragmented and further isolated itself, YAF was experiencing its own problems. Thormeyer, the organization's most dynamic leader, had had to devote less time to YAF, preparing himself for graduation and service in Vietnam. An Erie, Pennsylvania, undergraduate and devout Baptist, Denny Tanner, had assumed more organizational responsibilities but proved to be, as YAF activist Tom Bennett lamented, a terrible administrator. He did, however, remain true to Thormeyer's lead, insofar as he strongly supported the Vietnam War, while condemning students in February who mocked the SENSE peace fast. But unable to motivate the membership and recruit new followers, YAF entered two very lean years.[61]

With the Right and Left in disarray, moderate activists sought to exert their limited influence on the campus. The PSU Newman Club inspired the Student Ecumenical Council to sponsor a "Peace Pray-In." Pam Tross, an education major and council president, set forth the religious-minded students' view of the Vietnam War:

> We are concerned about the schism which war is causing in our own country and the inhuman suffering which it is causing in Vietnam. We surmise that the situation may grow worse. We wish to take positive actions to reunite the country and to push toward an honorable peace . . . .

At the Wesley Foundation, Rev. Cleeton, who had earned a reputation as a committed civil libertarian and friend of SENSE *and* YAF, launched in March a "Student-Faculty Roundtable" series on the war. Roundtable discussion participants included former SENSE member Roger Marsh, who described the philosophy of conscientious objection, and SDS faculty advisor Keddie, who denounced Selective Service for primarily drafting "the working classes" and "the culturally deprived."[62]

Clemson and twenty-five pacifist-oriented students who were attempting to keep SENSE viable, initiated an annual Saturday picket against the war in March. A few weeks later they demonstrated in front of a State College draft board. (One board member stated afterwards that he did not believe in awarding student draft deferments to liberal arts majors since society did not need "their kind," assuming that anyone who did not study engineering or medicine was a likely Communist.) The beleaguered SENSE activists also attempted to march in the April 30 State College Loyalty Day Parade, but irate police officers roughly removed them from the line.[63]

Few students participated in the campus clergy's roundtable discussions and peace pray-ins, and even fewer turned out for what became SENSE's final antiwar demonstrations. Consequently, the spring of 1966 did not seem to offer much promise to the campus antiwar movement. But then the unexpected happened: an awakening of long-dormant *mass* student discontent. Clemson, Ad hoc Committee for Student Freedom co-chair, called for a student rights rally in April. Two thousand students appeared in front of Old Main, the university administration building. Two weeks later, following another large rally, five hundred students occupied Old Main seeking an audience with Walker. But such action did not translate into support for the campus antiwar movement since the students were demonstrating for less strict curfew hours and dormitory visitation rules, and not protesting against the war and university military research. Still, many students had became comfortable with the idea of protest and learned that authority could be challenged.[64]

Changing PSU student attitudes towards protest and authority could also be seen in the columns of the *Daily Collegian*. By the spring of 1966, a group of left-leaning reporters were assuming positions of greater influence. News editor and Philadelphia undergraduate Julie Moshinsky urged further protest on behalf of student rights, accused the student government of attempting to co-opt the student rights movement, and ridiculed anti-Communist extremism which had led to American military intervention in Vietnam. The *Daily Collegian's* reform faction, led by Bill Lee, also gave front-page coverage to *Ramparts'* MSU-CIA exposé, subtly informing PSU students that state universities were greatly implicated in the conduct of the war.[65]

As greater numbers of PSU students championed student rights, and reformers took control of the campus newspaper, Davidson, who had been keeping abreast of developments in State College, charted new directions for the national SDS. At Clear Lake, Iowa, in August, Davidson characterized the universities as managerial training centers in which students were prepared to become "scabs" for "corporate liberalism." Critical of single-issue student reform groups, and dismayed with out-of-touch SDS intellectuals, Davidson advocated student syndicalism:

I use the term "syndicalism" for a crucial reason. In the labor struggle, the syndicalist unions worked for industrial democracy and worker's control, rather than better wages and working conditions. Likewise ... the issue for us is "student control. ... What we do not want is a "company union" student movement that sees itself as a body that, under the rubric of "liberalization," helps a paternal administration *make better rules for us.* What we do want is a union of students where the students themselves decide for themselves what king of rules they want or don't want. Or whether they need rules at all ... [66]

Even though Davidson's ideas would determine the direction of the national SDS for the next two years, few in the PSU SDS followed his lead or took his advice, a not uncommon situation as far as National Office and campus chapter relations went in the 1960s.

In the fall, SDS subsumed SENSE, despite Davidson's argument that a merger would only further isolate campus radicals and hinder the peace movement from broadening its membership base. However, SDS leader Neil Buckley did not welcome doves and libertarians into the movement unless they first recanted their political errors. Thus, with just sixty determined members, SDS claimed the campus antiwar movement as its own, and fraternizing with YAF, the enemy, became unthinkable.[67]

Having transformed SENSE into "the Vietnam arm of SDS," as Philadelphia SDSer Norman Schwartz so aptly put it, SDS launched its fall offensive. In October, SDSers attended Mass, wishing to illustrate that the Catholic church had a long history of supporting right-wing regimes, and not just in South Vietnam. While the liberal-dovish priest conducted services, SDSers placed in the pews copies of an article describing the ideological harmony between Nazism and Catholicism. Not content to defile a house of worship with anti-Catholic propaganda, SDSers also publicly denounced the "Pennsylvania primitives from the back woods and small towns" who debased the university's cultural and intellectual life. For an organization disproportionately represented by Jews and Philadelphians, and operating in a cultural milieu which was heavily Catholic, Protestant, and rural, such tactics were not at all conducive to expanding the movement's following.[68]

That fall Penn State SDS also devoted attention to other projects, including a boycott of the student government elections. Meanwhile, the PSU SDS affiliate, the Hillel Liberation Front, which Leverett Millen had founded in October, set to work. In contrast to the devout ex-Catholics, such as Neil Buckley, who had disrupted Mass, Millen and the HLF politely leafleted Sabbath services at the Hillel Foundation and sought to advance dialogue, not confrontation. Committed to reaching out to the local community, the HLF, in cooperation with Rev. Cleeton, documented white working-class poverty in Centre County. Millen, campus doves, and faculty activist John Withall also came together in a futile effort to elect Cleeton to Congress. Most SDSers scorned this undertaking, with Creegan arguing that electoral politics would not awaken the American people "to the facts of American imperialism" and enable them "to realize the revolutionary change necessary to destroy it."[69]

In addition to the tensions which were evident in SDS's contrasting ideological and tactical beliefs, personality politics severely hampered the organization. Neil Buckley, a "Hollywood version of a campus radical" his critics claimed, had an enormous ego as well as ambitions to become a national New Left figure. Jealous of Creegan's influence in the chapter, Buckley at one point had to be restrained from beating up his rival. When Buckley and Creegan were not fighting each other, they were locking horns with Pam Farley, who was increasingly disgusted with the male SDSers' sexism. In December 1965, at a national SDS conference in Illinois, Farley had encouraged the women delegates to meet separately in the ladies' restroom. This action won her few accolades and, when she took the same course of action at Penn State, made her highly unpopular with the male SDS leadership. There was also a problem with contrasting approaches to the developing counterculture since many SDSers enjoyed dope. Creegan had little patience with such self-indulgence and tried to set a refined tone, always wearing a white shirt, black tie, and black pants. Given the contentious example of the chapter's leaders, who were loosely tied to the National Office, few PSU SDSers were interested in joining and financially supporting the National SDS.[70]

In spite of the organization's personality and ideological conflicts in the fall of 1966, PSU SDSers realized that the chapter was too small and vulnerable to allow internal conflict to become debilitating. Just how vulnerable the chapter was became clear at its last 1966 antiwar demonstration. In November, President Walker invited former Austrailian prime minister Sir Robert Gordon Menzies to come to State College and defend America's Vietnam policy. Determined to challenge Menzies' prowar views, SDSers attended his lecture at Schwab Hall. As soon as the SDSers, who were seated in the balcony, quietly unfurled a protest banner, campus security officers demanded their identification cards and wrote down their names. Afterwards, Withall and the Centre County ACLU chapter issued a sharp condemnation of Walker for intimidating antiwar protestors. Walker ignored their criticism and took disciplinary action against the students.[71]

The winter of 1967 began miserably for SDS and then worsened. In January, Walker refused to reveal whether or not he had provided the names of SDSers to HUAC investigators. Further trouble developed from an unexpected quarter: John Warner, the black president of the Student Union for Racial Equality (SURE), expelled the organization's white members. Several white and black student civil rights veterans protested Warner's exclusionist policy, but white SDSers denounced them as racists. SDS's support for Black Power further alienated the campus from the radicals and led dovish students to wonder how SDS could oppose white, but not black, racism.[72]

SDS's unpopularity on the campus mounted throughout the winter. At a SDS dormitory forum in January, a student argued that if SDSers did not like the university then they should drop out of school. Buckley replied that such an action would be like "committing suicide if one does not like the world rather than trying to change it." The audience then urged Buckley to commit suicide. Following that incident, the chapter learned that it lacked even minimal student support when twenty SDSers protested against American use of napalm in Vietnam. Dozens of students wrote angry letters to the editors of the *Daily Collegian*, defending napalm as the "oozing salvation" from Communism. One typical letter writer contended that

the purpose of the Viet Cong is strictly terror; whereas the purpose of the bombing—of the napalm—is to flush out the VC and thus rid the country of terror. . . . The Viet Cong have shown their mettle by taking the leader of each village they terrorize and splitting his legs like we would a wishbone . . . how do you fight that kind of ungodly savageness? You fight it just as forcefully as it is provoked. You hit them with the same type of warfare that they are using—because it is the only thing those animals understand . . . [73]

The radicals' unpopularity was further driven home as they attempted to determine if Walker had been in contact with the HUAC. After the president declined to meet with SDS, seventeen students took over his office. Cleeton convinced the students to leave, which they did, only to resume their sit-in days later. Threatened with arrest at the second sit-in, and aware that their protest, in Buckley's words, "would have aroused no support from either faculty or students at the time and would have effectively ended SDS's campus operations for the rest of the year," they left. Buckley soon accused Cleeton of plotting with Walker to thwart the movement and slander SDS. Actually, Cleeton had convinced hawkish students not to charge into Old Main and assault the radicals.[74]

Fortunately for SDSers, they had a valuable ally in the *Daily Collegian*. Its editors devoted an entire week of front-page coverage to the state-wide SDS convention at PSU in February and carried an extended and sympathetic analysis of the New Left in April. *Daily Collegian* editor-in-chief Bill Lee, although occasionally critical of his friends, particularly for supporting SURE's exclusion of whites and for denigrating Cleeton, praised PSU SDSers for their intelligence and articulation. Vehemently opposed to the war, Lee pleaded for a negotiated peace settlement and condemned those students who supported the use of napalm in Indochina.[75]

Over the course of the winter a reaction to the *Daily Collegian* and SDS congealed. Hawkish faculty, administrators, and student government representatives denounced the campus paper for its leftist editorials. After Lee finished his term as editor in the spring of 1967, the *Daily Collegian* moved from a New Left to a dovish position and YAF members Linda Cahill and Laura Wertheimer became reporters. The YAF chapter was rejuvenated, thanks to the forceful leadership of Harold Wexler, a Levittown, Pennsylvania, political science major. YAF also benefited from the influx of hawkish students from Philadelphia and New York City. Many of these students were culturally conservative Jews who viewed SDSers, doves, and Black Power advocates as anti-Semitic fascists.[76]

Even though a number of SDSers, including Buckley and Millen, had grown weary of campus organizing and decided to drop out of school, they enthusiastically laid plans for a series of spring actions against the war. PSU SDS organized a teach-in on the war in April and invited David McReynolds of the War Resisters League to speak. Prior to the teach-in, which attracted four hundred students, SDS rallied one hundred students on the university mall while hecklers shouted obscenities and PSU maintenance crews sprayed the demonstrators with chemicals.[77]

A few days after the teach-in and campus rally, one hundred PSU students and faculty—the largest contingent of PSU students yet to take part in a protest outside of State College—went to New York City to participate in the Spring Mobilization march against the war. Eight PSU SDSers were among the two hundred youths who burned their draft cards in Central Park. Millen movingly proclaimed his opposition to the war:

I am opposed to the United States Government's immoral, illegal and genocidal war against the Vietnamese people in their struggle for self-determination ... All conscription is coercive and anti-democratic, and ... it is used by the United States Government to oppress people in the United States and around the world.

. . . I hope that a sense of urgency will move campus people to leave the campus to resist the draft and organize a movement of resistance to the draft and the war with its base in poor, working class, and middle class communities.

. . . I regret only that I had to strike a match and violate the holiness of the Sabbath in committing the act of draft card burning—I can only hope that God will look down upon what I did and say—Amen, brother. [Author's note: Orthodox Judaism prohibits starting fires on the Sabbath.]

Soon after the draft card burnings, the FBI once again descended upon State College in search of the resisters, their addresses provided to the agents by the university administration. At the same time, the Manhattan District Court subpoenaed seven PSU SDSers to stand trial for their acts.[78]

By far, the majority of PSU students who marched in New York City and attended the campus teach-in were liberal doves, not SDS partisans. It was obvious as early as the winter of 1966 that two separate and competing strains of antiwar dissent were emerging on the campus: one of the confrontational and radical SDS variety and the other nonconfrontational and dovish. In liberal doves' ranks, campus clergy played leading roles. Boyer and Cleeton organized peace fasts and antiwar ecumenical services, and provided draft counseling to anxious students. Dismayed with the collapse of SENSE, its former advisor Boyer, a World War II conscientious objector, sought to encourage a pacifist alternative to SDS's militancy. Following Boyer and Cleeton's lead, interns at the campus Presbyterian, United Church of Christ, and Lutheran churches established the "Jawbone," a place at which students could listen to folk music and discuss social justice issues.[79]

The doves and a few of the radicals set aside their philosophical differences while working on the local Vietnam Summer project which the State College Friends Meeting and Bill Lee coordinated. Three hundred student, faculty, and clergy volunteers canvassed central Pennsylvania, vainly attempting to mobilize sentiment against the war. Once summer ended, George Andrews, an assistant professor of mathematics, founded the Citizens for Peace in Vietnam in order to continue local antiwar organizing and convince the electorate to vote for dovish candidates.[80]

Meanwhile many SDSers not involved in the Vietnam Summer project, and utterly contemptuous of the electoral system, pursued their own forms of protest and organizing. On July 4, six SDSers joined an Independence Day parade in State College, displaying an American flag upon which the words, "Make Love, Not War," had been painted. Affronted, residents beat the protestors, after which the police arrested the SDSers for flag desecration and disorderly conduct. This spectacle so upset prowar faculty stalwart Henry Albinski that he testified on the SDSers' behalf at their trial. Centre County judge R. Paul Campbell fined and imprisoned the activists, but went easy on the one female defendant, Shelley Janoff, a Pittsburgh speech major: "Shelley's just a little, single gal," Judge Campbell intoned, "She's not quite as knowledgeable or sophisticated as the others and I felt she could become a victim of some of these over-zealous demonstrators."[81]

A number of PSU SDSers that summer eschewed street protests for their own version of community organizing, establishing a commune in nearby Bellefonte. Initially, Buckley, who had announced with much fanfare his intention to leave school in order to work for revolution, sought to create a communal environment which would serve to radicalize the working poor. However, the SDS commune quickly became a magnet for juvenile revelers. None of these teenagers were interested in SDS diatribes on revolution. Indeed, the often drunken street kids physically intimidated the middle-class SDSers. By August, the commune had disbanded, succeeding only in convincing the locals that SDS wished to corrupt the morals of their children.[82]

The beginning of the fall session saw PSU students presented with decidedly contradictory messages from their elders. Walker spoke to 5,000 entering freshmen, warning them to avoid self-righteous, deluded antiwar activists. A month later, Senator Joseph Clark, a Pennsylvania Democrat, appeared on the campus. He argued that a negotiated peace settlement in Vietnam was desirable and defended the patriotism of antiwar protestors. Coming from a hitherto uncritical supporter of Johnson, Clark's talk served to legitimate campus peace dissent.[83]

Clark's speech indicated that campus antiwar dissent had become almost acceptable; the student government even went so far as to criticize Selective Service director Hershey for wanting to draft immediately student antiwar protestors. Emboldened, SDS, having learned little, became more militant. (Certain members had learned, however, ways in which to promote themselves in the eyes of the National Office, falsely informing *New Left Notes*, the national SDS newspaper, in the fall that PSU SDS was the first party which uncovered naval research on the campus.) When CIA recruiters came to PSU, SDS sponsored a teach-in. At the teach-in, newly appointed political science instructor Jim Petras described the CIA as "an agency of subversion . . . minimizing social reform . . . subverting students they bring to the United States from foreign countries." Not content with just holding a teach-in, SDSers harassed the CIA recruiters. The *Daily Collegian's* editors chastised them for using "militancy to stop militancy" and "trampling over the rights" of others.[84]

Undeterred by criticism from SDS's only significant, albeit lukewarm, supporter, Jim Grant condemned those who, in the name of democratic pluralism, decried militant confrontation:

A society which can fight wars all over the globe making the world safe for colonialism and exploitation in order to maintain the wealth and power of those forces that control the society, is hardly democratic.

Such a society cannot be changed by nice, quiet peaceful methods. . . . Hitler could not be removed from power nonviolently nor can the forces of colonialism and imperialism be removed from the backs of the oppressed without a struggle. . . .

. . . Power comes only to those who take, whether on a university campus or in a tropical jungle whether "fair" or "foul" means is used . . . .

Such rhetoric had little appeal to most students, but Creegan attributed the lack of campus support to SDS's tactical moderation. Obviously, more intense protests were required for 1968.[85]

The State University of New York at Buffalo

Disturbed by Johnson's bombing of North Vietnam in February 1965, Rick Salter and Dave Gardiner sought out professors Ed Powell and Sid Willhelm. After quick deliberation, the graduate and faculty sociologists decided to distribute antiwar literature on the campus and enlisted the enthusiastic support of *Spectrum* editor Jerry Taylor. Since the university administration would not permit the activists to set up a literature table in the Norton Union unless they had a formal organizational name, Salter and Powell chose to call themselves the SUNY-Buffalo SDS.[86]

The SUNY-Buffalo SDS chapter immediately set out to publicize the antiwar message at the university, with Taylor using the *Spec-*

trum to condemn the war and inform students of the upcoming eleven-hour campus Vietnam teach-in. To the SDSers' delight, 1,500 students and faculty, instead of the fifty they had anticipated, turned out for the April 5 teach-in. In contrast to the MSU teach-in, only a handful of hawkish engineering students picketed the event and its organizers permitted prowar positions to be represented. Philosophy professor Marvin Zimmerman vigorously defended the war, arguing that while the American bombing of Vietnam was a cause for concern, the alternative to slaughtering thousands of Vietnamese would be a Communist victory followed by even greater bloodshed. Unfortunately for Zimmerman, most students were repulsed by his contention that killing was necessary to prevent further killing.[87]

Taylor, a teach-in participant as well as organizer, considered the event a great success and urged *Spectrum* readers to enlist in SDS and march for peace in Washington. One hundred and fifty students and faculty took his advice and demonstrated at the nation's capital. The energetic editor next organized an antiwar march down Main Street from the campus in early May, prompting Congressman Richard McCarthy to castigate the Soviet-inspired SDS and the editors of the Buffalo *Courier-Express* to demand that Furnas expel the disloyal demonstrators. Joining the hawkish chorus, a small number of students, with Zimmerman's assistance, circulated a prowar petition on the campus prior to the Buffalo rally. Although they garnered a respectable 3,200 signatures, this figure was far below the number of students who endorsed similar petitions at other state universities. Further, the overwhelming majority of prowar letters which appeared in the *Spectrum* advocated a negotiated peace settlement, not a military escalation of the conflict.[88]

By summer, SDSers realized that the most vehement supporters of the war would not be fellow students, but rather, community members. Congressman McCarthy championed U.S. foreign policy:

The right of a peaceful people to exist outside the Communist orbit is being brutally challenged.

The United States has intervened to uphold the right of this people to control its own future.

. . . the United States could not possibly withdraw from the war without a catastrophic let-down of the forces resisting Communism all over the globe . . .

The local press reiterated McCarthy's contentions and featured readers' letters which branded campus activists as disloyal and recommended that they be drafted and, hopefully, killed.[89]

Brushing aside the community's denunciations, the pacifist core of SDS urged adoption of nonviolent tactics to end the war. At a well-attended SUNY-Buffalo "Solve-In" on the Vietnam War in July, Taylor exhorted draft-age youth to "consider the alternative of conscientious objection . . . choose not to work in defense industries, choose not to pay the defense part of your taxes" and adopt "voluntary poverty as the moral equivalent to war." Although unwilling to take a vow of poverty, thirty SDSers committed themselves to the principle of civil disobedience and participated in the Committee for Non-Violent Action's (CNVA) Washington peace protest in August.[90]

Troubled that activists were confining their efforts to the campus and in Washington, YAWF chair and SDSer Gerry Gross urged students to "go to the people in the Buffalo and Niagara Falls areas with our literature . . ." because "polls indicate that there exists a large antiwar sentiment among the workers in these areas." Concurring with Gross, SDS, as part of the October International Days of Protest, organized rallies in Buffalo's LaFayette Square and in front of the U.S. Consulate in Toronto. But if the Buffalo protest was intended to pave the way for a student-worker peace coalition, then it failed miserably. As one hundred students and faculty picketed in downtown Buffalo, a larger crowd assembled on the steps of the city hall to listen to Mayor Chester Kowall read a "Proclamation of Vietnam Day in recognition of the patriotic, selfless and dedicated efforts of servicemen fighting daily in this great and noble cause of combating Communism." Catholic school children and members of the Buffalo Veterans of Foreign Wars waved American flags and loudly applauded Kowall. Meanwhile at the SDS protest, passing workers and teenagers shouted, "cowards, yellow bellies!" FBI and police officers were also present photographing the demonstrators.[91]

Paradoxically, the peace protest in Toronto proved to be better attended and received. Four hundred American students from SUNY-Buffalo, Cornell, Rochester, and Syracuse, and nine hundred Canadians, picketed the consulate. SUNY-Buffalo SDSer Steve Crafts, a graduate English student, delivered a ringing call for peace:

The United States is waging an immoral war against the people of Vietnam. We are asked to condone the indiscriminate slaughter of men, women and children in the name of peace and freedom. There are many Americans who have deluded themselves into believing that napalm, saturation bombing and trained killers are mechanisms of peace; and that news manipulations, violations of international law, and support of ruthless dictators . . .

are in the interests of freedom. Such beliefs are the product of a morally and spiritually bereft society.

Thoreau was to say of another war: "How does it become a man to behave toward this American government today? I answer, that he cannot without disgrace be associated with it." We have come today, refusing to associate with the disgraceful brutality in Southeast Asia.

But we cannot dissociate ourselves from the struggles of millions to attain true peace through freedom from social and economic oppression.

We mourn the deaths of Vietnamese and American people, and on their behalf and for all mankind, WE DECLARE PEACE.[92]

A few SUNY-Buffalo students, distressed with the extent of campus antiwar sentiment, began in the fall to voice loudly their complaints to the university administration. Receiving words of encouragement but no action from Richard Siggelkow, dean of students, they turned to Zimmerman for guidance. The philosopher, deeply concerned about the "misguided" campus pacifists and the Communist front SDS, helped them found in November the Students for U.S. in Vietnam. The organizers, thirty YAF and Young Democrat members, circulated a petition on the campus to have that "commie editor" of the *Spectrum* removed and prevent SDSers Salter and Powell from using the paper as a radical forum. One anti-Communist student suggested that the *Spectrum*, "this treason sheet," change its name to the *"Red Hanoi Express."* Sadly for the hawks, they were able to persuade just thirty-eight students to attend a prowar October YAF demonstration in Washington.[93]

Frustrated campus hawks, unable to acquire a mass following, formed in January 1966 a more militant organization, the Committee for Victory in Vietnam: "Having observed the complete lack of democracy, brutal totalitarianism, and persecution of opposition, which has taken place in Communist nations, we believe that the forces of Communism should be vigorously opposed." Although critical of Vietnamese Communist persecution, the hawks, largely YAF members, saw no moral contradiction in persecuting peace activists. During a January SDS campus peace vigil, YAF activists descended upon the SDSers screaming, "they don't even believe in God—let's kill them." This incident upset the student body and YAF subsequently became defunct.[94]

SDSers, assured that they had a solid base of support on the campus, began mailing moderately phrased fund-raising letters to community residents thought to be receptive to their peace message.

In addition to written appeals, pacifists in the chapter, grouped around Dan Katz, suburban Buffalo undergraduate and member of the Western New York chapter of the CNVA, championed community antiwar demonstrations. Their first community protest of 1966, picketing the appearance of Humphrey at the Statler Hilton, ended sourly in arrest and prosecution for disturbing the peace. At Katz's trial, a police officer testified that he had recognized the SDSer from previous protests and decided to arrest the chief troublemaker.[95]

Confronted with police and community hostility, the pacifists in SDS also increasingly found themselves engaged in an ideological struggle with more sanguine chapter members. Since the fall of 1965, with the influx of YAWF members into the chapter, SUNY-Buffalo SDS had been torn between two competing impulses. The first impulse, identified with Taylor, Salter, and Powell, embraced the ideas of ideological pluralism and tactical spontaneity. In contrast, the second impulse, represented by the YAWF partisans, dictated ideological rigidity and organizational discipline. By March of 1966, these competing impulses began to divide the chapter. Taylor published searing *Spectrum* editorials lambasting SDSer and Brooklyn native Barbara Brody for her "doctrinaire" and "authoritarian logic." He was particularly incensed by Brody's demands that SDS's alternative education project, the SUNY-Buffalo Free University, become "a training center for political radicals, and that it must include a 'revolutionary' (one must suppose 'Marxist-Leninist') bias." To Taylor, Salter and Powell, "no authority should be unquestioned," regardless of whether that authority was the American military-industrial complex or a revolutionary Marxist liberation movement. Further, they identified with the moral examples that pacifist Quaker faculty such as Newton Garver provided. Brody and YAWF, however, insisted that effective radicalism required a framework grounded in Marxist theory and championship of violent revolutionary change.[96]

Despite the Brody-YAWF challenge, the original core of SDS accelerated the pace of antiwar organizing. SDSers' efforts, in what had become a familiar pattern, were received with mixed responses: enthusiasm on the campus and hostility in the community. In late March, SDS and YAWF, temporarily setting aside their differences, rallied in LaFayette Square. During this protest, several Buffalo residents jumped on Willhelm and a number of other demonstrators as the spectators chanted, "Communist kikes go back to New York

City." Immediately after the confrontation, the Buffalo Common Council voted 12 to 1 in favor of a resolution calling for Furnas to "investigate the use of state facilities and agencies to conduct anti-Vietnam activities."[97]

On the other hand, campus antiwar protest proceeded with broad-based support. SDS sponsored a "Dialogue for Peace" in March and April which included a popular teach-in and soap box speeches. The *Spectrum* contributed to the peace education offensive by featuring a lengthy series on university-military research. Further, SDSers Salter, Bill Mayrl, and Carl Ratner formed a committee to promote draft resistance. Established in February, the Graduate Student-Faculty Committee on the Selective Service (GFCSS), with the aid of student government president Clinton Deveaux and the SUNY-Buffalo AAUP chapter, launched its attack on the draft in April:

> Since the probability of an individual attending college is greatly dependent on various factors, i.e.—his financial status, socio-economic background, etc., student deferment permits members of certain "classes" only to avoid military service. Not only is this undemocratic and unworthy of the theoretical American tradition, but it is also resented by many members of the non-academic community, resulting in increased anti-intellectualism. Sectors of the American population who are the most politically influential in our society, the middle and upper classes, may remain aloof from the calamity of war.
>
> . . . the military, through the Selective Service System, is undermining the autonomy of the university by establishing for the university the definitive qualities of intellectualism and intellectuals, using the coercive device of the 2–S deferment.
>
> Due to excessive pressures, many students are encouraged to conform academically, to cheat, and to plagiarize. Fear of low grades discourages experimentation in course work and selection. In these instances, the Selective Service System is destroying the idea of the university.[98]

The GFCSS organizers soon found themselves embroiled in controversy when they challenged university administration cooperation with Selective Service. Furnas resented the activists' insistence that he not forward student grades to Selective Service, as well as their calls for the university to cease administrating the Selective Service exam which decided whether or not students retained their draft deferments. Subsequently, after an initial meeting with the GFCSS, he declined further contact with SDS. Rising to the occasion, fifteen members of GFCSS in early May spontaneously occupied Furnas' Hayes Hall office. Taken by surprise, the president, who was preparing to retire and fearful that his law-and-order subordinates might overreact, agreed to negotiate, with Deveaux acting as a mediator. The SDSers consented to end their forty-five-hour sit-in, but not to forsake agitation. That week they held an open forum on the draft which attracted 350 sympathetic students and faculty. After the forum, three hundred students, led by Salter and GFCSS member Larry Faulkner, picketed Hayes Hall. They were quickly joined by an additional 1,000 students. Perplexed, Furnas chose to have his successor work out a solution.[99]

With summer break and Furnas' departure, the activists bided their time until the fall session and the installation of Martin Meyerson as the new university president. However, there was one major student antiwar protest in August, the CNVA's Hiroshima Day Peace Walk. This demonstration, like its predecessors, was marred by violence. As CNVA members marched from the campus to the American-Canadian Peace Bridge, residents screamed, "Jews! Jews! Show me a Jew commie and I'll show you a faggot!" and "Kill the Jews—to the ovens!" Buffalo police officers did nothing to calm the hecklers; indeed, they ignored the prowar partisans' provocations and chose to arrest CNVA marcher and sociology graduate student Bill Sander for blocking the sidewalk. During the arrest, an ethnic Italian policeman flung the pacifist against a patrol car, splitting open Sander's head.[100]

The fall session began on a hopeful note for antiwar activists as Meyerson pledged to promote dialogue on the campus. At his first campus press conference, the liberal educator propounded a new administrative philosophy and style: "I think students ought to take a major part in discussion of policy and of educational issues that face them." To reassure students that he was committed to his own version of participatory democracy, Meyerson set out to settle the issue of university cooperation with Selective Service. He worked closely with the student government to sponsor a university-wide forum on the draft and approved of the holding of a binding campus referendum to determine whether or not the Selective Service exam would be administered. After three days of balloting, 2,205 of 3,278 student and faculty voters (67 percent) approved university administration of the Selective Service exam.[101]

SDSers were not pleased with the referendum results. Unwilling to admit that the campus, while sympathetic to the Left, was firmly liberal-centrist, Salter and the new *Spectrum* editor and SDS member from Staten Island, New York, David Edelman, lashed out against Meyerson. Edelman and SDS characterized the president as "a slick liberal" who desired to preserve "the anti-democratic structure of the university" by using democratic trappings such as the referendum. In the same vein, Salter, in articles which appeared in the *Spectrum* and *New Left Notes,* claimed that Meyerson had scheduled the referendum at short notice before students had been fully apprised of the larger issues involved. Further, Salter contended, "the cooperation between military and university violated a fundamental principle of the university (autonomy from the state) and therefore was a question which could not be decided on by a referendum." Meyerson astutely replied that SDSers had been agitating against Selective Service for several months and, therefore, had had plenty of time to sway students to vote for a change in university policy. Additionally, Powell and Willhelm, admirers of Meyerson, felt that students had a right to vote in favor of something which the sociologists philosophically opposed. They were also uncomfortable with SDS's position that some issues were too fundamental to be subject to arbitration or a vote. Such a position, Powell and Willhelm believed, drastically redefined the concept of participatory democracy to mean that the people who were to decide would only be those with the correct ideological line.[102]

Recriminations from the disastrous referendum, on top of pacifist SDSers' ineffectiveness in attracting community support, gave much encouragement to YAWF partisans. Convinced that they could combat "corporate liberal fascists" like Meyerson better than SDS, YAWF members, now a significant presence in SDS, issued in October an ultimatum to the chapter: either accept discipline or quit. Angered, Edelman ridiculed YAWF while the majority of SDSers resigned from the organization. Carl Ratner smugly claimed that these ex-members would not be missed since they had "nothing to say about anything" and, in any event, were "red-baiters" and "McCarthyites." Jim Hansen, a graduate philosophy student, joined the fray, attacking participatory democracy as an ineffective means to fight Cold War liberalism. What was required, YAWF contended, was a new SDS which recognized the need for revolutionary violence and movement leadership. Not surprisingly, in November the Buffalo Common Council, which had barely tolerated the old pacifist-oriented SDS, prohibited the new SDS from demonstrating in La-Fayette Square.[103]

The Common Council's politically motivated ban on SDS-YAWF protests in Buffalo was just one of many setbacks experienced by campus activists. In particular, the more open-minded SDSers, already reeling from the YAWF conquest and purge of their chapter, lost Rick Salter's leadership. As early as August 1965, the Immigration Division of the Justice Department in Buffalo, responding to anonymous calls, had moved to revoke Salter's student visa and deport him to Canada. Although Salter assured the government that he was not a Communist party member, the Immigration and Naturalization Service (INS) was unconvinced. Salter and his four-year-old daughter were forced to leave the United States in October 1966.[104]

With Salter out of the way, the YAWF-SDS feared no serious campus opposition to the escalation of antiwar militancy. In addition to demanding that Meyerson overturn the results of the fall referendum, the radicals developed new tactics with which to oppose military recruitment on the campus. Subsequently, twenty-five activists maintained a sustained sit-in and set up literature tables next to military recruiters in the Norton Union. Intense discussions ensued among students and between radicals and army, marine, and navy personnel. Non-violent hippies joined the protests in April, distributing roses and lollipops to everyone and brushing aside the militant activists who thought they should be armed with baseball bats in case of trouble with the administration.[105]

Meyerson, counting on liberal student and faculty support for his sweeping educational reforms, chose not to provoke a violent confrontation by physically removing the activists from the union. Instead, he sent an eloquent letter to undergraduate SDSer Don Blank:

> The university can no more forbid one type of recruitment visit than it can forbid one kind of speaker. . . .
>
> It must be emphasized that our tradition has been to protect the right of students interested in any programs, as well as the right of dissent.
>
> However, all members of the university community must continue to share responsibility for maintaining a climate in which diverse views can be expressed, freely and without harassment, lest dissent become a form of minority tyranny.[106]

Meyerson's defense of civil liberties, and Blank's subsequent retort that free speech did not extend to a military which was engaged in killing, had little appeal to the campus countercultural forces. In the spring, Mike Aldrich, an undergraduate from South Dakota and flower power advocate, founded LEMAR. Countercultural students and faculty also organized an April "Angry Arts Festival" and May "Taurian Festival of the Druids" which included antiwar plays, poetry readings, dances, and body paintings. More than 2,000 people gathered in nearby Delaware Park to tune in, by far the largest campus peace demonstration up to that time. Convinced that they were constructing a free zone in fascist Buffalo, the politicized hippies proclaimed: "when the stench chokes the life of freedom and feeds the monster of conformity which stands guard over our great society, we must arise and unite to slap this beast."[107]

Buffalo residents observed the rise of the campus counterculture with dismay. Many locals cheered the arrest of LEMAR's faculty advisor, Leslie Fiedler, and wrote to Meyerson denouncing LEMAR and the radical *Spectrum* editors who published "filth, perversion and degeneration." Hawks in the student government, realizing that Deveaux's great involvement in national antiwar organizing left the liberals temporarily leaderless, made their play. These representatives, all engineering and business majors, denied funds for a campus Student Mobilization Committee (SMC) antiwar march in Washington and demanded Edelman's resignation. If Edelman did not resign, they vowed to withhold appropriations from the *Spectrum*, effectively abolishing the newspaper.[108]

The English department, which included some of the most determined civil libertarians on the campus, soundly rebuked the student government for seeking to control the newspaper's editorial policy. But such efforts mattered little, since Buffalo radio and television stations had joined the battle against the *Spectrum*. With community support, the conservative faction in the student government felt confident enough to ignore Meyerson's subsequent defense of free speech and a free press. Soon, Edelman and the New Left-oriented *Spectrum* reporters resigned. However, within a few months, other radicals had taken over the paper.[109]

As the battle for control of the *Spectrum* approached its climax, the Buffalo Mobilization, a loose coalition of ideologically diverse clergy, faculty, and students, defied the Common Council by rallying in LaFayette Square. Lutheran minister Ken Sherman and Catholic priest John Pietra read a joint statement to the crowd of 250:

The church in America can no longer preach peace in its sanctuary and then sanction, and send with blessing, its youth to kill.

God is the judge among nations and God wills that nations not lift up military might against nations.

Significantly, Buffalo police officers and locals, respectful of clergy-men, did not harass the antiwar demonstrators. After the rally, how-ever, the FBI exerted pressure on the Barnabite Order to have Father Pietra transferred to Toronto.[110]

Following the Mobilization peace rally, Rev. Sherman, SUNY-Buffalo biophysics instructor Donald Mikulecki, and SMC activist Bill Yates established a Vietnam Summer project in Buffalo and founded an alternative newspaper, the *Buffalo Insighter*. The SMC, in cooperation with Quakers and local clergy, provided draft coun-seling to area youths, showed antiwar films, distributed peace liter-ature and canvassed the community in order to nurture opposition to the war. Meanwhile, the *Buffalo Insighter* investigated university and community military research. Mobilization organizers also con-ducted a Hiroshima Day antiwar march through the city which attracted four hundred participants. This time, police officers and hecklers did not attack the marchers.[111]

The SUNY-Buffalo SMC, led by undergraduate and *Buffalo In-sighter* editor Mike McKeating and SDSer and Chicago native Carl Kronberg, championed a militant line governed by "the Marxian principle of democratic centralism." To demonstrate to Buffalo that the SMC was going to bring the war home, activists leafleted work-ing-class high schools. Far from revolutionizing city youth, how-ever, blue-collar juveniles, who resented the privileged radicals, mobbed the vanguard of the proletariat. Unchastened, Yates trum-peted that the radicals had won a significant victory at the high schools and called for more such revolutionary activity since "elec-toral politics are a fraud."[112]

Despite McKeating and Kronberg's disdain for electoral politics, there were some activists who retained faith in the electoral process. Don Mikulecki and twenty Vietnam Summer volunteers, supporters of the Citizens for a New Politics and the Black Panthers, labored mightily on behalf of Rev. Herman Coles' Common Council cam-paign. The radicals anticipated that Coles, the pastor of the Salem-Riverside United Church of Christ, would lose the election. Never-theless, Mikulecki argued that Coles' campaign served an important community education function:

Its main objective is to raise important issues before the city and point to the failure of other candidates to address themselves to these issues, which include:

The effect of the Vietnam War on Buffalo. . . . The rate of economic growth in Buffalo is lower when the nation is preoccupied by war produc-

tion, so that as the Vietnam War escalates, the Niagara Frontier begins to lag
behind in providing new jobs. . . .

The problems of the inner city and the need for the white man to
understand and support the concept of "Black Power." Mr. Coles sees a real
need for educating the white community to overcome racism and to learn
to trust the black man's ability to take the initiative in bringing about social
change.[113]

Unfortunately for the SMC, residents were not willing to support
Black Power. Republican Alfreda Slominski, appealing to her ethnic
constituency's desire for law and order, smashed Coles. Her victory,
in a predominantly Democratic city, was the product of a mounting
backlash against campus protest and the black uprising in Buffalo's
ghetto in June. According to the regional ACLU, Buffalo police
escalated the racial conflict by randomly gassing and clubbing blacks.
In response to such criticism, police officials blamed the riot on the
outside agitators who attended and taught at SUNY-Buffalo.[114]

Disturbed by the community backlash against the university, and
dreading the likelihood of increased campus unrest, Meyerson tried
to seize the initiative and please all discontented parties. To Buffalo's black community he promised university scholarships and programs to alleviate poverty. To the city's bitter ethnic populace Meyerson pledged that SUNY-Buffalo, with its enormous financial and
intellectual resources, would revitalize the region's economy. To
students the president offered expanded cultural facilities and the
creation of intellectually stimulating storefront colleges. And to
medical, biophysics, and engineering faculty, upset with the university's evolving commitment to the liberal arts, he approved of the
acquisition of a Themis grant. But in attempting to placate disparate
campus and community constituencies, Meyerson revealed his political weakness. Radical students and foes in the faculty, administration, and community realized that a politically secure university
president would not be so eager to please everyone.[115]

Meyerson's sense that campus unrest was about to enter a more
intense phase proved correct. In October, several hundred students,
faculty, and clergy gathered at the Norton Union to urge massive
draft resistance. Willhelm, having become more militant since his
beating and Salter's deportation, spoke of the necessity to "liberate
ourselves before we can go to another country and liberate them."
And liberation, the sociologist concluded, required draft resistance
so as to "dry up the military's ocean." Going one step further than

Willhelm, Mikulecki contended that "there is no difference between the American government (in this war) and the support the German people gave to the Nazi government when it destroyed six million innocent people."[116]

Following this protest, Larry Faulkner and a few friends announced their intention to resist induction into the military and published an open letter to the FBI:

Many of us have never before been involved in a political movement and have become resisters for strictly humanitarian reasons. We question the sincerity of a government that bombs and burns women and children in the name of freedom.

Originally, jails were built to protect peaceful citizens from those who would violate their basic rights. Now we place peaceful people in prison to protect a war-like majority from exposure to reason and sanity. Your soul . . . must surely recognize the obvious absurdity of this course.

Inspired by such well-reasoned defiance, fifty-one SUNY-Buffalo students turned in their draft cards, and several Resistance rallies, with the number of participants ranging up to six hundred, were held on the campus and in downtown Buffalo throughout the fall.[117]

The spirit of campus dissent seemed contagious. One hundred and forty activists took part in a "March on Buffalo's War Industries" in October and the SMC sponsored a two-day antiwar convocation which attracted five hundred participants. Answering the call to "Confront the Warmakers" in Washington, 525 SUNY-Buffalo students and faculty rallied at the Pentagon. Liberal student government representatives, caught up in this environment of escalating protest, routed their conservative opponents and passed a resolution demanding an end to the war. Two hawkish representatives resigned in disgust, paving the way for student government president and New York City resident Stewart Edelstein to call for a university ban on campus military recruiters.[118]

SDS-YAWF and the SMC, heartened by the momentum of campus activism, began a relentless crusade against military, Dow, and CIA recruiting at the university. SMC leaders McKeating and Kronberg responded to Meyerson's repeated defense of academic freedom for all:

We feel that you cannot take the bourgeois liberal position that you are against the napalming of children, but you defend Dow Chemical's right to recruit people to napalm. Or that you are against the CIA's murdering of thousands of people around the globe daily, but that you defend their right to come on campus and coerce people into doing the murdering.

This is not a matter of free speech. We are not talking about the CIA coming on campus to explain their philosophy or policy. We're talking about them coming on campus and holding secret meetings with a few potential murderers in the basement of the Placement Center.[119]

Twenty faculty, notably Powell, Willhelm, and Mikulecki, endorsed the essentials of the SMC's analysis and pledged in an open letter to the campus to "block access and in other ways to obstruct recruiters from Dow Chemical Company and the Central Intelligence Agency should they appear on our campus." Other faculty argued before the faculty senate that "recruitment is not an educational function of the university." Further, they contended that, "the chief cause of disorder on this or other campuses is not the irresponsibility of students. It is the stubborn continuation of an unjust and futile war by a government unresponsive to the moral torment this war inflicts upon the generation compelled to fight it." The faculty senate debated for three tense hours before voting 197 to 72 to permit recruiting. Meyerson influenced the outcome of the vote, warning that

Internal threats to the university through disorders can easily result in our losing control of our own affairs . . . disorder breeds further disorder . . . the use of force (even "non violent") breeds counterforce. The use of force more often than not is beyond the control of university authorities. The fabric of a university, even the strongest, is a fragile thing . . .[120]

But the Left would not heed Meyerson's warning, for, in Mikulecki's words, the university had played "into the hands of warmakers by dividing students over the question of academic freedom." In December, three hundred demonstrators, many of them dressed for battle in khaki green dungarees, dashed about the campus in search of Dow recruiters. The university spirited the men from Dow from one building to another, barely keeping ahead of the protestors. Rumors of the recruiters' whereabouts abounded, leading roving bands of up to five hundred students to search Hayes Hall and the Norton Union. Exhausted, the Dow representatives fled, causing Bill Mayrl to gloat, "clearly our movement has scored a victory in a battle that continues. . . . The movement will continue to struggle to stop the use of university facilities by war criminals."[121]

The SMC-Dow clash provoked wildly different responses. Pacifist philosophy professor Newton Garver, appalled by the protestors' mob spirit, praised campus police officers for their self-control. Students did not know what to make of the affair, registering their confusion in a student government-sponsored referendum. More than four hundred voted to ban CIA and Dow recruiters from the campus, while over 1,800 favored their presence. And a growing anti-Meyerson faction in the administration, convinced that he had encouraged disorder through his civil libertarian stances, forced a change in university policy. Henceforth, student disrupters would be suspended or expelled.[122]

As acrimony overcame the campus, Mayrl called for a final meeting of radicals prior to Christmas break. The 150 people in attendance were unsure as to whether or not new, less dramatic tactics should be developed. No consensus emerged. However, the group did agree that a right-wing reaction on the campus and off was unlikely. Violence and repression, they believed, would not occur in the New Year. Yet several leaders advised the activists "to wear heavy clothes and to bring helmets" at future demonstrations.[123]

Kent State University

Having acquired invaluable experience in campus organizing with the Kent State CORE chapter, Tony Walsh and Dave Edwards set out in the fall of 1964 to build a peace movement. The Kent Committee to End the War in Vietnam claimed just a dozen student members and received financial and moral support from a handful of faculty: Sidney Jackson, Bob Ehrlich, and English professors Doris Franklin, William Hildebrand, and Howard Vincent, a Quaker. Most students ignored the group while the faculty, who were, KCEWV member Joseph Jackson noted, "armchair academics and anti-Communists," maintained a contemptuous attitude towards the activists.[124]

Once the Vietnam War escalated, indifference and contempt gave way to hostility and persecution. At the first campus antiwar demonstration in the university's history, in February 1965, the dozen KCEWV and Young Socialist Alliance members were viciously mobbed. Over one hundred hawkish students pelted the activists with apples and oranges and kicked YSA secretary Barbara Brock in the face. Passions inflamed, the hawks grabbed the protestors' placards and confiscated and burned antiwar literature which the KCEWV had brought to the demonstration. Shocked, Joe Kuachta, a campus police officer and friend of Walsh, roped off the picketers to prevent further assaults. However, the crowd simply retreated a few yards and then threw rocks at the cold and terrified activists. President White declined to take disciplinary action against the assailants.[125]

Remarkably, the KCEWV and the YSA elected to continue demonstrating on the campus while Walsh and Joseph Jackson doggedly spoke against the war in the university's dining halls. Ehrlich, risking his continued employment, fired off a great number of letters to the *Daily Kent Stater*, most of which were not published, urging students to become informed and politically active:

> If Kent State University is going to produce students who are alive intellectually and emotionally, some kind of engagement with the very serious problems that transcend the now very limited boundaries of the university, problems that can be made to be "student activities" if the students want them to be, is absolutely essential.

Ehrlich, Walsh, and Jackson's efforts were not entirely unsuccessful. By April, the KCEWV's weekly demonstrations attracted twenty participants, as opposed to twelve, and thirty-six Kent State students attended the Washington peace rally. Of course, hawkish students continued to assault the activists, but now there were sufficient numbers of committed protestors to fend off attacks.[126]

The university community and the townspeople lashed out against the antiwar activists. In April, White described the KCEWV's organizers as publicity-seeking "martyrs" and opined that the YSA's goals "are distasteful to the overwhelming majority of us. Similarly, the mass of students within a true university process will come to see the shallowness of its arguments." Following White's lead, the editors of the *Daily Kent Stater* taunted the KCEWV and advised hawkish students to refrain from violence since this only made the nonviolent antiwar activists appear "mature," "respectable," and "sympathetic." The campus newspaper, as well as the *Record-Courier*, also prominently featured numerous hawkish letters and greatly publicized the Young Democrats and Young Republicans' May prowar campus rally which brought out two hundred students. And many community residents and faculty expressed their feelings in hateful letters to Sidney Jackson. He calmly responded to the correspondents who had the integrity to sign their names:

I do not believe we can defeat the Viet Cong any more than the French, because the VC's are local people fighting for their own territory and we are outsiders. Just because a few "operators" like our guns and dollars doesn't change that.

The Asian Communists have such a vast job to do to feed their millions that they are in no position to take us on, even if they wanted to—by attacking us at home.

The millions seem to respond in large measure to what the Asian Communists offer them. That is their privilege. I do not see that anyone appointed us to try to stop it. . . . Our presence in Asia makes no sense.[127]

Anti- and prowar demonstrations continued throughout the summer and fall of 1965, with the latter many times larger than the former. At the campus KCEWV demonstrations against the war and ROTC that fall, hawkish students in the dormitories flew American flags from their windows as they blasted the Star Spangled Banner on their stereos to drown out antiwar chants. KCEWV member Mike Van DeVere sought to reason with the hawks:

This country is based and evolved from demonstration, the right of every man to disagree, and the duty of these who dissent to publicly criticize.

I hear the words "American" and "freedom"—these words have a hollow and empty ring—when they come from those who attempt to crush criticism and apparently don't have any imagination and fear those who do. Do these concepts of "Americanism" mean—no dissent—a complete lack of imagination—and freedom to do only that which is popular?

Those few students and faculty members who truly believe in "freedom of speech" and the "American way" should . . . have the intestinal fortitude to support those who wish to exercise their right to free speech and dissent.[128]

Weary of the unrelenting persecution the KCEWV and the YSA faced at every protest, Barbara Brock instigated a demonstration in February 1966 against the *Daily Kent Stater*'s biased and hostile coverage of the antiwar movement. Although this action had no effect on the campus newspaper's hawkish editors, it did impress a number of students and faculty who paused in front of Bowman Hall to listen to Ehrlich, Van DeVere, and Walsh's pleas for fair play. Subsequently, ten faculty members bestirred themselves in April to form a committee on the draft and conscientious objection. Sensing a small change in campus opinion, Walsh and his compatriots felt emboldened to participate in the KSU spring parade. Transforming Walsh's ratty '58 Dodge convertible into an antiwar float, the KCEWV followed the parade queen through Kent's streets. Brock passed out peace buttons and literature on napalm while Edwards and Roy Iglee, who were dressed in black and wearing gasmasks, waved to the stunned spectators. Intrigued by the KCEWV display, two hundred students attended a May antiwar rally on Blanket Hill and loudly cheered the activists.[129]

Even though the KCEWV discovered that it was possible to mobilize sympathetic crowds, the number of committed activists remained small. Its ranks were also deplenished by Walsh's graduation and Barbara Gregorich's forced resignation from the faculty in June, a consequence of her arrest in November 1965 at a Cleveland Socialist Workers' party meeting. At the first peace vigil of the fall of 1966, only twenty students participated. But the disappointing turnout did not deter Joseph Jackson from speaking at dormitory functions and maintaining a lonely vigil at a KCEWV literature table in the union. His persistence paid off by October as a group of freshmen joined and reinvigorated the organization. Among the new recruits were two wildly different undergraduates who soon played leading roles in the KCEWV—Ruth Gibson, a lower-middle-class Methodist from West Virginia, and Howie Emmer, a Cleveland red diaper baby.[130]

The KCEWV soon stepped up the pace, as well as broadened the scope, of its activities. In the fall, the activists brought Dr. Benjamin Spock to the campus to speak against the war. In addition, one student peace partisan and a professor, in cooperation with a former KCEWV member and writer for an alternative Cleveland newspaper, established an underground network to conduct draft resisters to Canada. By the spring of 1967, the campus peace movement had made notable headway. One hundred and fifty students and faculty journeyed to New York City for the April Mobilization rally and the KCEWV had persuaded 240 students and eighty-one largely timid faculty members to sign an antiwar advertisement. And the KCEWV's weekly campus peace vigils began to bring out an average of thirty picketers. However, the activists realized that there was still much work to be done. In a March student government-sponsored referendum on the Vietnam War, 727 of 1,185 (61 percent) of students who cast ballots favored escalating the conflict. Moreover, demonstrators continued to be assaulted on the campus and in Kent's streets.[131]

To dampen further the spirits of antiwar activists, Kent police began in the fall to come onto the campus in order to photograph KCEWV picketers. Kent State security officer Donald Schwartz-miller argued that it was vital to photograph KCEWV members so as "to protect the university from professional demonstrators." Elaborating on this theme, Kent police chief Roy Thompson stated that the police were searching for "outside troublemakers." Gibson decried the photographing as "a form of intimidation and harassment." She also wryly observed that "it seems kind of ridiculous to look for professional demonstrators on this campus where there have never been any before." The activists soon learned that the Kent police had entered the campus at president White's invitation as well as at the behest of the Cleveland field office of the FBI.[132]

Campus, city, and federal police agents began to pay attention to the Kent State antiwar movement because by October 1967 it had become larger and, therefore, more threatening to the anti-Communist university president and board of trustees. Two hundred KSU students, the greatest contingent yet, marched on the Pentagon that fall. KCEWV members Jim Powrie and Howie Emmer came away from the Washington confrontation with significantly different perspectives. Powrie found the night he spent on the Pentagon grounds to be both "romantic and terrifying." The burly Irishman was sympathetic towards the soldiers who surrounded the demonstrators, perceiving that they were, like him, "scared working-class youth hoping to avoid violence." Reconciliation, not confrontation, Powrie believed, would end the war. Emmer, on the other hand, had charged into the soldiers and, exhilarated, thereafter championed active resistance against political authority:

We are willing to bodily disrupt and be arrested and maybe beaten because the war is escalating so rapidly and viciously. We still must work in our communities on an intellectual level, but we also have to be willing to engage in creative forms of disruption such as non-violently sitting in.[133]

While Emmer began to advocate confrontational tactics, Gibson maintained faith in peace education. The KCEWV received encouragement in this from the campus Newman Club, which sponsored antiwar lectures by Catholic clergy, and from Rev. Jacobs, who counseled students on the draft and took part in the KCEWV's November Vietnam teach-in. Several young faculty recently recruited to the university, including Ken Calkins, Tom Dubis, and Peter Churchill, joined with twelve protest veterans to give Kent State its first teach-in on the war. The teach-in brought out two hundred students, a small number compared to other universities. But it was a solid, albeit tardy, beginning, and the teach-in did encourage several additional faculty members to voice publicly their opposition to the war.[134]

Now that dissent was seeming to catch on, and respectable clergy and faculty had identified themselves with the peace movement, previously fearful students began to use the campus newspaper as a forum for criticizing the campus hawks. Overwhelmed by the volume of antiwar letters coming in, prowar *Daily Kent Stater* editors felt compelled to publish more than they had previously. Outraged at the newspaper for printing antiwar letters, right-wing students contended that the editors had "seen fit to prostitutionalize" the paper, making it "a wailing wall where the minority opinions . . . can gain prestige." Others, notably campus student politico Frank Frisina, warned that the newspaper and the KCEWV were in league with the Communists to undermine the free world.[135]

Inured to campus opposition by this point and, in any event, preferring written attack to physical assault, the KCEWV went beyond peace vigils to active protest against military and corporate recruiters who came onto the campus. In November, seventy-five students spent two hours peacefully demonstrating against a Dow representative who was conducting interviews in Stopher Hall. Spectators flung mud at the demonstrators and tore away and torched several of their "Dow Burns Babies'" placards while Emmer read aloud the group's statement:

Today a representative of the Dow Chemical Co. is interviewing candidates for employment. This company manufactures napalm, which is essentially jellied gasoline. This jellied gasoline is used as an anti-personnel weapon in Vietnam. Upon explosion it scatters, clinging to people and burning them.

In the rural villages which bear the brunt of the napalm attacks, everyone is considered the enemy and is subject to the indiscriminate burning of the napalm.

. . . We cannot stand by and let these atrocities be carried out in our name. You can help stop these atrocities by writing letters of protest to the Dow Chemical Co., Midland, Michigan, and by joining us in opposition to the war in Vietnam.[136]

With a sense of triumph, the demonstrators left the scene, some headed for the "Blind Owl" to listen to folk music and get stoned.

Others went home to plan an upcoming rally at a Cleveland military induction center. After three years of organizing and demonstrating, the KCEWV had grown from twelve to fifty members and dissent had become a part of the campus' cultural landscape. The movement, they believed, was at last on the move.[137]

"You Don't Need a Weatherman": 1968–1969

From the Tet Offensive to King's assassination, which produced a new round of race rioting, America in 1968 was disenchanted with the Vietnam War and tired of social protest and Great Society reform. In the wake of the spring student uprising and the summer violence at the Democratic National Convention in Chicago, antiwar activists and their opponents increasingly saw the vision of the apocalypse. Moderate forces in the campus-based peace movement competed against, and often lost ground to, the radical advocates of violent confrontation. American society in general became polarized in 1968–1969. President Nixon's pledges to restore law and order, and emotional pleas for support of his foreign policy among disgruntled blue-collar ethnic Democrats, furthered class, cultural, and political divisions in America.

With the failure of Eugene McCarthy's efforts to change the Democratic party's Vietnam War policy, and with the assassination of Democratic Senator Robert Kennedy of New York, the only national, mainstream politician who appealed to students, ethnics, and blacks, more disenchanted college youths flocked to SDS. Larger numbers of students became enamored with confrontational protest tactics. Throughout 1969 students and police clashed across the nation, draft resistance mounted, and ROTC and campus military research projects became focal points of protest. Simultaneously, SDS splintered and new movements on campus—Black Power, Gay Power, and women's liberation—divided students. A cult of extremism exerted itself as radicals attacked liberal doves and provoked com-

182

munity hostility. Events had taken a life of their own, sweeping up individuals and campus antiwar organizations and rushing all towards a Day of Judgment.

The trend towards violent antiwar protest in 1968–1969 was, as it had been in 1965–1967, strongest at the elite universities. At Berkeley, Columbia, Cornell, Michigan, and Wisconsin, upper-middle-class WASP and secularized Jewish radicals occupied or firebombed university buildings. Elite university adminstrators, disinclined to alienate wealthy liberal alumni by curbing the excesses of their children, did little to halt such activities. Morever, the majority of the student body and faculty at these schools tended to support the radicals and participate in violent protests, further limiting the effectiveness of university administrators and local police in restoring order.

Emboldened by the ease with which they assumed command of their campuses, elite educated activists, particularly Maoists from Harvard and Weathermen from Michigan, moved to wrest control of the national SDS from their less violent counterparts and to gain control of campus chapters at schools such as Michigan State and Kent State. Less privileged national New Left figures, notably Greg Calvert, Carl Davidson, and Carl Oglesby, unsuccessfully attempted to check their elite opponents' advance. Meanwhile at the state universities, SDS chapters, as a result of the efforts of Michigan and Columbia activists, divided along class and religious lines. State university students from upper-middle-class and red diaper baby backgrounds tended to follow the lead of the elite university radicals, while less affluent, and generally Catholic and "low-status" Protestant activists, tried to champion educational forums and non-violent protest.

Moderate antiwar activists at the state schools repudiated SDS, while hawkish students, usually a majority of the student body at these institutions, vigorously condemned, and frequently assaulted, peace activists. At the same time, many state university presidents, supported by a less affluent and more conservative alumni group than their elite university colleagues, and egged on by a number of faculty dependent upon military research contracts, often moved decisively to crush dovish and radical antiwar organizations. Elite university radicals desired campus polarization and university administration and community retribution in order to radicalize larger numbers of students for the revolution. They managed to polarize the state schools and provoke violence and campus and community hostility; the revolution, though, did not come.

Michigan State University

The United States, MSU SDSers agreed, was in serious trouble. Since the beginning of the Tet Offensive on January 29, 1968, thousands of American soldiers had lost their lives and Johnson saw his credibility with Establishment figures and the public evaporate. It was an angry, and apprehensive, MSU president who delivered his annual "State of the University" address:

The great dissenters in our history—such as Mr. Justice [Oliver Wendell] Holmes—have consistently sought to bring about reformation, not revolution. They have not challenged the fundamental assumptions. They accepted the necessity for order and orderly processes of change if our nation was to survive. . . .

But how different it is with the radical dissenters of our day! They would arrogate to themselves alone the right to dissent. They would confine the exercise of the freedom of speech to those who agree with them. Some boldly proclaim that they will not be content until the whole system is wrecked and brought down. . . .

Faced by the necessity to declare allegiance, each of us is free personally to choose his own loyalty. But for a university—this university—there is no choice. . . . It must be proud to be reviled as a part of "The Establishment."[1]

Equally concerned with escalating radical protest, but also opposed to the war, faculty activist Thomas Greer and the dovish historians Bill Hixson and Jim Hooker joined with radical academics Larrowe and John Masterson to advance McCarthy's presidential campaign. After McCarthy's unexpectedly strong showing in the New Hampshire Democratic primary, nearly four hundred MSU students flocked to his cause, canvassing for peace in the adjacent primary states of Indiana and Wisconsin. Prior to the McCarthy campaign, these dovish students, though critical of the Vietnam conflict, had not been the antiwar movement's most active participants. They had difficulty understanding SDS's Talmudic ideological discourses and, frustrated, seldom showed up for subsequent meetings. At the same time, the majority of McCarthy's volunteers were not attracted to the University Christian Movement, for they lacked the deep religious convictions that characterized Bill Skocpol and Dave Stockman. The McCarthy crusade offered student doves, who believed in the electoral process, a suitable place to channel their energies and anger with the war.[2]

While faculty McCarthy supporters organized a university-wide discussion of the Vietnam War during regular class meetings on April 16 and 17, concerned campus clergy established a draft counseling office. Rev. Pohl took over the new Draft Information Center (DIC) with the assistance of Larrowe and Masterson, a mathematics professor. By August, they had counseled over five hundred anxious MSU students on conscientious objection and alternative service. The DIC differed from the SDS draft counseling center in that the radicals urged students not to cooperate with the government by applying for conscientious objector status or volunteering for alternative service.[3]

The draft weighed heavily upon students, particularly those about to graduate. In a harried letter to his mother, Skocpol reviewed his options and expressed uncertainty about the future:

Coast Guard is swamped—they won't even send the stuff to finish the application. . . . I'm a *selective* objector not a co, and it's far too late for a believable application anyway. I *won't* change majors on the whim of tired old men—"channelling" is one of the worst features of the draft. Teaching I will continue to try to arrange. . . . Jail is out, but Canada is, like the draft, only an undesirable alternative. "Going in" may be easy, but the consequences aren't. Which is worse, burning my bridges or burning other peoples' villages?

. . . The truth is that if there are no legal alternatives, then I am stuck with a deck full of bad cards. . . . Until all hope is gone, my opinions on what part of my life I want amputated are bound to be transient.[4]

Campus security officers soon descended upon the DIC and accused Pohl of encouraging draft evasion. The former marine denied the accusation and stated that he only informed youths on the pacifist position and supplied them with literature on conscientious objection. The officers accepted his defense, but Pohl was deeply disturbed, for he believed, correctly, that the charges brought against him were the result of investigative work by undercover agents who had come to him posing as concerned students.[5]

The issue of police surveillance and infiltration exploded in late May on the campus following the arrest of thirteen students for marijuana possession. Two days after the arrests, four hundred students demonstrated in front of the Hannah Administration Building.

A militant faction of SDS, led by Beth Shapiro, a sociology major from Brookline, Massachusetts, and Rick Kibbey, a Justin Morrill student from San Mateo, California, stormed campus, city, and county police lines in an attempt to occupy the building. Twenty-six students, including a SDS member who was also a police informant, were arrested in the ensuing melee with the 120 police officers. According to Shapiro, the real issue was the presence of informants, not drugs, on the campus. The campus and East Lansing police often arrested students for drug possession and then offered to drop the charges if they would inform on other students and attend, and write reports on, SDS or UCM meetings.[6]

Michigan State had never experienced riot, or seen the black flag of anarchy raised on its buildings. A few short years ago, pristine sorority women serenaded madras-clad fraternity men, while faculty entertained each other with barbecues. But now it was the spring of 1968, a spring which began and ended with political assassinations and which saw one million college students on one hundred campuses engaged in antiwar protest. A mentality of confrontation overcame many students, surprising SDS. Andy Pyle was amazed that a few people could organize a rally of hundreds in just minutes by waving a black flag. More sanguine, Brad Lang warned of escalating government repression:

The cool heads seem to be losing control all over the country, and it shouldn't come as any surprise that MSU cannot maintain its cool any longer than anybody else. After all, MSU is not really a bastion of progressivism; it is, at best, just another urban complex, a microcosm of the nation as a whole. As that nation sinks deeper and deeper into a morass of riot-police, yahoos, paranoids, and warmongers, it is fitting and proper that our alma mater should not only keep up with the general trends, but at times actually lead the way. The university that trained Diem's palace guard is certainly capable of instituting a reign of terror against its more rebellious students.[7]

That exhilarating and tragic spring also witnessed the first campus protest against ROTC. During the May 25 ROTC Field Days, eighty largely religious-pacifist protestors and their children, many of whom carried small white crosses, marched across campus to the appropriately named Demonstration Hall, home of ROTC. Spotting a mock Vietnamese hut, a cardboard structure wired with dynamite, the James Anderson family, Larrowe, and others formed a circle around it and sat down, causing the parents of the cadets to boo.

Meanwhile, ROTC cadets staged a pitched battle, complete with Viet Cong dead. Every time an enemy cadet died, the children placed a cross on his chest. After the battle, Green Berets came out on the field and twirled their rifles, bayonets unsheathed. To Larrowe's horror, the children ran in between the performing soldiers, playing ball and illustrating the danger young Vietnamese faced every day. A major from ROTC approached the group and threatened either to arrest them or blow them to pieces. Larrowe went over to fellow economist Walter Adams and discussed the war with an upset Green Beret captain. Adams dryly recommended that the military level one less hamlet. The soldier reluctantly agreed after it became apparent that the administration, concerned about a public backlash against MSU for arresting clean-cut Quakers, did not wish to take a stand at Demonstration Hall.[8]

The reaction of the state legislature to the spring antiwar activities on campus was immediate and hostile. State Senator Charles Youngblood, D-Detroit, following MSU SDS's unsuccessful attempt to occupy the Hannah Administration Building, labeled SDS an organization of "bearded clowns," "hopheads," and "out-of-state" student agitators promoting anarchy and decadence on campus. Youngblood stated that MSU was the property of the authorities, not the activists, and suggested that Hannah reevaluate the admissions policy for out-of-state students or else university appropriations would be slashed. Hannah, however, could not drastically reduce the number of out-of-state agitators, for the majority of them were his cherished Merit Scholars.[9]

In a cruel twist of fate, the national SDS, catching Hannah by surprise, laid plans to hold its 1968 annual convention at MSU. State Representative Harold Clark, D-Warren, and State Senator John Bowman, D-Roseville, lashed out against Hannah, demanding his resignation if he had knowingly allowed the SDS convention to be held at MSU. Clark added that SDS was "teaching things we are all against in this country, and they should not be allowed at a state-supported university." The Michigan branch of the American Legion attacked Hannah for allowing an un-American organization to convene at MSU and build bombs and destroy Selective Service. Similarly, the Michigan Department of the Veterans of Foreign Wars condemned Hannah and argued that SDS was not entitled to constitutional guarantees of freedom of speech.[10]

The 1968 SDS convention evolved into a bizarre affair. Radical attorney and sultry Chicago activist Bernardine Dohrn paraded around the campus dressed in a black leather miniskirt while championing the cause of revolutionary Communism. State legislators who had come to the campus to denounce Hannah in person, when not gawking at Dohrn, walked through the student union gazing at posters of Che Guevara and picking up co-ed hippies. A group of anarcho-syndicalists from New York City, "The Motherfuckers," enhanced the convention atmosphere by distributing "diaphragms" (diagrams) which detailed the process by which the SDS "orgasm" (organization) could be restructured. Shapiro, noting the presence of a number of conference participants with crewcuts and suits, FBI agents she surmised, put together a workshop on "Sabotage and Explosives." All of the agents attended the faked workshop, thus being diverted from some of the real sessions.[11]

In addition to being strange, the convention was also noteworthy for its divisiveness, as the three hundred undercover police agents watched the five hundred authentic delegates contest the future of SDS. The Maoist Progressive Labor (PL), which had been boring within various campus chapters in the East, advanced a program to organize workers for revolution. In order to effect a "Worker-Student Alliance (WSA)," the PL insisted that SDSers would have to forsake drugs, long hair, and other middle-class countercultural accoutrements which alienated the proletariat. Another faction, grouped around Dohrn, Columbia SDSer Mark Rudd, and upper-middle and upper-class Ann Arbor-based radicals such as Jim Mellen, Bill Ayers, Diana Oughton, and Terry Robbins, sought to unite with the Black Panthers, the Viet Cong, and other Third Worlders in their struggle against "American imperialism." Shaken by the venomous exchanges which ensued between the PL and Ann Arbor factions, delegates departed from East Lansing convinced that the movement leaders were not in touch with reality. Still, they were prepared for some kind of increased militant action.[12]

In the aftermath of the convention, MSU SDS grew bolder as well as more ideologically divided. That fall, SDS marshaled 1,500 students in front of Hannah's campus residence to burn a black cardboard coffin containing 1,000 copies of the university's new, and more restrictive, rules governing campus protest. This well-attended rally, however, belied the fact that SDS had fragmented into four distinct groups. Mark Price and George Fish inclined towards the PL position, while upper-middle-class SDSers Lang and Scott Braley, with the assistance of Garskoff, advanced the Ann Arbor line. Shapiro, Dick Oestreicher, and many others floated between the PL and Ann Arbor camps. Meanwhile, Jack and Sue Sattel and their supporters sought less and less successfully to heal the breach, hoping for reconciliation. Their efforts failed since the MSU chapter was one of two which Ayers and Mellen had targeted for conquest.[13]

A metamorphosis overcame many in the campus student Left. In 1967, Oestreicher, the shy, clean-cut leader of the United Students, had been shocked when a small dormitory kiss-in protesting university rules against public petting degenerated into a 1,500–person passion pit. By 1968–1969, Oestreicher had grown his hair long and had marched into a hawkish history faculty member's office, saluted, and informed the incredulous professor that he would not serve as a teaching assistant in his "militaristic, imperialistic" courses. Chris Steensma, the petite and innocent roommate of Skocpol's precocious fiancée, began dating Lang and took to wearing leather jackets and combat gear. And then there was Linda Evans, a Justin Morrill student from Iowa. The daughter of affluent Republican parents, Evans, who had been groomed to attend Radcliffe, came under Braley's influence. She soon became tied into the Ayers-Mellen SDS network.[14]

As MSU SDS fragmented, a very small radical-pacifist group emerged on campus, The Resistance. The goal of the MSU Resistance was straightforward and defiant: to undermine "Selective Service by taking the position of complete and open non-cooperation with the draft." Resistance members denounced Selective Service "because it is an integral part of a system that pursues a brutal war in Southeast Asia, that actively opposes attempts at social revolution in the underdeveloped world, that exploits the black people of America, that maintains institutions over which ordinary citizens exercise virtually no control."[15]

SDSers admired the courage of the Resisters and agreed with their analysis of the function of Selective Service as a tool of imperialism, but contended that the effectiveness of a protest movement is severely limited if all of its members are in prison. Rick Kibbey, watching the Resisters depart for jail one by one, was reminded of a bizarre idea, current in the 1960s, that committing suicide, thus denying your mind and body to the "System," represented the ultimate in radical resistance.[16]

The half-dozen members of the MSU Resistance, largely Justin

Morrill and humanities majors, while sustaining each other's faith, worked to form a mutually supportive community. Steve Seick, a Tacoma, Washington, freshman, claimed that after years of fear of Selective Service and its coercive powers, his decision to resist the draft, along with his friends, had liberated him from terror and self-hatred. Mike Seraphinoff, a Justin Morrill senior, considered his renunciation of Selective Service to be a rejection of killing and an affirmation of right and human community.[17]

In a letter to his local draft board, Rick Kowall, a Justin Morrill student from Alabama, explained why he had became a resister:

You cannot begin to eliminate warfare by allowing yourself to participate in an organization dedicated to waging it. It was for that reason that I returned my draft card to this board in November 1968, knowing that I would willfully refuse to report for that induction, and knowing that the probable penalty for such an act would be arrest and imprisonment. But I wanted to use it as a public platform from which I might speak out and perhaps be heard, if only by one other, so that perhaps people would begin to pay heed to what was happening and to nurture the value of human life and resolve our problems with sanity and sensitivity.

The federal government subsequently imprisoned Kowall for sixteen months and then, upon his release, ordered him to report for induction into the military or else face another prison term. Kowall, however, continued his resistance.[18]

Outraged by a government which imprisoned nonviolent individuals and foisted two hawkish presidential candidates upon the electorate, the UCM joined forces with the Greater Lansing Community Organization (GLCO), a legacy of Vietnam Summer, in order to elect local dovish candidates. MSU SDSers, according to Don Mader, a working-class radical-pacifist activist, were scornful of the electoral process and distrustful of those "whose radicalism was religious/pacifist in origin" rather than "Marxist/sectarian." Subsequently, SDS began to purge members who were not sufficiently committed to revolution. Mader, Jeff Snoyer, and Jim Ebert, Kindman's successor as editor of *The Paper,* came under increased attack as "baggy-ass liberals." By late fall, Oestreicher and Dave Freedman, a suburban New Yorker, gained control of *The Paper.*[19]

Meanwhile, Braley and Evans endeavored to promote confrontation and militancy on the campus. Two opportunities to do so presented themselves in January and February of 1969: a retirement celebration for Hannah and the dismissal of Garskoff. From Ann

Arbor came Ayers, Mellen, and Oughton to incite violence. Six hundred students occupied the Administration Building and picketed Hannah's "Farewell Address." Concerned that events were becoming dangerously out of control, Jack Sattel and Carl Oglesby, who was passing through East Lansing on a speaking tour, sought to calm the protestors. Unfortunately for the two working-class radicals, the upper-class Michigan activists ignored their pleas to desist from smashing windows. Ironically, they escaped from the police patrols unscathed, while officers beat Oglesby and football players ambushed Sattel.[20]

The board of trustees, concerned with escalating radical activism on campus and unable to agree on whom to burden with the presidency, decided in March to appoint the politically moderate Walter Adams as interim university president. Urbane and erudite, Adams believed in limited reforms of the university and supported civil rights, while vigorously opposing sweeping radical change of existing social institutions. Adams had supported the Vietnam policy of Presidents Kennedy and Johnson, but as the war dragged on with no end in sight, he came to the conclusion that the war was no longer economically and politically viable.[21]

To deal with "irresponsible radicals" who threatened disorder and who increased the likelihood of a right-wing political reaction, Adams recommended cooptation:

Giving people a stake in the system by making them an integral part of the decision-making process is possibly the most deradicalizing strategy that can be followed. Participation gives them an understanding of the range and complexity of the problems which must be dealt with. It moderates extremist and unrealistic demands. It commits participants to support the decisions which have been reached.

The campus antiwar groups, particularly the bickering SDS, had understood Republican Cold Warrior Hannah and counted upon him to respond ineptly to protest, thus garnering greater student and faculty support for the antiwar movement. But in the course of his tenure as interim president, Adams changed the game. He adroitly confronted radicals with biting satire and tried to isolate them from the "moderate" student body.[22]

SDS, which had opposed the Vietnam War long before Adams became a dove, played into his hands. Adams showed up at every demonstration, defused potentially violent situations, eschewed police force, and successfully stole the show. Angered and frustrated, SDSers, instead of engaging Adams in rational dialogue, countered urbanity with profanity, screaming, "Eat shit Adams! Fucking son-ofabitch!" Their clumsy handling of the spring anti-ROTC rallies (at which one female SDSer kicked Adams in the groin), their hardening sectarian line, and their increased reliance upon profanity to express their feelings ruined SDS's reputation with antiwar liberals. In addition, the growing drug subculture on campus, according to SDS leaders, resulted in hundreds of students coming to demonstrations stoned and uncontrollable. Further, personality and ideological conflicts within SDS confused and disgusted potential recruits and crippled its effectiveness as a major student antiwar force. SDS effectively alienated broad campus support for radicalism.[23]

Ideological divisions within the campus Left became irreconcilable after the April ROTC protests. PL supporters firmly assumed command of MSU SDS and let it be known that the extremists grouped around Braley, Evans, and Lang were unwelcome. Faculty activists Anderson, Larrowe, and Masterson, who had assisted in the recent founding of the campus New University Conference (NUC) chapter, gave the SDS-PL their support. On the defensive, Braley attempted to forge an alliance with campus black militants, but discovered that "America's colonial subjects" did not want to overthrow the capitalist system, but rather, sought to be integrated into it. Sickened by the evolving political factionalism on the campus, key SDS leaders left East Lansing. Andy Pyle had already joined his girlfriend at Kent State while the Sattels prepared to take up residence in Detroit to work in the Radical Education Project (REP), one of the last SDS communities which had not been taken over by the Maoists or the Ann Arbor activists.[24]

The national SDS formally destroyed itself in Chicago at its June convention. Dohrn and Mellen announced their manifesto, "You don't need a weatherman to know which way the wind blows," whose title was taken from Bob Dylan's cryptic song, "Subterranean Homesick Blues." The "Weathermen Manifesto" condemned counterrevolutionary white working-class Americans, praised the Black Panthers, and sought to emulate the Viet Cong by waging guerilla warfare in the United States. To underscore their revolutionary zeal, the Weathermen chanted, "Ho, Ho, Ho Chi Minh! Dare to Struggle, Dare to Win!" Michigan and Kent State Weathermen swung motorcycle chains inches in front of the faces of the twenty-four members of the MSU delegation who remained riveted to their seats in the Chicago Coliseum. At the conclusion of this demonstration, three hundred of the 1,500 delegates marched out of the coliseum and founded the Weathermen Underground. Evans was quickly elected to the Weatherman National Interim Council.[25]

Determined to bring the word of the revolution to American youth, the Weathermen initiated invasions of schools from New York City to Chicago. In late July, ten women from the "Motor City" Weather collective, including MSU SDSer Denise Ryan, invaded Macomb County Community College in the working-class Detroit suburb of Warren. They interrupted a class and pummeled students who were not interested in learning "how the Vietnamese women carry on armed struggle together with Vietnamese men against U.S. imperialism." A month later, Evans, who had just returned from Hanoi, led an assault on Pittsburgh. The Weather contingent, comprised largely of WASPs, deemed Pittsburgh the perfect "pig city" in which to wage war against "racist" blue-collar ethnics. Seventy-five Weatherwomen, clad in leather jackets and carrying a Viet Cong flag, stormed through the corridors of the South Hills High School. It took a platoon of police officers to dislodge the club-wielding women and to capture Evans and national SDS organizer Cathy Wilkerson. Both women jumped bail and fled to Chicago in plenty of time to participate in the October "Days of Rage" protests. Having traveled across state lines to incite riot, Evans was now a federal fugitive, wanted in Chicago, Detroit, and Pittsburgh. Within a few months, authorities in San Francisco, St. Louis, and Tucson charged her with constructing bombs, and Cleveland sought Evans for firebombing a police officer's home.[26]

As Linda Evans' reputation grew in the Midwest, SDSers justifiably became increasingly concerned, even paranoid, about police surveillance. MSU police school students John Donnelly and David Epstein, in addition to several ROTC cadets, joined SDS in order to write reports on the radicals. State police troopers from the Red Squad tailed SDSers and faculty activists Larrowe and Robert Repas, recording the license plate numbers of cars parked near their residences. Red Squad agents also radioed in constant reports on the activists' every movement and compelled the First National Bank of East Lansing to provide information on SDS's checking account transactions. Not to be outdone, the East Lansing Police Department maintained a twenty-four-hour vigil in front of Shapiro's apartment, photographing all who came and left.[27]

With the beginning of the fall session, the GLCO, the Wesley Foundation, and the student government began to plan a local October 15 Moratorium march against the war. Student government leader Tom Samet, no fan of SDS, although W. C. Blanton had managed his successful spring 1968 campaign, requested Adams to suspend classes and make facilities available for discussion of the war prior to the march from the campus to the state capital. Adams divined MSU students' "incendiary mood," "frustration," and "sadness." The interim president realized that if he did not make a gesture of friendship, then the march would proceed without his steadying guidance. Worse, the students, by boycotting their classes to attend the rally, would have succeeded, *ipso facto,* in shutting down the university. Fearing that a shutdown would antagonize taxpayers and state legislators, Adams made class attendance optional and provided university facilities.[28]

Liberal Republican governor William Milliken defied a Nixon White House order and attended the mass antiwar meeting at the MSU Auditorium. At the auditorium, Michigan's Democratic Senator, Philip Hart, denounced the conflict that he had supported for years and Adams, disdaining moral and legal arguments against the war, discussed the negative impact of the conflict on America's economy. Following the antiwar speeches, Adams placed himself at the head of the mile-long procession of 8,000 students and faculty and made the trek to the capital. Hoping to reinforce the harmonious, moderate image of the march, Adams, a master of political theatre, carried a small American flag and inaccurately claimed that SDS had boycotted the Moratorium for reasons of Marxist ideological purity.[29]

Adams' pronouncements and efforts notwithstanding, the local Moratorium was anything but harmonious and moderate. Speaking to hundreds of MSU and high school students at the East Lansing High School gymnasium, Norman Pollack, radical historian and member of the NUC, systematically attacked Adams' economic analysis of the war. The Vietnam War, Pollack contended, *did* profit the nation, or at least the defense contractors and multinational corporations. And the student government, although grateful for Adams' cooperation, was disgusted with particular liberals' past and qualifed continued support of the war. On November 15, student government representatives sent black Christmas wreaths to Hart and other Michigan legislators. Further, the student government clashed with the university administration after Adams declined to suspend classes for the national Mobilization march on Washington in November.[30]

The November Mobilization in Washington was the largest peace protest in American history, attracting 800,000 demonstrators, including a seven hundred-person contingent from MSU. Antiwar liberals, smarting from Vice President Spiro Agnew's attacks on the moderate October Moratorium, declined to support the more radical November Mobilization. The national television networks, too intimidated by the White House to carry live coverage of the demonstration, reported that Nixon had ignored the protest and, instead, watched a televised football game. Angered and tired, MSU students returned to East Lansing, annoyed that Nixon had flippantly dismissed the antiwar movement. They were quickly dealt another blow. The board of trustees decided to replace Adams with Clifton Wharton.[31]

Despite the nearly unique success that Adams enjoyed in channeling student and faculty frustration with the war away from forms of violent expression, as well as his popularity with students—17,033 students endorsed a petition in support of his retention as president, and even a few SDSers admired their worthy opponent—the cigar-chomping WASP was simply too controversial to remain in office. Hawkish legislators and a few faculty applied pressure on the trustees to get rid of that "radical." Consequently, the campus was saddled with Wharton. A protégé of Nelson Rockefeller and an aloof administrator who had extensive ties to AID, Wharton could not hope, and would not try, to be a rallying point for liberal doves. Indeed, doves and radicals considered MSU's first black president to be an "Oreo Cookie"—black on the outside and white on the inside. With Adams removed from power, the SDS in disarray, the UCM now disbanded and absorbed into GLCO, and the McCarthy doves disfranchised by hawkish politicians, no unified campus voice spoke against the war. Anarchy and spontaneous, violent confrontations were bound to follow.[32]

Pennsylvania State University

Penn State's administrators wasted little time in the early days of 1968 to lay down the law. Biophysics department head Ernest Pollard argued before the faculty senate that "disrupters" should be suspended since most antiwar students had "a revolutionary point of view" and were "determined to overthrow the government." As part of the university's tougher policy, dovish student government representative Jim Womer revealed, federal narcotics agents had been stationed at the campus in order to plant dope on activists and then arrest them for drug possession. Further, Womer disclosed that university security forces were wiretapping radicals' telephones.[33]

The administration's stern pronouncements and extensive surveillance activities were wildly inappropriate given the fact that the radical dissenters were so small in number and had yet to engage in violent protest. Faculty activist Jim Petras pleaded with apathetic students to build a mass antiwar movement while campus hawks referred to peace demonstrators as "demonsTRAITORS." PSU SDSers were able to attract just a dozen students to their February rally against the university's IDA affiliation. Few people seemed to be interested in SDS's contention that

this university, through IDA and other military R & D projects such as the Ordnance Research Laboratory, directly aids in the process of genocide, now aimed at the Vietnamese and surely to be aimed in the next several years against the peoples of Laos, Thailand, Cambodia, Bolivia, Colombia . . . and the Afro-American population of U.S. urban ghettoes which shares the neo-colonial status of Third World peoples.[34]

Unanticipated developments on the campus in the spring, however, quickly brought forth protest on a larger scale and unleashed a wave of hatred. Black activists, following the lead of former SURE president John Warner, began demonstrating for the increased recruitment of black students, the establishment of a black studies program, and the lowering of university admissions standards. Warner, president of the campus black student organization, the Douglass Association, set forth his philosophy in no uncertain terms: "I hate whites. . . . It's just better to hate all whites and work from there. . . . The white man is useless to blacks." Subsequently, in May, one hundred blacks occupied Old Main. Fearing negative national publicity and, therefore, reluctant to employ force against black, as opposed to white, activists, Walker agreed to negotiate with Warner.[35]

The Douglass Association made it clear that blacks did not want to be identified in students' or administrators' minds with SDS radicals, even though SDSers, with the exception of campus clergy, were the organization's only white supporters. Indeed, a number of Catholic students protested the university's decision to cancel classes because of King's assassination in April, while compelling students to attend lectures on Good Friday, seemingly elevating the mortal above Christ. It did not help matters any when Warner accused all whites, including dovish clergy and SDSers, of being complicit in King's murder: "A white person mourning the death of Martin Luther King Jr., is like a man on death row mourning the death of the person whom he killed. He does not mourn because he is sorry; he mourns because he has been found out." Outraged, white students urged Warner and his supporters to return to Africa.[36]

In this environment of poisoned race relations, SDSers competed against Black Power activists and the 700 recently politicized McCarthy, and 225 Kennedy, student volunteers for campus attention. The radicals' need for publicity increased throughout the spring as student and faculty supporters of McCarthy moved towards forging a nascent peace coalition whose ideology was liberal dovish, rather than New Left. To promote the radical position, thirty SDSers escalated protest against the IDA. SDSers chose to focus on the IDA, instead of the ORL, in part because Socialist Club leader and SENSE partisan James Creegan viewed the former as more relevant to the issue of American exploitation of the Third World. Also, Neil Buckley, now a traveling national SDS correspondent, was one of the few State College activists excited by the Columbia uprising and, consequently, eager to follow Rudd's call for further anti-IDA protests. Fortunately for them, several student government representatives had become converted doves following the Tet Offensive and were willing to sponsor an IDA teach-in.[37]

The May 16 IDA teach-in included three Columbia SDSers, Jim Petras, and PSU SDSers Creegan and Jeff Berger, a Brooklyn graduate philosophy student. Pollard and university vice president for research, E. F. Osborn, defended the IDA. Five hundred doves listened to the acrimonious discussion, even though, overall, they had been underrepresented at the teach-in's afternoon session and not represented at all at the evening session. Creegan fired the first salvo, contending that the IDA supressed "nationalist revolutions which are formed by people trying to throw off the yoke of American domination and oppression," as well as perpetuated in Vietnam "an illegal, totalitarian puppet regime of the Americans." Pollard bristled at this speech and countered that university-military research was necessary to prevent the rise of future Hitlers. Similarly, Osborn claimed that such research had saved the United States from Nazi domination in the 1940s and vowed that the nation "won't be a sitting duck again for the countries that are preparing for war." Rejecting Osborn and Pollard's references to World War II which implicitly likened Hitler to Ho Chi Minh, Berger responded that America, not North Vietnam, was the "fascist nation." Osborn lost control of himself after a student in the audience questioned Walker's ties to the DoD. Incensed that anyone would suggest that Walker's motives were less than pure, Osborn snapped, "the hell with you." Surprised by his vehement retort, the audience hooted and jeered Osborn.[38]

At long last, PSU SDS scored a few points against the university administration. Campus support for SDS, however, remained limited. According to an opinion survey undertaken by the sociology department that spring, no more than 12 percent of students approved of civil disobedience tactics; the overwhelming majority of students thus repudiated the much-publicized SDS actions and campus building seizures which had taken place elsewhere. Further, 68 percent opposed an immediate U.S. military withdrawal from Vietnam and 37 percent termed themselves doves while another 37 percent considered themselves to be hawks. The remainder were undecided. Recognizing that at heart Penn State was a conservative campus, YAF leader and *Daily Collegian* reporter Laura Wertheimer agitated for the expulsion of SDSers. Grouped behind the presidential banners of Reagan and Nixon, YAFers declared war on the "anti-Semitic," "fascist," and "law-breaking," Left.[39]

Undeterred by SDS's minimal progress at Penn State, Buckley took off for the national SDS convention at Michigan State, convinced that "as a political movement, we are on to something, and They [The Establishment] know it." Concerned with the growing influence of the PL supporters in various campus SDS chapters, Buckley worked with National Office leaders Greg Calvert and Carl Davidson to eliminate the Maoist threat. Buckley, with the advice and assistance of Wells Keddie, began his anti-PL assault by outlining several important goals of SDS:

First, that this movement in general and SDS in particular is ultimately committed to the destruction of imperialism and therefore committed to the requisite destruction of capitalism; second, that our movement is an element of the revolutionary vanguard painfully forming from the innards of America; third, that the objective conditions for revolution are not with us, but are coming up (relatively) fast, and that our pre-revolutionary conditions must be conditioned for the coming struggle; fourth, that by the time the revolution is upon us, we will have transformed from the movement as we know it today into a revolutionary political party; fifth, that we have not fulfilled our potential as a political movement in the past and, if we continue to follow our past course, that we will suffer deeply as a total movement; sixth, that our failure, while in part a result of personal contradictions, is ultimately solvable in terms of organizational restructuring; and seventh, that now is the time to change our subjective conditions to meet new objective conditions realizing that simultaneously we must develop still newer forms of organization which will supplant those we now form when the former shall have outlived their political relevance.[40]

The call for the reorganization of SDS was key to Buckley's ideological agenda. To achieve this, the PSU activist urged every SDS chapter to create study groups, or cells, which would facilitate the education of political cadres. In order to coordinate the cells, central committees had to be established, thus providing firm, ideologically correct (i.e., anti-PL) leadership at the weekly executive sessions. PL forces at the convention had a field day with Buckley's position paper, pointing out the Soviet framework for control which informed his proposal. Even Davidson, no fan of the Maoists whom he considered to be largely privileged Harvard-educated elitists, was upset with the idea of cells and central committees. As Davidson observed, Buckley's terminology called up "visions of dark cellar meetings, stocking caps and buried weapons." Buckley's perceptions notwithstanding, 1968 America was not 1917 Russia. After much heated debate, the contest between the SDS National Office and the PL partisans remained unresolved.[41]

In August, PSU SDSers Norman Schwartz and Jeff Berger journeyed to the Chicago National Democratic Party Convention. Schwartz, accustomed to the low-key antiwar protests at State College, gaped in wonderment at the thousands of riot police. "Look at the busloads of cops," he remarked to a friend, "They're all over the place." And then he became scared, "Christ, look out, they're gonna charge." Pursued down Lake Shore Drive, Schwartz eluded the police without taking a single hit. Others were not so fortunate. Later, while marching towards the Hilton Hotel, a policeman arrested Schwartz "for molting and being a creep. It's a new law. I just made it up." Not amused, he broke free and spent the remainder of the protest ducking police billy clubs.[42]

Determined now more than ever to mobilize Penn State students against the "System," Schwartz saw a golden opportunity to do just that with the looming university and community housing shortage. As fall registration began, SDS set up three tents on the Old Main lawn and made camp. Five hundred curious and upset students, largely freshmen without a place to live, joined the SDS encampment. Soon, they erected a municipal sign, "Walkertown," and set up a sound system, playing rock 'n' roll music which blasted a good part of State College. Seizing the chance to politicize Walkertown's residents, Creegan distributed anti-IDA and ROTC leaflets. Newly elected student government president Womer joined SDS in Walkertown and urged students to become politically active. Keddie also spoke, encouraging the students to apply pressure on Walker and not to expect large faculty support since that would not happen "until hell freezes over or until you graduate." More direct, Berger told his audience that now was the time to eliminate Walker, for "the more militant we get, the better chance he has of losing his job."[43]

Walkertown elicited varying responses from the campus. Assailants beat up a non-SDS graduate student on the Old Main lawn, and hawkish students lobbed a tear gas capsule at SDSers Berger, Creegan, and Sue Davidoff, an undergraduate Philadelphia philosophy major. ROTC cadets also invaded the community, wrecking the Walkertown generator, and campus police refused to respond to complaints from students who were subsequently attacked. On the other hand, the *Daily Collegian* endorsed Walkertown and Schwartz was elected to the student government.[44]

Walker was not at all pleased with the honor which SDSers had bestowed upon him when they had selected the name for their city. The enraged president fired a young College of Human Development instructor who had brashly called for his resignation. He also exerted pressure on the Methodist church hierarchy to have Rev. Cleeton removed from the Wesley Foundation and sent packing from State College. Walker then read the riot act to 5,500 freshmen at a university convocation:

Penn State offers no sanctuary to any person or group which advocates the initiation of physical force or intimidation, or the takeover of classrooms or office buildings.

Such action is irresponsible, and to permit it would be equally irresponsible. We at Penn State will act immediately, firmly, and without hesitation to deal with any student or group guilty of such tactics.[45]

Despite Walker's warning, campus doves and radicals were unwilling to retreat from activism. In the past, opposition to the Vietnam War and the administration had been small and sporadic. This was no longer true by the fall of 1968. A change in campus attitudes towards authority had taken place, in part because the national political system had proven to be unresponsive to calls for change. Additionally, the evolving demographic composition of the university resulted in greater numbers of generally liberal Philadelphian students coming to Penn State. SDSers, now one hundred in number and finally in tune with a larger segment of the student body, wisely advocated popular actions: rent strikes against rapacious State College landlords and the creation of a student bill of rights to protect undergraduates from arbitrary disciplinary procedures imposed by the administration. Dovish faculty, chiefly John Withall, Marvin Rozen, and education professor Ken Wodtke, also began to develop strategies to bring about the abolition of the ORL. The *Daily Collegian's* editors enlisted in this cause, vowing to eliminate the ORL, "along with all other university collusion with the military."[46]

Although Penn State activists enjoyed a hitherto unthinkable level of support, they continued to be a distinct, besieged minority. Just sixty SDSers participated in an anti-election day protest in November and, as they marched through State College's streets, residents pelted them with eggs. SDSers also generated little community or campus sympathy when, to protest a visit to Walker by his close friend, General William Westmoreland, they blocked the president's driveway. Pennsylvania state troopers roughly removed the students and Wells Keddie as Walker laughed approvingly. In response, the seventy-five SDSers screamed "Heil Hitler" and "Gestapo" at the policemen. Enraged by the Left's increased militancy, YAF leaders warned Walker that they might file a legal suit against the university unless all student dissenters were expelled.[47]

The state legislature concurred with YAF, adopting sweeping laws to crush campus dissent after the Christmas-New Year recess. In 1969, conservative rural legislators empowered the Pennsylvania Education Department to deny financial aid to students who had been convicted of disrupting classes and other academic functions. The legislature also summoned Walker to Harrisburg in February. Senate majority whip Albert Pechan, the author of the 1950s Pennsylvania loyalty oath, informed Walker that state appropriations to PSU would be slashed unless he took stronger actions against campus activists. Other legislators vigorously denounced the Douglass Association and Philadelphia-based militants. Walker urged the legislators not to confuse the reasonable Douglass Association with the militant SDS, a ploy to further the black-white split on the campus. Further, he promised that "the ax will fall if classes are disrupted, interviewers harassed, property destroyed or buildings taken over."[48]

Walker, indeed, did let the ax fall in February. SDSers Tom Richdale, a New Jersey history major, Danny Gallo, a New York graduate mathematics student, and Malorie Tolles, a Wayne, Pennsylvania, native and former SENSE member, marched into Old Main to present Walker with a list of nonnegotiable demands, including the abolition of ROTC and *in loco parentis*. He refused to meet with the activists, prompting five hundred students, only a minority of them SDSers, to occupy Old Main for seven hours. As many as 1,500 hawkish students gathered outside screaming, "Throw the bums out," and "We want the coons," the latter in reference to the Douglass Association members who were maintaining their own separate sit-in. Walker sought a court injunction to prevent further sit-ins and filed a complaint against eight SDS leaders and 250 John Does. Subsequently, Centre County judge A. H. Lipez granted the injunction and denounced "mob rule."[49]

The administration simultaneously opened up a second front against campus activists, attempting to close down the underground newspaper, the *Water Tunnel*, and to prosecute its editors for publishing obscene material. Russ Farb, a New Hyde Park, New York, journalism major, Schwartz, Jay Shore, an Oreland, Pennsylvania, liberal arts major and former *Daily Collegian* columnist, and Alvan Youngberg had decided to establish an underground newspaper with money they solicited from Walkertown residents. Unable to find a printer in State College willing to publish a radical newspaper, whose name was taken from the campus' Garfield Thomas

Water Tunnel torpedo testing center, the SDSers made expensive publishing arrangements with friends in Philadelphia. The *Water Tunnel's* first issue in January featured on its cover a photograph of John Lennon and Yoko Ono, who were not wearing any clothes, and ran advertisements by students in search of others interested in group sex. Subsequent issues dealt with university-military research and provided scathing profiles of Walker and the board of trustees. Walker, not one to take criticism lightly, had State College and campus police on February 17 arrest the *Water Tunnel's* key staff members.[50]

Shore and his colleagues stood trial in Bellfonte in April, charged with distributing pornographic materials. Defense attorney Thomas Sterling pointed out to Judge R. Paul Campell and the jury that *Playboy* and various pornographic magazines could readily be purchased in State College. Therefore, he contended, it was legally inconsistent to apply Pennsylvania's obscenity law just to the *Water Tunnel*, unless there was an unconstitutional political motive behind the prosecution. To drive home his argument, Sterling compelled a prosecution expert witness on pornography, during cross examination, to read aloud sexually explicit literature which had been bought in State College. After arousing the jury, he shrewdly called as defense witnesses Rev. Dale Winter, a campus Wesley Foundation intern, and Rev. Robert Boyer. The respectable clergymen contended that the *Water Tunnel* was primarily political in nature and did not as a whole appeal to base sexual desires. Confused, the jury could not arrive at a verdict. Later Campell dismissed the charges since the prosecution's case was not strong enough to hold up in a court of law.[51]

In hoping that repression would quell campus dissent, Walker grievously erred. Instead, he gave much impetus to campus protest, particularly after banning the *Water Tunnel*, authorizing university police to record the names of all who sold the newspaper, and mailing threatening letters to the parents of the students involved in its publication. He also alienated a number of faculty by sending administrators to a meeting of seventy academics who were opposed to the *Water Tunnel* ban. Administrators informed the faculty that Walker did not believe that instructors, particularly those without tenure, had any business interfering in this matter. The student government condemned the ban and the *Daily Collegian* countered that the ORL was the real "obscenity" on the campus.[52]

As a result of university administration repression, SDSers were less and less willing to listen to Keddie's pleas to shun counterproductive, violent confrontations. Laurey Petkov, a Philadelphia history major, argued that SDS was justified in promoting confrontation since the chapter represented the people, while Walker and Nixon served the interests of racist, militaristic war criminals. In the same vein, Berger stated that there existed a right-wing conspiracy dedicated to perpetuating capitalist imperialism and oppression. To combat this conspiracy, SDSers argued, the "power structure" and its "reactionary, narrow-minded, and bigoted" supporters had to be overthrown. In order to accomplish this, nonviolent tactics had to give way to violent revolution. As Dianne Weiss, a graduate political science student from Philadelphia, reasoned, violent confrontation was actually less violent than pacifism:

What the pacifistic and non-violent position assumes is that if you don't act, you have not committed a violent act. Violence is committed every day in our society—in the ghettoes as well as in Vietnam. . . . Just because one doesn't pull the trigger doesn't absolve one of the guilt of compliance . . . .

Therefore, I take the position that an individual is *less* violent if he takes part in a violent demonstration either against the war in Vietnam or against racism than if he remains apathetic. For the first person's violent action, while it may have hospitalized a few policemen, may have caused his government to cease its war one day sooner, thereby saving twenty lives. In this situation, then, the first person through his violent actions actually saved several individuals' lives. The second person by his apathy was demonstrating compliance with the policies of his government, and thereby participating implicitly in the slaughtering of many people.[53]

Convinced that pacifism and nonviolent protest were no different from apathy and complicity, SDSers intensified their struggle against "American imperialism." A half-dozen SDSers stormed into the HUB in April to harass military recruiters and tear up their literature. Several hawkish students then beat up the radicals. In May, two hundred students, led by Barry Stein, a Huntingdon Valley, Pennsylvania, undergraduate, marched to Old Main and attempted to lower the American flag to half-mast in honor of a protestor who had been slain by police at Berkeley. A hostile crowd converged at the flagpole and, with campus and state police troopers, battled the SDSers. A few days later, fifty SDSers returned to the Old Main lawn, built a brick fireplace, and then, paying homage to their police adversaries, roasted a pig. Affronted by SDS's spring protests, YAF leader Laura Wertheimer obtained a court injunction to prevent the radicals from demonstrating on the campus. Since this marked the first time in the nation's history that one student group had sought a court injunction against another, President Nixon sent a letter of commendation to the PSU YAF.[54]

Committed to demonstrating solidarity with SDS, Keddie, Westby, Petras, Pam Farley, and Dianne Weiss founded a NUC chapter. Describing State College as "provincial, isolated," and "middle class," the PSU NUC vigorously defended students' rights to stage nonviolent occupations of Old Main. Following the flagpole confrontation, the NUC condemned the administration for arresting a SDSer while ignoring the provocations of hawkish students.[55]

Uncomfortable with the NUC's propensity to excuse radical extremism, as well as with SDS's nihilistic militancy, dovish students, faculty, and clergy founded in the spring the Coalition for Peace. In March, seven student members of the coalition reaffirmed their faith in nonviolent protest and rebuked SDS, maintaining that true "resistance embraces non-violent non-cooperation" and requires "overwhelming courage and a strong commitment to the future of mankind." At a student government-sponsored May Vietnam teach-in, Rev. Winter, a coalition supporter, decried ideological polarization, pleading with students to reunite the country and "restore to America the spirit it once possessed." That same month, Withall sharply criticized SDS:

The goals and objectives of the tiny group of provocateurs is to harass and disrupt, create disorder and thus bring down the existing political and economic structure that propagates human degradation and society's ills. They imagine they could start from scratch and build a better and more humane social order. These violent revolutionaries are terribly impatient with the slow pace of participatory and disciplined action. Their impatience has foundation and goads them to violent or fanatic acts. They tend to alienate people from their cause and set-back their cause by their excesses.[56]

SDS proved incapable of curbing its excesses. Buckley, concerned with purging the PL from the national SDS and eliminating the vestiges of Creegan's influence from the campus chapter (he left State College in 1968), succeeded only in dividing PSU SDS. The radical sought to restrict campus and national SDS membership to those who accepted revolutionary Marxist tenets. He also desired editorial control over the *Water Tunnel* which had been printing liberal-dovish articles by the Coalition for Peace. SDSers at Penn State, and at the national convention in Chicago, blasted Buckley's naked power play. Disgusted with Buckley, as well as with the PL "police agents," Pam Farley organized a new group in State College, the Women's Liberation Front (WLF), to promote feminist issues and work with the Coalition for Peace. Several female activists abandoned SDS and joined the WLF. Other SDSers became Weathermen. In July, Barry Stein and Sandy Rosenthall, a Philadelphia labor relations major, were arrested with several members of a Columbus, Ohio, Weathermen collective for inciting the black community to riot.[57]

The NUC attempted in the fall to check SDS's dissolution. Forming an alliance with the Black Student Union, the successor to the Douglass Association, the NUC and SDS issued a September "Manifesto on Repression." The manifesto called for "a dramatic increase in the number of black people at Penn State" and "an end to the Vietnam War and the university's complicity with such wars." Not everyone in the NUC, however, was eager to work with SDS. Although James Petras endorsed the Left's goal to bring about a "radical change in the distribution [of power] within social and economic, as well as political institutions," he had been less than thrilled with SDS's drift toward violent extremism. Similarly, Farley detested many male SDSers' sexism and deplored the chapter's ideological attacks on the Coalition for Peace. A segment of the chapter agreed with Farley and Petras and abandoned SDS for the Coalition for Peace. In turn, a SDSer physically threatened Petras and many snidely referred to Farley's feminist group as "the women's militia."[58]

Student leftists could take some cold comfort from the fact that the campus Right was experiencing its own divisions and acrimony. At the September national YAF convention in St. Louis, the Pennsylvania and California delegations were expelled for libertarian tendencies. Returning to State College, ex-YAF member Don Ernsberger, a Hatboro, Pennsylvania, undergraduate political science major, formed the Students for Individual Liberty (SIL). Ernsberger, who supported the abolition of the draft and an end to the war, had long been a source of embarrassment to the PSU YAF. Significantly, it was largely small-town Protestant YAFers who joined SIL. They were uncomfortable with Wertheimer and Harold Wexler's willingness to use the courts to stifle SDS's right to free speech and assembly and, further, could not relate to their intense hatred of apostate Jewish SDSers who supported Black Power and opposed Zionism. Contemptuous of their former friends, Jewish and Southern and Eastern European Catholic conservatives reaffiliated with the national YAF and intensified the struggle against those on the campus who supported Communists.[59]

While the campus Left and Right fragmented and engaged in internecine sectarian conflict, the two hundred members of the Coalition for Peace assumed leadership of the campus antiwar movement. *Daily Collegian* reporter and coalition activist Steve Soloman, a Lafayette Hill, Pennsylvania, undergraduate, wrote a penetrating series in October on the IDA, ORL, and PSU military research in general. Peter Wood, undergraduate co-chair of the coalition, established a State College Peace Center and coordinated a well-received draft counseling program. Other coalition members organized committees to educate the public on university-military research and planned the largest antiwar rallies and teach-ins in the university's history.[60]

The October 15 Moratorium proved to be a popular, albeit divisive, event. Walker refused to suspend classes for the PSU Moratorium. Two hundred faculty, a number of whom lacked tenure and were NUC members, defied Walker and canceled their classes. Additionally, 5,000 students boycotted lectures to spend most of the day at the HUB listening to folk music and participating in a continuous teach-in. Spot checks of the campus indicated that engineering and science classrooms were filled, while liberal arts and social science classrooms were deserted.[61]

Pennsylvania Democratic party activist Milton Shapp spoke against the war at Schwab Hall as 1,700 people listened:

Ours is a peaceful protest symbolizing the determination of an aroused people to return the nation to the true pursuit of peace. Our desire is to heal the gaping wounds inflicted upon all of us by this immoral war.

. . . If the reason why our soldiers patrol the rice paddies 10,000 miles away is to stop the spread of Communism, then the rulers in Moscow and Peking must be thrilled at our display of stupidity. They have yet to lose a single man in the Vietnam War. It is we, not they who are bogged down.

Following his speech, Shapp received a standing ovation. Keddie then went up to the podium and attacked Shapp, arguing that the war was not the result of a misguided policy of Communist containment, but rather a case study in American imperialism. The audience was unimpressed.[62]

ORL faculty accused the Moratorium organizers of encouraging further Communist aggression by their advocacy of appeasement. Residents were no less opposed to the Moratorium, arguing that students who sought to end the war should have "the hell beat outa them." Their loathing of the campus peace movement heightened as 4,000 candle-carrying protestors marched through the streets of State College and then set up a vigil outside of the Garfield Thomas Water Tunnel. At the head of the march, uninvited SDSers waved a Viet Cong flag. Campus Lutheran minister Fred Reisz tried to reason with them but was met with curses and clenched fists. Later, the coalition disassociated itself from SDS: "This is a peace march to end a day of concern over the war and a Viet Cong flag has no place here." New York City SDSer Dana Friedman defended the organization's action:

> By carrying the NLF flag, SDS declares open support for the aims of the Vietnamese people. We do not feel that the so-called "violence" of the oppressed Vietnamese is immoral or unjustified. In the face of U.S. imperialism, any and all methods of struggle are imperative in order to achieve their just revolutionary demands. We, the members of SDS, declare not only our support for the total victory of the NLF, but also for the liberation struggles of all people oppressed by U.S. imperialism.[63]

In spite of left- and right-wing criticism, the Coalition for Peace proceeded to organize a November 15 Mobilization against the war. The November protest was, however, much more subdued than the October Moratorium. Rev. Winter held an emotional memorial service for those who had died in the Vietnam War. But in general, fewer people participated in the Mobilization protest. Significantly, dovish and radical faculty and students held separate antiwar workshops. Student radicals lost what little credibility they had on the campus when they had bullied their way to the front of the October Moratorium march and displayed their Viet Cong flag. Further, Keddie's reputation with doves suffered when he lamely excused this action. Thus, even though the campus peace movement had grown greatly since the spring of 1968, it had reached an impasse.[64]

The State University of New York at Buffalo

In the wake of the Tet Offensive, liberal-dovish students and faculty sought to spark campus enthusiasm on behalf of McCarthy's presidential campaign. Fred Snell urged colleagues and students not to reject the American political system, but cautioned that they should be prepared to accept a limited victory; to wit, even if McCarthy proved unsuccessful, his crusade would galvanize dovish reform elements within the Democratic party. The biophysicist's realism and moderation, however, inspired little confidence in McCarthy and provoked ridicule from the campus Left. Philosophy graduate student Bob Cohen spoke for many in the SUNY-Buffalo SDS when he savaged McCarthy and accused doves of using the antiwar movement for their personal advantage. Further, he cried:

They won't bring us the changes in the society that we want.

Because the war in Vietnam is so reptilian, we jump at the first man who says he is going to stop the war. We forced ourselves on people, we developed new concepts, we were the ones who brought the issue to the people.[65]

Larry Faulkner, while disdainful of liberal doves' efforts to reform the Democratic party, was no fan of Cohen's. Joining forces with Rev. Kenneth Sherman and Renée Ferber, the mother of national Resistance founder Michael Ferber, Faulkner threw himself into community draft counseling. Although Buffalo police officers intimidated Faulkner and other volunteer draft counselors, many residents appreciated the fact that the pacifists, in contrast to Cohen and the SDS hardliners, did not reflexively call culturally conservative Catholics "racist, fascist pigs." Unfortunately for Faulkner, he could not devote the time necessary to counteract Cohen's growing power in the campus antiwar movement since the FBI and Selective Service had came down hard on him. To keep himself out of prison, Faulkner had to prepare for interminable government hearings and appeals.[66]

Greatly supportive of Faulkner's efforts to resist the draft, and equally determined to present alternatives to SDS's call for violent confrontations, faculty activists attempted to provide moral leadership to the campus antiwar movement. In March, Snell introduced a resolution to the faculty senate which urged

the President of the United States . . . to take all immediate steps to seek immediate negotiations for an immediate cessation of armed conflict and destruction in Vietnam, immediate de-escalation of the military forces present and immediate relief of human suffering. Furthermore, the faculty senate urgently recommends that all necessary action programs be instituted immediately to relieve the stress and indignation existent among the deprived people of this nation and thereby, hopefully, avoid further violent domestic confrontation.

The faculty senate adopted the resolution, the "strongest denunciation of the war by a major American university," observed the *Spectrum*, by a vote of 91 to 37. Hawkish philosophy professors Marvin Zimmerman and William Baumer attacked the resolution and sought unsuccessfully in April to have the faculty senate declare it null and void.[67]

Dovish and radical faculty, chiefly Snell, Ed Powell, and Sid Willhelm, also in March organized a "Strike for Knowledge" which promoted a variety of antiwar forums. The student government endorsed the strike and then went on to condemn the war, military recruiting on the campus, and university-military research. Outside speakers, including Jonathan Schell and indicted draft resistance leaders Michael Ferber, Mitchell Goodman, and Benjamin Spock, came to SUNY-Buffalo. This all-star lineup brought out hundreds, even though no faculty, and generally no students, from the chemistry, education, and engineering departments participated. Limited in its base of support, the forums also exposed ideological tensions within the campus peace movement. Snell and Cohen clashed at a panel discussion, while YAWF leader Gerry Gross called for activists to "bring the moral outrage of the war into the streets."[68]

SDS and YAWF, throwing caution to the wind, opted on August 7 to begin a dramatic antiwar protest in the community. Bruce Beyer, a Buffalo WASP, refused to be inducted into the military and took symbolic sanctuary inside the Elmwood Unitarian Church. He was accompanied by Gross and other members of the newly formed Buffalo Draft Resistance Union. Two hundred students and faculty, as well as Renée Ferber, enlisted in the cause. As Judy Collins sang folk songs and long-haired youths smoked dope on the church lawn, the demonstration assumed the appearance of a summer carnival. Even the Catholic high school students who picketed the church and carried placards which read, "Keep Marx out of the Church," were a source of amusement to the youths. Rev. J. D. Wright, assistant minister of the church, however, found little cause for merriment. Having reluctantly gone along with Ferber and other church members' request to grant sanctuary to the activists, he was receiving numerous threats. "If you want your church burned to hell," one anonymous resident informed Wright, "just keep on protecting draft evaders."[69]

Cohen stated that "if the authorities come to the church" to get the draft resisters, "they may have to do so over our dead bodies." Alarmed by such provocative rhetoric, Faulkner pleaded with Cohen and his followers to be less bloody-minded. He also demanded that they not bring baseball bats and motorcycle chains into the church. On August 19, dozens of FBI agents, Buffalo police officers, and federal marshals stormed the church. Using blackjacks to clear the center aisle of protestors, federal marshals captured Beyer. In all, eight youths were arrested for draft evasion and/or assaulting federal agents. Not coincidentally, among those charged with assault were prominent campus radicals Carl Kronberg and Gross. After a BDRU leader secretly met with FBI agents at the Forest Lawn Cemetery, the federal government also decided to indict SDS leader Bill Yates for assault. They quickly became known as the "Buffalo Nine."[70]

A state of war now existed between campus and community. The *Spectrum* conveyed campus attitudes towards Buffalo by featuring illustrations of armed soldiers with swastikas and running Ron Cobb's apocalyptic underground cartoons. Its editors also savaged Meyerson for not taking stands against racism, police repression, and military recruiting on the campus. The student government eschewed moderation and, further, abandoned its function as a deliberative, representative body by allowing all students who showed up for a meeting to vote. Subsequently, SDS and YAWF came to student government meetings in force to grant themselves money from the student activities fund and to pass resolutions condemning racism in Buffalo.[71]

SDS, claiming in the fall of 1968 five hundred members, many having recently joined the organization in reaction to the sanctuary confrontation, entered an intense phase of protest. Championing antiwar educational projects over violent confrontations, Charles "Speed" Powrie, brother of Kent State activist Jim Powrie, warned activists not to provoke further the anger of blue collar residents. Contemptuous of such counterrevolutionary sentiments, YAWF informed the working-class Irish Catholic radical that "we cast our lot with those who want to fight fascism, not those who bow down before it." Subsequently, in early October four hundred demonstrators, shouting "two, four, six, eight, we don't want a fascist state," marched into the War Memorial Auditorium to protest an appearance by Nixon. Buffalo police charged into the demonstrators' ranks. The next day, in response to the arrest of Gross and two others for assaulting police officers, one hundred students picketed the Buffalo City Courthouse prior to the arraignments. When the judge ordered the courtroom cleared of jeering spectators, SDSers chanted "Fascist judges must go!" Perturbed, the ethnic Polish judge threw the book at Gross and his comrades.[72]

With a militancy which surpassed that of SDS, Buffalo police and residents intensified their struggle against radicalism. On October 16, Police Sergeant Gerald Donovan nervously walked past the BDRU and Urban Action headquarters at Main and West Ferry streets as students shouted "pig," "oink," and "soowie." Angered, Donovan left the scene, returning a short while later with a special tactical squad. The officers seized Kronberg and allegedly vowed to kill him if he tried to escape. Then the police raided the Urban Action office, where the Buffalo Nine Defense Committee published its own newspaper, *Liberated Community News,* and arrested *Buffalo Insighter* editor Bill Mault. Taking six students back to the Cold Spring Station House, officers allegedly beat them for over an hour, made numerous anti-Semitic remarks, and threatened to carve a peace symbol on Kronberg's chest. The Buffalo ACLU demanded an investigation of police brutality, but Police Commissioner Felicetta countered that "the police officers involved acted in a manner compatible with their oath of office."[73]

Frightened by the October student-police battles, Meyerson held a special meeting of the faculty which he opened to students. The president once again warned that immoderate protest was provoking a violent community backlash over which he had no control. Unfortunately for Meyerson, few students, particularly SDSers, were in the mood to listen to him. English instructor and antiwar partisan Barbara Solomon captured the campus and community mentality in an October issue of *Harper's.* She described a growing collection of left-oriented scholars who commuted weekly via jet plane from New York City to Buffalo, unwilling to establish roots in the community and build a rapport with students. There was also, Solomon observed, disorientation and mania on the campus and mutual community-university paranoia and loathing. All in all, students and faculty, she concluded, were trapped in a simultaneously stimulating and stifling "Yellow Submarine."[74]

Lacking the resolve, as well as the ability, to bring order to an increasingly choatic campus, Meyerson had to accept the bitter consequences of the university's pell-mell expansion, acquisition of military research contracts, and ill-conceived quest for academic superstars who had no loyalty to the institution. SDS, cognizant of the president's powerlessness to influence events, drew up in the winter of 1969 an extensive list of nonnegotiable demands deliberately designed to be so unreasonable and unrealistic that Meyerson would be held up for ridicule regardless of whether he accepted or rejected the dictates. Among their demands, SDSers wanted: veto power over the faculty senate; the removal of the Buffalo police commissioner; an end to university-military research; the abolition of ROTC; and the withdrawal of federal charges against the Buffalo Nine.[75]

The beginning of the Buffalo Nine trial in February added to Meyerson's difficulties. As 150 students and faculty picketed the U.S. Courthouse, chanting "Free the Nine—The Trial's a Crime," residents commented that all of the radical "scum," not "just nine of 'em," should be imprisoned. Inside the courthouse, federal prosecutor Edgar NeMoyer presented the government's case. Prosecution witness Herman Erickson, a Buffalo *Courier-Express* reporter who had been present at the church on the day of the raid, testified that federal authorities had entered the sanctuary unarmed while Beyer carried a weapon with which he used to strike FBI agent Richard Schaller. When one of the defense attorneys showed Erickson photographs of armed FBI agents entering the church, the reporter reversed his testimony. Schaller gave further inconsistent testimony, claiming that the FBI had not used a house across from the church as a surveillance outpost. During cross-examination, Schaller acknowledged that he had been in error, forgetting about the movie cameras which he installed on the third floor of the house.[76]

Not content to discredit the government's weak case, the defendants and their lawyers decided to use the trial as "an organizing tool" with which to demonstrate that the judicial system was a vital component of "bourgeois domination." At campus rallies, and in the courtroom, defense attorney Michael Kennedy exhorted radicals to "stay in the streets" and not to expect justice from the judiciary. Beyer, Gross, Kronberg, and the other defendants informed the court that since they supported the "oppressed people all around the world," it was necessary to resist an "immoral, illegal, racist, politically insane war on the Vietnamese people." The defendants also stated that they were "of the working class; our acts were in opposition to the capitalist class because we want an end to capitalist rule and the building of socialism." (If the defendants were working class, their backgrounds indicated otherwise, for their ranks included graduates of the elite Manlius Military Preparatory School, the upper-middle-class Chicago Nicholseen High School, and MIT.) Judge John Curtin, who had worked his way up through the judicial system at a time when Buffalo's upper-middle-class Protestant professionals (e.g., the parents of some of the defendants) considered Irish Catholics to be barbarians at the gate, was visibly upset with the radicals. He found no joy in the knowledge that a new trial would have to be held in September since the jury could not arrive at a verdict for several of the defendants. Beyer, however, received a three-year prison sentence.[77]

Moved by the Buffalo Nine's rhetoric, campus activists worked to end bourgeois domination at the university. In late February, 1,000 students, protesting the trial and ROTC, staged an all-night sit-in at the Norton Union. For the next five days massive rallies were held on campus. Youth International Party (Yippie) leader Jerry Rubin captured the revolutionary imaginations of the protestors by waving a Viet Cong flag and showering his audience with marijuana joints. Seeking to calm inflamed passions, Meyerson and Warren Bennis sponsored in early March a week-long, university-wide teach-in. They encouraged all student groups to participate and hoped that dialogue would promote responsible dissent. Meyerson, however, miscalculated, for the teach-in became a forum which the radicals used to build up outrage against ROTC and the university's Themis research.[78]

A little more than a week after the teach-in, SDS and YAWF organized a boycott of classes and a rally against Themis and Judge Curtin. YAWF member Paul Dominick darkly informed fellow students that it was "up to us to stop them [the university administration] physically" from proceeding with construction of Themis research facilities. *Spectrum* college editor Dorie Kelin of New York City also encouraged students to drive Themis from the campus. Student government president Bill Austin added his voice to those of the demonstrators, demanding the "smashing of the military-industrial campus." Finally, SDS issued its manifesto on Themis:

It is time that we combat the dangerous and growing militarism in our society. . . . The demand to remove all military research from this campus was made several weeks ago . . . but the administration had ignored it completely! It is time we searched our consciences and began to act for the things we stand for before it is too late, and we go down the road of fascism as projects such as Themis grind on unopposed.[79]

Whipped into a frenzy, several hundred students descended upon the Themis construction site, demolishing the sheds which housed building materials. Then the demonstrators marched into Hayes Hall. While a few students climbed into the building's tower and rang the bells of liberation, others roughly ejected Newton Garver, unwilling to listen to the Quaker's objections to the occupation. The protestors smashed glass doors and windows until Meyerson, who had just returned from an out-of-town trip, made his way into the building. Escorted by several unarmed, and nervous, campus police officers, Meyerson tried to open negotiations. Unbeknownst to Meyerson, Peter Regan had summoned 150 Buffalo policemen to Hayes Hall. The students, angered by the presence of their mortal enemies, refused to negotiate. Exhausted, Meyerson left the building and that night, at the insistence of Regan and student affairs vice president Richard Siggelkow, who was complaining about the "radical fascist left," obtained a restraining order to halt the occupation. Five activists were singled out for their role in the protest, including Bob Cohen and YAWF leader Dan Bentivogli.[80]

The embattled president promptly requested that the faculty senate hold a special meeting to resolve the Themis controversy. Four hundred academics and a few hundred students crowded into the Kleinhans Music Hall on March 26 and participated in a marathon debate. Radical historian Gabriel Kolko vigorously attacked Themis. Snell, who had spoken at the March 19 rally, but had been appalled by the students' subsequent violence, also denounced Themis. Medical School and engineering faculty argued loudly on behalf of Themis and, in private, wrote blistering letters to Meyerson demanding the imprisonment of radical students and their faculty supporters. Unable to resolve the issue, the faculty senate agreed to discuss it again in late April. Prior to the second debate, Meyerson gave students the opportunity to vote on Themis and ROTC and render their verdict on the March 19 protest. A bare majority of voters favored Themis and ROTC and nearly two-thirds criticized the destruction of the Themis sheds and the Hayes Hall occupation. In response to the vote, which the *Spectrum* decried as an administration propaganda tool, a student flung two Molotov cocktails into the now fenced-in Themis site.[81]

By this point, the Buffalo Common Council and the state legislature had entered the fray. Councilmen Buyers and Lyman called for Meyerson's resignation and the legislature in April overwhelmingly passed a comprehensive antistudent riot bill. Given these developments, it was understandable that the administration refused to allow the national SDS to hold its 1969 convention at the university, even though SUNY-Buffalo SDS was still an officially recognized student organization and New York had the greatest number of chapters (thirty-five) in the nation. Subsequently, SUNY-Buffalo SDSer and *Spectrum* reporter Barbara Morrison, who attended the convention in Chicago, defended the expulsion of the PL and championed the Weathermen.[82]

In late September the second trial of the Buffalo Nine commenced. At a SDS-sponsored symposium on political repression, which featured Susan Sontag and other left-wing New York City luminaries, a Buffalo Nine defense attorney observed that the judges were the chief capitalist oppressors since they were the ones "who let the pigs operate." After the symposium, seven hundred students and faculty picketed the courthouse, screaming "Ho, Ho, Ho Chi Minh, NLF is Gonna Win!" SDSer and defendant Ray Malak, when called upon by Judge John Henderson to stand and be introduced to the court, raised his fist in a power salute. Bill Yates and Bill Berry followed suit, ignoring Henderson's caution that there was no need for any such gestures. With that, the relationship between the judge and the defense attorneys and defendants became stormy. Judge Henderson repeatedly overruled counsel's objections and strove to prevent the issue of the Vietnam War from being interjected into the case. The judge also cited Malak and Yates for contempt of court after they refused to stand when he called a recess. Malak then informed the judge that he could not stand and honor a judicial system which merited only contempt and "spit."[83]

After a month of, once again, inconsistent government testimony, the jury deliberated for two days before acquitting Berry and Kronberg and convicting Malak and Yates. Unable to arrive at a verdict on Gross, the government decided to drop his case. Malak and Yates, upon being sentenced to three years' imprisonment, rendered their own verdict. Defiant, Malak proclaimed that "you can jail a revolutionary, but you can't jail a revolution!" No less determined, Yates warned, "the American governing class has caused me to be branded a criminal. . . . The people in time will declare who really are the criminals. . . . I pledge to the people that I shall continue to act for freedom."[84]

As in the spring, the second Buffalo Nine trial coincided with, and fed into, another wave of revulsion against Themis. Beyer, out on bail pending appeals and now a SDSer, intoned in September that "Themis must fall again." More poetic, other SDSers chanted at rallies, "If Themis goes up, Themis blows up!" Joining SDS in opposition to Themis, Charlie Haynic and Chip Planck, political scientist and master of the storefront Tolstoy College, founded a loose organization of largely young, untenured instructors, the Radical Faculty Caucus. By now disillusioned with the political system, Snell joined the group. Kolko, on the other hand, disdained the Radical Faculty, for he believed that the nation was on the verge of a conservative counterrevolution and, therefore, the Left should not further antagonize the Right. Bewildered by Kolko's attitude, the Radical Faculty promoted anti-Themis sentiment on the campus and transformed the storefront colleges into radical organizing centers.[85]

In addition to anti-Themis agitation, the campus Left also stepped up protest against ROTC. On the day of the October 15 Moratorium, one hundred SDS and YAWF members ransacked the offices of the Air Force ROTC. After smashing office equipment and windows, the demonstrators carried away files and books which they burned in a gigantic bonfire. They then charged past the president's Hayes Hall office shouting "Up Against a Wall, Motherfucker!" Outraged, Regan, acting in place of Meyerson who had taken a leave of absence, called in the FBI. Within two weeks, nineteen activists were charged with burglary, conspiracy to incite riot, and vandalism.[86]

The campus reaction to the anti-ROTC protests was confused. Rev. Sherman, who had resigned his parish position to devote himself full-time to organizing the area Clergy and Laity Concerned about Vietnam, denounced SDS and contended that the peace movement should broaden its base of support, develop coalitions with liberals, and run dovish candidates for office. The minister also observed that the moderate peace movement had achieved some success in Buffalo, with Mayor Frank Sedita publicly endorsing the Moratorium. Even Congressman Richard McCarthy had urged Nixon to negotiate an end to the war. Cohen, exhibiting his contempt for Sherman and the doves, countered that "SDS is not a popular front. It has certain principles. One of these is to create a socialist revolution in this country." Given SDS's mission, Cohen told students, the movement must not join forces with liberal doves like Sherman and Sedita, but instead "move extremely to the left."[87]

Faculty members were also at odds with each other. The Radical

Faculty, committed to abolishing university-military research, set forth its position before an acrimonious faculty senate meeting in November:

We are convinced from our study of American foreign policy that the uses of ROTC graduates are insupportable on moral and political grounds. We do not wish to continue a program in which students from the University of Buffalo are put in a position where they either subject themselves to court martial or commit murder on the innocent to protect landlords and the wealthy in Vietnam, or perhaps in years to come, in South Africa, South America, Laos, Thailand, Indonesia, or wherever the theory and practice of counter-insurgency may send them. . . .

Acceptance of funds from the Defense Department sanctions and perpetuates the unwarranted importance of military money and perspectives in the structure of scholarly research in this country. This support structure needs opposition, not encouragement. The way to change it is to stop having anything to do with it . . . .

Conservatives on the faculty, many of them possessing DoD contracts, once again wrote vicious letters to the president in which they blasted Snell. Moderates answered that they could not "in good conscience take a stand in political roles: left, right or middle," because "when a university takes a stand it becomes a political instrument comparable to a political party." And doves such as Garver, smarting from his rough handling by SDS, adopted an antiwar and antiradical protest stance.[88]

Confronted with out-of-control student protest and an embittered faculty, the hard-liners in the administration consolidated their power as the liberals gathered around Bennis rapidly lost ground. Historian Theodore Friend, a dove, as well as an assistant to Regan, privately warned Bennis that the student Left was undermining the liberals' effectiveness in the administration. He also noted that "conversations with some of the violent radicals . . . give the impression of young men and women high on self-righteousness and narcissistic heroism, apt to get further and further involved with the euphoria of publicity and the ecstasy of violence."[89]

Meanwhile, the Buffalo community was working out its own ambiguous attitudes towards campus protest and the Vietnam War. Mayor Sedita's November re-election victory against law-and-order and hawkish candidate Slominski made it clear that the majority of voters were weary of the war. However, war weariness did not translate into warm support for the peace movement, particularly for its large campus component. Most residents did not distinguish between doves and violent radical students, hence they did not object when Buffalo police tried to break up an October Moratorium march of several thousand people from the campus to Niagara Square. In part, the local and national news media, by emphasizing violent rather than less visually dramatic nonviolent demonstrations, influenced residents against campus activists. But then, students and faculty were largely responsible for their poor public image. After all, what could blue-collar ethnic Catholics have made of a student body and faculty which published the *Buffalo Marijuana Review* (Leslie Fiedler and "Fugs" leader Ed Sanders, "consultant gurus,") and an alternative newspaper, the *Undercurrent* (Bill Mault and Barbara Morrison, editors), which carried photographs of homosexuals engaged in anal and oral sex? Residents were repulsed, venting their anger in anonymous hate letters to Meyerson, and then to the more receptive acting president:

Why kid yourself or any other of the law abiding people about the scum attending your school? A great many of the bums, black and white, red or yellow, stink to the high heavens. They are the filth of the New York state area.

Only way to treat the *BASTARDS*, crack down and throw the scum out. There isn't any way you can deal with this type but to get tough.

So they represent peace, they don't know the meaning of peace and decency. But sooner or later as one of your good stated after serving 3 years in Vietnam, they will have to get a hair-cut, take a bath, and go to work. What a big surprise when they find out they are totally unfitted to earn a living.[90]

And so, conservative and radical forces squared off against each other, with liberal doves caught in the middle and forced to take sides. Two years of escalating protest and violence—1968 and 1969 —had set the stage for an even more intense phase of confrontation.

Kent State University

The early months of 1968 were at once a time of success and frustration for the KCEWV. Antiwar education forums in the dormitories, as well as the KCEWV's determined pickets and vigils, raised the level of political consciousness on the campus. One thousand students participated in a campus memorial march for Rev. King in

April and 240 canvassed in Indiana in May on behalf of Robert Kennedy. But the campus Left, although encouraged by the fact that more students had at last became politically engaged, was not at all pleased that they had embraced a dovish, rather than a radical, intellectual approach to the Vietnam War and American race relations. Student peace activist Dave Edwards sharply criticized Kennedy's and McCarthy's supporters for viewing the Vietnam War as an aberration, the product of misguided American foreign policy. In reality, Edwards contended, the war was a carefully thought-out endeavor designed to promote U.S. imperialism and counterrevolution in the Third World. KCEWV members also took little comfort in the realization that while there were a number of students on the campus opposed to the use of napalm in Vietnam, only forty people in February chose to picket Dow recruiters at the union.[91]

Dissatisfied with the KCEWV's emphasis upon nonviolent, moral witness peace vigils and education projects, several activists began to call for more action. The advocates of action formed the core of the newly created Student Religious Liberals (SRL), a campus draft resistance group which was, despite its name, highly secularized and radical. Headquartered at the Kent Unitarian-Universalist Church on the floor above the Yellow Unicorn Coffeehouse, SRL and KCEWV activists George Hoffman and Vince Modugno, both Cuyahoga Falls, Ohio, residents, counseled students on conscientious objection and coordinated protests against Dow recruiters. Convinced that liberal doves had for too long acquiesced in the destruction of Vietnam, and critical of KCEWV leaders for clinging to ideological and tactical moderation which did nothing to halt it, the SRL established a SDS chapter at Kent State. Praising SDS as "basically anarchist, antiestablishment, anti-draft and action oriented," Hoffman and his allies committed themselves to building a radical movement at the university.[92]

KCEWV leaders Ruth Gibson and Joseph Jackson were determined to keep the organization and its nonviolent principles alive even as more of the membership drifted into SDS. In late April, the KCEWV organized a peaceful antiwar rally on the Commons which featured local folk singers and dovish clergy speakers. As a few hundred students reclined on Blanket Hill, hawkish athletes in Stopher Hall, armed with high-powered air rifles, opened fire on Rev. Peter Richardson and a visiting Catholic priest. After KCEWV secretary Carol Carson complained to campus security officers, the administration had Gibson arrested for having earlier that day chalked a rally notice on the library. Charged with vandalism and violating White's decree that the KCEWV could not publicize the rally on the campus, Gibson was taken to the Kent police station. Alone and frightened, the normally perky activist broke down and cried. White made no effort to prosecute Stopher Hall's vigilantes. Campus radio director Bob Carpenter waxed enthusiastic, praising the hawkish students and White for "turning the tables" on the KCEWV which for so long had infringed upon the "constitutional rights" of Dow by picketing its recruiters. Subsequently, SDSers pointed to Gibson's feminine weakness, and to White's indirect encouragement of right-wing violence on the campus, as compelling arguments for a more militant and masculine campus radical organization.[93]

Seizing the initiative from the moderates in the KCEWV, SDSers in early May staged a protest against Hubert Humphrey who was speaking at the university's Memorial Gymnasium. On cue, 150 white and black students, the latter belonging to the recently established Black United Students (BUS), marched out of the gym. The vice president angrily led the audience of 10,000 in a noisy booing session. Mim Jackson, a high school student, joined the walkout, anxiously awaiting attack. Her big brother Joseph, repulsed by SDS theatrics, was less concerned with the audience's ugly reaction. Far more disturbing to him had been the SDS-led heckling which had preceded the walkout. This denial of Humphrey's right to speak freely sent a "chill down his spine" and led him to view the radicals as "elitists" dedicated to silencing those who did not agree with them. Jim Powrie, who had refrained from heckling, plaintively responded that the protest "was not to victimize Mr. Humphrey nor deny him the right to speak. . . . It was, quite simply, an act of conscience" directed against "a supporter of an illegal and immoral war that continues to kill hundreds of people daily." However, Powrie did not speak for the entire chapter. Howie Emmer and Rick Erickson reasoned that Cold War liberals like Humphrey had no right to free speech and had to be silenced.[94]

Buoyed by the anti-Humphrey protest, Howie Emmer and Rick Erickson drove to Michigan State to participate in the National SDS convention. At East Lansing, the KSU SDSers became enamored of Dohrn, met with Bill Ayers and Jim Mellen, and re-established contact with Mark Rudd. (Erickson had become acquainted with Rudd while visiting Columbia during that campus' celebrated spring uprising.) It was decided by Ayers and Mellen, once they had purged the Ann Arbor SDS chapter of those opposed to aggressive, confrontational protests, to create a network of Michigan-Ohio SDS travelers. Excited by Emmer's accounts of the awakening white and black student movement at Kent State, and attracted to the town's flowering counterculture, Terry Robbins, a Kenyon College dropout who, Carl Oglesby observed, thought he was Butch Cassidy to Ayers' Sundance Kid, made the university his base of operations. The enormously wealthy Ayers donated a printing press which enabled the KSU and Northeast Ohio SDS to publish their own newspaper, *Maggie's Farm*. Emmer and Mark Lencl's parents, who were also former Ohio Communist party organizers, provided further assistance by leasing a Cleveland office building for the Michigan-Ohio SDS travelers. Armed with Black Panther and Third World revolutionary Communist principles, as well as with the collected works of Bob Dylan, Emmer and Erickson set out in the fall to intensify the struggle at Kent State. Paradoxically, the KSU SDS house where Erickson lived had been the model for the "Bates Motel" in Alfred Hitchcock's *Psycho*.[95]

To Emmer and Erickson's delight, 250 students came to SDS's first meeting in the fall of 1968. Among the crowd were about two dozen former members of the KCEWV, such as Bill Whitaker, the gregarious son of a U.S. Steel Corporation vice president. But by far the majority of students at the September SDS meeting had had little previous contact with the campus antiwar movement. Ken Hammond, a working-class suburban Cleveland undergraduate, did not associate with the activists until the spring of 1968 when he met Emmer and Modugno in a class. But it took the King and Kennedy assassinations, and the Chicago Democratic Convention, to move Hammond to join SDS. Similarly, Alan Canfora, a sophomore whose father was a Barberton, Ohio, Democratic councilman and vice president of his UAW local, became politically active only that fall. Even then, Canfora moved slowly into the SDS camp while maintaining ties to the KSU Young Democrats. His roommate, Tom Grace, a Syracuse, New York, freshman, eventually followed Canfora into SDS, but neither embraced, nor completely understood, New Left ideology.[96]

Grace and Canfora received their first exposure to KSU SDS action tactics on October 3. Traveling with the KSU Democrats to protest a Nixon appearance at the University of Akron, the two watched in awe as two hundred Kent State and Oberlin College SDSers on the hall balcony shouted, "Ho, Ho, Ho Chi Minh, NLF is Gonna Win!" Canfora turned to Grace and, calling the staid Young Democrats "really lame," suggested that they move up to the balcony. Sensing that the "SDSers were the more effective Nixon haters than the Young Democrats," Grace agreed. When the SDSers began to chant "Sieg Heil!" Nixon pointed to the balcony and vowed that decent Americans in November would "shout down the protestors." The audience wildly applauded and then, during a moment of silence before Nixon resumed speaking, a SDSer called back to the podium, "You fucking asshole!" Canfora and Grace accompanied SDS back to Kent, with the former enormously impressed by the radicals and the latter far less enthusiastic. It was difficult for a self-described Cold War Democrat, and Irish Catholic parochial school graduate, to identify with such a radical, as well as foul-mouthed, movement. But on the other hand, Grace realized, Kent State SDS had brought off, according to *Time* magazine, the "most successful disruption" of a Nixon speech during the campaign.[97]

Following the anti-Nixon protest, SDS sought to establish firmly in students' minds that the campus chapter was part of a larger, growing national radical movement. To accomplish this, and to fill the chapter's empty coffers, they brought Rudd to KSU and charged admission. Eight hundred students heard the media celebrity speak at the university auditorium. Grace and the majority of students were turned off by Rudd's profanity and incoherence. After the talk, Rudd and Emmer engaged in a battle of wits with campus radio reporter Maggie Murvay, refusing to let her leave with a tape she had made of the speech. That night, an undergraduate, who had been inspired by Rudd's rhetoric, sought him out at Erickson's home. He learned that Rudd could not speak to anyone at the moment since he was having sex with a groupie in a room off of the kitchen. Within minutes, Rudd came out of the kitchen and demanded that Erickson turn over to him all the money KSU SDS had collected. As Erickson and Rudd came close to blows, the incredulous undergraduate departed.[98]

KSU SDS also wished to broaden its political base on the campus. Since Ayers, Dohrn, and Robbins had taken the position that blacks represented the American revolutionary vanguard, Emmer and Mark

Real, a former Catholic seminarian, dutifully forged an alliance with BUS. Emmer provided the convoluted arguments on behalf of a SDS-BUS collaboration:

The American empire is *institutionally* racist and violent. All of us are affected by American racism. Some of us have taken that one step further and have decided that the task of the white radical must be to build a *white* radical movement.

. . . The black community in America is in fact a colony within the mother country and is *excluded* as such. Young white people are trained to perform the jobs needed to extend a racist society and older white people perform jobs which preserve a racist society. . . .

The black revolutionary movement and the white radical movement are building parallel liberation struggles against the same system of power, in which a few make the major decisions which clearly affect all of our lives. Eldridge Cleaver, minister of information for the Black Panther party has said, "The young people of America, black and white, have reaffirmed my faith in humanity." The soundest way in which we can aid our black brothers and sisters is to get our white shit together.[99]

SDS got its "white shit together" on November 13, blockading the Placement Office to protest the presence of two Oakland, California, Police Department recruiters. Considering the Oakland Police Department to be a racist organization which persecuted the Black Panthers, Emmer and 150 SDSers joined 150 BUS members in a five-hour sit-in. Real arrived with a portable loudspeaker, stating that any white student in the building who did not join the sit-in "would be considered a member of the Kent police force." Exactly what he meant by that statement required little imagination; Real took the Viet Cong concept of revolutionary justice very seriously.[100]

White termed the SDS-BUS demonstration "intolerable" and promptly filed legal charges against Emmer, Erickson, and eight other activists. Meanwhile, a few hundred hostile students gathered outside of the Placement Office screaming, "Kill the nigger-lovers!" Gibson, uncomfortable with SDS's tactics but a sit-in participant nonetheless, called several sympathetic faculty and asked them to escort the demonstrators through the vicious crowd. Their presence, however, did not deter several dozen counterprotestors, who were armed with motorcycle chains, from severely whipping the activists. Campus police and administrators made no attempt to halt the attack.[101]

Angered by the vigilante violence, as well as by the administration's actions, BUS leader Bob Pickett, a Perth Amboy, New Jersey, native, resigned his position as vice president of the student government and convinced 250 black students to leave the campus. As all but a dozen black Kent State students marched off the campus to exile in Akron, White and his subordinates issued press releases and circulated several presidential bulletins among the faculty which accused Pickett of coercing the majority of blacks into joining the walkout. SDS quickly organized a sympathy strike and a teach-in and demanded that the university grant amnesty to the activists:

We call on students to suggest to your professor at the beginning of class to devote the class to discussion of the issues of amnesty for SDS and BUS. ... IF YOUR PROFESSOR REFUSES, WE ASK YOU TO LEAVE YOUR CLASSROOM AND ASK YOUR CLASSMATES TO JOIN YOU. ...

Amnesty for all is the only position of integrity; for these times it is imperative that we do not allow these students who took the only real and moral position possible to be punished. THE PRECEDENT OF ARBITRARY PUNISHMENT FOR MORAL ACTS IS CLEARLY MORE SERIOUS THAN THE POSSIBILITY OF IMAGINARY ACTS OF FUTURE LICENSE.[102]

The majority of faculty, as well as the *Daily Kent Stater*, urged White to punish the SDS and BUS leaders. Only peace activists Sidney Jackson and Tom Lough openly praised the radicals for publicizing the issue of racism. In turn, many SDSers derided Jackson for his suggestion that they might be able to work successfully through "proper administration channels." Fortunately for the activists, the president, trying to stave off an investigation by the Ohio Civil Rights Commission, decided within a week of the BUS walkout to drop all charges. SDSers were exultant, feeling that, in Hammond's words, "a real victory had been won." Grace, who had declined to join Canfora in the sit-in, was duly impressed with the protest which convinced him that "if people joined together in numbers and stuck together," the forces of social change would emerge victorious. Pickett, however, had a different perspective. He was not impressed by the SDS antics which had preceded the demonstration, including invasions of classrooms in order to counter the teachings of hawkish faculty and an anti-ROTC protest which saw SDSers running alongside of cadets screaming, "Kill, Kill, Kill!" The black student leader and his followers thought that SDSers had used BUS as a "shield" to protect themselves from administration retribution and to further their own political agenda. They also concluded that Emmer and Erickson wanted "to live their fantasies out" and garner publicity: "Those cats loved their headlines. They would read the papers to each other about themselves. They wanted to use us to get themselves some big headlines." After BUS returned to campus, cooperation between the two groups ended and Pickett became an outspoken dove and critic of SDS.[103]

Powrie shared BUS's disenchantment with the SDS leadership. Although trained by Robbins to operate the SDS printing press, he did not identify himself with the Ayers-Dohrn faction in the campus chapter. Strongly opposed to the disruptive confrontations which Emmer and Erickson had staged, and planned to stage, Powrie contended that the chapter should appeal to doves and organize peace education forums such as a SDS "Free University," the latter undertaking eliciting Lough's strong endorsement. Seeing merit in Powrie's ideas, Hammond coordinated dormitory draft counseling and antiwar organizing sessions and, with the great assistance of Marilynn Davis, researched and published KSU SDS's most formidable recruiting document, a twenty-page pamphlet entitled, "Who Rules Kent?" Gibson and Melissa Whitaker, wife of Bill Whitaker, also added their voices, pleading with Erickson to eschew violence and to be more sensitive to women's issues. Erickson, who resented assertive women, ignored Gibson's entreaties, regarding her as "a pain in the ass." He also flippantly dismissed Whitaker's feminist concerns as nothing more than an insignificant "pots and pans revolution" when compared to the heroic anti-imperialist struggles of the Viet Cong and the Black Panthers. In the same vein, Emmer accused Powrie of being a timid liberal who would sell himself to the state if the price was right.[104]

To underscore their commitment to revolution, Emmer and Erickson spent the early days of 1969 developing the national SDS "Venceremos Brigade" which sent 216 student volunteers to Cuba to assist in the sugar cane harvest. They also organized a fifty-member KSU SDS contingent which went to Washington to protest Nixon's inauguration. Canfora and Grace joined the SDS caravan and viewed a fiery debate at St. Stephen's Church between Dave Dellinger and Rudd. As Rudd, in profane terms, called for violent disruption of the inauguration parade, Grace felt disgusted. The next day, after Emmer, Erickson, and Robbins had argued for militant action, the SDSers gathered in Franklin Park. With the approach of the presidential procession, someone in the crowd threw a bottle at Nixon's car. Washington police officers then charged the demonstrators.

Canfora and Grace broke into a run and wound up in the black ghetto which both considered "a much safer place to be than Pennsylvania Avenue." The police arrested four KSU SDSers and severely clubbed a young woman who had crossed their path. Having witnessed what was to him an unprovoked and thorough beating, Grace returned to Kent State firmly opposed to the Vietnam War.[105]

Canfora and Grace began to frequent some SDS functions, including films, slide shows, and lectures. Both were stirred by SDS's Saturday morning educational discussions on ROTC and the links between overseas imperialism and the domestic repression of the internal American black colony. But they were far less impressed by the increasingly acrimonious debates between Powrie and Emmer. The friends also received an unexpected shock when, at one meeting, Jim Mellen contended that "we have to really get down to the serious business of developing a Young Communist movement in this country." Feeling the pull of their Catholic, anti-Communist upbringings, Canfora and Grace left the meeting and for a while stayed away from SDS. But they then had a change of heart, with Canfora arguing "that SDS was the only group on campus that was coming out with any concrete analysis of things, especially the war, and they weren't afraid of action."[106]

Although Canfora and Grace may have been attracted to SDS's analysis of the war, they did not appreciate that the chapter had any number of conflicting analyses. In numerous photographs and illustrations, *Maggie's Farm* portrayed the Viet Cong as noble heroes. Powrie did not care for the Viet Cong, but their pictures were carried at Emmer's insistence. Kent State SDS leaflets were inevitably led off by a line from "Subterranean Homesick Blues" which Erickson's wife Candy played over and over again on her stereo, much to the neighbors' annoyance. The radicals' framed their appeals to students in soaring rhetoric which echoed Kennedy's Inauguration Address. But, at the same time, their phrasing tended to be weighted down by obtuse Marxist-Leninist analysis

We live in a world that is becoming increasingly restrictive—a world where we have less and less control over those things that most directly affect our lives. As young people living in America today, and, more especially, as students attending Kent State University, there are certain realities that to a greater or lesser degree we must face each day.

The Students for a Democratic Society is an education and social action anti-imperialist organization dedicated to increasing democracy in all phases of common life. It seeks to promote the active participation of young people in the formation of a movement to build a society free from poverty, ignorance, war, exploitation and the inhumanity of man to man.

This strange combination of Kennedy and Lenin reflected the ideological diversity of the campus chapter, but also, more importantly, pointed to Powrie and Emmer's irreconcilable worldviews and cultures. Powrie looked to a tradition of triumphant, nonviolent, Irish-American political activism. In contrast, Emmer could only reflect upon an Eastern European Jewish cultural experience whose highlights included pogroms, forced emigration, and death camps.[107]

Such cultural and ideological divisions notwithstanding, the SDS militants launched their "Spring Offensive" in April. SDS demanded, among other things, the abolition of ROTC and the Liquid Crystals Institute, in its eyes genocidal institutions which contributed "to the repression of people of color all over the world who are struggling against exploitation and oppression by the American ruling class." On April 8, three SDSers requested a meeting with White in order to discuss the university's "complicity with the War Machine." When he refused to talk with the activists, 250 students marched to the administration building. Fistfights between hawkish students and the activists broke out and the president ordered Emmer and Erickson's arrest and suspension.[108]

On April 16, Mellen, standing on top of an overturned trash can, warned jeering campus hawks that

I know that there are some pigs out there who still think we should occupy Vietnam. And there are some pigs out there who still think they can go into the ghettoes and push people around. Well, what we're telling you is that you can't do it anymore! We are no longer asking you to come and help us make a revolution. We're telling you that the revolution has begun, and the only choice you have to make is which side you're on. And we're also telling you that if you get in the way of that revolution, it's going to run right over you.

As soon as Mellen finished, two hundred SDSers, insisting that Emmer and Erickson's closed suspension hearings be opened to the public, marched to the Music and Speech Building. There they clashed with three hundred students, some of whom carried baseball bats. Discovering an unlocked side entrance to the building, the SDSers proceeded to the third floor. Once they arrived at the hearing room, the activists discovered that the university had stationed a large body of Ohio highway patrolmen in the basement. Facing arrest, many SDSers were rescued by speech professor Carl Moore and young faculty member Ken Calkins who showed them a service elevator which the police had overlooked.[109]

Canfora and Grace, who, caught up in the heat of the moment, had entered the building, were relieved to have been extricated from White's trap. Fifty-nine SDSers, however, were not so fortunate. Those arrested, with the exception of a female black student whom the administration released so as not to push SDS and BUS back together, were quickly suspended or expelled and later placed on trial for conspiracy, trespassing, and riot. The campus AAUP chapter endorsed White's actions and warned that continued SDS disruptions would only antagonize legislators and taxpayers who already resisted funding state higher education. Calkins, despite having rescued many of the activists, also condemned the radicals. Satisfied that he had the support of the majority of the faculty, White concluded the incident by banning any campus group that sponsored SDS meetings and speakers. The president chose not to punish the prowar students who had, while assaulting the SDSers, accidentally destroyed university property.[110]

With the core SDS membership expelled, and many leaders remaining in jail until they could post bail, the chapter was financially and politically crippled. At one point, the radicals were so strapped for funds, what little money they had raised going for legal expenses, that they requested the phone company to shut off service to the SDS house. The FBI, having put a great deal of effort into tapping the students' phones, promptly paid their phone bills and restored service. A few activists who had taken backseats to the leadership, Joyce Cecora, a strikingly beautiful student from Cleveland, Candy Erickson, Gibson, Hammond, and former MSU SDSer Andy Pyle, sought to rally the campus. Dovish students, outraged by the SDS ban and White's thwarted attempt at the Music and Speech Building to trap and prosecute the entire chapter, formed the Concerned Citizens of Kent State. Despite being confronted by faculty who came to meetings in order to report on its activities to the administration, and contending with student informants working for the campus police, the committee's efforts were not fruitless. Several hundred hitherto apolitical students, enraged by the faculty and White's tactics of intimidation, and disgusted with the administration for doing nothing to halt hawkish right-wing violence, participated in campus protest rallies.[111]

Not realizing that his actions, rather than those of SDS, had radicalized a significant minority of students, White joined Maggie Murvay in Washington to testify on campus subversion before the House Internal Security Committee (formerly HUAC). Revealing that administrators had met in secret as early as July 1968 to lay the groundwork for dealing with campus activists, White then launched a tirade against SDS, "an enemy of democratic procedure, of academic freedom, and of the essential university characteristics of study, discussion, and resolution." After he had finished, Murvay testified that, while a campus radio reporter, she had also been a Kent undercover police officer responsible for taping activists' conversations. She provided the committee with the names of thirty-two Kent State SDSers, focusing particularly on Jewish members. The congressmen shared Murvay's obsession with Jewish radicals and also commented upon the ties Emmer and Mark Lencl, both Jewish, had to the Communist party through their parents. Other witnesses inadvertently disclosed to the committee the extent of the political surveillance apparatus the university had established, which included using *Daily Kent Stater* reporters as informants.[112]

Warped by their campus experiences, the KSU activists made their presence felt at the National SDS convention in Chicago. Parading through the hall with their Michigan allies, Kent State SDSers heaped abuse upon their Michigan State opponents and then departed with Ayers and Dohrn. Powrie, unhappy with Emmer, but also angered by the elitist PL organizers, who "all went to Harvard and were straight-looking and came to the convention in chartered planes," left the convention in disgust. As the last of the Weathermen made their exit, MSU SDSer Dick Oestreicher wryly observed that "in an organization known for its crazies, Kent State SDS was in a class by itself."[113]

The Weathermen quickly appointed Kent State SDSer "Corky" Benedict to its National Interim Council, and Emmer, Erickson, Lencl, Colin Nieburger, Real, and Robbins assumed national Weathermen leadership positions. Deciding that summer to bring the revolution to Ohio's oppressed blacks, Kent State Weathermen established communal houses in Akron, Athens, Cleveland, and Columbus. In the Columbus commune, which was under Emmer, Erickson, and

Robbins' command, the Weathermen, when not engaged in group sex, committed such revolutionary acts as parading with a Viet Cong flag through a local park on Independence Day and spray-painting the walls of a high school with the slogans, "Off the Pigs," "Viet Cong Will Win," and "Fuck U.S. Imperialism." Since the men of the house were busy with these activities, as well as hanging out on street corners discussing revolution with local youths, one female SDSer had to obtain a job in a striptease club in order to pay the rent. The situation was the same in Akron, compelling Kent State SDSer Robin Marks, the daughter of a successful New York City writer, to get work as a barmaid in a Lebanese tavern. One night the Akron radicals urged everyone to get guns to fight the police. Appalled, Marks argued with the commune's leaders and then, shouted down, fled. Columbus commune activists went one step further than their Akron counterparts, actually bringing a .22, a shotgun, and an M-1 into the house. The Akron commune soon collapsed and the Columbus Weathermen were finally driven from the city by their unresponsive, impoverished neighbors. Adding insult to injury, Columbus police authorities charged the Weathermen with having fanned the flames of the city's July 21 race riot. A few months later, in October, Emmer and Benedict were arrested for their roles in the "Days of Rage" trashing of Chicago.[114]

Disturbed by the direction in which SDS was heading, Powrie spirited the chapter's printing press to his brother in Buffalo so that it would not fall into Emmer's hands. Powrie and his supporters also carried baseball bats in case of attack by the Weathermen. Sectarian lines hardened to the point where Andy Pyle's girlfriend, the daughter of a Kent State faculty member, broke off their relationship in order to join the Weathermen underground. Powrie and Hammond's repeated attempts to bring about a reconciliation of the campus chapter failed miserably. As early as May, the working-class activists had invited Emmer and his upper-middle-class supporters to share ice cream and comradeship. Bobbi Smith, who was white, denounced Powrie for serving vanilla—instead of chocolate—ice cream, a crime only a blue-collar racist would commit. The irony of the Kent State Weathermen and anti-Weathermen relationship was further driven home when the activists were convicted for their roles in the Spring Offensive. Powrie, the advocate of political education, spent a year in an institution for the criminally insane. Emmer and Erickson, the proponents of violence, served forty-five days of jail time. But then, Powrie's father was a meter reader, not, like Erickson's, a former Akron mayor with clout in the Ohio Democratic party.[115]

With the beginning of the 1969 fall session, White finally realized that his efforts to crush student activism had backfired. The cumulative impact of four years of escalating war, and university and community hostility towards even the most politically moderate activists, had outraged and mobilized a hitherto unthinkable number of students. Viet Cong flags were displayed in the windows of the Tri-Towers dormitory complex and its halls were thick with marijuana smoke. Liberal student government representatives, led by Craig Morgan, an Upper Arlington, Ohio, resident, criticized the war and President White. The new editors and reporters of the *Daily Kent Stater*, sickened by the role their predecessors had played as police informants, followed Morgan's lead. Mike Alewitz, the president (and only member) of the Young Socialist Alliance, Pickett, and Hammond were given special *Daily Kent Stater* antiwar columns and they eagerly cooperated with Morgan to organize an October 15 Moratorium march in Kent. Calkins, Sidney Jackson, and Lough, a founder of the newly established campus NUC chapter, delivered impassioned addresses against the war, and Joe Walsh and the "James Gang" performed antiwar rock songs. Afterwards, 3,000 students peacefully marched through Kent and 5,000 boycotted their classes. A month later, 240 KSU students, the largest contingent in the university's history, marched on Washington.[116]

But the opposition to the campus antiwar movement remained large and vehement. In an April student government-sponsored referendum, 4,745 students had endorsed White's banning of SDS, with 3,012 students opposed. This polarization of the campus continued into the fall. Hawkish student government leader Frank Frisina, with paper and a printing press provided by the administration, distributed anti-SDS scare circulars on the campus. In these circulars, Frisina red-baited his dovish rivals in the student government and accused them of being "fronts" for SDS and the Communists. It did not matter to the hawk that two of the people he denounced as subversives were Vietnam veterans. Campus, city, and county police authorities, as well as the judiciary, also had decided to expand their political surveillance activities, with Kent State security officer Schwartzmiller, Kent police chief Thompson, and Judge Robert Kent meeting at the Twinlakes Country Club to prepare a plan for dealing with future campus incidents. And White condemned SDSers and "bleeding heart" liberals who gave comfort to the radical "culprits." He also refused to cancel classes in recognition of the October Moratorium and November Mobilization and warned students not to interfere with normal university functions.[117]

In addition to hawkish opposition, the campus antiwar movement also contended with ideological divisions. By far the majority of antiwar students were nonviolent doves, whose ranks included a Jewish fraternity, anti-Nixon Young Republicans, and the local ACLU chapter. Their position was best summed up by the campus newspaper editors who urged an immediate end to the war lest "idealists" became "more frustrated" and wound up believing "that violence is the only way to accomplish anything." In contrast, a hard core of radicals, all members of the NUC and the banned SDS chapter, identified with the Viet Cong. The radicals castigated the doves for claiming that the NLF committed atrocities in Vietnam, not appreciating, they argued, that Communist violence was far less severe than American violence and was necessary to defeat U.S. imperialism. Liberals and radicals competed against each other for the allegiance of the campus, but the latter group was too small, and largely without forceful leadership, to be effective.[118]

As the Kent State antiwar movement bickered and coalesced, events had been taking place in Columbus which would have serious ramifications for the university. Ohio legislators drafted anti-student riot bills and called for investigations of antiwar activism at the state's public and private universities. Major General Sylvester Del Corso, commander of the Ohio National Guard, warned that the antiwar movement was part of "the international Communist conspiracy" which sought to destroy America. And Governor James Rhodes, who was to face the formidable Robert Taft Jr., in the state Republican Senate primary in the spring, was desperately searching for a popular campaign issue. Aware of a mounting public reaction against campus activism, and a desire for law and order, Rhodes decided to get tough with student demonstrators. In December 1969, after three black students at the University of Akron had staged a nonviolent Black Power protest, Rhodes sent seven hundred National Guardsmen to occupy the campus. The Guardsmen provided

the news media and the public with dramatic pictures which underlined Rhodes' decisive leadership and bolstered his popularity with
the electorate. If there were to be any more campus disturbances,
the governor let it be known that he was prepared to employ whatever force necessary to restore order.[119]

PART THREE

"Disciplined by a Hard and Bitter Peace"

"Tin Soldiers and Nixon's Coming": 1970

On the evening of February 17, 1970, 250 students assembled in the MSU Union to discuss ways of protesting the convictions of the Chicago Seven, the antiwar activists who had disrupted the 1968 Democratic convention. The MSU Weathermen, led by Brad Lang, showed up in leather jackets and carried six-foot-long iron fence posts. Although it was only seventeen degrees outside, the protestors marched over to the East Lansing City Hall singing (to the Beatles' "Come Together") "Trash Together":

> We are the Trashmen we've got
> Rocks and bottles we've got
> Stones and sticks and right on
> Politics!
> We fight the pigs, they try to bust,
> One thing I can tell you is the winner
> is us!
> Trash together, right now, off the pig!

Radio reports that a mob had gathered at city hall brought out a few hundred curious student and faculty spectators. Angry and excited, the Weathermen began smashing the city hall's windows with their fence posts. The sound of shattering glass, shouting, and cheering attracted even more spectators, swelling the crowd to 1,200. Twenty minutes elapsed before police officers, equipped with billy clubs and tear gas, stormed out of city hall. The officers indiscriminately clubbed and gassed everyone in sight. Reinforced with Lansing police and state troopers, they slowly pushed the unruly crowd down

Abbott Street towards the campus. In the course of their retreat, students, who before being gassed had had no intention of making trouble, angrily trashed the East Lansing State Bank and Jacobson's department store. As tear gas shrouded Grand River Avenue and the police arrested hundreds of students, Bill Hixson slid madly about on the icy pavement as he dragged to safety the fallen wife of a colleague. Finding refuge, the dovish history professor watched the Kafkaesque scene unfold. He stared at a thermometer which registered at zero degrees and wondered apprehensively what warm spring days would bring to MSU.[1]

As East Lansing recovered from the Chicago Seven protest, SUNY-Buffalo became a combat zone. On February 25, forty students rallied to protest the presence of Buffalo police at the previous evening's basketball game. Marching to Hayes Hall, they demanded to meet with Regan. When he refused to talk to them, several students pitched rocks at his office window. Suddenly, Buffalo police officers appeared and chased the vandals back to the Norton Union. One hundred and fifty students were milling around the union when a breathless student flew into the building and shouted that the police were coming. Reflexively, the students piled couches, chairs, and trash cans against the doors. But the barricades did not slow down the club-wielding officers. Many students were beaten until they lost consciousness.[2]

When the police, with several handcuffed students in tow, left the union, they were greeted by four hundred protestors who threw rocks, traffic signs, and trash cans at them. Frightened, the officers fled to the Lockwood Library, using their prisoners as shields. Soon, more policemen arrived on the campus and made a second bloody sweep of the union where three hundred students had rebuilt the barricades. By this point, eight hundred students had gathered in the area, exchanging curses and blows with the police. The officers fired so much tear gas that Charlie Haynie's wife and two little girls, who were leaving the union after having watched a movie, nearly collapsed for want of fresh air. Student government representative Janet Cohen, a suburban New Yorker, attempted to administer first aid to the injured students. Frenzied officers, yelling, "Get that fucking cunt!" slammed her into the side of a van. She had to be hospitalized. At the 16th Precinct, eighteen students were booked for inciting riot. Surveying the bleeding demonstrators, many of whom were Jewish, the policemen allegedly muttered that America "should have let Hitler win, he'd have known how to take care of fuckers."[3]

The next day, 1,000 students attacked Hayes Hall, campus police headquarters, the Themis construction sheds, and the ROTC offices. Setting afire a pickup truck parked at the Themis site, the demonstrators then trashed a university police car. Thirty Buffalo police officers at the Winspear Avenue campus entrance, sensing that the screaming students charging towards them meant no good, fled. But before the protestors could savor their victory, two hundred police reinforcements arrived, this time equipped with riot guns, grenade launchers, a K-9 corps, and a helicopter. The crowd, now swollen to 1,500, chanted "Pigs go home!" and "Power to the People!" Several tense minutes passed before the students disbanded. Regan obtained a court order to restrain Bob Cohen, Terry Keegan, Carl Kronberg, and other SDSers from leading further protests. Disgusted with the radicals, Regan's assistant, Theodore Friend, signed an affidavit in support of the restraining order.[4]

Convinced that the presence of Buffalo policemen on the campus had provoked subsequent student rioting, Warren Bennis tried to find out who had summoned them to the university. Regan assured his subordinate that the police had came on their own volition. However, the *Spectrum* unearthed secret adminstration memorandums which clearly indicated that Regan and Ed Doty, vice president for operations and systems, had requested the city to send the officers. Disturbed by Regan's actions, Bennis resigned. Other liberal administrators, feeling isolated and betrayed after Meyerson announced his intention to leave SUNY-Buffalo, followed Bennis' lead.[5]

Meanwhile, hundreds of students blocked the entrances to numerous university buildings and smashed one hundred windows. Three days later, on March 2, 4,000 students marched to Hayes Hall where they burned Regan in effigy. Two hundred liberal arts faculty voted to boycott classes while other professors bitterly debated the issues of police force, student suspensions, ROTC, and Themis. Faced with the firebombing of several buildings, and informed that some faculty were carrying loaded revolvers to defend themselves from student radicals, Regan requested the city to restore order at the university. Regan also suspended twenty students, including Dan Bentivogli, Bob Cohen, and Barbara Morrison. Subsequently, on March 8, four hundred Buffalo policemen occupied the campus. Richard Siggelkow warned that, if necessary, the officers would remain at SUNY-Buffalo indefinitely. Then the Erie County grand jury, based upon information provided by the administration, indicted many SDS and YAWF members for inciting riot.[6]

A number of politically moderate professors established the Faculty Peace Patrol to prevent students from firebombing more buildings and to persuade the police to be less violent. Their efforts proved fruitless. On the extremely cold night of March 12, hundreds of students engaged in a four hour-long running battle with police occupation forces. The evening's spectacle began with a bonfire in front of the ROTC offices where students torched an American flag. Then the demonstrators marched towards police lines chanting, "Ho, Ho, Ho Chi Minh—NLF is Gonna Win!" and "Up Against a Wall, Motherfucker!" A group of Peace Patrol members placed themselves between the students and the police. Surprised, the crowd, after hurling a Molotov cocktail at the academics, turned to march on the Themis site. There, the protestors tore down a fence. Afterwards, they ran to Hayes Hall, smashing windows along the way. When three Peace Patrol volunteers attempted to halt the rampage, the students screamed "Pigs!" and "Strikebreakers!" and beat them. The police, no more fond of the professors than were the students, also attacked several Peace Patrol members. With the scent of fresh blood in their nostrils, officers stormed about Main Street dragging nonprotesting students from restaurants and slamming them into the pavement. At the same time, they clubbed local news reporters as well as an Associated Press photographer.[7]

The student uprising provoked a variety of responses. Members of the SUNY-Buffalo Veterans Club blasted Regan for turning the campus into an "American Vietnam." Further, 263 professors at a faculty senate meeting called for Regan's resignation while the Graduate-Undergraduate Student Judiciary charged the administration with engaging in "disruptive, illegal, unconscionable violence." In contrast, the university alumni association praised Regan and the Buffalo police. The state legislature also extended its regards to the acting president and launched an investigation into the role the storefront colleges had played as agents of campus chaos.[8]

Desiring to express support for the student strike, and shocked by Regan's resort to police force, seventy faculty members convened a special meeting. Peace Patrol organizers David Hays and Nick Goodman announced that the time for action was overdue; $200,000 worth of property damage had already been done to the university and 125 students, faculty, and police had been hospitalized. Goodman argued that Regan was insane for having played into the hands of the radical lunatics. If Regan and SDS were not stopped, he warned, student-police confrontations would eventually culminate in shootings and death. A debate then ensued between the younger, and more militant, faculty and their somewhat older, and more cautious, colleagues. Haynie and radical historian Michael Frisch urged the faculty to occupy Hayes Hall to protest Regan's use of police force and court injunctions. Fearful that Regan would arrest, fire, and possibly shoot faculty demonstrators, Gabriel Kolko informed Haynie that he could not support a sit-in. Nearly half of the faculty concurred with Kolko, leaving forty-five to occupy Hayes Hall.[9]

The professors trooped over to Hayes Hall on March 15, prompting Doty to summon the police and to arrest that "bastard" Fred Snell and "his graduate students." Sitting around a table in the president's office, the faculty were warned to leave. Ray Federman, a French Jew and former World War II Resistance fighter, became agitated. Attempting to calm him, Max Wickert read aloud all too appropriate selections from Kafka's *The Trial*. One by one, the police lifted the academics from their chairs and passed them out of the crowded office. It was not too long before they were in jail, facing prison sentences of up to six years for criminal trespass and violating Regan's court injunction. Kolko went to the jail and proceeded to dress down Haynie. Afterwards, Kolko informed him that he had put his house up on bond in order to raise bail money and retain a lawyer.[10]

Students, shocked by the arrest of so many faculty, quieted down for a while. However, the university remained unsettled. In April, hawkish philosopher William Baumer swore out an affidavit against two radical academics, accusing them of assisting students in blockading the entrances to university buildings. An embittered faculty senate, many of its hitherto neutral members radicalized by the arrests of their colleagues, voted to abolish ROTC and convinced Regan to resign. Harsh feelings among faculty, administrators, and students mounted after the grand jury indicted Bruce Beyer and additional SDSers and YAWF members for their roles in the winter riots. Not content with that, jurors also demanded the personnel records and academic transcripts of ninety-one faculty and students, including draft resister Larry Faulkner who had not engaged in any violent activities on the campus. Further, the grand jury, noting that many SDSers and a number of the faculty arrested on March 15 were affiliated with the storefront colleges, ordered SUNY-Buffalo to turn over the appropriate class rosters, lecture notes, and course descriptions. Anyone on the campus who had taken a public stand against Themis, ROTC, or the Vietnam War, whether liberal or radical, pacifist or violent, was to be investigated and perhaps sent to prison. Community residents cheered the grand jury and began a popular petition campaign demanding that the university expell its dissidents.[11]

After six years of worsening campus-community relations, the winter riots at SUNY-Buffalo were, perhaps, to be expected. But that such disruption also occurred at a relatively calm campus like Penn State, highlighted the pervasiveness of American student disaffection in the early months of 1970. Ironically, the antiwar movement at Penn State appeared stalled and divided in February. Division was all too evident that month following a SDS raid on a ROTC dance and protest in the HUB against navy recruiters. The Peace Coalition condemned SDSers for shouting obscenities at the cadets and their dates, and chastised the radicals for punching counterdemonstrators in the HUB. Pam Farley also denounced SDS. In turn, SDS leader Jeff Berger characterized the Peace Coalition and other campus critics as "fascists."[12]

SDSers' responses to the campus Black Power movement deepened dissension between liberals and radicals. The radicals supported Black Student Union leader Alan "Commander Ali" Cunningham, a Philadelphia undergraduate, who described the Peace Coalition's Jewish members as "Kosher Nationals." According to Commander Ali, the dovish Jews expressed their "demented white supremacy complex" by criticizing the Viet Cong and promoting the cause of "racist Zionism." Outraged, YAF condemned Commander Ali and SDS's "racism" and "anti-Semitic fascism." In response, SDSers argued that since their chapter was "30 percent Jewish," they could not possibly be anti-Semitic or racist. Further, SDS contended, given the fact that PSU YAF was "90 percent WASP," the conservatives were by culture and breeding natural anti-Semites and white supremacists. Thoroughly provoked, YAF pointed out that not only was a third of its membership Jewish, but moreover, the chapter's Jews were religiously observant, as opposed to SDS's Jewish apostates. To the campus, the Jewish, black, dovish, radical, and YAF charges and countercharges were unfathomable. Peace Coalition activists warned that these rancorous public exchanges were tarnishing the reputation of the campus antiwar movement.[13]

With the coming of warm spring days, a deeply divided campus movement engaged in vigorous protest activities. On April 14, seventy black students occupied a university building. They excluded whites from the antiracism sit-in. The next day, the Peace Coalition, with no black students present, picketed the ORL. Of the three hundred protestors, only a minority were SDSers. However, the radicals made up for their lack of numbers through the boisterous shouting of, "Off the pigs!" Following the ORL picket, the demonstrators marched to Old Main and requested a meeting with Walker in order to discuss university-military research. When he refused to talk with the Peace Coalition's representatives, 250 students entered Old Main. Several radicals began running through the building, smashing vending machines until stopped by Wells Keddie. Gradually, the bulk of students, not wishing to spark a violent confrontation, left the building. The one hundred remaining students listened to SDSers make impassioned speeches from the second floor balcony. Meanwhile, Walker obtained a court injunction to halt the occupation and brought eighty-five state troopers to the campus. Offering no resistance, the students consented to be taken into custody and transported to jail in the five police buses parked behind Old Main.[14]

The word spread quickly around the campus that Walker had brought in outside force. Within fifteen minutes, 1,000 students assembled outside of Old Main. Individually, and then in groups, students smashed the vehicles' headlights and windows. As policemen escorted the arrested students to the buses, the crowd began screaming "pigs off campus" and throwing rocks. Then students used street signs, trash cans, and construction materials to erect barricades on the street. Officers grabbed long boards and formed a flying wedge to sweep clear Pollock Road. The buses slowly got under way, periodically stopping so policemen could jump out and beat the rock-throwing protestors who lined the route. In all, twenty-nine students were arrested and scores injured.[15]

Deploying state troopers against a small number of students transformed a limited, nonviolent protest into a massive, brutal riot. The next day, 2,000 angry students rallied outside of Old Main, demanding amnesty for the quickly dubbed "Penn State Twenty-Nine" and calling for the abolition of the ORL and ROTC. Moderates in the Peace Coalition urged students to remain calm and sought to open negotiations with Walker. However, the president maintained that there was nothing to negotiate. His uncompromising stance prompted one hundred students on April 20 to smash the windows of his campus residence. Desiring retribution, Walker spent the next morning helping 280 state troopers set up base at Beaver Stadium. At 5 P.M., five busloads of police surrounded Old Main where a delegation of students was vainly trying to arrange a meeting with Walker. Rebuffed, the delegates left the building where they were met by the riot squad. Once again, the campus grapevine hummed with the news that a bust was imminent. Soon, 2,000 students converged on Old Main. Another round of rock throwing ensued, prompting the police to flail the students. The buses headed back to the stadium amidst chants of "Sieg Heil!" A more tame group of students sang "America the Beautiful" and offered marijuana joints to the police.[16]

A few hours later, a crowd of 5,000 students and faculty marched through the campus and Pam Farley and Geoff Sill, a graduate English student from Ohio and NUC member, organized a strike committee. The following day, 6,000 people peacefully rallied on the Old Main lawn. Concerned that Republican governor Raymond Shafer would make good his threat to send the Pennsylvania National Guard to PSU, Democratic gubernatorial candidate Milton Shapp came to the campus on April 22. Speaking to a crowd of 2,000 which had gathered outside of Old Main, Shapp criticized Walker's use of excessive force and pleaded with students to avoid provoking further administration violence.[17]

By the last week of April, the entire campus, not just the antiwar movement, had become divided and embittered. Walker's decision to obtain a permanent injunction against campus protest, and move to suspend Farley and Sill, worsened the deteriorating situation. Both had been the campus voice of relative political moderation and they had intervened, at some risk to themselves, to prevent SDSers from vandalizing university property. The president's credibility with many students declined rapidly after the television magazine show "60 Minutes" aired an exposé of ORL cost overruns and administrative corruption. Further, to Walker's chagrin, an unprecedented number of faculty (293) publicly joined the *Daily Collegian* and the student government in an anti-administration and antiwar chorus.[18]

But still, many faculty endorsed Walker's actions and 250 students signed a petition praising the state police and demanding that all members of campus antiwar organizations be expelled. Seventy-five percent of these student hawks were business and science majors, 98 percent came from Pennsylvania, 74 percent claimed small-town residences, and 87 percent were of Northern and Western European extraction. They were the polar opposites of the antiwar students. The two rival worlds of the campus, the one local, heavily Protestant and Catholic, and career-oriented, and the other cosmopolitan, disproportionately Jewish, and concerned with abstract ideals, had come into open cultural and ideological conflict.[19]

The protests and violence which had taken place since February at PSU, SUNY-Buffalo, and MSU graphically illustrated that the universities had lost their institutional stability and could no longer claim the status of neutral Ivory Towers which rose above national discord. Initiatives at the local level to introduce outside police force to the university, or U.S. military escalation of the war, invariably sparked spontaneous, uncoordinated campus protests. This was the reality which many educators, and even a few astute politicians, recognized. Tragically, however, this reality did not penetrate through the walls of the White House. On April 30, Nixon announced that American military forces had invaded Cambodia. Thus, Nixon expanded the war which he had been elected to end. The campus response came swiftly as students firebombed ROTC buildings at Maryland, Michigan State, Washington, Wisconsin, and Yale.[20]

While campus protests erupted across the nation, five hundred Kent State students gathered at the Commons on May 1. It was an upset crowd which, claiming that Nixon had killed democracy, buried a copy of the constitution. BUS held a separate rally highlighted by black Ohio State students who, speaking from recent experience, warned that if the National Guard came to Kent, "brothers and sisters" would be the first shot. In the evening, as thousands of students celebrated the first warm spring night of the term by drinking themselves into a stupor, a fist fight broke out at J.B.'s, a Water Street bar. The fight quickly spilled into the street and turned into a riot after a middle-aged Kent resident attempted to use his car to run down the students. A mob of four hundred students and out-of-town revelers then rampaged through downtown Kent, smashing windows and causing $7,500 worth of property damage. By 12:30 A.M., Mayor LeRoy Satrom, without notifying the university administration, declared a state of civil emergency and requested assistance from the Ohio National Guard. Meanwhile, city police arrested fourteen students and, with the aid of tear gas, pushed 1,500 back to the campus. Weathermen leaders Howie Emmer and Rick Erickson, both just released from jail, had been spotted among the crowd.[21]

Kent State was quiet on the morning and afternoon of May 2. But that night a peaceful rally at the Commons degenerated into a riot. Unidentified individuals—unidentified because anyone with a camera was beaten in order to prevent pictures from being taken—set fire to the ROTC building. Conservative geology professor and World War II veteran Glenn Frank, who was working with NUC member and New York graduate student Steve Sharoff to check violent outbreaks on the campus, unsuccessfully defended the building. When several students assaulted Frank, Ruth Gibson fought her way through the crowd and rescued the academic. Firemen who came onto the scene were pelted with rocks and their water hoses cut. They returned shortly afterwards with a police escort and extinguished the flames. Later that night, the ROTC building was again torched, the fire visible for miles away and giving the impression that the entire campus was aflame. At that point, Troop G of the National Guard occupied the campus, eerily silhouetted by the fire. With tear gas and fixed bayonets, the soldiers quickly dispersed a crowd of five hundred students. The arsonists would subsequently be described as police agent provocateurs, Weathermen, or ordinary students, depending upon whom one asked. In any event, notable Kent State Weathermen fled the vicinity.[22]

The uprising had caught Gibson and Ken Hammond by surprise. Indeed, on the morning of May 2, Hammond, his wife, and Bill Whitaker had gone to Buffalo to attend a radical conference and did not return to Kent State until Monday, May 4. The activists had been aware of mounting student frustration with the university administration and the war. Earlier that spring, Craig Morgan had been elected student government president, defeating Frank Frisina's hawkish political machine. The campaign had been the most bitter in the university's history, with the hawks engaging in vicious redbaiting. Conservatives had also attacked "Hanoi, Ohio," the Tri-Towers dormitory complex where many antiwar students lived. Under cover of darkness, vigilantes sneaked into the dormitory and dumped broken glass throughout the halls. In mid-April, 250 students had rallied at the Commons to protest the war and 2,000 turned out to listen to Jerry Rubin.[23]

Despite this evidence of campus discontent, Gibson had not anticipated violence and abhorred its very prospect. When Terry Robbins, Diana Oughton, and Ted Gold had blown themselves up on March 2 in New York City while constructing a bomb to be used against army personnel, she had breathed a sigh of relief. If the Weathermen had been successful, Gibson believed that their action would have initiated unprecedented government repression directed against all activists. But still, she was gravely concerned. While there was a large antiwar movement at Kent State, and though that movement had never been overtly violent, students lacked leadership and organizational discipline. White's decision to prosecute even moderate activists such as Jim Powrie, and sustained hostility towards campus peace groups, had created a leadership and organizational vacuum. The campus situation, she feared, could become even more violent and chaotic.[24]

When the soldiers occupied the university, a number of students who lived off campus took refuge in the Tri-Towers. Several faculty met with Guard officers and then assured the students that they could safely return home. As Alan Canfora and his roommates walked across the campus, they were blocked by an armored personnel carrier. Having just buried his best friend who had been killed in Vietnam, Canfora attempted to engage a soldier in a discussion of the war. The Guardsman slammed him to the ground with the butt of his M-1 combat rifle. Other students quickly learned that the soldiers, exhausted and tense after having spent the previous weeks being shot at by striking Teamsters, were in no mood to talk. Requesting a meeting with Satrom and White, several hundred students on May 3 staged a sit-in at the intersection of East Main and Lincoln Streets. Egged on by Governor Rhodes's press conference in Kent at which he bellowed that he intended to "eradicate" the "Communist element," Guardsmen charged the students. With bayonets unsheathed, they stabbed several students and arrested fifty-one. Allison Krause, a dovish Pittsburgh undergraduate, had earlier given a flower to a soldier and begged him to refrain from violence.[25]

Andy Pyle and several friends passed much of Sunday night spreading the word on campus that the May 4 rally at the Commons would go on as previously scheduled in spite of the mayor's ban on campus rallies. Throughout the night they dodged tanks and helicopter searchlights to ensure a good turnout. Early Monday morning, an anxious Mike Alewitz called Hammond. The YSA leader suggested that the activists hold an emergency meeting to see if the 11:30 A.M. rally should be canceled. They opted to proceed with the antiwar and anti-Guard demonstration. Meanwhile, BUS activist Bob Pickett had assisted in evacuating the entire black student population from Kent. White, who had been out of town when the troubles began, joined several other administrators at the Brown Derby restaurant for early morning cocktails. The administration had decided to allow the Guard to deal with the rally, unwilling to go to the Commons and calm students' and soldiers' passions.[26]

Mourning his friend, and angry with the soldiers, many of whom had political connections which enabled them to join the Guard and thus avoid service in Vietnam, Canfora arrived at the Commons with a black flag which he had fashioned from his apartment's drapes. Tom Grace, returning from an exam, joined Canfora. By noon, 2,000 students had gathered around the victory bell and 10,000 stood off and watched the rally. Prior to speaking, Hammond and his wife separated, lest both were arrested together and unable to bail the other out of jail. As he climbed up on the bell housing and spoke, the Guardsmen fired tear gas and drove students to the parking lot. Peace activists Bob Lewis and Jerry Casale watched in terrified awe, mixed with disgust, when "middle-class" student "crazies" lobbed rocks and spent tear gas canisters at the distant Guardsmen. One group of soldiers forced students behind Taylor and Johnson halls and then marched onto the practice playing field. Another group of Guardsmen kept vigil between Taylor and Prentice halls. Spotting Canfora, who was defiantly waving his flag, several soldiers at the football field knelt and aimed their rifles at him. Jeff Miller, a transfer student from MSU and liberal antiwar Republican, stood near Canfora and Hammond and shouted epithets at the Guardsmen. A handful of faculty, largely those who had issued a public condemnation of the Guard on May 3, stood by as ineffective peace marshals.[27]

The soldiers assembled, conferred among themselves, and marched away from the students and towards Blanket Hill. Arriving at the top of the hill near the pagoda, they turned and fired into the crowd. In thirteen seconds the Guardsmen expended sixty-one rounds. A few hundred feet away in the parking lot, Allison Krause fell mortally wounded. Jeff Miller's face was blown off. Canfora took a bullet in the wrist and Grace, shot in the foot, writhed in agony. Loaded onto an ambulance, Grace watched as medical attendants pulled a sheet over Sandy Scheuer's head. Four dead, nine wounded. A young female runaway knelt beside Miller and, arms outstretched, wept.[28]

Stunned silence. Then hysterical crying. Marilynn Hammond frantically searched for her husband and, finding him unharmed, fainted. An antiwar student and Vietnam veteran, with blood all about him, stared into the distance. The students spontaneously sat down on the ground. When the Guard commander ordered them to move or be fired upon again, freshman Mim Jackson stoically awaited death. Glenn Frank pleaded with the officer to desist, but was curtly dismissed. With tears welling in his eyes and voice cracking, he urged students to leave the Commons: "They're going to shoot us again. We're going to be slaughtered. They've got guns and the guns are at our throats. . . . " Slowly, the students arose and dispersed. A colleague then helped the trembling professor home.[29]

As soon as the national news media relayed the story from Kent State, America's campuses experienced a second, even more convulsive, wave of protest. At 1,350 universities and colleges, 4,350,000 students participated in demonstrations against the shootings and the invasion of Cambodia. At SUNY-Buffalo, 2,500 students marched down Main Street on May 6 and later that evening a handful firebombed the ROTC offices. City police promptly laid siege to the university. From careening patrol cars, officers shot several students who were walking to their classes. None were engaged in protest activities. Other policemen fired tear gas into university buildings. Warren Bennis, on his way to a first aid station to offer assistance to injured students, was gassed. The level of unprovoked police violence became so great as spring term wound down that Regan filed an official protest. In response to university criticism of the police, Common Councilman Gerald Whalen exclaimed, "The hell with gas, bring out the bullets!"[30]

The Penn State activists who had been arrested during the April riots were embroiled in a losing legal battle with Walker when the Kent State shootings occurred. Linking this legal contest with the Ohio slayings, the Coalition for Peace called for a strike. Organized and mobilized as never before, activists enlisted the aid of several dynamic speakers. On the evening of May 5, two hundred students listened to SUNY-Buffalo professor and Hayes Hall sit-in participant

William Fleischmann argue that events at Kent State and Buffalo were part of a national pattern of government repression. The next day, 4,000 students marched across campus in a funeral procession to honor the Kent State victims. Two KSU faculty doves, Jerry Lewis and Richard Taylor, a Quaker, spoke movingly to the demonstrators, criticizing the Ohio Guardsmen and imploring students to eschew violent protest.[31]

The extent of student and faculty disaffection soon dawned on Walker, leading him to proclaim May 6 to be a day of mourning. However, many students were not convinced that he had suddenly became supportive of dissent. Indeed, Walker's decision to proceed with the university hearings on the April protests, which culminated in the expulsion of seven students, the suspension of five for up to two years, and the placing of nineteen on disciplinary probation, illustrated his actual feelings towards activists. The president also won few accolades in the wake of a bitter May 12 faculty senate meeting. At this meeting, all but a handful of academics voted in favor of a sharp antiwar resolution. Administration supporter and faculty senate chair Arthur Lewis declared the resolution void since a unanimous vote was required. Eight hundred students who had been observing the meeting loudly booed Lewis, and many professors coldly realized that Walker considered their opinions to be superfluous.[32]

Such administration actions only served to provide further momentum to the student strike. Class attendance in the Colleges of Education, Human Development, and Liberal Arts plummeted to below 50 percent and many liberal arts and social science faculty joined the strike. In a student government-sponsored referendum held on May 12 and 13, 18,000 students, the largest turnout in the university's history, voted on whether or not to support the strike. More than 11,000 opted to substitute regular classes with antiwar teach-ins. But in spite of this unprecedented level of campus support for antiwar activism, the university was just as polarized in May as it had been in April. Class attendance in the Colleges of Agriculture, Business Administration, and Engineering remained high and very few business and science faculty participated in the teach-ins. Campus division and tension carried on through to the end of the spring term.[33]

Campus polarization was not unique to Penn State. Within hours of the Kent State shootings, Michigan State students and faculty were organizing one of the most successful, as well as divisive, antiwar strikes in the nation. On May 5, 1,000 people marched through the campus chanting, "On strike—shut it down! 1, 2, 3, 4 —we don't want your fucking war! 5, 6, 7, 8—we don't want your fascist state!" Small groups cut through the classroom buildings, their shouts emptying the lecture halls. Soon, 3,000 students surrounded the Hannah Administration Building, demanding that President Wharton honor the slain Kent State students and urge Nixon to withdraw from Cambodia.[34]

The MSU student government immediately held an emergency meeting, disrupted by the heckling of prowar engineering and business majors. At Rick Kibbey's insistence, the student government hammered out a unanimously supported resolution calling for a strike until Nixon withdrew from Cambodia and MSU terminated ROTC. Even the *State News* editorial staff, angered by the Kent State tragedy and the invasion of Cambodia, broke ranks with Wharton and supported the strike.[35]

That evening, 7,000 people went to the auditorium and for six confusing, exhausting hours debated and voted on strike issues. Black militants, seizing an opportunity to exploit the guilt of white students and threatening to continue to drag out the meeting, successfully added their demands—free Black Panther leader Bobby Seale, increase minority enrollment, and lower admissions standards for blacks—to the white antiwar students' proposals to drive ROTC off campus. Similarly, the emerging gay-liberation advocates blurred the antiwar message of the student uprising with their call for protection from police harassment and brutality.[36]

Initially, Wharton perceived himself as a sane mediator between anti- and prostrike factions, trying to take a middle course, but this irked all involved, particularly the American Legion and the state legislature. Therefore, two weeks into the strike, Wharton succumbed to the pressure of law-and-order state legislators and newspaper editors. At first, he tried threats, declaring that striking faculty would be fired and activist students would be flunked out of the university. When threats proved ineffective, Wharton resorted to more direct intimidation. On May 15, he called in the state police to gas the participants of a Demonstration Hall sit-in and, three days later, to arrest 134 white students attending a discussion on racism at the union. The president, aware of his Buffalo counterpart's mistakes, waited until faculty activists had left before sending in the police.[37]

Significant as they may have been seen at the time, Wharton's tactics of threatening and intimidating students and faculty were not the most important factors contributing to the strike's collapse by the third week of May. In retrospect, the strike movement was not as strong and unified as it initially appeared. Although 12,000 people went on strike May 5, this represented only 32 percent of the student body. According to the MSU Social Science Research Bureau, 51 percent of graduate students and 32 percent of undergraduates vigorously opposed the student government's prostrike resolution. Fifty-five percent of graduate students and 40 percent of undergraduates denounced the Demonstration Hall sit-in, and fully 53 percent of undergraduates and 63 percent of faculty concurred, in varying degrees, that withdrawal from Vietnam would undermine America's prestige and credibility.[38]

MSU's strikers were largely social science or humanities majors, while very few hard science or business majors, who constituted 46 percent of the student body, participated in the strike. The conservative, competitive hard science and business majors, concerned about finding well-paid positions in respectable corporations or in government, generally did not wish either to wreck their grade point averages or risk arrest by striking. They were also more hawkish and to the political right of liberal arts majors. The relatively popular antiwar movement had been unable to penetrate the "New Campus," built by DoD and AID contracts, and convert large numbers of students and faculty. The conservative ethical and political makeup of the hard sciences was not receptive to the liberal-left arguments that the liberal arts put forward.[39]

Even on the "Old Campus," the heart of the MSU antiwar movement, not all departments, faculty, and students supported the strike. Even if one assumes that all of the 12,000 strikers majored in the social sciences or the humanities, this still accounts for only 59 percent of such majors. Consequently, at least 41 percent of these majors did not participate in the strike. James Madison students boycotted their classes, but the dean and many of the college's faculty considered the strike "inappropriate to the learning process" and in violation of the university's "political neutrality." The history faculty, like their counterparts in political science, had been bitterly divided ever since Johnson's escalation of the war.[40]

Another problem with the strike was students' rapidly decreasing commitment to holding out against Wharton until their demands were met. Prior to May 8, 32 percent of undergraduates and 56 percent of graduate students strongly opposed the strike. After May 8, 42 percent of undergraduates and 65 percent of graduate students strongly opposed striking. The trauma of the Cambodia invasion and Kent State had temporarily drawn together radical, antiwar liberal, and hitherto apolitical students and faculty. After the first week of the strike, however, as the shock over Cambodia and Kent State subsided, the mood of the campus took on a holiday spirit. This was understandable, for 71 percent of the strikers had never participated in an antiwar demonstration. Their roots in the antiwar movement were shallow and easily severed.[41]

Flagging commitment to the strike might also be explained by the campus perception of the strike leaders' motives and ideology. Seventy-two percent of undergraduates believed to some extent that the demand to release Seale was the strike leaders' deliberate attempt to include black students in the strike. Another 70 percent of undergraduates said that strike leaders had exploited the Kent State tragedy in order to radicalize them. The majority of faculty (61 percent), graduate students (54 percent), and undergraduates (54 percent) called themselves liberal or moderate. Very few faculty (2 percent), graduate students (3 percent), and undergraduates (5 percent) considered themselves to be radical. Yet it was this minority of radical faculty and students, notably NUC members Charles Larrowe and Norman Pollack, and SDSers Rick Kibbey and Beth Shapiro, who organized the strike. Among antiwar liberals and moderates, SDS, and to a lesser extent the NUC, stood in ill repute, for the radicals had barred liberals from speaking at antiwar rallies and had bored audiences with their complicated, polemical worldview of capitalism, racism, and the Vietnam War. In the wake of SDS's disastrous confrontations with Adams and the Weathermen's trashing of East Lansing, 72 percent of undergraduates, 92 percent of graduate students, and 91 percent of faculty, in varying degrees considered the New Left too hostile and antagonistic to be effective.[42]

As the radicals were not respected, unable to gain a committed following, and incapable of overcoming negative perceptions and misperceptions, it was inevitable that the strike would peter out. Once the passions of the moderate majority of strikers receded, the out-of-touch radical minority was left to stand alone. Wharton only needed to wait out what was really a spontaneous reaction, and not a rooted, coherent movement. When the moderate masses defected from the strike, Wharton cracked down freely on the die-hard minority.[43]

Although the nation's campuses had become deeply divided, American society as a whole was overwhelmingly of one mind in the aftermath of the Kent State tragedy: more students should have been shot. From Nixon on down, a consensus emerged. The consensus was that because campus dissent had turned violent since 1968, legal authority had to reassert itself by any means necessary. Not surprisingly, this reaction against campus protest was greatest in the city of Kent and Portage County. Within hours of the shootings, Kent policemen raided the houses of suspected radicals. It seemed that a radical was anyone under the age of 30. Rhodes, Del Corso, and newspaper publisher and KSU trustee Robert Dix added fuel to the fire by claiming that student snipers had shot and killed at least one Guardsman. The Hammonds, fearful that "a real reign of terror" was beginning in Kent, fled to Buffalo and stayed briefly with Speed Powrie. Andy Pyle took off for Oberlin where a few hundred Kent State students had proclaimed themselves in exile from America. When Arthur Krause arrived in Kent to collect his daughter's possessions, her landlord, after praising the Guardsmen, demanded the balance of the rent. Krause and all of the parents of the shooting victims received numerous hate letters, many of which were postmarked from Kent. Community residents also spread the word about town that Allison Krause "deserved to die" since she was "pregnant," had "syphilis" and, worst of all, was a "Jew." Only the last part of this litany was accurate.[44]

Portage County Republican party chair Seabury Ford, who had a local reputation for telling funny "nigger jokes," pushed for the criminal indictments of well-known Kent State activists. Subsequently, the Portage County grand jury indicted twenty-four students and sociology professor Tom Lough for conspiracy to commit riot. Weathermen were not among those indicted; only doves and radicals with a reputation for advocating nonviolent protest. (Since local law enforcement agencies claimed to have eliminated the

Weathermen presence in Kent in 1969, county officials could not in 1970 indict people who no longer officially existed.) Canfora, by virtue of having been shot by the Guard, was indicted along with Gibson, Hammond, and Craig Morgan. Lough had attracted attention for having drawn up the May 3 faculty critique of the Guard. Sidney Jackson and Ken Calkins were not indicted since, in contrast to Lough, they had neither supported SDS nor prominently involved themselves in the NUC. Jurors also condemned the Scranton Commission which, reluctantly appointed by Nixon to investigate the shootings, had exonerated activists and condemned the Guardsmen. Ford and his allies were further enraged when the FBI, after sending one hundred agents to Kent, concluded that the soldiers had fired without due cause. At no time, the FBI observed, were Guardsmen in danger, and subsequent Guardsmen stories stating otherwise were contrived.[45]

With the beginning of the fall term, rumors abounded at Kent State that fifty FBI undercover agents were enrolled as students. Kent and campus police, their ranks swelled and their equipment upgraded thanks to the state legislature's unusual generosity, routinely stopped and searched any youth with long hair or blue jeans. Grace, who now had a permanent limp, began to place pebbles on the hood of his car. If the pebbles were gone when he returned from class, then he knew that a resident had opened the hood to tamper with the brakes and engine. Faced with such intense police and community harassment, hundreds of students began wearing T-shirts which had a bitter logo emblazoned on them: "Kent Police State University."[46]

The shootings, and the subsequent reaction, had radicalized thousands of Kent State students. Determined to fight the grand jury, Hammond returned and helped to found a defense committee and the Kent Liberation Front (KLF). Former Kent antiwar leader Tony Walsh, now a lawyer, offered legal assistance. Bill Arthrell and Jerry Persky, a former SDSer, established a popular Yippie chapter which combined radical analysis with countercultural attributes. Working together, the activists organized an October 16 campus march which brought out 2,000 students who demanded the abolition of ROTC and the LCI, and called for the dropping of the indictments. That same month, 4,000 students participated in a "Kent 25" campus rally. White refused to meet with the students, but did issue a position paper in which he condemned activists and defended ROTC and the Liquid Crystals Institute. Most faculty, with the vocal exceptions of Sidney Jackson and Glenn Frank, followed White's lead.[47]

Despite White's efforts to dismiss the activists and salvage the university's reputation with the state legislature, he had to live with the fact that Kent State had become an international symbol of antiwar protest and government repression. A decisive point in history had been reached. All of the cultural ambiguities of Cold War-Vietnam War America which had been building up for years were suddenly and viciously expressed. Americans hated the peace movement and despised the war; supported Nixon but demanded that U.S. military forces withdraw from Cambodia and ultimately Vietnam. For a few brief weeks the mounting crescendo of campus dissent across the nation had become linked and activists spoke as one. This development was to be short lived. Campus activists turned away from Kent State and once again confronted the problems of dealing with national developments as they affected their localities. But the Kent State tragedy was never far from students' minds. The bitter taste of death had forever changed the mentality of the campus-based antiwar movement. One had only to tune in to a rock 'n' roll radio station to hear Crosby, Stills, Nash, and Young blast out "Ohio" to realize that an angry and alienated generation had been reborn in 1970:

> Tin soldiers and Nixon's coming,
> This summer I hear the drumming,
> Four dead in Ohio!
> Four dead in Ohio!

Epilogue: "We Stand against Fear, Hate, Systems, and Structures Not in the Service of Man": Legacies of Protest

In the months following the 1970 strike, the campus Left collapsed. MSU SDS, crippled by ideological divisions and the loss of its most dynamic leaders and members, faded away. Steve Badrich and George Fish had left MSU, and Brad Lang and Linda Evans had gone underground. Evans, however, was soon captured by the FBI. Released, she disappeared until 1983 when she was arrested and charged with planting a bomb in the U.S. Capitol Building. The Paper ceased publication and the alternative newspaper which took its place, the Bogue Street Bridge, was more oriented towards countercultural than political issues. Significantly, the most popular antiwar organizations at MSU after the strike were largely community-directed and based: the Greater Lansing Community Organization and the Lansing-MSU Vietnam Veterans Against the War (VVAW). The two groups were also liberal-dovish and sought to work through the electoral system to achieve social change and peace.[1]

Penn State SDS also fell upon hard times, losing membership and discontinuing publication of the Water Tunnel for lack of funds. Nonetheless, it continued to be active, filing legal suit against the university in connection with the 1970 student-police riot. The radicals also tried to build up campus opposition to Walker's successor, John Oswald, who had annoyed many activists by declaring that the "university must not allow itself to become an instrument for social or political change." He also created some bitterness by concurring with Walker's decision to deny tenure to Wells Keddie.

However, the majority of campus dissenters regarded the new president as a benign figure. They would never be able to promote opposition to Oswald to the same degree that SDS had mobilized sentiment against Walker.[2]

In contrast to the PSU SDS, the Coalition for Peace had become somewhat more popular and an increasingly assertive force at the university. In 1971, dovish and radical pacifists affiliated with the Coalition for Peace founded an underground newspaper, the *Henderson Station*. Its editors embraced the desirability of cultural and ideological diversity and sought to build a just society. Towards those ends, the editors and writers, among them Rev. Fred Reisz, advocated a variety of nonviolent tactics to oppose the war. Larry Smuckler, an undergraduate psychology major from Philadelphia, urged readers not to pay their "war taxes," and other writers publicized the Coalition for Peace's student voter registration drive. The editors were also careful to avoid the *Water Tunnel's* controversial example, refusing to print articles which contained obscenities. Finally, in spite of the polemics directed against the Coalition for Peace by the radicals, the *Henderson Station* published articles by SDSers such as Geoff Sill.[3]

Even though the Coalition for Peace had grown, the Penn State antiwar movement did not have the strength to rout its conservative foes. In 1971, a Republican Centre County judge undercut the liberals' voter registration efforts by ruling that, regardless of federal law to the contrary, PSU students were not to be considered community residents. Therefore, students could not register to vote in State College and those who had registered prior to this ruling were required to place their ballots in separate boxes. When the polls closed, county officials destroyed the students' ballots. Meanwhile, residents organized a prowar "March for Victory" in Washington.[4]

Mounting ideological and cultural divisions further limited the PSU antiwar movement's effectiveness. Coalition member Steve Soloman crossed swords with SDS leader Don Sassoon, a British political science graduate student who viciously denounced the doves and their ideology of peaceful change. Pam Farley outraged SDSers by arguing that while the Vietnam War was imperialistic, the movement had to embrace nonviolent protest and reject the philosophy of revolutionary violence. On the cultural front, black militants scorned the Coalition for Peace, yet demanded that white activists support their political agenda: increased black student enrollment, lowered admissions standards for blacks, and the employment of more black faculty regardless of academic qualifications. In addition, a new activist group appeared on the campus, Homophiles of Penn State (HOPS), whose intent was to promote homosexual lifestyles and rights in State College. To be politically correct, antiwar leaders had to support the black and homosexual militants, or be branded racists and homophobes. Thus, the majority of PSU students came to the erroneous conclusion that peace, affirmative action, and homosexuality were interconnected causes. In reality, blacks and homosexuals insisted upon financial and moral aid from the Coalition for Peace and SDS, but did not reciprocate by participating in antiwar organizing and protest.[5]

Cultural and ideological divisions, as well as the conservative local environment, ensured that the antiwar movement would have great difficulty in recapturing the momentum gained in 1970. An attempt in February 1971 to organize a student strike to protest the American-backed South Vietnamese Army invasion of Laos fizzled. Campus demonstrations against university-military research, scheduled to coincide with the May Day civil disobedience peace actions in Washington, fared somewhat better and attracted six hundred participants. Unfortunately, the rally in front of Old Main on April 19 degenerated into a farce when a SDSer denounced an administrator as an "enemy of the people" and shot him with a squirt gun. A subsequent attempt by two hundred students to block traffic on South Atherton Street and College Avenue succeeded in further alienating residents. The editors of the *Daily Collegian* were particularly alarmed by this action which resulted in 120 state policemen descending upon State College. It was evident that a handful of militants were intent upon provoking renewed confrontations with the police in order to radicalize the campus. Unlike the previous spring, however, the police were on their best behavior. Additionally, PSU VVAW members made sure that the militants did not take control of the situation. One veteran, Lou Redden, was greatly disturbed by the advocates of confrontation and argued that "anyone who starts any violence is a pig."[6]

In stark contrast to Penn State, the antiwar movement at Michigan State, perhaps because of the disappearance of the self-defeating radical student Left, expanded. On the first anniversary of the Kent State slayings, 3,000 MSU students peacefully protested against the war. Defying President Wharton, who had threatened to dock the pay of any faculty who canceled classes in recognition of the event, New University Conference organizers John Masterson, Norman Pollack, and Charles Larrowe coordinated the demonstration. Standing in front of Demonstration Hall, seventy Vietnam veterans pinned their combat medals on a dummy corpse which symbolized the MSU students who had died in Vietnam. Former president Walter Adams then read aloud the lengthy list of Michigan residents who had been killed in Indochina. Afterwards, the sobbing World War II veteran, no longer able to criticize the war in terms of cold economics, delivered an impassioned moral appeal for peace: ". . . end this war which is destroying this country and that for which it stands. Let us honor the memory of those who have lost their lives by bringing their living brothers home."[7]

Wharton could not have been pleased with the antiwar activities of his predecessor. But then, Adams was not the only person at MSU defying the president. When Wharton fired natural scientist and NUC organizer Eileen van Tassel for her role in the 1970 strike, he had expected the professor to depart meekly from the campus. After all, whenever Hannah had dismissed a faculty member for leftist political activism, the academic quickly and quietly left town. Unfortunately for Wharton, van Tassel was not a meek academic. She retained a lawyer and successfully sued MSU to get back her job. The president also discovered that he could no longer maintain the university's policy of *in loco parentis*. In the spring of 1971, Justin Morrill students removed the bolted doors separating the men and women's sections of their dormitory and cast them into the Red Cedar River. Then the residential college students instituted the gender integration of their suites. Other dormitory residents followed their lead. Wharton appeared even less infallible after the courts dismissed the charges he had brought against the students arrested at Demonstration Hall and the union in 1970. Finally, the editors of the *State News,* savoring the days of editorial freedom which they had enjoyed during the strike, refused any longer to submit to administration censorship. Recognizing that he had become the most ineffectual and powerless president in MSU's history, Wharton wearily gave the campus newspaper its independence.[8]

In Buffalo, the student Left had descended into irrationality and chaos. SDSers, following the lead of a former Trotskyist who later took the alias of Lyndon LaRouche, invaded classrooms in order to prevent "racist" and "imperialist" professors from teaching. YAWF went into rapid decline after its adult leaders expelled Gerry Gross and most of the student membership for deviating from the Marxist-Maoist line. Student leftists lost one of their best leaders when convicted Buffalo Nine defendant Bruce Beyer jumped bail and fled to Sweden. The radical editors of the *Spectrum* exhibited their contempt for religiously observant Jewish students, and community moral sensibilities in general, by denouncing Zionism as a racist ideology and featuring an advertisement which depicted Dorothy of *The Wizard of Oz* saying, "Which way to the gang bang? Don't go wrong the first week! Join the *Spectrum* and go bad the second week!" Later, the *Spectrum* carried full-page photographs of couples engaged in sexual intercourse, informing students that if they joined the paper's staff, they too could have a good time.[9]

As the student Left fell apart, demoralization and ideological division set in among the faculty. Marvin Resnikoff, a radical physicist, and Tom Rainey, a historian and member of the People's Coalition, a community peace organization, were denied tenure. A number of dovish faculty, including Theodore Friend and Newton Garver, joined forces with former president Peter Regan to endorse local Conservative party candidates who championed law and order in the city and on the campus. Meanwhile, five university officials resigned, discontented with President Robert Ketter's attempts to undo Meyerson's reforms. Throughout the university, faculty and graduate students denounced one another in the columns of the *Spectrum* and in department meetings. On the defensive, the radical faculty scored one major victory: Meyerson quietly convinced Ketter not to continue with the prosecution of the forty-five faculty who had been arrested in 1970.[10]

SUNY-Buffalo faculty and student antiwar activists also endured unrelenting community attack. The Erie County grand jury recommended the dismissal of faculty who refused to sign loyalty oaths, described the storefront colleges as a "radical nucleus" which threatened the university, and implicity blamed Meyerson's liberal, permissive administration for setting the stage for the 1970 riots. Buffalo politician Alfreda Slominski added her voice to that of the grand jury, arguing that: "The good kids who live in our community can't go to college because there's no room for them. I'm quite sure that if we would eliminate this radical element and put the decent kids of our community [in], we would be better off. The whole nation would gain." Additionally, a right-wing vigilante group fire-bombed a student cooperative in the Allentown district of Buffalo and police officers on motorcycles charged through a crowd of 1,500 university peace protestors at a May Day antiwar demonstration in Niagara Square.[11]

Buffalo residents and policemen, though eager to denounce and assault middle-class peace protestors, avoided confrontations with the university's two hundred antiwar Vietnam veterans. Over-whelmingly blue-collar, Catholic, and from the Niagara Frontier, the SUNY-Buffalo VVAW defied the community's image of the privi-leged New York City antiwar protestor. Indeed, the hawkish Buffalo *Courier-Express* wrote sympathetic accounts of the activist veterans and Buffalo policemen stood by in uncomfortable silence whenever VVAW members staged antiwar demonstrations in the city. Scorn-ing what remained of the campus student Left, veterans such as Gail Graham, a working-class SUNY-Buffalo VVAW organizer, kept order at antiwar rallies to make sure that left- and right-wing extremists did not provoke confrontations.[12]

The difficulties which confronted Buffalo antiwar partisans were nearly as great as those which Kent State activists faced after 1970. With the approach of the first anniversary of the shootings, the new university president, Glenn Olds, attempted to control memorial observances, unsuccessfully banning outside speakers and restrict-ing the number of students and activists from across the nation who wished to come to Kent State. Kent police officers infiltrated the campus VVAW chapter and, with the advent of spring, swept the city's streets clear of what seemed to them to be outside agitators. They accomplished this by indiscriminately firing wooden pellets at students and clubbing anyone who got in their way, including Rev. Tom Taggart of the United Christian Fellowship. The student government began to instruct the campus on first aid and civil disobedience tactics and criticized many faculty for spying on activ-ists and helping the Kent police single out particular protestors for beatings.[13]

Even though the first memorial observance passed largely without great incident, the campus remained unsettled because prosecution had begun of the twenty-five individuals who had been indicted in 1970. Thoroughly disgusted with Governor Rhodes and Seabury Ford, Ohio Democratic senator Stephen Young denounced the Por-tage County grand jury as "a fraud and a fakery." Radical attorney

William Kunstler followed suit and offered to defend KSU student government president and Kent 25 defendant Craig Morgan. Ultimately, after glaring national news media exposure and frequent, bitter protest rallies, Ohio attorney general William Brown decided not to continue with the prosecutions. Despite this development, Tom Lough concluded that the shootings and the subsequent indictments had "succeeded in stamping out the *political* vitality of the nation, and particularly of the nation's youth." The United States, Lough concluded, was "beyond salvaging."[14]

Not everyone in the antiwar movement was as sanguine as Lough. In East Lansing, by the spring of 1972, campus antiwar activists had organized successful student voter registration drives which resulted in the election of doves to the city council and the Ingham County board of commissioners. George Griffiths, a GLCO leader who, as a Lansing ACLU member had championed student rights' activist Paul Schiff in 1966, used his city council seat to promote the cause of peace. On April 18, the city council's dovish majority passed a resolution calling for Nixon "to immediately cease all bombing of North Vietnam, and to accelerate the withdrawal of all American forces in Southeast Asia." Meanwhile, Adams and Larrowe joined forces with the 385–member MSU VVAW. After donning their World War II uniforms, the professors and a VVAW delegation met with the university board of trustees and demanded that MSU go on record against the war. Unable to resist a group of activists whose patriotism was unassailable, the trustees adopted a strongly worded antiwar resolution.[15]

With the fall of the two bastions of prowar sentiment and political conservatism in East Lansing—the board of trustees and the city council—it seemed as if everyone accepted the idea that change could be wrought through moral suasion and the electoral system. Moreover, SDS was dead and GLCO and the VVAW were far more moderate, polite, and effective. Consequently, many students and faculty believed that the era of mass, disruptive protesters was over. It therefore came as a shock when subsequent events proved otherwise.

In the waning days of April, Nixon ordered American naval forces to mine Haiphong Harbor, North Vietnam's major port. Concerned that American mines would sink Soviet and Chinese ships and thus precipitate World War III, the nation's campuses exploded. At the University of Massachusetts, demonstrators attacked ROTC offices and protestors at the University of Maryland became so disruptive that the governor called out the National Guard. Eight hundred Kent State students occupied the new ROTC offices, resulting in the arrest of 129 protestors, the bulk of them former SDSers and activists who had been present at the Commons on May 4, 1970. In East Lansing, four hundred doves and veterans met in the union to discuss the latest escalation of the war. The crowd overflowed outside of the building. Local police officers, thinking that they were witnessing a reprise of the 1970 strike, promptly gassed everyone in the vicinity. Enraged, the students fled, only to return an hour later with 3,000 reinforcements and a number of laundry carts which had been taken from Justin Morrill and James Madison colleges. The protestors positioned the carts at the intersection of Abbott Street and Grand River Avenue and set up camp.[16]

Governor William Milliken, in response to the blockade of the major highway leading to the capital, reluctantly declared a state of emergency. Not wishing to emulate the example of Rhodes, for whom Milliken had nothing but contempt, and displeased with Nixon, the liberal Republican governor initially hoped that a *display* of force might calm the situtation. Subsequently, he sent state police helicopters to hover over East Lansing, an action which, in the eyes of numbers of students, conjured up images of a "banana republic coup." During the second evening of the blockade, students bought out merchants' liquor stocks and thumbed their noses at seething East Lansing police officers who had received reprimands from the city council. Members of the VVAW talked with policemen and students in an attempt to relieve tensions. They also dealt with some former Michigan Weathermen who came to East Lansing to promote violent confrontation. Not wishing to see MSU become another Kent State, the veterans, who regarded the Weathermen as "a bunch of upper-middle-class faggots who wanted to fuck each other," chased the radicals out of town.[17]

Towards the morning of the third day of the protest, two hundred East Lansing, Lansing, and state police officers moved in with bulldozers, tear gas, and clubs, quickly re-opening Grand River Avenue to traffic. Eight hundred students leapt on bicycles and circled a section of the highway until police violently pulled them from their seats. State police troopers then deployed on the roof of Jacobson's department store, training their rifles on the street below. Thousands of students, careful not to set foot on Grand River Avenue, the free fire zone, glared silently at the troopers. Suddenly, a student threw something at Jacobsen's, causing the crowd to gasp and the troopers to stiffen. A trooper, crouching on the roof, put aside his gun and caught the object. He smiled and tossed the frisbee back towards the campus. The blockade was over and the crowd sensed that the war at home had also ended.[18]

At Penn State, in response to the mining of Haiphong Harbor, the Coalition for Peace called for a rally in front of Old Main. To the organizers' surprise, the initial crowd of two hundred grew to 2,000 chanting students who soon marched through the streets of State College and picketed the ORL and the Garfield Thomas Water Tunnel. Residents were irate that students were blocking traffic along College Avenue and Atherton Street, prompting several motorists to accelerate and plow into the crowd. Other locals careened through State College in pickup trucks, swinging baseball bats at students. Enraged by such actions, which injured dozens of youths, 5,500 protestors turned out the next day and blocked the main streets of the town. Sympathetic to the students' cause, newly elected Governor Milton Shapp ordered the temporary shutdown of the ORL and dispatched Lt. Governor Ernest Kline to talk to the demonstrators.[19]

The campus remained tense for the next week, but once students' anger and enthusiasm waned, mass protest collapsed permanently. As attendance at subsequent rallies tapered off, the Coalition for Peace realized that it could not sustain political momentum. Worse, the activists had to close their Peace Center in September because of lack of funds. The university administration quickly reopened the ORL. With the doves utterly demoralized, SDSers seized control of the *Henderson Station*. Immediately, the radicals purged moderates from the staff and began publishing anonymous, strange articles, including a piece which contended that Jews were treated better in the "democratic" Soviet Union than in the "racist," "imperialistic" state of Israel. Within a few months the paper ceased publication. SDS and the Coalition for Peace, as well as YAF, faded from the scene by late 1972, killed by student apathy and a hostile local political environment.[20]

If the great postprotest letdown at Penn State in 1972 proved anything, it demonstrated that in America all politics really are local. Although national developments shaped the framework in which events took place at Penn State and other campuses in the 1960s, local values and actors determined the substance of, and gave enormous variety to, the historical texture. Consequently, sweeping generalizations of the period are suspect, for historical patterns and sociological paradigms do not always fit the actual local situation. Every university, and every community in which that institution was located, was different in terms of ethnic composition, physical size, history, and ideological orientation. Communities unprepared, or unwilling, to embrace change and tolerate dissent—State College, Buffalo, and Kent—reacted harshly to antiwar protest.

Moreover, at these schools, the community viewed faculty, students, and, sometimes, university administrators as outsiders subverting the traditional order. This was not true at MSU, but the State of Michigan generally had a polity imbued with the spirit of progressivism. Even though New York could claim to be the bastion of modern liberalism and the font of cultural pluralism, this ignores the fact that there are two New Yorks: New York City and everything else. Buffalo was not New York City and the majority of SUNY-Buffalo administrators, faculty, and students who wanted it to be so were rudely awakened to that reality.

There were other realities which informed the era of campus protest. One of the most important of those realities was that America's institutions of higher education, desiring to promote national security and to further the cause of global Communist containment, involved themselves in military research. Federal grants transformed quiet agricultural and teaching colleges into sprawling academic complexes and enabled an unprecedented number of Americans from differing class and cultural backgrounds to obtain a university education. From the MSU Vietnam Project to the Penn State ORL and Project Themis, state universities seized the opportunity to achieve an institutional greatness on a par with that of more prestigious schools while championing democracy around the world. Yet these developments sowed the seeds of discontent, brought to fruition by the Vietnam War and ultimately blooming at Kent State.

The state university administrators responsible for transforming their schools into academically comprehensive institutions of higher education, and who also tied their campuses to the DoD, did not anticipate the long-term political consequences of their actions. John Hannah, Eric Walker, and Robert White failed to understand the mounting revolt of students, faculty, and campus clergy who rejected university-military research on the grounds that it made the academy complicit in what they considered to be an unjust and unnecessary war. Subsequently, state university administrators determined that protest against the war, ROTC, and the ORL or MSU technical assistance programs in the Third World, was Communist-inspired. If Communist-inspired, they reasoned, political surveillance and/or repression directed against campus peace activists was required. Less sanguine and somewhat more in tune with dovish antiwar sentiment, Martin Meyerson thought that he could reason with protestors. Tragically, most of his rebellious students, and some of his faculty, were not reasonable.

When confronted with disruptive student protest, elite university administrators were far less prone to introduce police force than their state university counterparts. Cornell administrators in 1969 did nothing to stop black militants from carrying rifles on the campus and physically intimidating white faculty and students. Similarly, Columbia officials in 1968 allowed students to occupy buildings and disrupt classes for days until finally, and reluctantly, bringing in city police forces. In part, the reluctance of elite university administrators to check irresponsible protest stemmed from strongly held civil libertarian values acquired during their own liberal arts training at Ivy League schools. More important, given the prominent social origins of the majority of elite university student activists, administrators were careful not to arouse the wrath of economically and politically powerful parents by having the police club and gas their children. State university administrators, generally less well-educated and often unexposed to the humanities, did not place a high value on civil liberties. Further, since the bulk of state university students were middle to working class, such administrators did not have to worry about serious economic and political retaliation from parents whose children had run afoul of the police. This reality meant that if National Guardsmen were to come onto a campus and bayonet or kill students, then the institution involved would not be a Harvard, but rather a Kent State.

While university administrators tried to cope with social forces beyond their control and experience, faculties polarized over the issue of the Vietnam War and campus antiwar protest. At the onset of the U.S. military escalation of the war, many academics who supported American foreign policy in Indochina tended to have vested interests in the continuation of the Cold War. This was particularly true at the state universities where engineering and science departments defined their schools' academic and cultural mindset and which became dependent upon military research contracts. Affiliation with the IDA, participation in technical assistance programs in the Third World such as the MSU Vietnam Project, and DoD research contracts, were all powerful incentives for academics seeking to further their careers while serving the national interest. Academics who were the most vocal in their opposition to the war, and loud in their criticism of military research-oriented faculty, were those without DoD ties. Cold War funding policies created at least two streams of faculty: those who looked to Washington and the Pentagon and those who believed in separation of university and Defense Department. The Vietnam War brought the two streams of faculty into open, bitter conflict. When student protest became increasingly violent after 1967, the faculty Cold War dissenters fragmented into various ideological factions. The academy still has not recovered from the intellectual, political, and cultural aftershocks of the war.

In addition to the war and university-military research, the nation's faculty also polarized in response to mass, unprecedented student revolt. Student activists such as Tom Hayden credited American college youth with abolishing racial segregation, ending the Vietnam War, reforming the Democratic party, and compelling the federal government to reconsider its Cold War foreign policy. He also noted that from 1965 to 1971, 26,358 students were arrested, fourteen killed, and thousands injured or expelled for protesting against the war. While Hayden's claims are overdrawn, he is correct in pointing to the pivotal role university students played in American politics. Over four million Americans participated in antiwar protest, with students representing a vital component of the peace movement. And SDS, on the extreme left of the antiwar movement, had 100,000 members in 1968 at hundreds of nonelite state universities, a significant number and development given that in 1962 the organization was just a small collection of elite college-educated radicals. Of course, Johnson's Vietnam policy made SDS popular, rather than the organization's ideological agenda. But despite SDS's remarkable progress, it took Nixon's invasion of Cambodia, and the killings at Kent State, to mobilize millions of students against the war.

Initially, student activists such as Carl Davidson, Jack Sattel, Jerry Taylor, and Tony Walsh sponsored teach-ins, collected signatures for peace petitions, published antiwar literature, and organized rallies. In 1965, they believed that if "the Establishment" could only see patriotic citizens' concerns about the war, it would end. Instead, the war escalated. Frustrated with trying to educate the government, student activists sometimes forged campus populist alliances (the UCM and SDS at MSU) and others turned to electoral channels. Liberal doves, in the aftermath of the aborted McCarthy campaign, found that political leaders restricted access to the power structure. The war continued to escalate and entered more intense stages of violence. Radicals bickered with their liberal allies, fought with each other, fragmented, and ultimately opted for either class or guerilla war against the power structure.

The 1960s student antiwar movement caught up great numbers of culturally diverse partisans who shared a general sense of idealism mixed with feelings of alienation from society. Cultural diversity gave the student peace movement an enriched political vision seldom seen in the history of mass movements in America. In Carl Davidson, Dave Stockman, Leverett Millen, and Carl Oglesby, the student antiwar movement could choose from, or attempt to combine, the currents of labor syndicalism, social gospel, Old Testament prophecy, and populism. But at the same time, history weighed heavily upon students. Antiwar student activists, reflecting the larger society, were profoundly divided along class, ethnic, religious, and racial lines and, subsequently, the products of many often irreconcilable cultural heritages. Such cultural divisions ultimately fragmented SDS and other antiwar groups, and spawned movements within movements. Cultural and class divisions were also evident between campus antiwar groups and, in SDS, informed chapter relationships with the National Office. The tensions between elite and nonelite university SDS chapters (the upper-class Michigan and Columbia Weathermen and their working-class Kent State and Michigan State opponents) contributed further to the cultural and class struggle waged in antiwar student ranks.

At the state universities, a variety of local and nationally affiliated student antiwar groups emerged in the 1960s and early 1970s. Each organization possessed a particular critique of the war and American society, a product of the different cultural values and experiences students brought to the groups. The Resistance attracted largely middle- to upper-middle-class Protestant pacifists who embraced the concept of individual moral witness against perceived evil.

Members of the UCM, overwhelmingly working to lower middle class, found pacifism appealing, but were willing to support violent revolutionary movements abroad to an extent if they furthered the cause of social justice and were not totalitarian. Rhetorically revolutionary, the UCM at MSU and other campuses in practice avoided violent confrontations with authority and stressed the desirability of working to achieve peaceful change through the electoral process.

It is important to keep in mind that the great majority of antiwar students either involved themselves in dovish local national political campaigns and/or participated in campus and community peace demonstrations, but did not formally affiliate with any organization. This organizationally and ideologically unaffiliated mass represented SDSers' hopes for building a large radical movement. Occasionally, SDSers succeeded in mobilizing and radicalizing the mass, but only temporarily and then only because national political developments and the introduction of outside police force to the campus aroused students. In general, most students rejected SDS's increasingly violent style and championship of revolutionary Communism, being much more comfortable with a moderate Coalition for Peace or GLCO. Further, SDSers, regardless of which campus chapter they belonged to, castigated the democratic electoral process, criticized pacifism, and by the late 1960s expended great energy attacking dovish organizations. By being against everything, it was difficult for students and faculty to discern exactly what SDS was for.

Beyond ideological contests, the relative success or failure of an antiwar organization often depended upon the cultural ambiance of the campus. Michigan State, while not, as *Ramparts* noted in 1966, "the Paris of the Midwest," was far more liberal and cosmopolitan than Kent State and Penn State. Consequently, MSU activists were able to found and sustain a variety of peace organizations which spanned the ideological spectrum from SDS on the vaguely Marxist left to the social gospel-oriented UCM and the dovish GLCO on the right. Conservative and prowar student groups did not thrive at MSU. This was in stark contrast to PSU and KSU where the student and faculty antiwar movement remained small, isolated, and under ideological and often physical attack throughout the 1960s. In response to a hostile environment, Penn State SDS became increasingly strident, while the Weathermen tendency subsumed much of Kent State SDS.

Such differences in political outcomes were also bound up in the nature of the institutions. MSU and SUNY-Buffalo placed great emphasis upon the liberal arts, creating more philosophically diverse campuses. These institutions were academically comprehensive in real terms and had student bodies more inclined to peace activism. Kent State and Penn State, however, though enrolling larger numbers of liberal arts majors, never transcended their origins as engineering or education colleges. Both institutions enrolled largely engineering and education majors who tended to be conservative and hawkish. The pool of potential antiwar supporters was limited and the cultural environment of these schools conventional, as well as hostile towards dissent. All of this points to the fact that while state university students were much more vocationally minded and hawkish than their elite liberal arts university peers, there were gradations among such schools in terms of academic emphasis and cultural diversity. The more liberal arts oriented and intellectually diverse the institution, the more dovish or radical the students and faculty.

Nowhere is the influence of the campus and community environment on the university-based antiwar movement more evident than in Buffalo. As an urban-industrial center populated largely by anti-Communist Catholics, Buffalo in the 1960s was a cultural battleground. SUNY-Buffalo students and faculty in the 1960s were increasingly drawn from the ranks of the middle and upper-middle classes, had secularized Protestant and Jewish backgrounds, and came largely from cosmopolitan, liberal New York City. Class, ethnicity, religion, and political orientation divided campus and community to an extent far beyond that experienced in East Lansing, Kent, and State College. Cultural animosities dating from the 1930s and the early years of the Cold War were brought to the surface by the escalating Vietnam War and SUNY-Buffalo peace protest. The campus antiwar movement responded to community hostility by moving further to the left and adopting violent tactics.

SUNY-Buffalo antiwar students, who were far to the left of their counterparts at MSU, PSU and Kent State prior to the escalation of the Vietnam War, also contended with an established Old Left in the city. This Old Left quickly seized control of, and then intellectually corrupted, SDS. Jerry Taylor's vision of an independent, ideologically inclusive, pacifistic New Left could not endure attack from the community and undermining from within by the sectarian, violence-prone YAWF.

Advocates of nonviolent antiwar protest fared no better at Kent State. The working- and lower-middle-class supporters of peace education and nonviolent protest were no match for upper-middle-class sectarian activists such as Howie Emmer, Bill Ayers, and Terry Robbins. Jim Powrie, Ken Hammond, and Ruth Gibson, brought up in households which stressed the importance of civility and compromise, were incapable of responding with sufficient vigor to opponents who had been taught that control, manipulation, and confrontation were positive cultural attributes. With Emmer's and Robbins' rise to power in the Kent State SDS, forces were set in motion which culminated in the tragic confrontation with the Ohio National Guard in 1970.

Where student and faculty antiwar activists cooperated with campus and local clergy and rejected radical extremism and violent confrontation, the peace movement achieved some success. At MSU, the UCM and later GLCO, supported by Revs. Keith Pohl and Lynn Jondahl, captured political control of their community. Religious-oriented peace protestors also conveyed a positive image on and off the campus which earned the respect, if not always the endorsement, of residents and some important state politicians such as Governor William Milliken. The same may be said to a lesser extent for Penn State, where the Coalition for Peace and its dovish clergy and faculty supporters were able to build, temporarily, a mass, nonviolent antiwar movement.

In Buffalo, the VVAW generated sympathy and some support from the community. But then, the student activists who joined the VVAW were drawn from the area and came largely from Catholic and working-class backgrounds. These were not alien SDSers, but rather the children of the Buffalo community. For this reason, they did not experience community attacks. Further, their actions received a fair hearing from Buffalo's ethnic residents. In general, however, the campus-based antiwar movement failed to appeal to off-campus constituencies, thus severely limiting its effectiveness while provoking a cultural and political backlash across the nation.

It would be somewhat misleading to close on this note of post-1960s backlash, or to observe that campus-based mass protest ended in the spring of 1972. Certainly after 1970 the national news media devoted less attention to the peace movement and the Vietnam War. But the peace movement was not finished in 1972 and, moreover, many students remained politically active, canvassing for liberal doves such as George McGovern rather than taking their protest to the streets. Beyond the McGovern presidential campaign, there was a much less commented upon antiwar strain which had emerged in the nation: the Catholic New Left.

In Buffalo, a group of Irish Catholic youths, largely products of the city's parochial schools, began in 1971 to raid area draft boards. Over the next several months they stole 32,000 draft files. Following each nocturnal break-in, the youths mailed the files to draft-aged males, explaining to them that they could not be inducted into the military if Selective Service did not have their files. It was up to each individual, the activists stated, to decide if he wished to return the file to his draft board. Profoundly pacifistic, the youths called themselves "The Buffalo" and informed the local news media that: "We stand against fear, hate, systems, and structures not in the service of man, the military industrial complex which has run rampant and at the verge of destroying our life system—our mother the earth."[21]

One night in the fall of 1971, five of The Buffalo were apprehended during a draft board break-in. Among the five was Jeremiah Horrigan, the son of the Buffalo Bills general manager. Ed Powell put his house up on bond to help with legal expenses and Horrigan's father enlisted the aid of a local Irish Catholic attorney, Vincent Doyle. A John Kennedy Democrat who had fought his way into the Protestant Establishment, Doyle met with his clients and attempted to put together a traditional legal defense. However, the youths politely told Doyle that they did not wish to contend the federal government's criminal charges. Rather, they were willing to admit their guilt, but wanted to argue that their actions had been necessary to end the war. Aghast, Doyle futilely argued with them and finally concurred. Then the activists urged Doyle not to worry about jury examination and selection; they would accept whatever jury the prosecuting attorney chose. Another passionate exchange occurred, but once again Doyle threw up his hands. Consequently, the jury was, according to Doyle, composed entirely of "WASPs—White Anglo Saxon Protestants." The Irish jurist was particularly disturbed by this development; he could not say WASP without spitting.[22]

The trial of The Buffalo commenced in the spring of 1972, Judge John Curtin presiding. Throughout the trial, the youths were respectful towards the judge and jury and explained their actions in moderate tones. Impressed by the youths, Curtin, in a dramatic turnabout from the Buffalo Nine proceedings, allowed the defendants to put the war on trial. Citing Catholic church teachings on peace and social justice, as well as the lessons of the Nuremberg War Crimes trials, The Buffalo pleaded for an end to war and man's inhumanity to man. Day after day testimony concerning the war, particularly the stories of local Vietnam veterans, weighed more and more heavily upon Curtin and the Buffalo Catholic community which expressed sympathy for its co-religionists. Finally, the defense rested and the jury deliberated. Quickly, the jury found the defendants guilty, paving the way for sentences ranging up to twelve years' imprisonment.[23]

After a moment of silence, Curtin, voice cracking and fighting back tears, stated, "Your love of country is above that of most other citizens. If others had the same sense of morality, the war would have been over a long time ago." Curtin vacated the sentences and released the defendants. With this decision, he established a legal precedent which recognized that federal laws may have to be broken to ensure that justice and peace prevail.[24]

Notes

Introduction

1. James Miller, *"Democracy Is in the Streets": From Port Huron to the Siege of Chicago* (New York: Simon and Schuster, 1987); Tom Hayden, *Reunion: A Memoir* (New York: Random House, 1988); Todd Gitlin, *The Sixties: Years of Hope, Days of Rage* (New York: Bantam, 1989); Godfrey Hodgson, *America in Our Time: From World War II to Nixon, What Happened and Why* (New York: Vintage Books, 1978); Kenneth Keniston, *Youth and Dissent* (New York: Harcourt, Brace, Jovanovich, 1971); Michael Miles, *The Radical Probe: The Logic of Student Rebellion* (New York: Atheneum, 1971); J. Anthony Lukas, *Don't Shoot—We Are Your Children!* (New York: Dell, 1971); "Making Sense of the Sixties," produced by Ricki Green and David Hoffman, WETA-TV Washington, D.C., and Varied Directions International, 1990.

2. Peter Collier and David Horowitz, *Destructive Generation: Second Thoughts about the Sixties* (New York: Summit Books, 1990); Hayden, *Reunion*; Patrick J. Buchanan, *Right from the Beginning* (Washington, D.C.: Regnery Gateway, 1990); Allan Bloom, *The Closing of the American Mind: How Higher Education Has Failed Democracy and Impoverished the Souls of Today's Students* (New York: Simon and Schuster, 1988).

3. Nancy Zaroulis and Gerald Sullivan, *Who Spoke Up? American Protest against the War in Vietnam, 1963–1975* (New York: Doubleday, Inc., 1984); Charles DeBenedetti and Charles Chatfield, *An American Ordeal: The Anti-War Movement of the Vietnam Era* (New York: Syracuse University Press, 1990); Hayden, *Reunion*.

4. Collier and Horowitz, *Destructive Generation*; Buchanan, *Right from the Beginning*; Bloom, *The Closing of the American Mind*; Hodgson, *America in Our Time*; Christopher Lasch, *The Culture of Narcissism: American Life in an Age of Diminishing Expectations* (New York: Warner Books, 1979); Dinesh D'Souza, *Illiberal Education: The Politics of Race and Sex on Campus* (New York: The Free Press, 1991).

5. Michael Novak, *The Rise of the Unmeltable Ethnics: Politics and Culture in the Seventies* (New York: Macmillan, 1972); Kevin P. Phillips, *The Emerging Republican Majority* (New Rochelle, N.Y.: Arlington House, 1970); Michael W. Miles, *The Odyssey of the American Right* (New York: Oxford University Press, 1980); Everett

275

Carll Ladd, Jr., *Where Have All the Voters Gone? The Fracturing of America's Political Parties* (New York: W. W. Norton, 1978).

6. Max Heirich, *Spiral of Conflict: Berkeley, 1964* (New York: Columbia University Press, 1971); Miller, *"Democracy Is in the Streets"*; Irwin Unger, *The Movement: A History of the American New Left, 1959–1972* (New York: Harper and Row, 1974); Kirkpatrick Sale, *SDS* (New York: Random House, 1973); W. J. Rorabaugh, *Berkeley at War: The 1960s* (New York: Oxford University Press, 1989); Jerome H. Skolnick, *The Politics of Protest* (New York: Ballantine Books, 1970); George R. Vickers, *The Formation of the New Left: The Early Years* (Lexington, Mass.: D. C. Heath, 1975); Stanley Rothman and S. Robert Lichter, *Roots of Radicalism: Jews, Christians, and the New Left* (New York: Oxford University Press, 1982); Gitlin, *The Sixties*; Richard Flacks, "The Liberated Generation," in Shirley M. Clark and John P. Clark, eds., *Youth in Modern Society* (New York: Holt, Rinehart and Winston, 1972), 319–39; Hayden, *Reunion*.

7. S. Robert Lichter, Stanley Rothman and Linda S. Lichter in *The Media Elite: America's New Power Brokers* (Bethesda, Md.: Adler and Adler, 1986), provide an extensive analysis of the class and cultural backgrounds, and political values, of hundreds of influential journalists who began their careers in the 1960s. Overwhelmingly, the journalists are East Coast WASPs and Jews, graduates of elite universities, and cultural liberals. Todd Gitlin in *The Whole World Is Watching: Mass Media in the Making and Unmaking of the New Left* (Berkeley: University of California Press, 1980), details the symbiotic relationship between upper-middle-class reporters and activists in the 1960s. As for the backgrounds and consequent biases of activists turned memoir writers and scholars, consider the following: James Miller, scholar, was a member of the Brandeis SDS; Todd Gitlin, scholar, attended Harvard, Michigan, and Berkeley and was a member of the Michigan and national SDS; Richard Flacks, scholar, attended Michigan and was a founder of that school's SDS chapter; and Tom Hayden, memoir writer, was also a founder of the Michigan and national SDS. On the other side of the political divide, Peter Collier and David Horowitz spent their days of radical youth in the Berkeley area, while Allan Bloom was a faculty member at Cornell in 1969.

8. H. Edward Ransford, "Blue Collar Anger: Reactions to Student and Black Protest," *American Sociological Review* 27 (June 1972): 333–46; J. Michael Ross, Reeve D. Vanneman, and Thomas F. Pettigrew, "Patterns of Support for George Wallace: Implications for Racial Change," *Journal of Social Issues* 36 (Spring 1976): 69–91; Sheldon G. Levy, "Polarization in Racial Attitudes," *Public Opinion Quarterly* 36 (Summer 1972): 221–34; Samuel Lubell, *The Hidden Crisis in American Politics* (New York: W.W. Norton, 1971).

9. Carl Davidson, PSU-SENSE-Students for Peace and national vice president of SDS, telephone conversation with author, 6 May 1988; Carl Davidson, Formal Remarks Made at the Kent State University Students for a Democratic Society Reunion, Kent, Ohio, 6 May 1989; Carl Davidson, "Toward a Student Syndicalist Movement or University Reform Revisited," working paper prepared for the National Convention of the Students for a Democratic Society at Clear Lake, Iowa, August 1966 (Thomas Bennett Personal Papers—copy in author's possession); Victor Rabinowitz, attorney at law, New York City, letter to author, 25 February 1988. Rabinowitz defended Stapp at his military court-martial.

10. Steve Badrich, MSU SDS, letter to author, 4 October 1987; Donald Mader,

MSU SDS, letter to author, 4 August 1988; Abe Peck, *Uncovering the Sixties: The Life and Times of the Underground Press* (New York: Pantheon, 1985); Warren Hinckle, Robert Scheer, and Sol Stern, "The University on the Make," *Ramparts* 4 (April 1966): 54–57; Donna Lloyd Ellis, "The Underground Press in America: 1955–1970," *Journal of Popular Culture* 5 (Summer 1971): 102–24; Bertram Garskoff, MSU SDS faculty advisor, telephone conversation with author, 5 November 1988; Unger, *The Movement*, 138; Thomas Powers, *Diana: The Making of a Terrorist* (Boston: Houghton Mifflin, 1971); Larry Grathwohl, *Bringing Down America: An FBI Informer With the Weathermen* (New Rochelle, N.Y.: Arlington House, 1976); DeBenedetti and Chatfield, *An American Ordeal*, 109.

11. *Spectrum* (Buffalo, New York), 29 September 1967; Milton Viorst, *Fire in the Streets: America in the 1960s* (New York: Simon and Schuster, 1979), 383–420; Fred Snell, SUNY-Buffalo antiwar faculty activist, letter to author, 3 January 1988; Sale, *SDS*, 618; Stephen M. Kohn, *Jailed for Peace: The History of American Draft Law Violators, 1658–1985* (New York: Praeger, 1987), 89–90; Maureen Considine, The Buffalo, Buffalo, New York, interview with author, 26 August 1988; Vincent Doyle, attorney for The Buffalo, Buffalo, New York, interview with author, 26 August 1988; *Griffin* (Buffalo, New York), 17 September 1971. *Griffin* is the student newspaper of Buffalo's Jesuit college, Canisius.

12. Tony Walsh, KCEWV, telephone conversation with author, 14 January 1989; Joseph Jackson, KCEWV, telephone conversation with author, 25 September 1989; Andy Pyle, KSU and MSU SDS, Kent, Ohio, interview with author, 5 May 1989; *Daily Kent Stater* (Kent, Ohio), 7 July 1964; Sale, *SDS*, 576, 580–83, 603, 648.

1. "Bastions of Our Defense"

1. Clark Kerr, *The Uses of the University* (Cambridge, Mass.: Harvard University Press, 1963), 53; *Liberation News Service* (Washington, D.C.), 31 October 1967; Miller, "Democracy Is in the Streets," 25; Lawrence Wittner, *Cold War America: From Hiroshima to Watergate* (New York: Praeger, 1974), 124, 320.

2. Martin J. Oppenheimer, ed., *The American Military* (New York: Aldine, 1971), 5; Adam Yarmolinsky, *The Military Establishment: Its Impact on American Society* (New York: Harper and Row, 1971), 304–6, 310.

3. James Ridgeway, *The Closed Corporation: American Universities in Crisis* (New York: Random House, 1968), 223–35.

4. Vannevar Bush, *Pieces of the Action* (New York: William Morrow, 1972), 31, 39; Robert L. Geiger, *To Advance Knowledge: The Growth of American Research Universities, 1900–1940* (New York: Oxford University Press, 1986), 246–67; Robert C. Cook, ed., *Presidents of American Colleges and Universities, 1933–1934*, 1st ed. (New York: Robert C. Cook, 1933); Robert C. Cook, ed., *Presidents and Professors in American Colleges and Universities, 1935–1936*, 1st ed. (New York: Robert C. Cook, 1935).

5. Cook, ed., *Presidents of American Colleges and Universities, 1933–1934*; Cook, ed., *Presidents and Professors in American Colleges and Universities, 1935–1936*; *Who's Who in America, 1932–1933*, vol. 17 (Chicago: Marquis Who's Who, 1932).

6. Jacques McKeen Cattell et al., eds., *Leaders in Education: A Biographical Directory, 1941*, 2d ed. (New York: Science Press, 1941); Cattell and E. E. Ross, eds.,

Leaders in Education: A Biographical Directory, 1948, 3d ed. (Lancaster, Penn.: The Science Press, 1948); Cook, ed., *Presidents of American Colleges and Universities, 1952–1953,* 2d ed. (Nashville, Tenn.: Who's Who in American Education, 1952); Cook, ed., *Presidents and Deans of American Colleges and Universities, 1964–1965,* vol. 7 (Nashville, Tenn.: Who's Who in American Education, 1964); Cattell, ed., *Directory of American Scholars: A Biographical Directory, 1957,* 3d ed. (New York: R. R. Bowker, 1957); *Who's Who in America, 1952–1953,* vol. 27 (Chicago: Marquis Who's Who, 1952); Iowa State Government, *Iowa Official Register, 1959–1960,* 48th Number (Des Moines, Iowa: Iowa State Government, 1960), 237–39; Iowa State Government, *Iowa Official Register, 1963–1964,* 50th Number (Des Moines, Iowa: Iowa State Government, 1964), 256–57.

7. Cook, ed., *Who's Who in American Education: An Illustrated Biographical Directory of Eminent Living Educators of the United States and Canada, 1965–1966,* 22d ed. (Nashville, Tenn.: Who's Who in American Education, 1966); Cook, ed., *Who's Who in American Education, 1967–1968,* 23d ed. (Hattiesburg, Miss.: Who's Who in American Education, 1968); Russell W. Calkins, ed., *Who's Who in American College and University Administration, 1970–1971* (New York: Cromwell-Collier Educational, 1970); Jacques McKeen Cattell et al., eds., *Leaders in Education, 1970–1971,* 4th ed. (New York: Jacques Cattell Press and R. R. Bowker, 1971); *Who's Who in America, 1972–1973,* vol. 37 (Chicago: Marquis Who's Who, 1972); *Who's Who in America, 1966–1967;* "Themis: DoD Plan to Spread the Wealth Raises Questions in Academe," *Science* 155 (3 February 1967): 584; Ridgeway, *The Closed Corporation,* 146.

8. Seymour E. Harris, *A Statistical Portrait of Higher Education* (New York: McGraw-Hill, 1972), 267, 277; Wittner, *Cold War America,* 124, 319.

9. Wittner, *Cold War America,* 124; Sale, *SDS,* 501.

10. Kerr, *The Uses of the University,* 88.

11. Miller, "*Democracy Is in the Streets,*" 25.

12. Cook, ed., *Presidents and Deans of American Colleges and Universities, 1964–1965;* John A. Hannah, "The State of the University in February, 1969," address at the Michigan State University Faculty Convocation, 10 February 1969 (Robert Repas Personal Papers—copy in author's possession); Michigan State University, "John A. Hannah Retrospective," *Format,* 1969 (Robert Repas Personal Papers—copy in author's possession); Lansing *State Journal* (Lansing, Mich.), 9 January 1969.

13. John A. Hannah, *Memoirs* (East Lansing, Mich.: Michigan State University Press, 1980), 54.

14. John A. Hannah, "The State of the University in February, 1968," address at the Michigan State University Faculty Convocation, 12 February 1968 (Robert Repas Personal Papers—copy in author's possession); *State News* (East Lansing, Mich.), 19 January 1968; Michigan State University Office of the Registrar, *Budget for Fiscal Year 1966* (East Lansing, Mich.: Michigan State University Office of the Registrar, 1966); Michigan State University Office of the Registrar, *Student Enrollment* (East Lansing, Mich.: Michigan State University Office of the Registrar), 1950–1970; Ridgeway, *The Closed Corporation,* 223–35.

15. *The Paper* (East Lansing, Mich.), 17 November 1966.

16. Hannah, "The State of the University in February, 1968"; Hinckle et al., "The University on the Make," 54–57; Michigan State University Advisory Group, *Final Report Covering Activities of the MSU Vietnam Advisory Group for the Period May*

20, 1965 - June 30, 1962 (Saigon, Vietnam: Michigan State University Advisory Group, 1962), 23–26, 61–64, 77; Robert Scigliano and Guy Fox, *Technical Assistance in Vietnam: The MSU Experience* (New York: Praeger, 1965), 4, 40, 41; MSU Vietnam Project, "Requisitions," "Civil Police," "Administration," "Budget," "Refugees" (MSU Vietnam Project Papers, Box 17, Boxes 53–68, MSU Archives).

17. Hinckle et al., "The University on the Make," 54–60; Adrian Jaffe and Milton C. Taylor, "The Professor-Diplomat: Ann Arbor and Cambridge Were Never Like This," *New Republic* 146 (5 March 1962): 28–30; *State News*, 6 January 1965.

18. Charles Larrowe, MSU SDS faculty advisor, East Lansing, Mich., interview with author, 17 November 1983; Robert Repas, MSU faculty antiwar activist, East Lansing, Mich., interview with author, 13 October 1983; John A. Hannah, president of Michigan State University, letter to Dr. Robert Repas, MSU School of Industrial and Labor Relations, 18 March 1959 (Robert Repas Personal Papers—copy in author's possession).

19. Larrowe interview.

20. James T. Selcraig, *The Red Scare in the Midwest, 1945–1955: A State and Local Study* (Ann Arbor, Mich.: University of Michigan Press, 1982), 103–4, 116.

21. George Griffiths, GLCO, telephone conversation with author, 15 October 1983; Repas interview; "Report of the Special Committee on Political Surveillance by the East Lansing Police Department, Larry Owen, Chairman," East Lansing, Mich., City of East Lansing, 1977 (George Griffiths Personal Papers—copy in author's possession); *Lansing State Journal*, 14 February 1962.

22. Repas interview; Robert Repas letter to author, 29 December 1987; John W. Truitt, director, Men's Division of Student Affairs, Michigan State University, letter to James R. Humphrey, director of Life Marketing, Mutual Service Insurance Companies, St. Paul, Minn., 3 March 1961 (Robert Repas Personal Papers—copy in author's possession); Sale, *SDS*, 329; *State News*, 29 April 1965, 23 August 1966.

23. Repas interview; Larrowe interview; Calkins, ed., *Who's Who in American College and University Administration, 1970–1971*; Cattell et al., eds., *Leaders in Education*, 4th ed.

24. Repas interview; Larrowe interview; Selcraig, *The Red Scare in the Midwest, 1945–1955*, 4; Harris, *A Statistical Portrait of Higher Education*, 280–83, 728. For the correspondence of MSU president John Hannah, see "Hannah Papers" in the Michigan State University Archives.

25. Stephen E. Ambrose and Richard H. Immerman, *Milton S. Eisenhower: Educational Statesman* (Baltimore: Johns Hopkins University Press, 1983), 108–45.

26. Ambrose and Immerman, *Milton S. Eisenhower*, 146–65; Ellen W. Schrecker, *No Ivory Tower: McCarthyism and the Universities* (New York: Oxford University Press, 1986), 115–16, 290, 313, 317; Dr. Ellen W. Schrecker, Department of History, Yeshiva College, New York City, letter to author, 7 October 1988. In her letter, Schrecker graciously identified the PSU AAUP representative and anti-Semite.

27. Vance Packard, *The Status Seekers: An Exploration of Class Behavior in America and the Hidden Barriers That Affect You, Your Community, Your Future* (New York: David McKay, 1959), 174; *Who's Who in America, 1973–1974*, vol. 38 (Chicago: Marquis Who's Who, 1973).

28. *Daily Collegian* (State College, Penn.), 17 November 1965, 6 October 1966, 26 February 1970; The Pennsylvania State University Office of the Vice President for Research, *Sponsored Research, Fiscal Year 1961–1962* (University Park, Penn.:

Pennsylvania State University, 1962), 12; Cook, ed., *Presidents and Deans of American Colleges and Universities, 1964–1965*; Oppenheimer, ed., *The American Military*, 6; "Harvard Underwater Sound Laboratory," *Noise Level* 1 (July 1981): 1–2 (newsletter of the Pennsylvania State University Applied Research Laboratory); Pennsylvania State University, *The Garfield Thomas Water Tunnel: 25 Years, 1949– 1974* (University Park, Penn.: Pennsylvania State University, 1974). *Noise Level* and the *Garfield Thomas Water Tunnel* were provided to the author by the Department of the Navy.

29. Ambrose and Immerman, *Milton S. Eisenhower*, 108–45; *Daily Collegian*, 14 April 1965, 1 July 1965, 3 May 1972; Cook, ed., *Presidents and Deans of American Colleges and Universities, 1964–1965*.

30. *The Water Tunnel* (State College, Penn.), 10 March 1969; Eric Walker and Buckminster Fuller, *Approaching the Benign Environment* (New York: Macmillan, 1970), 115.

31. *Daily Collegian*, 30 March 1965, 25 September 1966, 18 October 1971.

32. *Daily Collegian*, 6 January 1965, 20 September 1967.

33. Calkins, ed., *Who's Who in American College and University Administration, 1970–1971*; Cattell et al., eds., *Leaders in Education*, 4th ed.

34. *Daily Collegian*, 11 January 1967, 16 February 1967, 10 January 1968; Neil Buckley, Penn State SDS, letter to Greg Calvert, National President of SDS, 11 February 1967 (Neil Buckley Papers, Historical Collections and Labor Archives, PSU Library).

35. Pam Farley, PSU NUC, telephone conversation with author, 3 October 1988; Sale, *SDS*, 643; *Daily Collegian*, 30 January 1968, 12 February 1969, 14 November 1969; John Finnegan, PSU Young Democrats Club, FBI file (John Finnegan Personal Papers—notes from file in author's possession).

36. *Daily Collegian*, 29 October 1969, 2 April 1970.

37. Warren Bennis, *The Leaning Ivory Tower* (San Francisco: Jossey-Bass, 1973), 23.

38. Ibid., 87–145.

39. Cook, ed., *Presidents and Deans of American Colleges and Universities, 1964–1965*; Ridgeway, *The Closed Corporation*, 128–30; Stephen Strickland, ed., *Sponsored Research in American Universities and Colleges, 1967* (Washington, D.C.: American Council on Education, 1967), 33–44; Sparkle Moore Furnas, *Memorial Biographical Record of Clifford C. Furnas*, 2 vols., privately printed by Sparkle Moore Furnas, 1975. Furnas' wife, Sparkle, taped extensive interviews with her husband prior to his death. She did not, however, bother to edit the transcripts. Consequently, one is given great insight into President Furnas' critical attitude towards SUNY chancellor Gould and a number of SUNY-Buffalo administrators and faculty.

40. *Spectrum*, 18 September 1964, 14 April 1966; Bennis, *The Leaning Ivory Tower*, 112–28.

41. Schrecker, *No Ivory Tower*, 113–14; *Spectrum*, 4 December 1964, 15 June 1965; Furnas, *Memorial Biographical Record of Clifford C. Furnas*, vol. 2; Clifford C. Furnas, president of the State University of New York at Buffalo, letter to Samuel B. Gould, SUNY chancellor, 10 November 1964 (Office of the Chancellor-President, Central Files, Permanent Files, 1938–1969, Box 7, SUNY-Buffalo Archives).

42. Hon. Doris Varn, House of Representatives, State of Arizona, letter to the president of the University of Buffalo, 27 February 1963 (Office of the Chancellor-

President, Central Files, Permanent Files, 1938–1969, Box 7, SUNY-Buffalo Archives); Dr. Clifford Furnas, president of SUNY-Buffalo, letter to the Hon. Doris Varn, 11 March 1963 (Office of the Chancellor-President, Central Files, Permanent Files, 1938–1969, Box 7, SUNY-Buffalo Archives); Statement Concerning Dr. William T. Parry, associate professor of philosophy at the University of Buffalo, by T. R. McConnell, chancellor of the university, 1953 (Office of the Chancellor-President, Central Files, Permanent Files, 1938–1969, Box 7, SUNY-Buffalo Archives); Clifford C. Furnas, president of the State University of New York at Buffalo, Statement to the News Media, 26 May 1964 (Office of the Chancellor-President, Central Files, Permanent Files, 1938–1969, Box 7, SUNY-Buffalo Archives); Spectrum, 25 September 1964; Furnas, Memorial Biographical Record of Clifford C. Furnas, vol. 2; Niagara Frontier Civil Liberties (Buffalo, New York), October, 1963 (Elizabeth Olmsted Smith Papers, Box 15, SUNY-Buffalo Archives).

43. Spectrum, 14 April 1966; Bennis, The Leaning Ivory Tower, 112–27; Calkins, ed., Who's Who in American College and University Administration, 1970–1971; Martin Meyerson, The City and the University (New York: St. Martin's Press, 1969), 7–16.

44. Martin Meyerson, Office of the President, University of New York at Buffalo, Press Release on Project Themis, 18 April 1969 (Campus Unrest, 1965–1970, Box 1, SUNY-Buffalo Archives); Snell letter to author, 8 March 1988; Bennis, The Leaning Ivory Tower, 129–45; Dr. Paul Ehrlich, Department of Chemical Engineering, SUNY-Buffalo, letter to Martin Meyerson, 21 March 1969 (Office of the President, Central Files, Research, Box 38, SUNY-Buffalo Archives); Dr. Raymond Ewell, vice president for Research, SUNY-Buffalo, memorandum to Martin Meyerson, 22 October 1968 (Office of the President, Central Files, Research, Box 38, SUNY-Buffalo Archives); Dr. William J. Walbesser, Department of Electrical Engineering, SUNY-Buffalo, letter to Martin Meyerson, 22 March 1969 (Office of the President, Central Files, Research, Box 38, SUNY-Buffalo Archives).

45. Spectrum, 17 November 1967.

46. Oppenheimer, ed., The American Military, 9; Dr. Raymond Ewell, vice president for Research, SUNY-Buffalo, "Funding of Sponsored Research at the State University of New York at Buffalo, 1960–1969," internal memorandum (Office of the President, Central Files, Research, Box 38, SUNY-Buffalo Archives).

47. Bennis, The Leaning Ivory Tower, 129–45; A. P. Aversano, vice president of the Foster-Milburn Company and president of the SUNY-Buffalo General Alumni Board, letter to Martin Meyerson, 25 September 1968 (Office of the President, Central Files, Administration, Box 9, SUNY-Buffalo Archives); Spectrum, 1 April 1966, 8 April 1966, 18 September 1967, 26 September 1967, 27 February 1970, 6 March 1970, 9 March 1970, 20 April 1970, 8 May 1970, 12 June 1970, 10 July 1970; Snell letter, 8 March 1988; Elwin Powell, SUNY-Buffalo SDS faculty advisor, letters to author, 12 November 1987, 19 December 1987; Sidney Willhelm, SUNY-Buffalo SDS faculty advisor, letter to author, 17 January 1988.

48. Spectrum, 16 September 1966, 28 June 1968, 7 November 1969, 24 January 1972, 7 February 1972; Richard O'Connor, SUNY-Buffalo undergraduate student, "Student Association Bail Fund Service" information card issued along with student identification card, 1970 (Richard O'Connor Personal Papers—copy in author's possession).

During the February-May, 1970, upheaval at SUNY-Buffalo, a student stole a campus security officer's logbook from an unoccupied police cruiser. This logbook records in great detail Snell's daily activities. The logbook is in Campus Unrest, 1965–1970, Box 1, SUNY-Buffalo Archives.

49. Larry Faulkner, BDRU, telephone conversation with author, 25 May 1988; *Spectrum,* 23 September 1966; John L. Duffy, Special Agent in Charge, Federal Bureau of Investigation, Department of Justice, Buffalo, New York, letter to author, 30 September 1987; Sharon Fischer, BDRU, and Karl Meller, SUNY-Buffalo YAWF, FBI files (Elwin Powell Personal Papers—notes from files in author's possession).

50. Sale, *SDS,* 499–500, 645–46; Joe Eszterhas and Michael D. Roberts, *13 Seconds: Confrontation at Kent State* (New York: College Notes and Texts, 1970), 34, 48–49, 67; *Daily Kent Stater,* 14 January 1970; Ruth Gibson, KCEWV, telephone conversation with author, 4 February 1989.

51. Selcraig, *The Red Scare in the Midwest, 1945–1955,* 33–36, 102, 124; Lionel S. Lewis, *Cold War on Campus: A Study of the Politics of Organizational Control* (New Brunswick, N.J.: Transaction Books, 1988), 83–84; Harris, *A Statistical Portrait of Higher Education,* 728. Schrecker informed me that she discovered no political firings of Kent State faculty in the AAUP Archives. She suspects, as do I, that given the example of Ohio State and the fact that Ohio had its own Un-American Activities Committee, Kent State took the precaution of not knowingly hiring politically questionable faculty. Since access to Kent State administration files is restricted, there is no way to prove or disprove this contention.

52. *Daily Kent Stater,* 21 July 1964, 3 October 1967, 23 October 1968; *Big US* (Cleveland, Ohio), 26 April 1969; Scott L. Bills, *Kent State, May 4: Echoes through a Decade* (Kent, Ohio: Kent State University Press, 1982), 141–42.

53. *Daily Kent Stater,* 20 May 1969.

54. *Daily Kent Stater,* 6 April 1969, 20 May 1969, 30 October 1969; Eszterhas and Roberts, *13 Seconds,* 45–70; Gibson conversation; Calkins, ed., *Who's Who in American College and University Administration, 1970–1971*; *Daily Collegian,* 20 August 1970; Tom Grace, KSU SDS, telephone conversation with author, 3 March 1989.

55. *Daily Kent Stater,* 30 April 1968; Gibson conversation. Having consulted every reference work available on American educators, I could find little or no information on Kent State's administrators in 1970. What biographical data were available indicated that Kent State's administrators claimed no special academic accomplishments.

56. Joseph Jackson conversation; Gibson conversation; *Daily Kent Stater,* 27 October 1967, 22 May 1969.

57. Eszterhas and Roberts, *13 Seconds,* 100–3; *Daily Kent Stater,* 10 December 1969.

2. "Those People Would Do the Damndest Things"

1. Harvey Klehr, *The Heyday of American Communism: The Depression Decade* (New York: Basic Books, 1984), 69–84, 349–64; Schrecker, *No Ivory Tower,* 12–83.

2. Klehr, *The Heyday of American Communism,* 349–409; Schrecker, *No Ivory Tower,* 63–125; Christopher Lasch, *The Agony of the American Left* (New York: Vintage Books, 1969), 61–114.

3. Theodore Draper and Nathan Glazer, in separate reviews of Schrecker's study of McCarthyism and the universities *(New Republic,* 6 October 1986 and 26 January

1987, respectively), provide an insight into the lingering bitterness liberal and non-Communist radical faculty feel for their Communist colleagues from the 1950s. Leslie Fiedler, in *Being Busted* (New York: Stein and Day, 1969), described his disgust with Communists in the 1930s and 1940s. For a good discussion of New Left academic analyses of Third World Communist wars of national liberation, see Viorst, *Fire in the Streets*, 465–504. An excellent primary source is Staughton Lynd and Tom Hayden, *The Other Side* (New York: New American Library, 1967).

4. Michael Frisch, SUNY-Buffalo faculty antiwar activist, letter to author, 30 April 1989.

5. Alan E. Bayer, *College and University Faculty: A Statistical Description* (Washington, D.C.: Carnegie Commission on Higher Education, 1970), 12–13; Hodgson, *America in Our Time*, 53.

6. Bayer, *College and University Faculty*, 20–21.

7. Ibid., 19.

8. Seymour Martin Lipset and Everett C. Ladd, Jr., "The Politics of American Sociologists," *American Journal of Sociology* 78 (July 1972): 67–104.

9. Lipset and Ladd, "The Politics of American Sociologists," 67–104.

10. *New University Conference Newsletter* (Chicago, Illinois), May 1968 (Samuel P. Hays Collection, University of Pittsburgh Archives); Sale, *SDS*, 412–13; *New University Conference Newsletter*, November 1968 (Samuel P. Hays Collection, University of Pittsburgh Archives); Lynn Jondahl, *Unrest on Campus: A Christian Perspective* (New York: Friendship Press, 1970), 68–69.

11. Hinckle et. al., "The University on the Make," 55; Thomas Greer, MSU faculty antiwar activist, East Lansing, Mich., interview with author, 13 October 1983.

12. "Michigan State University Vietnam Project Briefing Information, 1 October 1958" (MSU Vietnam Project Papers, Box 16, MSU Archives).

13. Wesley R. Fishel, "Vietnam's Democratic One-Man Rule," *New Leader* 42 (2 November 1959): 10–13; Repas interview. Repas witnessed Fishel's performance at the state legislature.

14. Adrian Jaffe and Milton C. Taylor, "A Crumbling Bastion: Flattery and Lies Won't Save Vietnam," *New Republic* 144 (19 June 1961): 17–20; *Washington Post*, 17 June 1962.

15. While working on my senior history thesis in 1983–1984 at MSU on the MSU anti-Vietnam War movement, my roommate, John Wesley Rowden, and I started a landscaping business. In the spring of 1984 one of our clients turned out to be Dr. Ralph Turner. After work, Turner would invite us into his den and talk about the MSU Vietnam Project.

16. *Washington Post*, 17 June 1962; *State News*, 1 April 1965; John D. Donoghue, *Cam An, A Fishing Village in Central Vietnam* (East Lansing, Mich.: Michigan State University Advisory Group, 1960).

17. *State News*, 1 April 1965, 8 April 1965, 12 April 1965; Greer interview.

18. *State News*, 20 April 1965, 28 April 1966.

19. Greer interview; *State News*, 12 May 1965, 14 April 1966, 20 April 1966, 12 May 1966; *Newsweek* 67 (25 April 1966): 78; MSU Faculty antiwar petition addressed to President Lyndon Johnson, 27 February 1967 (Student Radicalism Collection, MSU Special Collections).

20. Repas interview; Larrowe interview; Robert Repas, "Open Letter to the MSU Campus on University Political Surveillance, 10 April 1967" (Robert Repas Personal

Papers—copy in author's possession); John A. Hannah, president of Michigan State University, letter to Dr. Robert Repas, School of Labor and Industrial Relations, concerning compulsory ROTC, 18 March 1959 (Robert Repas Personal Papers—copy in author's possession).

21. Repas letters, 29 December 1987 and 30 June 1988; Robert Repas, Michigan State Police Red Squad File (Robert Repas Personal Papers—copy in author's possession); Jan Garrett, MSU Young Socialist Club, letter to author, 5 August 1988.

22. Repas interview; Robert Repas, "Summary of Phone Conversation between President John Hannah and Bob Repas, 25 June 1965" (Robert Repas Personal Papers —copy in author's possession); Larrowe interview.

23. Larrowe interview; *State News*, 28 March 1968.

24. *State News*, 2 June 1965; Greer interview; Thomas Greer, "What Is the War Doing to Us in the World of International Politics?" Address presented to the Interfaith Convocation on War and Peace, East Lansing, Mich., 15 January 1967 (Student Radicalism Collection, MSU Special Collections).

25. James Anderson, MSU Resistance faculty advisor, East Lansing, Mich., interview with author, 7 November 1983; *The Paper*, 17 April 1968.

26. Bertram E. Garskoff, "Who Says the Curriculum Is Irrelevant! ROTC and the University," *New University Conference Newsletter*, November 1968 (Samuel P. Hays Collection, University of Pittsburgh Archives); *State News*, 1 November 1966, 7 November 1966; Garskoff conversation.

27. Garskoff conversation; George Fish, MSU SDS, telephone conversation with author, 16 March 1989; Repas interview; Unger, *The Movement*, 138.

28. *State News*, 28 February 1967; MSU Faculty antiwar petition; Michigan State University Bureau of Social Science Research, "Omnibus Survey #2, 1970," 11–13, 19, 57 (William Hixson Personal Papers, Department of History, Michigan State University). The MSU antiwar faculty database, as well as the databases for the other schools, was compiled by consulting the relevant campus newspapers, both mainstream and underground, antiwar petitions and other arcane documents found in the various archives and in individuals' possession. Oral interviews also generated names and provided an insight into the leadership and ideology of liberal-dovish and radical faculty. Core faculty is defined as those academics whose activism went a great deal beyond signing antiwar petitions. Affiliation with various peace organizations, and demonstrations and teach-ins in which faculty participated, were the chief criteria used to select the core faculty. Departmental affiliations and academic ranks were determined by consulting the appropriate university faculty directories from 1964 to 1973.

The categorization of antiwar faculty activists as liberal dovish or radical is based upon the following methodology: first, oral interviews of faculty and students who identified faculty as falling into one or the other broad groupings; second, speeches and position papers put out by particular faculty indicating their ideological leanings; and third, faculty membership in organizations which were explicitly radical, e.g., the New University Conference.

29. Repas interview; Larrowe interview; *The Paper*, 16 May 1967; Ferency Campaign, Fact Sheet, 1982 (Zolton Ferency Personal Papers—copy in author's possession).

30. Keith Pohl, MSU UCM advisor, East Lansing, Mich., interview with author, 4

October 1983; Lynn Jondahl, GLCO, Lansing, Mich., interview with author, 10 November 1983; Repas interview; Larrowe interview.

31. John Withall, PSU faculty antiwar activist, letter to author, 18 December 1987.

32. Ibid.

33. Ibid.

34. Ibid.; *Daily Collegian*, 25 October 1968.

35. James Andrews, State College, PSU Friends, letter to author, 27 October 1987. Andrews attended the Quaker session at which Kennedy's Cuban policy was debated in October 1962.

36. *Daily Collegian*, 20 November 1965, 15 October 1969.

37. David Westby, PSU NUC, letter to author, 14 December 1987; James Petras, PSU NUC, telephone conversation with author, 7 July 1988; *Daily Collegian*, 27 September 1971.

38. *Daily Collegian*, 2 November 1965, 29 October 1968; *Henderson Station* (State College, Penn.), 3 November 1971.

39. Petras conversation; *Daily Collegian*, 24 July 1969.

40. *Henderson Station*, 1 January 1971.

41. James Creegan, PSU SDS, telephone conversation with author, 11 July 1988.

42. Petras conversation; *Daily Collegian*, 12 October 1966, 17 October 1969; Victor Marchetti and John D. Marks, *The CIA and the Cult of Intelligence* (New York: Dell, 1975), 11.

43. *Daily Collegian*, 29 May 1969, 23 October 1969, 24 October 1969.

44. *Daily Collegian*, 12 November 1965, 16 February 1967, 22 October 1969.

45. *Daily Collegian*, 27 May 1966, 15 October 1969.

46. Dr. Newton Garver, Department of Philosophy, SUNY-Buffalo, letter to Dr. David S. Price, State University of New York, Albany, New York, 11 August 1964 (Office of the Chancellor/President, Central Files, Permanent Files, 1938–1969, Box 7, SUNY-Buffalo Archives); Dr. Netwon Garver, Statement of Act of Civil Disobedience in 1948, to Department of Philosophy and SUNY-Buffalo president Clifford Furnas, May 1965 (Office of the Chancellor/President, Central Files, Permanent Files, 1938–1969, Box 7, SUNY-Buffalo Archives); Dr. Newton Garver, letter to SUNY-Buffalo president Clifford Furnas, 11 August 1964 (Office of the Chancellor/President, Central Files, Permanent Files, 1938–1969, Box 7, SUNY-Buffalo Archives).

47. *Spectrum*, 22 October 1971; Faulkner conversation; Powell letter to author, 16 April 1988. The FBI file of Sharon Fischer notes that a SDS and BDRU leader met with federal agents at the Forest Lawn Cemetery in Buffalo on 10 September 1968. Although the name of the SDS leader is blacked out, the description of the person in question, his activities, and whereabouts, coupled with the suspicions of Faulkner and Powell, make it clear who the informer was.

48. Fiedler, *Being Busted*, 93.

49. Ibid. 136; Charlie Haynie, SUNY-Buffalo faculty antiwar activist, Buffalo, New York, interview with author, 26 August 1988.

50. Fiedler, *Being Busted*, 96.

51. Snell letter, 3 January 1988.

52. Dr. Donald W. Rennie, Department of Physiology, SUNY-Buffalo, Buffalo, letter to SUNY-Buffalo acting president Peter Regan, 20 October 1969 (Office of the President, Central Files, Administration, Box 8, SUNY-Buffalo Archives); *Spectrum*, 16 June 1967, 22 October 1968; Snell letters, 3 January 1988, 8 March 1988.

53. Snell letter, 3 January 1988; SUNY-Buffalo Radical Faculty Caucus, "Substitute Motion on the Moratorium, 11 November 1969" (Office of the President, Central Files, Administration, Box 8, SUNY-Buffalo Archives); Haynie interview; *Spectrum*, 26 January 1968, 15 October 1969.

54. Dr. Robert E. Mates, chair, Department of Mechanical Engineering, SUNY-Buffalo, letter to SUNY-Buffalo president Martin Meyerson, 20 March 1969 (Office of the President, Central Files, Research, Box 38, SUNY-Buffalo Archives); Dr. Daniel H. Murray, dean of the School of Pharmacy, SUNY-Buffalo, "A Unanimous Resolution by the Executive Committee of the School of Pharmacy, 21 March 1969" (Office of the President, Central Files, Research, Box 38, SUNY-Buffalo Archives); "Unanimous Resolution by the Faculty of the Department of Pathology, SUNY-Buffalo, 21 March 1969" (Office of the President, Central Files, Research, Box 38, SUNY-Buffalo Archives); Dr. Ernest Hausmann, assistant dean of the School of Denistry, "A Resolution by the Executive Committee of the School of Denistry, 21 March 1969" (Office of the President, Central Files, Research, Box 38, SUNY-Buffalo Archives); *Spectrum*, 18 December 1964, 12 December 1967; Dr. Marvin Zimmerman, Department of Philosophy, SUNY-Buffalo, "Common Sense: Addressed to the Academic Community, December 1967" (Campus Unrest, 1965–1970, Box 1, SUNY-Buffalo Archives).

55. Calkins, ed., *Leaders in Education, 1970–1971*, 4th ed.; *Spectrum*, 28 July 1967, 14 April 1969, 3 March 1970, 29 April 1970, 7 October 1970, 26 April 1971.

56. Powell letter, 12 November 1987; Sidney Willhelm, SUNY-Buffalo SDS advisor, letter to author, 17 January 1988.

57. Powell letter, 19 December 1987; Willhelm letter; Frisch letter, 8 December 1987.

58. *Spectrum*, 2 April 1965.

59. Ibid., 20 October 1969; Haynie interview.

60. Haynie interview.

61. Ibid.; Powell letter, 12 November 1987; Frisch letter, 30 April 1989. An excellent analysis of the 1960s counterculture is Lasch, *The Culture of Narcissism*.

62. Haynie interview; Powell letter, 12 November 1987; Frisch letter, 30 April 1989.

63. Mim Jackson, KSU antiwar student, Kent, Ohio, interview with author, 7 May 1989; Joseph Jackson conversation; Tim Smith and Scott L. Bills, "My Perspective Is Socialism: An Interview with Clara Jackson about the Life and Political Perspective of Sidney Jackson," *Left Review* 4 (Fall 1979): 1–7. Mim and Joseph Jackson are the children of the late Sidney Jackson.

64. Mim Jackson, Kent, Ohio interview with author, 7 May 1989; Joseph Jackson conversation; Dr. Sidney L. Jackson, Kent State University, letter to Hon. John F. Kennedy, president of the United States, 7 January 1962 (Sidney L. Jackson Papers, Box 1, Kent State University Archives).

65. Mim Jackson interview; Joseph Jackson conversation.

66. Harris Dante, Kent State antiwar faculty activist, letter to author, 2 February 1988; Ottavio Casale, Kent State antiwar faculty activist, letter to author, 2 February 1988; Harris Dante, "The Kent State Tragedy: Lessons for Teachers," *Social Education* 35 (April 1971): 357–361. The controversy surrounding antiwar protest and the slayings at Kent State has continued unabated since 1970. Most faculty, anti- or prowar, never responded to my research inquiries. Casale and Dante, while opposed

to the war, vigorously defended White after the shootings and argued that the university was politically inactive and had a history of promoting free speech.

67. *Daily Kent Stater*, 2 March 1967, 7 April 1967, 29 November 1967; Gibson conversation.

68. *Daily Kent Stater*, 17 October 1967, 20 October 1967, 9 November 1967.

69. Ibid., 16 April 1968; Bills, *Kent State*, May 4, 100–104.

70. *Daily Kent Stater*, 11 October 1968, 15 May 1969.

71. Ibid., 13 November 1969.

3. "The Genius of a Nation"

1. Nathan C. Belth, *A Promise to Keep: A Narrative of the American Encounter with Anti-Semitism* (New York: Schocken Books, 1981), 188–89; Hodgson, *America in Our Time*, 53; William E. Leuchtenberg, *Franklin D. Roosevelt and the New Deal, 1932–1940* (New York: Harper and Row, 1963), 129, 187, 257, 336; Robert A. Caro, *The Path to Power: The Years of Lyndon Johnson* (New York: Vintage Books, 1983), 238, 338–39, 349–51, 417–18; E. Digby Baltzell, *The Protestant Establishment: Aristocracy and Caste in America* (New York: Vintage Books, 1964), 335–52.

2. Miller, "Democracy Is in the Streets," 24–26; Kerr, *The Uses of the University*; Lasch, *The Agony of the American Left*, 61–114; Hodgson, *America in Our Time*, 67–98, 186, 460–61, 469.

3. Hodgson, *America in Our Time*, 53, 67–69; Vickers, *The Formation of the New Left*, 111–13; Miller, "Democracy Is in the Streets," 100–102, 123–25, 151, 205, 331–33; Keniston, *Youth and Dissent* and *The Uncommitted: Alienated Youth in American Society* (New York: Dell, 1965).

4. Hodgson, *America in Our Time*, 315–16, 334–41.

5. Lasch, *The Culture of Narcissism*, 256–58; Skolnick, *The Politics of Protest*, 93, 103–4, 117.

6. Heirich, *Spiral of Conflict*, 53–54. Daniel Yankelovitch's survey of university students, and Americans at large, in *Fortune*, vol. 80, January 1969, confirms this argument.

7. For astute analyses of news media class biases and the 1960s, see Herbert J. Gans, *Deciding What's News: A Study of CBS Evening News, NBC Nightly News, Newsweek and Time* (New York: Vintage Books, 1980), and Gitlin, *The Whole World Is Watching*, 30–31. Standard scholarly works on the 1960s student movement which focus on privileged youths include: Powers, *Diana*; Flacks, "The Liberated Generation," 319–39; Rothman and Lichter, *Roots of Radicalism*; Sale, *SDS*; Gitlin, *The Sixties*; Miller, "Democracy Is in the Streets."

8. Nathan Glazer, "The New Left and the Jews," *Jewish Journal of Sociology* 11 (December 1969): 121–32; John Higham, *Strangers in the Land: Patterns of American Nativism, 1860–1925* (New York: Atheneum, 1978), 66–67, 92–94, 160–61; Packard, *The Status Seekers*, 264–83; Rothman and Lichter, *Roots of Radicalism*, 82.

9. Glazer, "The New Left and the Jews," 121–32; Gitlin, *The Sixties*, 25–26; Miller, "Democracy Is in the Streets," 136–37; Rothman and Lichter, *Roots of Radicalism*, 82; Hayden, *Reunion*, 96; Packard, *The Status Seekers*, 264–83.

10. Hayden, *Reunion*, 96; Packard, *The Status Seekers*, 122–23, 203–4; Allen Gutman, *The Wound in the Heart: America and the Spanish Civil War* (New York:

Free Press of Glencoe, 1962), 43; George Q. Flynn, *Roosevelt and Romanism: Catholics and American Diplomacy, 1937–1945* (Westport, Conn.: Greenwood Press, 1976), 9; Father Charles Owen Rice, "The Dynamite of the Encyclicals," radio address, KDKA, Pittsburgh, Pennsylvania, 15 May, 1937 (Rice Papers, Box 27, University of Pittsburgh Archives).

11. Rothman and Lichter, *Roots of Radicalism*, 83; Miller, "*Democracy Is in the Streets*," 179, 237, 242, 310–11; Sale, *SDS* 204–5, 207, 279–80; Miles, *The Radical Probe*, 174.

12. Richard Sennett and Jonathan Cobb, *The Hidden Injuries of Class* (New York: Vintage Books, 1973), 26–27; Fish conversations, 16 August 1988, 16 March 1989; James Powrie, KSU SDS, Formal Remarks Made at the KSU SDS Reunion, Kent, Ohio, 5 May 1989.

13. Carl Oglesby, national president of SDS, Formal Remarks Made at the KSU SDS Reunion, Kent, Ohio, 5 May 1989; Carl Davidson conversation and Formal Remarks Made at the KSU SDS Reunion, Kent, Ohio, 6 May 1989; Robert Lewis, KCEWV and KSU SDS, Kent, Ohio, interview with author, 6 May 1989; Fish conversations, 16 August 1988 and 16 March 1989; Powrie, KSU SDS Reunion; Sue Sattel, MSU SDS, letter to author, 10 July 1988.

14. Sale, *SDS*, 206.

15. Gitlin, *The Sixties*, 87–101; Hayden, *Reunion*, 102; Walsh conversation; Jack Sattel, MSU SDS, letter to author, 5 July 1988; Badrich letters, 4 October 1987 and 18 March 1989.

16. Garrett letter.

17. Ibid.

18. Ibid.; Jan Garrett, "Chronology of the Young Socialist Club-Hannah Confrontation," no date (Jan Garrett Personal Papers—copy in author's possession); *State News*, 22 May 1976.

19. Garrett, "Chronology of the Young Socialist Club-Hannah Confrontation;" Repas letters to author, 29 December 1987 and 30 June 1988; Ellis, "The Underground Press in America," 102–24.

20. Larry Lack, MSU Friends of SNCC, telephone conversation with author, 17 August 1988.

21. *State News*, 28 May 1965; William Skocpol, MSU UCM, letter to author, 21 November 1983; William Skocpol, "Report on Summer Experience with STEP for Honors College," 1965 (William Skocpol Personal Papers—copy in author's possession).

22. *State News*, 28 May 1965; Michigan State University Student Directory, 1964–1965 (East Lansing, Mich.: Michigan State University, 1964); Jack Sattel letter.

23. Jack Sattel letter.

24. Ibid.

25. Ibid.; Sue Sattel letter.

26. Jack Sattel letter; Sue Sattel letter; Fish conversations, 16 August 1988 and 16 March 1989.

27. Sue Sattel letter; Skocpol letter to author; Melissa Whitaker, KSU SDS, Kent, Ohio, interview with author, 6 May 1989. For a good discussion of sexism in the New Left, see Sara Evans, *Personal Politics: The Roots of Women's Liberation in the Civil Rights Movement and the New Left* (New York: Alfred A. Knopf, 1970).

28. Bruce Douglass, "The Student Christian Movement and Student Politics," in

Bruce Douglass, ed., *Reflections on Protest* (Richmond, Va.: John Know Press, 1967), 13; William Skocpol, letter to Theda Barron (Skocpol), 6 September 1966 (William Skocpol Personal Papers—copy in author's possession); Pohl interview.

29. Pohl interview; Keith Pohl, Michigan Red Squad File (in author's possession).

30. Pohl interview.

31. Ibid.; Jondahl interview; *State News*, 21 April 1967.

32. Mary Bivins, MSU antiwar student, East Lansing, Mich., interview with author, 4 October 1983; Keniston, *Youth and Dissent*, 345; Skocpol letter to author; Pete Canon, letter; Pyle interview. Bivins and Canon were discontented National Merit Scholarship winners. Bivins was one of the Merit Scholars interviewed by Keniston in *Youth and Dissent*.

33. *The Paper*, 6 March 1967, 12 April 1967; Badrich letters, 4 October 1987 and 18 March 1989; Ellis, "The Underground Press in America," 102–24.

34. Pyle interview; Badrich letter, 13 May 1988.

35. The student anti- and prowar databases for each of the campuses were compiled by recording every single name I came across in the mainstream, underground and conservative alternative newspapers, appropriate materials located in the universities' archives, individuals' FBI and Michigan Red Squad files which they shared with me, and oral interviews. Organizational affiliations were noted as I consulted these sources. Ethnicity was derived from a conservative surname analysis, consulting Patrick Hanks and Flavia Hodges, *A Dictionary of Surnames* (New York: Oxford University Press, 1988) and Benzion C. Kagonoff, *A Dictionary of Jewish Names and Their History* (New York: Schocken Books, 1977). Northern-Western European includes English and German Protestants as well as Irish and German Catholics. Frequently lacking activists' middle names, it was impossible to segregate German Catholics and Protestants—e.g., Catholics' middle names are frequently Saints' names.

Majors were garnered from the student directories for the years 1961–1973, campus newspapers and university administration documents (often civil complaint forms). Liberal arts/social science majors include the departments of art, English, history, political science, sociology, and social work. Business/science majors include those students studying accounting, agriculture, business, chemistry, engineering, and physics. Activists' residences were determined by consulting the student directories. Residential subcategories were based on the U.S. population in 1960. A metropolitan area is defined as an area with a population of over one million, (e.g., New York City, Chicago, Philadelphia, Detroit); a large city is one with a population between 500,000–999,000 (e.g., Pittsburgh); a medium-size city is one with a population of 100,000–499,000; a small city is one with a population of 50,000–99,000; and a small town is one with a population of 2,000–49,000.

36. The data on the overall MSU student body are based upon figures reported in 1969–1970 by the MSU Office of the Registrar. Females, 42 percent; males, 58 percent; liberal arts/social science majors, 54 percent; business-science majors, 46 percent; in-state, 83 percent; out-of-state, 17 percent; National Merit Scholars/Honors College students, 2 percent; residential college students (James Madison and Justin Morrill only), 2 percent. I determined the proportion of Jewish students on campus by taking a random sampling of names from the MSU student directories and then employing a conservative surname analysis.

37. The data on the overall student body are drawn from information published in 1969 by the MSU Office of the Registrar.

38. The classic work on labor politics, particularly in Pennsylvania in the 1930s, is Arthur Schlesinger, Jr.'s, volumes on the New Deal. Transcripts of Father Charles Owen Rice's prolabor radio speeches may be found in the University of Pittsburgh Archives.

39. Davidson conversation and KSU SDS Reunion.

40. Ibid.

41. Ibid. Sale made some disparaging remarks about the location of the 1966 National SDS convention in Clear Lake, Iowa. He obviously did not know the history of the region and how appropriate that site was to the "prairie power" activists.

42. Davidson conversation; Neil Buckley letter to Carl Davidson, 1967 (Neil Buckley Papers, Historical Collections and Labor Archives, PSU Library); *Daily Collegian,* 17 April 1965.

43. *Daily Collegian,* 22 September 1965, 25 April 1966, 18 November 1966; Creegan conversation.

44. Creegan conversation; Thomas Bennett, PSU YAF, Pittsburgh, Penn., interview with author, 25 March 1989; Farley conversation; Carl Thormeyer, PSU YAF, letter to author, 25 October 1988.

45. David L. Westby and Richard G. Braungart, "Class and Politics in the Family Backgrounds of Student Political Activists," *American Sociological Review* 31 (October 1966): 690–92. PSU SENSE members in 1965 were identified by consulting the *Daily Collegian* and then determining their various characteristics, residence, and majors by using the PSU student directories.

46. Andrews letter.

47. Creegan conversation; Farley conversation.

48. Thormeyer letter; Bennett interview; Newsletter of the Young Americans for Freedom at Penn State, *The Student Conservative* (State College, Penn.), Summer Issue, 1967 (Thomas Bennett Personal Papers—copy in author's possession); Westby and Braungart, "Class and Politics in the Family Backgrounds of Student Political Activists," 690–92; Penn State Ad hoc Committee for Student Freedom, "Open Letter to President Eric Walker," 10 May 1965 (Thomas Bennett Personal Papers—copy in author's possession).

49. *Daily Collegian,* 18 February 1970; Westby and Braungart, "Class and Politics in the Family Backgrounds of Student Political Activists," 690–92.

50. Data on the overall composition of the PSU student body in 1969 were kindly provided to me by the PSU Office of the Registrar. While the data provided by the PSU Office of the Registrar did not break students down by specific home residences, the data did provide county totals. This proved to be quite useful, as Philadelphia is a county as well as a city. Here are some basic data on the overall PSU student body in 1969: 31 percent female; 54 percent liberal arts/social science majors; 12 percent out-of-state; 7 percent Philadelphia residents; 84 percent undergraduates.

51. Westby and Braungart, "Class and Politics in the Family Backgrounds of Student Political Activists," 690–92.

52. U.S. Congress, House Committee on Un-American Activities, *Investigation of Communist Activities in the Buffalo, New York Area, part I,* 85th Congress, 2 October 1957.

53. United Anti-Communist Action Committee of Western New York, "Membership Roster, 1964" (Elwin Powell Personal Papers—copy in author's possession); Albert J. Weinert, director, Speakers' Bureau, United Anti-Communist Action Com-

mittee of Western New York, letter to the Hon. John R. Pillion, 19 April 1964 (Elwin Powell Personal Papers—copy in author's possession); Hon. John R. Pillion, letter to Mr. Kenneth Maher, Jr., United Anti-Communist Action Committee of Western New York, 22 April 1964 (Elwin Powell Personal Papers—copy in author's possession).

54. Walter Goodman, *The Committee: The Extraordinary Career of the House Committee on Un-American Activities* (Baltimore: Pelican Books, 1969), 453–55.

55. *Spectrum*, 2 October 1964, 23 October 1964, 30 October 1964, 29 January 1965, 19 February 1965, 5 April 1965.

56. *Spectrum*, 30 April 1965, 8 April 1966, 29 September 1967.

57. *Spectrum*, 4 December 1964, 11 December 1964, 23 April 1965, 10 December 1965, 10 October 1967; Willhelm letter.

58. *Spectrum*, 12 April 1966, 17 October 1967; SUNY-Buffalo YAWF leaflet, "Escalation in Vietnam Today, World War III Tomorrow," January 1965 (Elizabeth Olmsted Smith Papers, Box 17, SUNY-Buffalo Archives); *Spirit and the Sword*, "End the War in Vietnam," 1965 (Elizabeth Olmsted Smith Papers, Box 17, SUNY-Buffalo Archives).

59. Gerald Gross, SUNY-Buffalo YAWF, FBI File (Elwin Powell Personal Papers —notes from file in author's possession); Gerald Gross, letter to the Peoples' Republic of China representative in Canada, included in Gross's FBI File (copy of letter in author's possession); Fischer FBI File. Fischer's FBI file mentions a police informant in the Buffalo YAWF. She noted in the margins of the file the probable identity of the informant, a Buffalo YAWF founder.

60. Haynie interview; Faulkner conversation.

61. *Spectrum*, 11 March 1966, 11 February 1970.

62. *Spectrum*, 7 May 1965, 30 July 1965, 8 February 1966, 8 April 1966, 5 July 1968, 13 December 1968.

63. *Spectrum*, 5 August 1966; Faulkner conversation; Powell letter, 16 April 1988.

64. *Spectrum*, 15 October 1965, 28 January 1966, 1 February 1966, 8 April 1966, 15 April 1966; Marcella Branagan, SUNY-Buffalo antiwar student, letter to author, 28 July 1989.

65. *Spectrum*, 19 April 1965.

66. Oglesby KSU SDS Reunion.

67. Oglesby KSU SDS Reunion; Carl Oglesby and Richard Shaull, *Containment and Change* (New York: Macmillan, 1967), 112–39; Paul Jacobs and Saul Landau, *The New Radicals: A Report with Documents* (New York: Vintage Books, 1966), 257–66.

68. *Daily Kent Stater*, 7 July 1964. The KSU student directories did not provide information on students' majors. Since the KSU Office of the Registrar never responded to my inquiries concerning the social characteristics of the KSU student body in 1969–1970, I was forced to select at random 240 students from the 1969–1970 KSU student directory and compile my own profile of the overall student body: Northern-Western European, 74 percent; Southern-Eastern European, 22 percent; Jewish, 5 percent; undergraduate, 93 percent; graduate, 7 percent; in-state, 83 percent; out-of-state, 17 percent; metropolitan area, 17 percent; Cleveland and its suburbs, 9 percent; Cleveland residents, 4 percent; female, 43 percent; male, 57 percent.

69. Walsh conversation.

70. Ibid.

71. Ibid.; *Daily Kent Stater,* 12 January 1965; Joseph Jackson conversation.

72. Walsh conversation; Joseph Jackson conversation; Gibson conversation; *Daily Kent Stater,* 27 October 1967, 14 February 1968.

73. Walsh conversation; Joseph Jackson conversation; Gibson conversation.

74. Gibson conversation; Howie Emmer, KCEWV and KSU SDS, Formal Remarks Made at the KSU SDS Reunion, Kent, Ohio, 5 May 1989; Powrie KSU SDS Reunion; Robin Marks, KSU SDS, Formal Remarks Made at the KSU SDS Reunion, Kent, Ohio, 6 May 1989.

75. Gibson conversation; Lewis interview.

76. Heirich, *Spiral of Conflict,* and Hodgson, *America in Our Time,* among others, contend that the Berkeley FSM represented the birth of white student activism.

77. Gitlin, *The Sixties,* Miller, *"Democracy Is in the Streets,"* and Sale, *SDS,* as well as other scholars, have argued that the state university student activists were generally intellectually inferior to their elite educated counterparts.

78. Rothman and Lichter, *Roots of Radicalism,* and Richard Flacks, "The Liberated Generation," in Clark and Clark, eds., *Youth in Modern Society,* profiled radical activists at Chicago, Columbia, and Michigan and concluded that in general Jews were heavily represented in the ranks of the New Left. They were, but far less so at the less prestigious state universities.

4. "Let Us Try to Succeed with Reason"

1. Zaroulis and Sullivan, *Who Spoke Up?* 106.

2. Unger, *The Movement,* 103; Sale, *SDS,* 302; Richard Flacks, "The Liberated Generation," in Clark and Clark, eds., *Youth in Modern Society,* 319–39; F. Chandler Young, "The Importance of Students, 1949–1974," in Allan G. Bogue and Robert Taylor, eds., *The University of Wisconsin: One Hundred and Twenty-Five Years* (Madison: University of Wisconsin Press, 1975), 131–56; Lukas, *Don't Shoot—We Are Your Children!* 9–61.

3. Young, "The Importance of Students, 1949–1974," 131–56.

4. *State News,* 8 March 1965.

5. Ibid., 9 March 1965.

6. Ibid., 8 April 1965, 12 April 1965; Greer interview; Bivins interview.

7. Dr. John Donoghue, Department of Anthropology, Michigan State University, letter to MSU president John Hannah, 12 April 1965 (Hannah Papers, MSU Archives); Resolutions of the MSU Vietnam Teach-in, 11 April 1965 (Hannah Papers, MSU Archives); Greer interview.

8. *State News,* 20 April 1965.

9. Ibid., 12 April 1965, 21 April 1965, 22 April 1965; DeBenedetti and Chatfield, *An American Ordeal,* 109.

10. *State News,* 12 May 1965; Greer interview.

11. *State News,* 13 October 1965, 18 October 1965; Michigan Free Speech Defense Circular, 1966 (Student Radicalism Collection, MSU Special Collections); Fish conversation, 16 August 1988.

12. *State News,* 17 November 1965; *The Paper,* 3 December 1965.

13. Jacobs and Landau, *The New Radicals,* 258–59.

14. *State News,* 11 October 1966.

15. *The Paper*, 28 March 1966.

16. Detroit *Free Press*, 2 April 1966; Michigan Free Speech Defense Circular, 1966.

17. *State News*, 30 March 1966, 31 March 1966; Detroit *Free Press*, 2 April 1966.

18. Detroit *Free Press*, 2 April 1966; Michigan Free Speech Defense Circular, 1966.

19. Hinckle et al., "The University on the Make," 53–55; *Newsweek* 67 (25 April 1966): 78; *New York Times*, 14 April 1966; *State News*, 14 April 1966, 20 April 1966, 12 May 1966.

20. Lansing *State Journal*, 24 April 1966.

21. Ibid.

22. Repas interview; Michigan State University Advisory Group, *Final Report Covering Activities of the MSU Vietnam Advisory Group for the Period May 20, 1955–June 30, 1962*, 23–26, 61–64, 77; Scigliano and Fox, *Technical Assistance in Vietnam*, 4; *State News*, 20 April 1966; *The Paper*, 7 April 1966, 19 May 1966.

23. Badrich letters, 4 October 1987, 13 May 1988, 17 May 1988; *State News*, 20 April 1966; *The Paper*, 7 April 1966.

24. Badrich letters, 4 October 1987, 13 May 1988, 17 May 1988; Fish conversation, 16 August 1988; Pyle interview; Jack Sattel letter; Sue Sattel letter.

25. Skocpol letter to author; Skocpol letter to Theda Barron; Pohl interview.

26. Badrich letters, 4 October 1987, 13 May 1988, 17 May 1988; Jack Sattel letter; Sue Sattel letter; George Fish conversation, 16 August 1988.

27. *The Paper*, 27 January 1967.

28. Harvey Goldman, "MSU-SDS Announcement of National SDS Draft Resolution," 18 January 1967 (Student Radicalism Collection, MSU Special Collections); SDS, "SDS Draft Resolution," 28 December 1966 (Student Radicalism Collection, MSU Special Collections).

29. *The Paper*, Fall Orientation Issue, August 1968; Skocpol letter to author.

30. Greer interview; Larrowe interview; *State News*, 16 November 1966.

31. Interfaith Convocation on War and Peace Circular, 30 November 1966 (Student Radicalism Collection, MSU Special Collections); Greer, "What Is the War Doing to Us in the World of International Politics?"

32. *The Paper*, 4 April 1967; UCM, Regional Headquarters Staff of Vietnam Strategy Committee, "General Policy Statement of the Peace Strategy Committee," Spring 1967 (Lynn Jondahl Personal Papers—copy in author's possession).

33. MSU-UCM, "1967 Student Elections Proposal," Spring 1967 (Lynn Jondahl Personal Papers—copy in author's possession); MSU-UCM, "Peace Strategy Committee Report," 20 February 1967 (Lynn Jondahl Personal Papers—copy in author's possession); Pohl interview; Jondahl interview.

34. *State News*, 10 March 1967; Badrich letters, 4 October 1987, 13 May 1988, 17 May 1988.

35. *The Paper*, 25 April 1967.

36. J. Robert Nelson, "Vietnam Summer," *Christian Century* 84 (24 May 1967): 678–79; Lansing Vietnam Summer Project, "Lansing Vietnam Summer Newsletter," East Lansing, July 1967 (Lynn Jondahl Personal Papers—copy in author's possession).

37. Lansing Vietnam Summer Project, "Lansing Vietnam Summer Letter to the

Public," East Lansing, 26 May 1967 (Lynn Jondahl Personal Papers—copy in author's possession); *Towne-Courier Enterprise* (East Lansing, Mich.), 1 August 1967; Sue Sattel letter.

38. "Lansing Vietnam Summer Newsletter"; Lansing Vietnam Summer Project, "Things You Can Do to Express Your Concern," July 1967 (Lynn Jondahl Personal Papers—copy in author's possession); Dave Stockman letter to Friends of Lansing Vietnam Summer, July 1967 (Lynn Jondahl Personal Papers—copy in author's possession); *The Paper*, 16 May 1967.

39. "Things You Can do to Express Your Concern;" Stockman letter; *The Paper*, 16 May 1967.

40. Lansing Vietnam Summer, "Perspectives for Action," 21 August 1967 (Lynn Jondahl Personal Papers—copy in author's possession); Unger, *The Movement*, 138; Garskoff conversation.

41. *The Paper*, 7 November 1967.

42. *Daily Collegian*, 6 January 1965.

43. Ibid., 15 February 1965, 24 February 1965, 25 February 1965.

44. Ibid., 17 February 1965, 18 February 1965.

45. Ibid., 24 February 1965.

46. Withall letter; *Daily Collegian*, 7 April 1965, 9 April 1965, 10 April 1965.

47. *Daily Collegian*, 20 April 1965, 21 April 1965.

48. Ibid., 27 April 1965, 28 April 1965, 30 April 1965.

49. Ibid., 19 August 1965; *Student Conservative*, 1 March 1965, 12 April 1965, 26 April 1965, 20 May 1965 .

50. Thormeyer letter; Bennett interview; Newsletter of the YAF at Penn State, *Freedom!* 20 May 1963 (Thomas Bennett Personal Papers—copy in author's possession); *Daily Collegian*, 29 September 1965, 29 October 1965.

51. *Daily Collegian*, 28 October 1965, 30 October 1965; Creegan conversation.

52. Creegan conversation; *Daily Collegian*, 19 October 1965.

53. *Daily Collegian*, 23 October 1965, 28 October 1965.

54. Ibid., 20 October 1965, 2 June 1967; Rabinowitz letter; Bennett interview.

55. *Daily Collegian*, 10 November 1965.

56. Ibid., 17 April 1965, 11 September 1965, 25 September 1965, 12 October 1965, 22 October 1965, 23 October 1965, 27 October 1965, 6 November 1965, 24 November 1965; Bennett interview; PSU YAF, "Report of the Penn State YAF," 1966 (Thomas Bennett Personal Papers—copy in author's possession).

57. *Daily Collegian*, 2 October 1965, 15 October 1965, 20 November 1965.

58. Ibid., 28 January 1966, 8 February 1966, 10 February 1966, 19 February 1966; Farley conversation.

59. *Daily Collegian*, 28 January 1966, 29 January 1966, 1 February 1966, 11 February 1966; Creegan conversation.

60. *Daily Collegian*, 1 February 1966; Creegan conversation.

61. Bennett interview; PSU YAF Memorandums from Carl Thormeyer to Dennis Tanner, 7 July 1965, 10 August 1965, 27 July 1965 (Thomas Bennett Personal Papers—copies in author's possession); Thormeyer letter; *Daily Collegian*, 9 February 1966.

62. Bennett interview; *Daily Collegian*, 18 February 1966, 23 February 1966, 29 April 1966, 30 April 1966.

63. *Daily Collegian*, 8 March 1966, 5 May 1966, 4 October 1966.

64. Ibid., 30 April 1966, 11 May 1966; PSU Ad hoc Committee for Student

Freedom, Open Letter to the President of the University, 10 May 1966 (Carl Thormeyer Personal Papers— copy in author's possession).

65. *Daily Collegian*, 2 April 1966; *Daily Collegian*, 19 April 1966, 23 April 1966, 30 April 1966.

66. Davidson, "Toward a Student Syndicalist Movement or University Reform Revisted," working paper prepared for the National Convention of the Students for a Democratic Society at Clear Lake, Iowa, August 1966 (Thomas Bennett Personal Papers-copy in author's possession).

67. Thormeyer letter; Bennett interview; *Daily Collegian*, 7 October 1966.

68. *Daily Collegian*, 7 October 1966; Steve Accardy and Neil Buckley et al., "The Movement, Part I," Students for a Democratic Society, Penn State chapter, December 1966 (Thomas Bennett Personal Papers—copy in author's possession); *New Left Notes*, 16 December 1966.

69. *Daily Collegian*, 6 October 1966, 13 October 1966, 19 October 1966, 22 October 1966, 1 November 1966, 19 November 1966, 22 November 1966.

70. Bennett interview; Farley conversation; Creegan conversation; Neil Buckley letter to Cathy Wilkerson, SDS National Office, 18 February 1967 (Neil Buckley Papers, Historical Collections and Labor Archives, PSU Library).

71. Withall letter; *Daily Collegian*, 22 November 1966, 29 November 1966, 2 December 1966.

72. *New Left Notes*, 27 January 1967; *Daily Collegian*, 17 January 1967, 18 January 1967, 19 January 1967, 20 January 1967, 26 January 1967, 7 February 1967, 2 March 1967.

73. *Daily Collegian*, 12 January 1967, 16 February 1967, 21 February 1967; PSU SDS circular on napalm, "How Dow Chemical Serves You," 1967 (Neil Buckley Papers, Historical Collections and Labor Archives, PSU Library).

74. *Daily Collegian*, 1 February 1967, 2 February 1967, 3 February 1967, 4 February 1967; *New Left Notes*, 20 February 1967; Neil Buckley, "Penn State SDS Sit-in . . . 2/5/67, Summary of Events" (Neil Buckley Papers, Historical Collections and Labor Archives, PSU Library).

75. *Progress* (Clearfield, Penn.), 7 January 1967 (Neil Buckley Papers, Historical Collections and Labor Archives, PSU Library); Neil Buckley letter to Greg Calvert, National SDS president, 11 February 1967 (Neil Buckley Papers, Historical Collections and Labor Archives, PSU Library); *Daily Collegian*, 18 January 1967, 21 January 1967, 2 February 1967, 21 February 1967, 22 February 1967, 23 February 1967, 24 February 1967, 28 February 1967, 12 April 1967.

76. Bennett interview; PSU YAF circular on the DeJaegher debate, "Unprecedented Debate," May 1967 (Thomas Bennett Personal Papers—copy in author's possession); Don Ernsberger, PSU YAF, Ogontz campus of PSU, letter to Tom Bennett, PSU YAF, PSU main campus, 3 February 1967 (Thomas Bennett Personal Papers —copy in author's possession); PSU YAF circular, "Join Young Americans for Freedom," 1967 (Thomas Bennett Personal Papers—copy in author's possession); *Daily Collegian*, 2 March 1967, 17 March 1967.

77. *Daily Collegian*, 22 February 1967, 8 March 1967, 11 April 1967; Neil Buckley letter to his sister, 28 March 1967 (Neil Buckley Papers, Historical Collections and Labor Archives, PSU Library).

78. *Daily Collegian*, 15 April 1967, 18 April 1967, 20 April 1967, 21 April 1967, 22 April 1967, 14 November 1967, 17 November 1967; Creegan conversation.

79. Robert Boyer, PSU clergy antiwar activist, letters to author, 9 December 1987 and 26 January 1988; *Daily Collegian*, 14 February 1967, 15 February 1967, 28 February 1967, 2 March 1967.

80. *Daily Collegian*, 31 May 1967, 29 June 1967, 17 August 1967, 27 September 1967, 28 September 1967.

81. Ibid., 6 July 1967, 13 July 1967, 20 July 1967, 26 September 1967, 18 September 1968.

82. Creegan conversation; Neil Buckley letter to Carl Davidson, 1967 ; Sale, *SDS*, 141–42; Neil Buckley Press Release-letter to Dr. Henry W. Sams, head, English Department, PSU, 8 March 1967 (Neil Buckley Papers, Historical Collections and Labor Archives, PSU Library).

83. *Daily Collegian*, 20 September 1967, 24 October 1967.

84. Ibid., 18 October 1967, 19 October 1967, 24 October 1967, 25 October 1967, 2 November 1967, 22 November 1967; Sale, *SDS*, 380. Sale, relying on *New Left Notes* for a great deal of his information on campus activism, credited SDS for being the first group at PSU to "uncover" the ORL. This should serve as a warning to scholars that *New Left Notes'* reports of SDS chapter activities and achievements must be taken with a grain of salt. It may be that the publication functioned as a forum for self-serving and publicity-seeking individuals.

85. *Daily Collegian*, 1 November 1967, 7 November 1967.

86. Willhelm letter; Powell letter, 12 November 1987.

87. Powell letter, 12 November 1987; *Spectrum*, 26 March 1965, 5 April 1965, 9 April 1965.

88. *Spectrum*, 23 April 1965, 30 April 1965, 7 May 1965.

89. Ibid., 30 July 1965, 8 October 1965.

90. Ibid., 16 July 1965, 30 July 1965, 13 August 1965.

91. Ibid., 24 September 1965, 1 October 1965, 8 October 1965, 15 October 1965, 22 October 1965; Gross FBI File.

92. *Spectrum*, 22 October 1965.

93. Ibid., 1 October 1965, 15 October 1965, 22 October 1965, 5 November 1965, 12 November 1965, 23 November 1965, 10 December 1965, 8 April 1966.

94. Ibid., 28 January 1966, 1 February 1966, 15 April 1966.

95. Ibid., 4 February 1966, 11 March 1966; SUNY-Buffalo SDS, Fund Raising Letter to the Buffalo Community, 1966 (Elizabeth Olmsted Smith Papers, Box 17, SUNY-Buffalo Archives).

96. *Spectrum*, 22 February 1966, 15 March 1966; Powell letter, 16 April 1988.

97. Ibid., 1 April 1966, 8 April 1966.

98. Ibid., 28 January 1966, 25 February 1966, 1 April 1966, 8 April 1966, 12 April 1966, 26 April 1966, 5 May 1966, 6 May 1966.

99. Ibid., 3 May 1966, 5 May 1966, 9 May 1966, 10 May 1966; *New Left Notes*, 6 May 1966; Willhelm letter; Faulkner conversation; see Furnas, *Memorial Biographical Record of Clifford C. Furnas*, for the president's running commentary on his subordinates.

100. *Spectrum*, 12 August 1966.

101. Ibid., 7 September 1966, 30 September 1966, 4 October 1966.

102. Ibid., 27 September 1966, 30 September 1966, 4 October 1966, 15 November 1966; *New Left Notes*, 28 October 1966; Faulkner conversation; Willhelm letter; Powell letter, 12 November 1987; Haynie interview.

103. *Spectrum*, 21 October 1966, 25 October 1966, 28 October 1966, 1 November 1966, 4 November 1966, 31 October 1967; Gross FBI File; SUNY-Buffalo YAWF leaflet, "U.S. Bombs Hanoi!" 1966 (Elizabeth Olmsted Smith Papers, Box 17, SUNY-Buffalo Archives); Powell letter, 16 April 1988.

104. *Spectrum*, 28 October 1966; Elwin H. Powell, "Promoting the Decline of the Rising State: Documents of Resistance and Renewal from the Alternative Community, Buffalo, 1965–1976," *Catalyst* 9 (1977): 63–65; Powell letter, 12 November 1987.

105. *Spectrum*, 31 January 1967, 7 February 1967, 14 February 1967, 28 February 1967, 3 March 1967, 7 March 1967, 7 April 1967.

106. Ibid., 3 March 1967, 11 April 1967.

107. Ibid., 3 March 1967, 7 April 1967, 11 April 1967, 5 May 1967, 22 September 1967; Powell letter, 19 December 1987.

108. *Spectrum*, 31 January 1967, 14 April 1967, 18 April 1967; George C. Cox, Buffalo community resident, letter to SUNY-Buffalo president Martin Meyerson, 17 March 1967 (Campus Unrest, 1965–1970, Box 1, SUNY-Buffalo Archives); Anna O'Connor, Buffalo community resident, letter to SUNY-Buffalo president Martin Meyerson, 10 April 1967 (Campus Unrest, 1965–1970, Box 1, SUNY-Buffalo Archives).

109. *Spectrum*, 4 April 1967, 21 April 1967, 25 April 1967, 23 June 1967; Faculty-Student Committee to Oppose Censorship, letter to SUNY-Buffalo president Martin Meyerson, 25 April 1967 (Campus Unrest, 1965–1970, Box 1, SUNY-Buffalo Archives).

110. *Spectrum*, 14 March 1967, 11 April 1967, 4 August 1967, 27 October 1967; *Buffalo Insighter* (Buffalo, New York), 20 November 1967 (Campus Unrest, 1965–1970, Box 1, SUNY-Buffalo Archives).

111. *Buffalo Insighter*, 25 September 1967; Vietnam Summer, Erie County, circular, 1967 (Elizabeth Olmsted Smith Papers, Box 17, SUNY-Buffalo Archives).

112. Carl Kronberg, SUNY-Buffalo YAWF, FBI File (Elwin Powell Personal Papers—notes from file in author's possession); *Spectrum*, 23 June 1967; *Buffalo Insighter*, 1 July 1967, 25 September 1967.

113. *Buffalo Insighter*, 25 September 1967; *Spectrum*, 11 August 1967, 26 September 1967, 17 October 1967.

114. *Spectrum*, 14 June 1967.

115. Ibid., 26 September 1967; Branagan letter; Snell letter, 8 March 1988; Bennis, *The Leaning Ivory Tower*, 129–45; Meyerson, *The City and the University*, 7–16.

116. *Spectrum*, 17 October 1967, 20 October 1967.

117. Ibid., 8 December 1967; *Buffalo Insighter*, 20 November 1967; Faulkner conversation.

118. *Spectrum*, 20 October 1967, 27 October 1967, 17 November 1967, 15 December 1967; *Buffalo Insighter*, 25 September 1967.

119. *Spectrum*, 3 November 1967, 17 November 1967; SUNY-Buffalo president Martin Meyerson, Open Letter to Faculty Colleagues and Students, 30 October 1967 (Campus Unrest, 1965–1970, Box 1, SUNY-Buffalo Archives).

120. SUNY-Buffalo president Martin Meyerson, Open Letter to Students and Faculty Colleagues, 13 December 1967 (Campus Unrest, 1965–1970, Box 1, SUNY-Buffalo Archives); Dr. George Hochfield et al., A Statement for the Approval of the Faculty Senate, November 1967 (Campus Unrest, 1965–1970, Box 1, SUNY-Buffalo Archives); *Spectrum*, 17 November 1967, 12 December 1967.

121. *Spectrum*, 7 November 1967, 15 December 1967, 19 December 1967; Sharon Edelman, Review of Student Activism, 1965–1967 (Campus Unrest, 1965–1970, Box 1, SUNY-Buffalo Archives).

122. SUNY-Buffalo Student Senate Referendum, Campus Recruitment, Results, December 1967 (Campus Unrest, 1965–1970, Box 1, SUNY-Buffalo Archives); Dr. Newton Garver, Department of Philosophy, Open Letter to Colleagues, 19 December 1967 (Campus Unrest, 1965–1970, Box 1, SUNY-Buffalo Archives); *Spectrum*, 3 November 1967, 8 December 1967, 12 December 1967, 15 December 1967, 19 December 1967.

123. *Spectrum*, 19 December 1967.

124. Joseph Jackson conversation; Walsh conversation.

125. Joseph Jackson conversation; Walsh conversation; *Daily Kent Stater*, 12 February 1965.

126. Joseph Jackson conversation; Walsh conversation; *Daily Kent Stater*, 20 April 1965, 19 May 1965, 8 April 1965, 14 April 1965, 15 April 1965.

127. Joseph Jackson conversation; Walsh conversation; *Daily Kent Stater*, 6 April 1965, 15 April 1965, 11 May 1965, 12 May 1965; Dr. Sidney L. Jackson, School of Library Science, Kent State University, letter to Mrs. Henry Lewis, Kent community resident, 2 April 1965 (Sidney Jackson Papers, Box 1, Kent State Archives).

128. Joseph Jackson conversation; Walsh conversation; *Daily Kent Stater*, 11 November 1965, 16 November 1965.

129. Joseph Jackson conversation; Walsh conversation; *Daily Kent Stater*, 24 February 1966, 8 April 1966.

130. Joseph Jackson conversation; Walsh conversation; Gibson conversation.

131. Joseph Jackson conversation; Gibson conversation; *Daily Kent Stater*, 1 March 1967, 18 April 1967, 25 May 1967, 2 June 1967.

132. Joseph Jackson conversation; Gibson conversation; *Daily Kent Stater*, 27 October 1967, 31 October 1967, 2 November 1967.

133. Powrie KSU SDS Reunion; Emmer KSU SDS Reunion; *Daily Kent Stater*, 20 October 1967, 2 November 1967.

134. Gibson conversation; *Daily Kent Stater*, 17 October 1967, 20 October 1967, 27 October 1967, 3 November 1967, 9 November 1967, 29 November 1967.

135. *Daily Kent Stater*, 31 October 1967, 8 November 1967, 14 November 1967, 21 November 1967.

136. Ibid., 1 November 1967, 2 November 1967, 14 November 1967.

137. Joseph Jackson conversation; *Daily Kent Stater*, 6 December 1967, 7 December 1967.

5. "You Don't Need a Weatherman"

1. Badrich letter, 24 July 1988; MSU president John A. Hannah, "State of the University," address to Faculty Convocation, 12 February 1968 (Robert Repas Personal Papers—copy in author's possession).

2. Badrich letter, 13 May 1988; *State News*, 15 February 1968; William Hixson, MSU faculty antiwar actvist, East Lansing, Mich., interview with author, 4 April 1984.

3. *The Paper*, 10 April 1968, 17 April 1968, 24 April 1968; Academic Days of

Conscience, circular, April 1968 (Student Radicalism Collection, MSU Special Collections); *State News*, 17 April 1968; Pohl interview; Pohl Red Squad File.

4. William Skocpol letter to his mother, 18 June 1968 (William Skocpol Personal Papers—copy in author's possession).

5. Pohl interview; Pohl Red Squad File.

6. Beth Shapiro, MSU SDS, East Lansing, Mich., interview with author, 2 February 1984; Rick Kibbey, MSU SDS, telephone conversation with author, 21 November 1983; Skocpol letter to author; *State News*, 30 May 1968, 19 June 1968, 26 September 1968; Fish Red Squad File.

7. *State News*, 20 June 1968, 26 September 1968; Pyle interview; Larrowe interview.

8. Larrowe interview; *State News*, 26 May 1968; Mader letter.

9. Lansing *State Journal*, 14 June 1968, 15 June 1968.

10. American Legion, Department of Michigan, letter to MSU president John Hannah, 2 August 1968 (Hannah Papers, MSU Archives); Veterans of Foreign Wars, Department of Michigan, letter to MSU president John Hannah, 30 June 1968 (Hannah Papers, MSU Archives); Lansing *State Journal*, 15 June 1968.

11. The Motherfuckers, "The Destructuring of SDS," June 1968 (Student Radicalism Collection, MSU Special Collections); MSU SDS, "General Agenda for Panels, Workshops, National Convention and National Council," and "Specific Area Workshops," June 1968 (Student Radicalism Collection, MSU Special Collections); Lansing *State Journal*, 15 June 1968; Shapiro interview; Hixson interview; Sale, *SDS*, 455–70; Fish Red Squad File; George Fish FBI File (George Fish Personal Papers—copy in author's possession).

12. Sale, *SDS*, 455–70.

13. *State News*, 30 September 1968, 1 October 1968; Fish conversations, 16 August 1988, 3 September 1989 and 16 March 1989; Garskoff conversation.

14. Pyle interview; Skocpol letter to author; *State News*, 1 March 1967, 2 March 1967; Jack Sattel letter; Sue Sattel letter. For information regarding Linda Evans' background, I am indebted to the Ft. Dodge, Iowa, public library for providing me with excerpted copies of the following: *The Dodger '65*, Ft. Dodge, Iowa, High School Yearbook, and the *1964 Ft. Dodge, Iowa, City Directory*. The 2 December 1990 issue of the Des Moines *Register* (Des Moines, Iowa) carried a lengthy article on Evans and her trial that year for planting eight bombs between 1983 and 1985.

15. MSU Resistance Newsletter, November 1968 (Student Radicalism Collection, MSU Special Collections); *State News*, 15 October 1968.

16. MSU Resistance circular, 1968 (Student Radicalism Collection, MSU Special Collections); Kibbey conversation.

17. Resistance circular; *State Journal*, 15 November 1968.

18. Rick Kowall letter to his draft board, 11 January 1970 (James Anderson Personal Papers—copy in author's possession); Anderson interview.

19. Mader letter.

20. Fish Red Squad File; Fish conversations, 16 August 1988 and 3 September 1989; Pyle interview; Andy Pyle, Michigan State Police Red Squad File (Andy Pyle Personal Papers—notes from file in author's possession); Garskoff conversation; Carl Oglesby, Kent, Ohio, interview with author, 5 May 1989; *State News*, 11 February 1969, 12 February 1969.

21. Larrowe interview; Repas interview; Shapiro interview; *The Paper*, 1 May 1969.

22. Associated Students of Michigan State University Minutes (ASMSU, MSU student government), 11 February 1969 (East Lansing, Mich.: ASMSU); Walter Adams, *The Test* (New York: Macmillan, 1971), 118.

23. Adams, *The Test*, 52; Kibbey conversation; Larrowe interview; Pohl interview; Shapiro interview; Fish conversation, 16 August 1988; MSU SDS, "Abolish ROTC," 29 October 1969 (Student Radicalism Collection, MSU Special Collections); *New York Times*, 5 January 1969; *State News*, 21 January 1971.

24. Jack Sattel letter; Sue Sattel letter; Fish conversation, 16 August 1988; Pyle interview; *State News*, 29 April 1969, 1 May 1969, 9 May 1969; Jack Sattel, Sue Sattel, Janet Dowty, Stu Dowty et al., Radical Education Project, Detroit, letter to supporters, July 1969 (Neil Buckley Papers, Historical Collections and Labor Archives, PSU Library.)

25. Fish conversation, 16 August 1988; Shapiro interview; Fish Red Squad File; Sale, *SDS*, 557–80.

26. Sale, *SDS*, 576, 588, 589, 624, 648, 649.

27. Report of the Special Committee on Political Surveillance by the East Lansing Police Department; Pyle Red Squad File; Fish interview, 3 September 1989; Shapiro interview; Frank Donner, "Spies on Campus," *Playboy* 15 (March 1968): 108, 115, 144–45, 147–50; James Ridgeway, "Patriots on the Campus," *New Republic* 156 (25 March 1967): 12–13. David Epstein had joined SDS in 1968, ostensibly to write a Master's Thesis, "The Students for a Democratic Society at Michigan State University, 1968–1969: A Case Study" (Michigan State University School of Police Administration and Public Administration, 1970). However, he did not, according to Shapiro and Fish, inform SDSers of his intentions; they only discovered his purpose by accident. Further, prior to 1968 he had been an outspoken hawk, then he informed SDSers that he had changed his mind and was drawn to the radicals. Activists later discovered that Epstein had been with the Army Military Police in Vietnam.

28. Tom Samet, MSU antiwar student, letter to author, 12 July 1988; Adams, *The Test*, 47–48, 98–107; ASMSU Minutes, 30 September 1969.

29. Adams, *The Test*, 102–7; Kibbey conversation.

30. ASMSU Minutes, 28 October 1969 and 18 November 1969; Kibbey conversation; Norman Pollack, MSU NUC, telephone conversation with author, 14 October 1983.

31. Anderson interview.

32. Larrowe interview; Repas interview; Fish conversation, 16 August 1988; *State News*, 6 May 1969, 9 October 1969; Clifton Oreo Wharton Research Committee, "Clifton Oreo Wharton: A Fact Sheet," Fall 1970 (Student Radicalism Collection, MSU Special Collections); *Who's Who in America, 1973–1974.*

33. *Daily Collegian*, 10 January 1968, 6 February 1968; *New Left Notes*, 12 February 1968; Farley conversation.

34. *Daily Collegian*, 19 January 1968, 21 February 1968, 22 February 1968, 29 February 1968, 1 March 1968; PSU SDS leaflet on the IDA, "Walker Attends Secret Meeting Today," February 1968 (Thomas Bennett Personal Papers—copy in author's possession).

35. *Daily Collegian*, 3 May 1968, 14 May 1968.

36. *Daily Collegian*, 6 April 1968, 9 April 1968, 9 May 1968, 14 May 1968, 15

May 1968, 17 May 1968; PSU SDS, *Southpaw* (State College, Penn.), 13 May 1968 (Student Activism Records, Box 1, PSU Library).

37. Creegan conversation; *Daily Collegian*, 7 March 1968, 29 March 1968, 2 April 1968, 4 April 1968, 6 April 1968, 11 April 1968, 8 May 1968, 9 May 1968; *Southpaw*, 13 May 1968.

38. Creegan conversation; *Daily Collegian*, 15 May 1968, 16 May 1968, 17 May 1968.

39. Bennett interview; *Daily Collegian*, 16 January 1968, 6 February 1968, 3 April 1968, 16 May 1968, 10 October 1968, 20 November 1968.

40. Creegan conversation; Sale, *SDS*, 459, 463–64; Greg Calvert, national president of SDS, letter to Neil Buckley, 22 January 1968 (Neil Buckley Papers, Historical Collections and Labor Archives, PSU Library); Neil Buckley, position paper for the 1968 National SDS convention, "Burning Questions of Our Movement," June 1968 (Neil Buckley Papers, Historical Collections and Labor Archives, PSU Library).

41. Davidson conversation; Buckley, "Burning Questions of Our Movement."

42. *Daily Collegian*, 27 September 1968.

43. Creegan conversation; Withall letter; *Daily Collegian*, 18 September 1968, 25 September 1968, 27 September 1968, 1 October 1968, 12 October 1968, 15 October 1968, 18 October 1968.

44. Creegan conversation; *Daily Collegian*, 24 September 1968, 28 September 1968, 18 October 1968, 8 November 1968, 20 November 1968.

45. *Daily Collegian*, 18 September 1968, 5 November 1968, 8 November 1968; Creegan conversation; Petras conversation; Dale Winter, PSU clergy antiwar activist, letter to author, 28 January 1988.

46. *Daily Collegian*, 2 October 1968, 4 October 1968, 9 October 1968, 23 October 1968, 26 October 1968, 1 November 1968, 5 November 1968.

47. Ibid., 12 October 1968, 5 November 1968, 6 November 1968, 7 November 1968, 12 November 1968.

48. Ibid., 25 February 1969; Joseph E. Gonzalez, Jr., special assistant for Legislative Relations, Rutgers, The State University, "State Laws of 1969 Dealing with Student Unrest," 5 November 1969 (Office of the President, Central Files, Administration, Box 8, SUNY-Buffalo Archives).

49. *Daily Collegian*, 18 February 1969, 25 February 1969, 27 February 1969, 8 May 1969; Statement of Judge A. H. Lipez in Centre County Court, 28 February 1969 (Student Activism Records, Box 1, PSU Archives); In the Court of Common Pleas of Centre County, Pennsylvania, *The Pennsylvania State University vs. Alvin Youngberg, et al., defendants,* Complaint, April Term, 1969 (Student Activism Records, Box 1, PSU Library).

50. *Daily Collegian*, 20 November 1968, 18 February 1969; *Water Tunnel*, 27 January 1969, 10 February 1969, 24 February 1969, 10 March 1969.

51. *Daily Collegian*, 24 September 1969; In the Court of Common Pleas of Centre County, Pennsylvania, *Commonwealth vs. Stephen Alvan Youngberg, Russell Steven Farb, Jay Robert Shore,* Transcript of Trial, 14 April 1969 (Student Activism Records, Box 1, PSU Library).

52. *Daily Collegian*, 14 January 1969, 28 January 1969, 31 January 1969, 11 February 1969, 12 February 1969, 18 February 1969, 19 February 1969; Petras conversation.

53. *Water Tunnel*, 24 February 1969; *Daily Collegian*, 18 April 1969, 21 May

1969; PSU SDS circular on SDS ideology and student government elections, "The Platform—The Candidates," 1969 (Student Activism Records, Box 1, PSU Library).

54. *Daily Collegian,* 25 April 1969, 2 May 1969, 22 May 1969, 23 May 1969, 27 May 1969; Bennett interview; President Richard M. Nixon, letter to Mr. Douglas Cooper, 13 May 1969 (Thomas Bennett Personal Papers—copy in author's possession); Charles L. Lewis, vice president for Student Affairs, letter to Barry Stein, Scott F. Gibbs, Malorie Tolles, Cletus J. Wineland, 23 May 1969 (Student Activism Records, Box 1, PSU Library).

55. *Daily Collegian,* 26 April 1969, 30 April 1969, 27 May 1969; PSU NUC, "Organizing an NUC Chapter at PSU," 1969 (Pam Farley Personal Papers—copy in author's possession); Farley conversation; Petras conversation.

56. *Daily Collegian,* 8 May 1969, 28 May 1969; *Water Tunnel,* 10 March 1969.

57. Farley conversation; Creegan conversation; *Daily Collegian,* 14 August 1969; Neil Buckley proposal for restructuring SDS, "Get Organized," 1969 (Neil Buckley Papers, Historical Collections and Labor Archives, PSU Library).

58. Farley conversation; Petras conversation; *Daily Collegian,* 24 September 1969, 17 October 1969, 23 October 1969, 24 October 1969, 31 October 1969; *Water Tunnel,* 21 September 1969, 13 November 1969.

59. Bennett interview; *Daily Collegian,* 3 October 1969, 9 October 1969, 17 October 1969, 1 November 1969.

60. *Water Tunnel,* 21 September 1969; *Daily Collegian,* 24 September 1969, 26 September 1969, 15 October 1969, 22 October 1969, 24 October 1969.

61. *Daily Collegian,* 15 October 1969, 16 October 1969; PSU NUC, "NUC Supports Call for Antiwar Strike on October 15th," 1969 (Pam Farley Personal Papers—copy in author's possession).

62. *Daily Collegian,* 16 October 1969.

63. Petras conversation; *Daily Collegian,* 16 October 1969, 22 October 1969, 23 October 1969, 28 October 1969, 30 October 1969; *Water Tunnel,* 2 November 1969.

64. *Daily Collegian,* 23 October 1969, 13 November 1969, 15 November 1969, 20 November 1969; PSU NUC circular on November 15, 1969 Mobilization (Student Activism Records, Box 1, PSU Library); PSU Coalition for Peace, "Final Instructions for People Going to Washington, November 13–15," November 1969 (Student Activism Records, Box 1, PSU Library); PSU Coalition for Peace, "Program for November Mobilization at State College," November 1969 (Student Activism Records, Box 1, PSU Library).

65. *Spectrum,* 26 January 1968, 2 February 1968, 19 March 1968, 26 March 1968; Snell letter, 3 January 1988.

66. Faulkner conversation; *Spectrum,* 26 January 1968, 16 February 1968; Buffalo Draft Counselling Center circular, "Draft Counselling Seminar," 28 November 1967 (Elizabeth Olmsted Smith Papers, Box 16, SUNY-Buffalo Archives).

67. Resolution Proposed by the Faculty Senate of the State University of New York at Buffalo, March 8, 1968 (Campus Unrest, 1965–1970, Box 1, SUNY-Buffalo Archives); *Spectrum,* 12 March 1968, 15 March 1968, 19 March 1968, 30 April 1968.

68. *Spectrum,* 15 March 1968, 19 March 1968, 22 March 1968; Faculty Committee for Peace in Vietnam circular, "Strike for Knowledge," March 1968 (Campus Unrest, 1965–1970, Box 1, SUNY-Buffalo Archives); SUNY-Buffalo Student Senate, Student Senate Statement on the War and the Draft, March 1968 (Campus Unrest, 1965–1970, Box 1, SUNY-Buffalo Archives); SUNY-Buffalo Graduate Student Association, Reso-

lution of the Graduate Student Association on the Strike for Knowledge, March 1968 (Campus Unrest, 1965–1970, Box 1, SUNY-Buffalo Archives).

69. *Spectrum*, 8 March 1968, 16 August 1968, 24 February 1969; Michael Ferber and Staughton Lynd, *The Resistance* (Boston: Beacon Press, 1971), 193; Buffalo Nine Defense Committee, "Buffalo's Chicago, or When the Gloves Came off in Buffalo," 1968 (Campus Unrest, 1965–1970, Box 1, SUNY-Buffalo Archives); Buffalo Nine Defense Committee, "Nine Protesters Brutally Attacked Need Your Help," 1968 (Campus Unrest, 1965–1970, Box 1, SUNY-Buffalo Archives); Buffalo Nine Defense Committee Newsletter, "Draft Resistance and Symbolic Sanctuary," 1969 (Elizabeth Olmsted Smith Papers, Box 15, SUNY-Buffalo Archives).

70. Faulkner conversation; Powell, "Promoting the Decline of the Rising State," 69–70; *Spectrum*, 9 August 1968, 10 September 1968, 17 February 1969; Gross FBI File; Fischer FBI File; Buffalo Nine Defense Committee, "Nine Protestors Brutlly Attacked Need Your Help;" Buffalo Nine Defense Committee Newsletter, "Draft Resistance and Symbolic Sanctuary;" *Liberated Community News* (Buffalo, New York), 21 August 1968 (Campus Unrest, 1965–1970, Box 1, SUNY-Buffalo Archives).

71. *Spectrum*, 27 September 1968, 4 October 1968, 8 October 1968, 18 October 1968, 5 November 1968.

72. Ibid., 17 September 1968, 27 September 1968, 11 October 1968, 1 October 1968.

73. Ibid., 8 October 1968, 22 October 1968, 8 November 1968, 14 March 1969; *Liberated Community News*, 21 August 1968.

74. *Spectrum*, 22 October 1968; Barbara Probst Solomon, "Life in the Yellow Submarine: Buffalo's SUNY," *Harper's* 237 (October 1968): 96–102.

75. *Spectrum*, 21 February 1969, 3 March 1969; Joe Striker circular, "Where is Meyerson At?" 1969 (Campus Unrest, 1965–1970, Box 1, SUNY-Buffalo Archives).

76. *Spectrum*, 19 February 1969, 21 February 1969, 24 February 1969.

77. Ibid., 26 February 1969, 3 March 1969, 21 March 1969, 11 April 1969, 27 June 1969, 19 September 1969; Buffalo Nine Defense Committee Press Release, 1 March 1969 (Campus Unrest, 1965–1970, Box 1, SUNY-Buffalo Archives); Buffalo Nine Defense Committee, "Fact Sheet," 1969 (Campus Unrest, 1965–1970, Box 1, SUNY-Buffalo Archives); Buffalo Nine Defense Committee, "The Political Declaration of the Buffalo Nine: Non-cooperation with 'our' Government," 1969 (Campus Unrest, 1965–1970, Box 1, SUNY-Buffalo Archives); Buffalo Nine Defense Committee Newsletter, "Draft Resistance and Symbolic Sanctuary."

78. *Spectrum*, 28 February 1969, 3 March 1969, 7 March 1969; Committee to Transform UB (SUNY-Buffalo SDS and YAWF), "Strike? The Decisions of the Mass Meeting," February 1969 (Campus Unrest, 1965–1970, Box 1, SUNY-Buffalo Archives); Stewart Edelstein, Acting Chairman of Graduate Student Association Executive Committee et al., "Open Letter to the University Community," March 1969 (Campus Unrest, 1965–1970, Box 1, SUNY-Buffalo Archives); SUNY-Buffalo Office of the vice president for Academic Development, Memorandum to all Department Heads, 3 March 1969 (Campus Unrest, 1965–1970, Box 1, SUNY-Buffalo Archives); Warren Bennis et al., Office of the vice president, Memorandum to the University Community, 10 March 1969 (Campus Unrest, 1965–1970, Box 1, SUNY-Buffalo Archives); SUNY-Buffalo Graduate Student Association and Student Association demands, "Strike?" 1969 (Campus Unrest, 1965–1970, Box 1, SUNY-Buffalo Archives,);

Col. John J. Herbert, Jr., professor of aerospace studies, SUNY-Buffalo, Open Letter to the Campus and Air Force ROTC Fact Sheet, 10 March 1969 (Campus Unrest, 1965–1970, Box 1, SUNY-Buffalo Archives).

79. Community for Real Change (SUNY-Buffalo SDS and YAWF) circular, "Let's Get the Military Off!" March 1969 (Campus Unrest, 1965–1970, Box 1, SUNY-Buffalo Archives); Community for Real Change circular, "A Call to Action," March 1969 (Campus Unrest, 1965–1970, Box 1, SUNY-Buffalo Archives); Community for Real Change circular, "Policy State of the Community for Real Change," March 1969 (Campus Unrest, 1965–1970, Box 1, SUNY-Buffalo Archives); *Spectrum*, 7 March 1969, 10 March 1969, 19 March 1969.

80. *Spectrum*, 24 March 1969, 26 March 1969, 18 April 1969, 7 May 1969; SUNY-Buffalo SDS circular, "Join to Fight the Injunction Now!" March 1969 (Campus Unrest, 1965–1970, Box 1, SUNY-Buffalo Archives).

81. Snell letter, 3 January 1988; *Spectrum*, 21 March 1969, 26 March 1969, 11 April 1969, 14 April 1969, 16 April 1969, 18 April 1969, 21 April 1969, 5 May 1969; SUNY-Buffalo president Martin Meyerson, Open Letter to the Campus, 18 April 1969 (Campus Unrest, 1965–1970, Box 1, SUNY-Buffalo Archives); SUNY-Buffalo president Martin Meyerson letter to the Executive Committee, Faculty Senate, 22 April 1969 (Campus Unrest, 1965–1970, Box 1, SUNY-Buffalo Archives); Dr. Robert J. Good, Department of Chemical Engineering, letter to Martin Meyerson, 24 March 1969 (Office of the President, Central Files, Research, Box 38, SUNY-Buffalo Archives); Dr. Paul Ehrlich letter to Martin Meyerson, 24 March 1969; Dr. James English, Dean, School of Denistry, letter to Martin Meyerson, 1 April 1969 (Office of the President, Central Files, Research, Box 38, SUNY-Buffalo Archives); Dr. Robert E. Mates letter to Martin Meyerson, 20 March 1969; Dr. William J. Wallbesser letter to Martin Meyerson, 22 March 1969; Internal SUNY-Buffalo administration memorandum on security precautions and use of police force, 3 April 1969 (Office of the President, Central Files, Administration, Box 8, SUNY-Buffalo Archives).

82. Sale, *SDS*, 530; *Spectrum*, 17 March 1969, 24 March 1969, 26 March 1969, 16 April 1969, 13 June 1969, 3 July 1969; State of New York, 6610–A in Assembly, February 18, 1969, An Act, Article 129–A, Regulation by Colleges of Conduct on Campus and Other College Property Used for Educational Purposes (Campus Unrest, 1965–1970, Box 1, SUNY-Buffalo Archives); Gonzalez, State Laws of 1969 Dealing with Student Unrest.

83. *Spectrum*, 19 September 1969, 22 September 1969, 24 September 1969, 26 September 1969, 6 October 1969, 8 October 1969, 24 October 1969.

84. *Spectrum*, 29 September 1969, 3 October 1969, 10 October 1969, 13 October 1969, 17 October 1969, 20 October 1969, 22 October 1969, 24 October 1969, 3 November 1969, 12 November 1969.

85. Ibid., 19 September 1969, 15 October 1969; Haynie interview.

86. *Spectrum*, 12 September 1969, 17 October 1969, 20 October 1969, 31 October 1969, 5 December 1969.

87. Ibid., 13 October 1969, 31 October 1969, 24 November 1969.

88. Ibid., 31 October 1969, 3 November 1969, 7 November 1969; Radical Faculty Caucus, "Abolish ROTC at SUNYAB: Statement of the Radical Faculty," 3 November 1969 (Campus Unrest, 1965–1970, Box 1, SUNY-Buffalo Archives); Radical Faculty Caucus, "Substitute Motion on the Moratorium," 11 November 1969; SUNY-Buffalo Moratorium leaflet, October 1969, with accompanying note from Newton Garver to

Acting President Peter Regan (Office of the President, Administration, Central Files, Box 8, SUNY-Buffalo Archives); Dr. Ronald Rennie letter to Acting President Peter Regan, 20 October 1969.

89. *Spectrum,* 7 November 1969, 12 November 1969; SUNY-Buffalo provost Rollo Handy, letter to Morris L. Horowitz (October 1969 Moratorium organizer), president, University Union Activities Board, 12 October 1969 (Office of the President, Administration, Central Files, Box 8, SUNY-Buffalo Archives); Morris L. Horowitz letter to Dr. Peter Regan, 10 October 1969 (Office of the President, Administration, Central Files, Box 8, SUNY-Buffalo Archives); Theodore Friend, office of assistant to the president, memorandum to Dr. Warren Bennis, 29 October 1969 (Office of the President, Administration, Central Files, Box 8, SUNY-Buffalo Archives); SUNY-Buffalo Acting President Peter F. Regan, Open Letter to Members of the University Community, 10 November 1969 (Campus Unrest, 1965–1969, Box 2, SUNY-Buffalo Archives); Acting President Peter Regan, bulletin and memorandum to university community, 10 November 1969 (Campus Unrest, 1965–1969, Box 2, SUNY-Buffalo Archives); acting president Peter Regan bulletin to the university community, 4 December 1969 (Campus Unrest, 1965–1969, Box 2, SUNY-Buffalo Archives).

90. *Spectrum,* 7 November 1969; 14 November 1969, 17 November 1969, 17 December 1969; *Griffin,* 21 March 1969, 23 April 1969, 18 September 1969; anonymous hate letter to Acting President Regan, 16 October 1969 (Office of the President, Administration, Central Files, Box 8, SUNY-Buffalo Archives); see *Buffalo Marijuana Review* (Buffalo, New York), 1969–1971 (Underground Newspaper Collection on Microfilm, University of Pittsburgh Library); *Undercurrent* (Buffalo, New York), 1969–1972 (Underground Newspaper Collection on Microfilm, University of Pittsburgh Library).

91. Joseph Jackson conversation; Gibson conversation; *Daily Kent Stater,* 9 February 1968, 23 February 1969, 9 April 1968, 8 May 1968.

92. Joseph Jackson conversation; Gibson conversation; *Daily Kent Stater,* 17 January 1968, 23 January 1968, 22 February 1968, 23 February 1968, 8 May 1968.

93. Joseph Jackson conversation; Gibson conversation; *Daily Kent Stater,* 30 April 1968, 7 May 1968.

94. Joseph Jackson conversation; Gibson conversation; Mim Jackson interview; *Daily Kent Stater,* 7 May 1968, 8 May 1968.

95. Sale, *SDS,* 3, 490, 577–78; Gitlin, *The Sixties,* 386–87; Gibson conversation; Powrie KSU SDS Reunion; Emmer KSU SDS Reunion; Eszterhas and Roberts, *13 Seconds,* 58; James A. Michener, *Kent State: What Happened and Why* (New York: Ballantine Books, 1971), 76–77; Hearings before the Committee on Internal Security, Ninety-First Congress, First Session, June 24 and 25, 1969, *Investigation of Students for a Democratic Society, Part 2, Kent State University* (Washington, D.C.: U.S. Government Printing Office, 1969). Michener's book must be used with care; activists insist that he deliberately misquoted them and listened too much to Kent's Republican civic leaders.

96. Grace conversation; Ken Hammond, "History Lesson: Kent State, A Participant's Memoir," March 1974 (May 4th Collection, Box 21, KSU Archives); Viorst, *Fire in the Streets,* 510; Eszterhas and Roberts, *13 Seconds,* 45–69.

97. Grace conversation; Viorst, *Fire in the Streets,* 511–12.

98. Grace conversation; Eszterhas and Roberts, *13 Seconds,* 48–49; Michener, *Kent State,* 92–93.

99. KSU SDS, *Maggie's Farm* (Kent, Ohio), 12 November 1968 (May 4th Collection, Box 20, KSU Archives).

100. *Daily Kent Stater,* 14 November 1968; *Maggie's Farm,* 12 November 1968.

101. Gibson conversation; *Daily Kent Stater,* 14 November 1968.

102. KSU SDS leaflet, "I Read the News Today, Oh Boy: 250 Black Students Exiled from KSU," November 1968 (May 4th Collection, Box 20, KSU Archives); KSU SDS leaflet, "Say Yes to Boycott! Say No to Business as Usual," November 1968 (May 4th Collection, Box 21, KSU Archives); Robert I. White, KSU Office of the President, Special Bulletin to all Faculty and Staff, 18 November 1968 (May 4th Collection, Box 20, KSU Archives); Robert I. White, KSU Office of the President, Special Bulletin to All Faculty and Staff, 25 November 1968 (May 4th Collection, KSU Archives); Robert E. Matson, Dean of Students Office, press release, 18 November 1968 (May 4th Collection, Box 20, KSU Archives).

103. Hammond, "History Lesson"; Grace conversation; Viorst, *Fire in the Streets,* 512–13; Eszterhas and Roberts, *13 Seconds,* 57; *New Left Notes,* 11 December 1968; *Daily Kent Stater,* 1 November 1968, 5 November 1968, 14 November 1968, 21 November 1968; KSU Faculty Senate, Statement by the University Committee of the University Faculty Senate, 22 November 1968 (May 4th Collection, Box 21, KSU Archives); KSU Faculty Senate, University Faculty Senate Minutes, 19 December 1968 (May 4th Collection, Box 21, KSU Archives); Pyle interview.

104. Whitaker interview; Grace conversation; Powrie KSU SDS Reunion; KSU SDS, "Who Rules Kent?" (May 4th Collection, Box 20, KSU Archives); KSU SDS, "SDS Draft Committee," December 1968 (May 4th Collection, Box 21, KSU Archives); KSU SDS leaflet, "Kent Free University," no date (May 4th Collection, Box 21, KSU Archives); Sale, *SDS,* 489; Gibson conversation; *Daily Kent Stater,* 8 October 1968, 11 October 1968.

105. Grace conversation; Viorst, *Fire in the Streets,* 513–15; Sale, *SDS,* 517.

106. Grace conversation; Viorst, *Fire in the Streets,* 515–16.

107. Grace conversation; Pyle interview; Powrie KSU SDS Reunion; KSU SDS leaflet, "20 Years of Schooling and They Put You on the Day Shift," no date (May 4th Collection, Box 20, KSU Archives); *Maggie's Farm,* printing press plates on display at the Kent State SDS Reunion, Kent, Ohio, 5 May 1989.

108. Grace conversation; Emmer KSU SDS Reunion; Powrie KSU SDS Reunion; Pyle conversation; Gibson interview; Viorst, *Fire in the Streets,* 516–18; *Big US,* 26 April 1969; *Daily Kent Stater,* 6 April 1969, 9 April 1969, 10 April 1969; KSU SDS leaflet, "Liquid Crystals Chained Shut!" Spring 1969 (May 4th Collection, Box 21, KSU Archives); KSU SDS leaflet, "Abolish Liberalism!" Spring 1969 (May 4th Collection, Box 20, KSU Archives); KSU SDS position paper, "Now Is the Time of the Furnaces, and Only Light Should be Seen," Spring 1969 (May 4th Collection, Box 20, KSU Archives).

109. *New Left Notes,* 24 April 1969; Sale, *SDS,* 555; KSU SDS leaflet, "Open it Up, or Shut it Down!" 15 April 1969 (May 4th Collection, Box 21, KSU Archives); Bills, *Kent State, May 4,* 100–104; KSU SDS leaflet, "Kent Thugs," Spring 1969 (May 4th Collection, Box 20, KSU Archives); Grace conversation; Pyle interview; Emmer KSU SDS Reunion; Powrie KSU SDS Reunion; Viorst, *Fire in the Streets,* 516–18.

110. *Daily Kent Stater,* 6 April 1969; Powrie KSU SDS Reunion; Emmer KSU SDS Reunion; Grace interview; Dr. Gene Wenninger, Department of Sociology and Anthropology, Memorandum to All Staff, 21 April 1969 (May 4th Collection, Box 20,

KSU Archives); Executive Committee of the Kent State Chapter, American Association of University Professors, Memorandum to Kent State University Community, 21 April 1969 (May 4th Collection, Box 20, KSU Archives).

111. Pyle interview; Whitaker interview; Gibson conversation; *Daily Kent Stater*, 15 May 1969, 16 May 1969, 21 May 1969, 22 May 1969; Hammond, "History Lesson"; Committee of the Concerned Citizens of Kent State leaflet, "Rally," Spring 1969 (May 4th Collection, Box 20, KSU Archives); Committee of the Concerned Citizens of Kent State leaflet, "Seek the Truth! Act on Your Conscience!" Spring 1969 (May 4th Collection, Box 20, KSU Archives); KSU SDS leaflet, "Mind F.U.C.K*" May 1969 (May 4th Collection, Box 20, KSU Archives); Wenninger, Memorandum to All Staff, 21 April 1969.

112. House Internal Security Committee, *Investigation of Students for a Democratic Society, Part 2, Kent State University*, 477–568.

113. Sale, *SDS*, 558–74; Emmer KSU SDS Reunion; Powrie KSU SDS Reunion; Richard Oestreicher, MSU SDS, Pittsburgh, Penn., interview with author, 11 January 1989.

114. Sale, *SDS*, 576, 580–83, 603, 648; *Daily Kent Stater*, 10 October 1969, 23 October 1969; *Daily Collegian*, 14 August 1969; Marks KSU SDS Reunion.

115. Hammond, "History Lesson"; Powrie KSU SDS Reunion; Pyle interview; Gibson conversation; Eszterhas and Roberts, *13 Seconds*, 68–69.

116. Pyle interview; *Daily Kent Stater*, 9 October 1969, 10 October 1969, 16 October 1969, 31 October 1969, 11 November 1969, 12 November 1969, 13 November 1969, 14 November 1969, 5 December 1969; Pyle FBI File.

117. *Daily Kent Stater*, 15 May 1969, 20 May 1969, 14 October 1969, 16 October 1969, 14 November 1969, 20 November 1969, 14 January 1970; [Frank Frisina] Anti-SDS scare circulars, no title, 1969 (May 4th Collection, Box 21, KSU Archives); Committee of Concerned Citizens of Kent State, "Seek the Truth! Act on Your Conscience!" (May 4th Collection, Box 20, KSU Archives): Concerned Students for Ohlweiler-Goodwin (Committee of Concerned Citizens of Kent State) circular, "Appeal to Justice!" 1969 (May 4th Collection, Box 20, KSU Archives); Dr. Gene Wenninger, Department of Sociology and Anthropology, Memorandum to All Staff, Graduate Assistants, etc., on Referendum, 24 April 1969 (May 4th Collection, Box 20, KSU Archives); Eszterhas and Roberts, *13 Seconds*, 67; Chief Roy Thompson, Security Officer Schwartzmiller, Judge Robert Kent et al., "Recap of Meeting of Twinlakes Country Club, May 7, 1969" (May 4th Collection, Box 21, KSU Archives).

118. *Daily Kent Stater*, 3 October 1969, 7 October 1969, 8 October 1969, 14 October 1969, 17 October 1969, 29 October 1969, 30 October 1969, 18 November 1969; KSU NUC leaflet, "New University Conference," no date, spring 1969 (May 4th Collection, Box 21, KSU Archives); KSU NUC leaflet, "Keepers of the Faith," 1969 (May 4th Collection, Box 21, KSU Archives).

119. *Spectrum*, 10 December 1969; *Daily Kent Stater*, 15 May 1969, 20 May 1969, 14 January 1970; Eszterhas and Roberts, *13 Seconds*, 100–103, 136–44.

6. "Tin Soldiers and Nixon's Coming"

1. Fish conversation, 16 August 1988; Larrowe interview; Hixson interview; Kibbey conversation; *State News*, 19 February 1970; A Song from the Weather Ma-

chine, "Trash Together," 1969 (Student Radicalism Collection, MSU Special Collections).

2. Bennis, *The Leaning Ivory Tower*, 88–89; James Beckley, Graduate Student, State University of New York at Buffalo, Statement of Events of 25 February 1970 (Campus Unrest, 1965–1970, Box 2, SUNY-Buffalo Archives).

3. Beckley, Statement of Events of 25 February 1970; Haynie interview; *Spectrum*, 26 February 1970, 15 March 1970.

4. *Spectrum*, 20 February 1970, 27 February 1970, 10 March 1970; SUNY-Buffalo Press Packet, "Summary of Campus Security Activities, February 25, 1970" (Campus Unrest, 1965–1970, Box 2, SUNY-Buffalo Archives); State University of New York at Buffalo vs. Terry Keegan et al., Order to Show Cause with Temporary Restraining Order, 5 March 1970 (Campus Unrest, 1965–1970, Box 2, SUNY-Buffalo Archives); Transcript of Remarks Made by Dr. Peter F. Regan, acting president, State University of New York at Buffalo, over WBEN-TV, Sunday, March 1, 1970 (Campus Unrest, 1965–1970, Box 2, SUNY-Buffalo Archives).

5. Bennis, *The Leaning Ivory Tower*, 89–95; *Spectrum*, 30 January 1970, 4 February 1970, 27 February 1970; Warren G. Bennis, acting executive vice president, letter of resignation addressed to Acting President Peter F. Regan, 9 March 1970 (Campus Unrest, 1965–1970, Box 2, SUNY-Buffalo Archives).

6. *Spectrum*, 2 March 1970, 3 March 1970, 4 March 1970, 6 March 1970, 9 March 1970, 10 March 1970, 11 March 1970; SUNY-Buffalo Faculty of Engineering and Applied Sciences, Referendum Concerning Campus Demands, 11 March 1970 (Campus Unrest, 1965–1970, Box 2, SUNY-Buffalo Archives); Open Meeting of Faculty, Students and Staff, Department of Biology, SUNY-Buffalo, Friday, March 6, 1970 (Campus Unrest, 1965–1970, Box 2, SUNY-Buffalo Archives); Peter F. Regan, acting president, letter to commissioner Frank N. Felicetta, Police Department, City of Buffalo, Buffalo, New York, 7 March 1970 (Campus Unrest, 1965–1970, Box 2, SUNY-Buffalo Archives); SUNY-Buffalo Acting President Peter F. Regan, Notice of Suspension, 5 March 1970 (Campus Unrest, 1965–1970, Box 2, SUNY-Buffalo Archives); Acting President Peter F. Regan, Open letter to Colleagues, 8 March 1970 (Campus Unrest-1965–1970, Box 2, SUNY-Buffalo Archives).

7. *Spectrum*, 9 March 1970, 13 March 1970; SUNY-Buffalo, The Faculty-Student Campus Peace Patrol circular, March 1970 (Campus Unrest, 1965–1970, Box 2, SUNY-Buffalo Archives).

8. *Spectrum*, 6 March 1970, 13 March 1970, 16 March 1970; SUNY-Buffalo Graduate-Undergraduate Student Judiciary, Order for a Permanent Injunction against the SUNY-Buffalo administration, 17 March 1970 (Campus Unrest, 1965–1970, Box 2, SUNY-Buffalo Archives); John M. Carter, vice president for alumni affairs, letter to Acting President Peter F. Regan, 12 March 1970 (Office of the President, Central Files, Administration, Box 8, SUNY-Buffalo Archives).

9. *Spectrum*, 16 March 1970; Haynie interview; Bennis, *The Leaning Ivory Tower*, 27.

10. *Spectrum*, 16 March 1970; Haynie interview.

11. Erie County, New York, Grand Jury Subpeona issued to Peter F. Regan, acting president of the State University of New York at Buffalo, 1 April 1970 (Office of the President, Central Files, Administration, Box 8, SUNY-Buffalo Archives); *Spectrum*, 3 April 1970, 6 April 1970, 10 April 1970, 15 April 1970, 20 April 1970; Mrs. Joseph Lang, Buffalo community resident, letter and enclosed antiriot petition addressed to

Dr. Peter Regan, 4 April 1970 (Office of the President, Central Files, Administration, Box 8, SUNY-Buffalo Archives).

12. Farley conversation; *Daily Collegian*, 10 February 1970, 13 February 1970, 17 February 1970, 19 February 1970, 20 February 1970.

13. Farley conversation; Petras conversation; *Daily Collegian*, 16 January 1970, 20 January 1970, 22 January 1970, 18 February 1970, 20 February 1970.

14. Petras conversation; *Daily Collegian*, 2 April 1970, 9 April 1970, 10 April 1970, 14 April 1970, 15 April 1970, 16 April 1970, 29 September 1970.

15. Petras conversation; *Daily Collegian*, 16 April 1970, 17 April 1970, 29 September 1970.

16. Petras conversation; *Daily Collegian*, 17 April 1970, 18 April 1970, 21 April 1970, 22 April 1970.

17. *Daily Collegian*, 22 April 1970, 23 April 1970, 24 April 1970, 28 April 1970.

18. Pam Farley, letter to the head of the English department describing her involvement with the student strike committee, April 1970 (Pam Farley Personal Papers—copy in author's possession); James A. Rhodes, dean of student affairs office, Penn State, letter of suspension to Geoffrey Sill, 29 April 1970 (Pam Farley Personal Papers—copy in author's possession); *Daily Collegian*, 14 April 1970, 15 April 1970, 17 April 1970, 18 April 1970, 21 April 1970, 22 April 1970, 23 April 1970, 28 October 1970, 18 November 1970.

19. Penn State student petition praising the state police and denouncing antiwar students, 16 April 1970 (Student Activism Records, Box 1, PSU Library). The social characteristics of the petition signers were garnered from the appropriate PSU student directories.

20. *US News and World Report* 68 (29 June 1970): 20–22; *State News*, 29 April 1970, 30 April 1970.

21. May 4th Task Force, A Chronology—Kent, Ohio, May 1–4, 1970, n.d. (May 4th Collection, Box 20, KSU Archives); LeRoy M. Satrom, mayor, City of Kent, letter to commander of troops, Ohio National Guard, 2 May 1970 (May 4th Collection, Box 21, KSU Archives); LeRoy M. Satrom, mayor, City of Kent, Proclamation of Civil Emergency, 2 May 1970 (May 4th Collection, Box 21, KSU Archives); Michener, *Kent State*, 47–63.

22. Michener, *Kent State*, 125–28, 174–98; A Chronology—Kent, Ohio, May 1–4, 1970.

23. Hammond, "History Lesson"; Bills, *Kent State, May 4*, 82–91; Pyle interview; *Daily Kent Stater*, 15 April 1970, 16 April 1970.

24. Gibson conversation; Bills, *Kent State, May 4*, 82–91.

25. A Chronology—Kent, Ohio, May 1–4, 1970; Viorst, *Fire in the Streets*, 532–34; Pyle interview; Michener, *Kent State*, 245–51.

26. Pyle interview; Hammond, "History Lesson." For White's behavior before, during, and immediately after the shootings, see his testimony in, President [Scranton] Commission on Campus Unrest, *Report*, (Washington, D.C.: U.S. Government Printing Office, 1970).

27. A Chronology—Kent, Ohio, May 1–4, 1970; Hammond, "History Lesson"; Viorst, *Fire in the Streets*, 534–37; Joan Morrison and Robert K. Morrison, eds., *From Camelot to Kent State: The Sixties Experience in the Words of Those Who Lived It* (New York: New York Times Books, 1987), 329–35; Lewis interview; Bills, *Kent State, May 4*, 100–104.

28. A Chronology—Kent, Ohio, May 1–4, 1970; Hammond, "History Lesson"; Viorst, *Fire in the Streets*, 537–39; Morrison and Morrison, *From Camelot to Kent State*, 329–35; Eszterhas and Roberts, *13 Seconds*, 161–64.

29. A Chronology—Kent, Ohio, May 1–4, 1970; Hammond, "History Lesson"; Mim Jackson interview; Eszterhas and Roberts, *13 Seconds*, 165–76.

30. Hayden, *Reunion*, 501, 505; Sale, *SDS*, 479, 636; *Spectrum*, 6 May 1970, 8 May 1970; Peter F. Regan, SUNY-Buffalo acting president, letter to Frank N. Felicetta, commissioner, Buffalo Police Department, 13 May 1970 (Office of the President, Central Files, Administration, SUNY-Buffalo Archives).

31. *Daily Collegian*, 5 May 1970, 6 May 1970, 7 May 1970; Pyle FBI File.

32. *Daily Collegian*, 5 May 1970, 6 May 1970, 7 May 1970, 13 May 1970, 22 May 1970, 29 September 1970; Petras conversation; Farley conversation.

33. *Daily Collegian*, 8 May 1970, 9 May 1970, 14 May 1970, 21 May 1970, 22 May 1970.

34. *State News*, 5 May 1970, 6 May 1970.

35. Kibbey conversation; Shapiro interview; ASMSU Minutes, May 5, 1970; *Bogue Street Bridge*, Summer Orientation Issue, 1970; *State News*, 5 May 1970.

36. *Bogue Street Bridge*, Summer Orientation Issue, 1970; Larrowe interview; Pollack conversation; *State News*, 7 May 1970, 8 May 1970.

37. Committee to Abolish ROTC, "ROTC Sit-in Fact Sheet," 18 May 1970 (Student Radicalism Collection, MSU Special Collections); ASMSU Minutes, May 5, 1970; *State News*, 5 May 1970, 6 May 1970, 7 May 1970, 8 May 1970, 14 May 1970, 15 May 1970; Larrowe interview; Pollack conversation; Repas interview; John Masterson, MSU NUC, telephone conversation with author, 31 October 1983; MSU-SDS Worker Student Alliance, "The Meaning Behind the May 19th Bust," September 21, 1970 (Student Radicalism Collection, MSU Special Collections).

38. "MSU Omnibus Survey #2, 1970," 44, 55, 58, 59.

39. Lansing *State Journal*, 7 May 1970.

40. Richard Zinman, MSU conservative faculty member, interview with author, 18 October 1983; Michigan State University Office of the Registrar, *Student Enrollment, Spring, 1970*.

41. "Omnibus Survey #2," 44, 47; Pollack conversation.

42. "Omnibus Survey #2," 11–13, 19, 57; *Bogue Street Bridge*, Fall Orientation Issue, 1970.

43. Larrowe interview; Repas interview; Shapiro interview; Pollack conversation.

44. Hammond, "History Lesson"; Pyle interview; Sale, *SDS*, 638–39; Eszterhas and Roberts, *13 Seconds*, 189–211, 295–305; Michener, *Kent State*, 369–84, 389–423, 439–90; Kent State in Exile leaflets, Oberlin, Ohio, May 1970 (Christopher Densmore Personal Papers—copies in author's possession).

45. Michener, *Kent State*, 475–96; *Spectrum*, 30 September 1970, 21 October 1970, 26 October 1970, 26 October 1970, 28 October 1970; *Daily Collegian*, 17 October 1970, 21 October 1970.

46. Grace conversation; Pyle interview; Gibson conversation; Bills, *Kent State, May 4*, 92–99.

47. Hammond, "History Lesson"; Bills, *Kent State, May 4*, 92–99; Walsh conversation; Kent Liberation Front and Yippie leaflet, "Fight for Change, Support the Demands," Fall 1970 (May 4th Collection, Box 21, KSU Archives); KSU Yippie leaflet, "The Price of Liberty Is Less than the Cost of Oppression," Fall 1970 (May 4th

Collection, Box 20, KSU Archives); Kent State president Robert I. White, KSU Position Paper, October 1970 (May 4th Collection, Box 20, KSU Archives); Kent Liberation Front circular on Portage County Grand Jury, Fall 1970 (May 4th Collection, Box 21, KSU Archives).

Epilogue

1. Sue Sattel letter; Shapiro interview; Grathwohl, *Bringing down America*.

2. Farley conversation; *Daily Collegian*, 5 February 1970, 25 June 1970, 9 July 1970, 28 September 1970, 29 September 1970, 30 September 1970, 3 October 1970, 15 October 1970, 10 November 1970, 11 November 1970, 12 November 1970, 17 November 1970.

3. *Daily Collegian*, 2 September 1971; *Henderson Station*, 15 July 1971, 6 October 1971, 19 October 1971, 25 January 1972, 8 February 1972, 5 April 1972.

4. *Daily Collegian*, 11 February 1971, 16 April 1971, 13 October 1971, 1 November 1971; *Henderson Station*, 19 October 1971.

5. *Henderson Station*, 6 October 1971, 19 October 1971, 3 November 1971, 25 January 1972, 8 February 1972, 5 April 1972; *Daily Collegian*, 13 February 1971, 17 February 1971, 19 February 1971, 15 November 1971; Pam Farley, Violence Workshop Report of Discussion: Preliminary Draft, 1971 (Pam Farley Personal Papers—copy in author's possession); Pam Farley, Nixon's New Plans for the War, 1971 (Pam Farley Personal Papers—copy in author's possession); Farley conversation.

6. *Daily Collegian*, 9 February 1971, 11 February 1971, 12 February 1971, 13 February 1971, 16 April 1971, 20 April 1971, 28 April 1971, 6 May 1971, 7 May 1971, 8 May 1971, 14 May 1971, 2 September 1971; *Henderson Station*, 6 October 1971; Coalition for Peace, Fact Sheet on Protest Rally on April 19, 1971 (PSU Student Activism Records, Box 1, PSU Library); David A. Dankovic et al., Coalition for Peace, letter to Dean Russell E. Larson, 19 April 1971 (PSU Student Activism Records, Box 1, PSU Library).

7. *State News*, 30 April 1971, 3 May 1971, 6 May 1971.

8. Larrowe interview; Pollack conversation; Sue Korlan, MSU antiwar student, East Lansing, Mich., interview with author, 14 February 1984.

9. *Spectrum*, 23 September 1970, 30 September 1970, 25 June 1971, 2 July 1971, 5 November 1971, 23 February 1972; Faulkner conversation; Fischer FBI File; Bruce Beyer FBI File (Elwin Powell Personal Papers—notes from file in author's possession).

10. Haynie interview; *Spectrum*, 10 February 1971, 12 February 1971, 4 October 1971, 8 October 1971, 22 October 1971, 18 February 1971, 3 March 1972, 8 March 1972.

11. *Spectrum*, 29 January 1971, 1 February 1971, 24 February 1971, 5 May 1971, 7 May 1971, 15 November 1971.

12. Gail Graham, SUNY-Buffalo VVAW, letter to author, 22 January 1988; *Buffalo Courier-Express* (Buffalo, New York), 27 February 1972; *Spectrum*, 29 October 1971; *Column Left, March!* (Buffalo, New York), 1971 (Gail Graham Personal Papers—copy in author's possession). *Column Left, March!* was the publication of the SUNY-Buffalo VVAW.

13. Kent State Student Government handout, "Bleeding and Shock," 26 April 1971 (May 4th Collection, Box 20, KSU Archives); Kent State Student Government

handout, "Tear Gas and Mace," 26 April 1971 (May 4th Collection, Box 20, KSU Archives); Craig Morgan, president of the KSU student government, "Memorial to the Slain Students of Kent State University," 3 May 1971 (May 4th Collection, Box 20, KSU Archives); Kent May Day Coalition, "Open Kent!" May 1971 (May 4th Collection, Box 21, KSU Archives); Kent May Day Coalition, "May 4th Revival!" May 1971 (May 4th Collection, Box 21, KSU Archives); Kent May Day Coalition, "The Hour's Getting Late," May 1971 (May 4th Collection, Box 21, KSU Archives); KSU Yippies, "A Strong Wind Blows in Kent!" May 1971 (May 4th Collection, Box 20, KSU Archives); KSU administration position paper, "Memorial Observance," May 1971 (May 4th Collection, Box 20, KSU Archives); Paul Kriese, "Committee for Non-Violence Activities for Water Street Nights," 9 June 1971 (Mary Vincent Personal Papers—copy in author's possession); Paul Kriese, Kent Friends Meeting, report on activities, winter and spring quarters, August 1971 (Mary Vincent Personal Papers—copy in author's possession); Rev. Tom Taggart, Campus United Christian Fellowship, account of Kent police violence, May 1971 (Mary Vincent Personal Papers—copy in author's possession); KSU student government, "Keeping Kent Open," May 1971 (Mary Vincent Personal Papers—copy in author's possession); Pyle interview.

14. Thomas Lough letter to Jon Krosnick, 19 November 1975 (May 4th Collection, Box 21, KSU Archives); *Spectrum*, 10 December 1971; KSU Yippies, *Stump City* (Kent, Ohio), 1971 (May 4th Collection, Box 20, KSU Archives); Craig Morgan, Press Release, 15 March 1971 (Mary Vincent Personal Papers—copy in author's possession); U.S. Senator Stephen M. Young letter to Ohio Adjutant General Dana L. Stewart, 16 August 1971 (May 4th Collection, Box 20, KSU Archives).

15. *State News*, 20 April 1972, 21 April 1972, 24 April 1972, 5 May 1972; Griffiths conversation; Jondahl interview; East Lansing City Council, "A Resolution Concerning the War in Southeast Asia," 18 April 1972 (George Griffiths Personal Papers—copy in author's possession).

16. Korlan interview; Hixson interview; *State News*, 10 May 1972; Jerry M. Lewis and Raymond J. Adamek, "Anti-ROTC Sit-in: A Sociological Analysis," *Sociological Quarterly* 15 (Autumn 1974): 542–47; *Spectrum*, 21 April 1972, 24 April 1972, 26 April 1972.

17. Korlan interview; Terry Heineman, Lansing VVAW, Seattle, Wash., interview with author, 22 December 1987.

18. Korlan interview; *State News*, 10 May 1972.

19. *Daily Collegian*, 3 May 1972, 5 May 1972, 8 May 1972, 10 May 1972, 11 May 1972, 12 May 1972, 19 May 1972; Coalition for Peace, "May 4—Schedule of Events," 4 May 1972 (Student Activism Records, Box 1, PSU Library); Pennsylvania State University Department of Public Information, "Chronology of May 1972 Events," May 1972 (Student Activism Records, Box 1, PSU Library).

20. "Chronology of May 1972 Events;" Richard G. Cunningham, "Information Statement on the Ordnance Research Laboratory," 15 May 1972 (Student Activism Records, Box 1, PSU Library); *Henderson Station*, December 1972, March 1972; *Daily Collegian*, 2 May 1972, 16 May 1972, 17 May 1972, 18 May 1972, 30 June 1972; Bennett interview.

21. The Buffalo, "Statement of The Buffalo," 1971 (Elizabeth Olmsted Smith Papers, Box 15, SUNY-Buffalo Archives); *Spectrum*, 1 November 1971, 19 November

1971; *Griffin,* 17 March 1971, 17 September 1971, 19 November 1971, 18 February 1972.

    22. Considine interview; Doyle interview; *Griffin,* 18 February 1972.

    23. *Spectrum,* 24 April 1972, 28 April 1972; Considine interview; Doyle interview.

    24. *Spectrum,* 2 June 1972; Considine interview; Doyle interview.

Bibliography

Primary

Manuscript Collections
Anderson, James. Papers. Author's files, Lancaster, Ohio.
Bennett, Thomas. Papers. Author's files, Lancaster, Ohio.
Buckley, Neil. Papers. Historical Collections and Labor Archives, Pennsylvania State University Library, State College, Pennsylvania.
Densmore, Christopher. Papers. Author's files, Lancaster, Ohio.
Farley, Pam. Papers. Author's files, Lancaster, Ohio.
Ferency, Zolton. Papers. Author's files, Lancaster, Ohio.
Fish, George. Papers. Author's files, Lancaster, Ohio.
Garrett, Jan. Papers. Author's files, Lancaster, Ohio.
Graham, Gail. Papers. Author's files, Lancaster, Ohio.
Griffiths, George. Papers. Author's files, Lancaster, Ohio.
Hannah, John A. Papers. Michigan State University Archives, East Lansing, Michigan.
Hays, Samuel P. Papers. University of Pittsburgh Archives, Pittsburgh, Pennsylvania.
Hixson, William. Papers. Author's files, Lancaster, Ohio.
Jackson, Sidney. Papers. Kent State University Archives, Kent, Ohio.
Jondahl, Lynn. Papers. Author's files, Lancaster, Ohio.
May 4th Collection. Kent State University Archives, Kent, Ohio.
Michigan State University Student Radicalism Collection.
Michigan State University Special Collections, Michigan State University Library, East Lansing, Michigan.
Michigan State University Vietnam Project Papers. Michigan State University Archives, East Lansing, Michigan.
O'Connor, Richard. Papers. Author's files, Lancaster, Ohio.
Office of the Chancellor/President, Central Files, Permanent Files, 1938–1969. State University of New York-Buffalo Archives, Buffalo, New York.
Office of the President, Central Files, Administration. State University of New York-Buffalo Archives, Buffalo, New York.

Office of the President, Central Files, Research. State University of New York-Buffalo Archives, Buffalo, New York.
Pennsylvania State University Student Activism Records. Penn State Room, Pattee Library, Penn State University, State College, Pennsylvania.
Pohl, Keith. Papers. Author's files, Lancaster, Ohio.
Powell, Elwin. Papers. Author's files, Lancaster, Ohio.
Pyle, Andy. Author's files, Lancaster, Ohio.
Repas, Robert. Papers. Author's files, Lancaster, Ohio.
Skocpol, William. Papers. Author's files, Lancaster, Ohio.
Smith, Elizabeth Olmsted. Papers. State University of New York-Buffalo Archives, Buffalo, New York.
State University of New York-Buffalo Campus Unrest Records, 1965–1970. State University of New York-Buffalo Archives, Buffalo, New York.
Thormeyer, Carl. Papers. Author's files, Lancaster, Ohio.
Vincent, Mary. Papers. Author's files, Lancaster, Ohio.
Waltzer, Kenneth. Papers. Author's files, Lancaster, Ohio.

Interviews
Anderson, James. Interview with author. East Lansing, Michigan, 7 November 1983.
Bennett, Thomas. Interview with author. Pittsburgh, Pennsylvania, 25 March 1989.
Bivins, Mary. Interview with author. East Lansing, Michigan, 4 October 1983.
Considine, Maureen. Interview with author. Buffalo, New York, 26 August 1988.
Creegan, James. Telephone conversation with author, 11 July 1988.
Davidson, Carl. Telephone conversation with author, 6 May 1988.
Doyle, Vincent. Interview with author. Buffalo, New York, 26 August 1988.
Farley, Pam. Telephone conversation with author, 3 October 1988.
Faulkner, Lawrence. Telephone conversation with author, 25 May 1988.
Fish, George. Telephone conversations with author, 16 August 1988, 16 March 1989, 3 September 1989.
Garskoff, Bertram. Telephone conversation with author, 5 November 1988.
Gibson, Ruth. Telephone conversation with author, 4 February 1989.
Grace, Tom. Telephone conversation with author, 3 March 1989.
Greer, Thomas. Interview with author. East Lansing, Michigan, 13 October 1983.
Griffiths, George. Telephone conversation with author, 15 October 1983.
Haynie, Charlie. Interview with author. Buffalo, New York, 26 August 1988.
Heineman, Terry. Interview with author. Seattle, Washington, 22 December 1987.
Hixson, William. Interview with author. East Lansing, Michigan, 4 April 1984.
Jackson, Joseph. Telephone conversation with author, 25 September 1989.
Jackson, Mim. Interview with author. Kent, Ohio, 7 May 1989.
Jondahl, Lynn. Interview with author. Lansing, Michigan, 10 November 1983.
Kibbey, Rick. Telephone conversation with author, 21 November 1983.
Korlan, Sue. Interview with author. East Lansing, Michigan, 14 February 1984.
Lack, Lawrence. Telephone conversation with author, 17 August 1988.
Larrowe, Charles. Interview with author. East Lansing, Michigan, 17 November 1983.
Lewis, Robert. Interview with author. Kent, Ohio, 6 May 1989.
Oestreicher, Richard. Interview with author. Pittsburgh, Pennsylvania, 11 January 1989.
Masterson, John. Telephone conversation with author, 31 October 1983.

Oglesby, Carl. Interview with author. Kent, Ohio, 5 May 1989.

Petras, James. Telephone conversation with author, 7 July 1989.

Pohl, Keith. Interview with author. East Lansing, Michigan, 4 October 1983.

Pollack, Norman. Telephone conversation with author, 14 October 1983.

Pyle, Andy. Interview with author. Kent, Ohio, 5 May 1989.

Repas, Robert. Interview with author. East Lansing, Michigan, 13 October 1983.

Shapiro, Beth. Interview with author. East Lansing, Michigan, 2 February 1984.

Walsh, Tony. Telephone conversation with author, 14 January 1989.

Whitaker, Melissa. Interview with author. Kent, Ohio, 6 May 1989.

Zinman, Richard. Interview with author. East Lansing, Michigan, 18 October 1983.

Correspondence

Andrews, James. Letter to author, 27 October 1987.

Badrich, Steve. Letters to author, 4 October 1987, 13 May 1988, 17 May 1988, 24 July 1988, 18 March 1989.

Boyer, Robert. Letters to author, 9 December 1987, 26 January 1988.

Branagan, Marcella. Letter to author, 28 July 1989.

Canon, Pete. Letter to author, 30 November 1983.

Casale, Ottavio. Letter to author, 2 February 1988.

Dante, Harris. Letter to author, 2 February 1988.

Duffy, John L. Letter to author, 30 September 1987.

Farley, Pam. Letter to author, 4 November 1988.

Frisch, Michael. Letters to author, 8 December 1987, 30 April 1989.

Garrett, Jan. Letter to author, 5 August 1988.

Graham, Gail. Letter to author, 22 January 1988.

Mader, Donald. Letter to author, 4 August 1988.

Powell, Elwin. Letters to author, 12 November 1987, 19 December 1987, 16 April 1988.

Rabinowitz, Victor. Letter to author, 25 February 1988.

Repas, Robert. Letters to author, 29 December 1987, 30 June 1988.

Samet, Tom. Letter to author, 12 July 1988.

Sattel, Jack. Letter to author, 5 July 1988.

Sattel, Sue. Letter to author, 10 July 1988.

Schrecker, Ellen. Letter to author, 7 October 1988.

Skocpol, William. Letter to author, 21 November 1983.

Snell, Fred. Letters to author, 3 January 1988, 8 March 1988.

Thormeyer, Carl. Letter to author, 25 October 1988.

Westby, David. Letter to author, 14 December 1987.

Willhelm, Sidney. Letter to author, 17 January 1988.

Winter, Dale. Letter to author, 28 January 1988.

Withall, John. Letter to author, 18 December 1987.

Speeches

Davidson, Carl. Formal Remarks Made at the Kent State University Students for a Democratic Society Reunion, Kent, Ohio, 6 May 1989.

Emmer, Howie. Formal Remarks Made at the Kent State University Students for a Democratic Society Reunion, Kent, Ohio, 5 May 1989.

Marks, Robin. Formal Remarks Made at the Kent State University Students for a Democratic Society Reunion, Kent, Ohio, 6 May 1989.
Oglesby, Carl. Formal Remarks Made at the Kent State University Students for a Democratic Society Reunion, Kent, Ohio, 6 May 1989.
Powrie, James. Formal Remarks Made at the Kent State University Students for a Democratic Society Reunion, Kent, Ohio, 5 May 1989.

Government Documents
Iowa State Government. *Iowa Official Register, 1959–1960*. Des Moines, Iowa: Iowa State Government, 1960.
———. *Iowa Official Register, 1963–1964*. Des Moines, Iowa: Iowa State Government, 1964.
Michigan State University Advisory Group. *Final Report Covering Activities of the MSU Vietnam Advisory Group for the Period May 20, 1955–June 30, 1962*. Saigon: Michigan State University Advisory Group, 1962.
Michigan State University Office of the Registrar. *Budget for Fiscal Year 1966*. East Lansing, Mich.: Michigan State University Office of the Registrar, 1966.
———. *Student Enrollment*. East Lansing, Mich.: Michigan State University Office of the Registrar, 1950–1970.
Pennsylvania State University Office of the Vice President for Research. *Sponsored Research, Fiscal Year 1961–1962*. University Park, Penn.: Pennsylvania State University, 1962.
United States Congress. Committee on Internal Security. *Investigation of Students for a Democratic Society, Part 2, Kent State University*. Washington, D.C.: U.S. Government Printing Office, 1969.
———. House Committee on Un-American Activities. *Investigation of Communist Activities in the Buffalo, New York Area, Part 1*. Washington, D.C.: U.S. Government Printing Office, 1957.
United States President. (Scranton) Commission on Campus Unrest. *Report*. Washington, D.C.: U.S. Government Printing Office, 1970.

Newspapers
Boston *Resistance*
Buffalo *Column Left, March!*
Buffalo *Courier-Express*
Buffalo *Evening News*
Buffalo *Griffin*
Buffalo *Insighter*
Buffalo *Liberated Community News*
Buffalo *Marijuana Review*
Buffalo *Spectrum*
Buffalo *Undercurrent*
Chicago *New Left Notes*
Chicago *New University Conference Newsletter*
Cleveland *Big US*
Des Moines *Register*
Detroit *Free Press*

East Lansing *Bogue Street Bridge*
East Lansing *Paper, The*
East Lansing *State News*
East Lansing *Towne-Courier Enterprise*
Kent *Daily Kent Stater*
Kent *Maggie's Farm*
Kent *Stump City*
Lansing *State Journal*
New York *Times*
Pittsburgh *Press*
Ravena, Ohio, *Record-Courier*
State College *Daily Collegian*
State College *Freedom!*
State College *Henderson Station*
State College *Southpaw*
State College *Student Conservative*
State College *Water Tunnel*
Washington, D.C. *Liberation News Service*
Washington, D.C. *McCarthy Advance*
Washington Post
Washington, D.C. *Student Mobilizer*

Books
Adams, Walter. *The Test*. New York: Macmillan, 1971.
Bennis, Warren. *The Leaning Ivory Tower*. San Francisco: Jossey-Bass, 1973.
Besag, Frank, and Philip Cook. *The Anatomy of a Riot: Buffalo, 1967*. Buffalo, New
    York: University Press at Buffalo, 1970.
Casale, Ottavio, and Louis Paskoff, eds. *The Kent Affair: Documents and Interpreta-
    tions*. Boston: Houghton Mifflin, 1971.
Clark, Shirley M., and John P. Clark, eds. *Youth in Modern Society*. New York: Holt,
    Rinehart and Winston, 1972.
Collier, Peter, and David Horowitz. *Destructive Generation: Second Thoughts about
    the Sixties*. New York: Summit Books, 1990.
Divale, William Tulio. *I Lived Inside the Campus Revolution*. New York: Cowles,
    1970.
The Dodger '65. Ft. Dodge, Iowa: n.p., 1965.
Donoghue, John D. *Cam An: A Fishing Village in Central Vietnam*. East Lansing,
    Mich.: Michigan State University Advisory Group, 1960.
Fiedler, Leslie. *Being Busted*. New York: Stein and Day, 1969.
Furnas, Sparkle Moore. *Memorial Biographical Record of Clifford C. Furnas*, 2 vols.
    n.p.: privately printed, 1975.
Grathwohl, Larry. *Bringing Down America: An FBI Informer with the Weathermen*.
    New Rochelle, New York: Arlington House, 1976.
Hannah, John A. *Memoirs*. East Lansing, Mich.: Michigan State University Press,
    1980.
Hayden, Tom. *Reunion: A Memoir*. New York: Random House, 1988.
Hurwitz, Ken. *Marching Nowhere*. New York: W. W. Norton, 1971.

Jacobs, Paul, and Saul Landau. *The New Radicals: A Report with Documents.* New York: Vintage Books, 1966.

Jondahl, Lynn. *Unrest on Campus: A Christian Perspective.* New York: Friendship Press, 1970.

Keniston, Kenneth. *The Uncommitted: Alienated Youth in American Society.* New York: Dell, 1965.

————. *Young Radicals: Notes on Committed Youth.* New York: Harcourt, Brace & World, 1968.

————. *Youth and Dissent.* New York: Harcourt, Brace, Jovanovich, 1971.

Kerr, Clark. *The Uses of the University.* Cambridge, Mass.: Harvard University Press, 1963.

Luce, Phillip Abbott. *The New Left Today: America's Trojan Horse.* Washington, D.C.: The Capitol Hill Press, 1971.

Lukas, J. Anthony. *Don't Shoot—We Are Your Children!* New York: Dell, 1971.

Lynd, Staughton, and Tom Hayden. *The Other Side.* New York: The New American Library, 1967.

Meyerson, Martin. *The City and the University.* New York: St. Martin's Press, 1969.

Miles, Michael. *The Radical Probe: The Logic of Student Rebellion.* New York: Atheneum, 1971.

Morrison, Joan, and Robert K. Morrison, eds. *From Camelot to Kent State: The Sixties Experience in the Words of Those Who Lived It.* New York: New York Times Books, 1987.

1964 Ft. Dodge, Iowa, City Directory. Ft. Dodge, Iowa: n.p., 1964.

Oglesby, Carl, and Richard Shaull. *Containment and Change.* New York: Macmillan, 1967.

Packard, Vance. *The Status Seekers: An Exploration of Class Behavior in America and the Hidden Barriers that Affect You, Your Community, Your Future.* New York: David McKay, 1959.

Peck, Abe. *Uncovering the Sixties: The Life and Times of the Underground Press.* New York: Pantheon Books, 1985.

Powers, Thomas. *Diana: The Making of a Terrorist.* Boston: Houghton Mifflin, 1971.

Scigliano, Robert, and Guy Fox. *Technical Assistance in Vietnam: The MSU Experience.* New York: Praeger, 1965.

Skolnick, Jerome H. *The Politics of Protest.* New York: Ballantine Books, 1970.

Stockman, David A. *The Triumph of Politics: Why the Reagan Revolution Failed.* New York: Harper and Row Publishers, 1986.

Strickland, Stephen, ed. *Sponsored Research in American Universities and Colleges, 1967.* Washington, D.C.: American Council on Education, 1967.

Walker, Eric, and Buckminster Fuller. *Approaching the Benign Environment.* New York: Macmillan, 1970.

Articles

Dante, Harris. "The Kent State Tragedy: Lessons for Teachers." *Social Education* 35 (April 1971): 357–61.

Donner, Frank. "Spies on Campus," *Playboy* (15 March 1968): 108, 115, 144–45, 147–50.

Fishel, Wesley R. "Vietnam's Democratic One-Man Rule," *New Leader* 42 (2 November 1959): 10–13.

Garskoff, Bertram E. "Who Says the Curriculum Is Irrelevant! ROTC and the University," *New University Conference Newsletter*, November 1968.

Glazer, Nathan. "The New Left and the Jews," *Jewish Journal of Sociology* 11 (December 1969): 121–32.

Hinckle, Warren, Robert Scheer, and Sol Stern. "The University on the Make," *Ramparts* 4 (April 1966): 54–57.

Jaffe, Adrian, and Milton C. Taylor. "A Crumbling Bastion: Flattery and Lies Won't Save Vietnam," *New Republic* 144 (16 June 1961): 17–20.

———. "The Professor-Diplomat: Ann Arbor and Cambridge Were Never Like This," *New Republic* 146 (5 March 1962): 28–30.

Lewis, Jerry M., and Raymond J. Adamek. "Anti-ROTC Sit-in: A Sociological Analysis," *Sociological Quarterly* 15 (Autumn 1974): 542–47.

Lipset, Seymour Martin, and Everett C. Ladd, Jr. "The Politics of American Sociologists," *American Journal of Sociology* 78 (July 1972): 67–104.

Nelson, J. Robert. "Vietnam Summer," *Christian Century* 84 (24 May 1967): 678–79.

Powell, Elwin H. "Promoting the Decline of the Rising State: Documents of Resistance and Renewal from the Alternative Community, Buffalo, 1965–1976," *Catalyst* 9 (1977): 59–98.

Ridgeway, James. "Patriots on the Campus," *New Republic* 156 (25 March 1967): 12–13.

Smith, Tim, and Scott L. Bills. "My Perspective is Socialism: An Interview with Clara Jackson about the Life and Political Perspective of Sidney Jackson," *Left Review* 4 (Fall 1979): 1–7.

Solomon, Barbara Probst. "Life in the Yellow Submarine: Buffalo's SUNY," *Harpers* 237 (October 1968): 96–102.

"Themis: DoD Plan to Spread the Wealth Raises Questions in Academe," *Science* 155 (3 February 1967): 584.

Westby, David L., and Richard G. Braungart. "Class and Politics in the Family Backgrounds of Student Political Activists," *American Sociological Review* 31 (October 1966): 690–692.

Yankelovitch, Daniel. "What They Believe," *Fortune* 80 (January 1969): 70–71, 179–81.

Thesis

Epstein, David. "The Students for a Democratic Society at Michigan State University, 1968–1969: A Case Study." M.S. thesis, Michigan State University, 1970.

Secondary

Books

Ambrose, Stephen E., and Richard H. Immerman. *Milton S. Eisenhower: Educational Statesman*. Baltimore: Johns Hopkins University Press, 1983.

Baltzell, E. Digby. *The Protestant Establishment: Aristocracy and Caste in America*. New York: Vintage Books, 1964.

Bayer, Alan E. *College and University Faculty: A Statistical Description*. Washington, D.C.: Carnegie Commission on Higher Education, 1970.

Belth, Nathan C. *A Promise to Keep: A Narrative of the American Encounter with Anti-Semitism*. New York: Schocken Books, 1981.

Bills, Scott L. *Kent State, May 4: Echoes through a Decade.* Kent, Ohio: Kent State University Press, 1982.

Bloom, Allan. *The Closing of the American Mind: How Higher Education Has Failed Democracy and Impoverished the Souls of Today's Students.* New York: Simon and Schuster, 1988.

Bogue, Allan G., and Robert Taylor, eds. *The University of Wisconsin: One Hundred Twenty-Five Years.* Madison: University of Wisconsin Press, 1975.

Buchanan, Patrick J. *Right from the Beginning.* Washington, D.C.: Regnery Gateway, 1990.

Calkins, Russell W., ed. *Who's Who in American College and University Administration, 1970–1971.* New York: Cromwell-Collier Educational, 1970.

Caro, Robert A. *The Path to Power: The Years of Lyndon Johnson.* New York: Vintage Books, 1983.

Cattell, Jacques McKeen. *Directory of American Scholars: A Biographical Directory, 1957.* 3d ed. New York: R. R. Bowker, 1957.

Cattell, Jacques McKeen, et al., eds. *Leaders in Education: A Biographical Directory, 1941,* 2d ed. New York: The SciencePress, 1941.

Cattell, Jacques McKeen, and E. E. Ross, eds. *Leaders in Education: A Biographical Directory, 1948,* 3d ed. Lancaster, Penn.: The Science Press, 1948.

Caute, David. *The Year of the Barricades: A Journey through 1968.* New York: Harper and Row, 1988.

Cook, Robert C., ed. *Presidents and Deans of American Colleges and Universities, 1964–1965.* Nashville, Tenn.: Who's Who in American Education, 1964.

———. *Presidents and Professors in American Colleges and Universities, 1935–1936.* New York: Robert C. Cook, 1935.

———. *Presidents of American Colleges and Universities, 1933–1934.* New York: Robert C. Cook, 1933.

———. *Presidents of American Colleges and Universities, 1952–1953,* 2d ed. Nashville, Tenn.: Who's Who in American Education, 1952.

———. *Who's Who in American Education: An Illustrated Biographical Directory of Eminent Living Educators of the United States and Canada, 1965–1966,* 22d ed. Nashville, Tenn.: Who's Who in American Education, 1966.

———. *Who's Who in American Education, 1967–1968,* 23d ed. Hattiesburg, Miss.: Who's Who in American Education, 1968.

DeBenedetti, Charles, and Charles Chatfield. *An American Ordeal: The Anti-War Movement of the Vietnam Era.* Syracuse: Syracuse University Press, 1990.

D'Souza, Dinesh. *Illiberal Education: The Politics of Race and Sex on Campus.* New York: Free Press, 1991.

Eszterhas, Joe, and Michael D. Roberts. *13 Seconds: Confrontation at Kent State.* New York: College Notes and Texts, 1970.

Evans, Sara. *Personal Politics: The Roots of Women's Liberation in the Civil Rights Movement and the New Left.* New York: Alfred A. Knopf, 1970.

Farber, David. *Chicago, '68.* Chicago: University of Chicago Press, 1988.

Flynn, George Q. *Roosevelt and Romanism: Catholics and American Diplomacy, 1937–1945.* Westport, Conn.: Greenwood Press, 1976.

Fussell, Paul. *Class.* New York: Ballantine Books, 1990.

Gans, Herbert J. *Deciding What's News: A Study of CBS Evening News, NBC Nightly News, Newsweek and Time.* New York: Vintage Books, 1980.

Geiger, Robert L. *To Advance Knowledge: The Growth of American Research Universities, 1900–1940.* New York: Oxford University Press, 1986.

Gerber, David A., ed. *Anti-Semitism in American History.* Urbana: University of Illinois Press, 1987.

Gitlin, Todd. *The Sixties: Years of Hope, Days of Rage.* New York: Bantam, 1989.

———. *The Whole World Is Watching: Mass Media in the Making and Unmaking of the New Left.* Berkeley: University of California Press, 1980.

Goodman, Walter. *The Committee: The Extraordinary Career of the House Committee on Un-American Activities.* Baltimore: Pelican Books, 1969.

Gutman, Allen. *The Wound in the Heart: America and the Spanish Civil War.* New York: Free Press of Glencoe, 1962.

Hanks, Patrick, and Flavia Hodges. *A Dictionary of Surnames.* New York: Oxford University Press, 1988.

Harris, Seymour E. *A Statistical Portrait of Higher Education.* New York: McGraw-Hill, 1972.

Heirich, Max. *Spiral of Conflict: Berkeley, 1964.* New York: Columbia University Press, 1971.

Higham, John. *Strangers in the Land: Patterns of American Nativism, 1860–1925.* New York: Atheneum, 1978.

Hodgson, Godfrey. *America in Our Time: From World War II to Nixon, What Happened and Why.* New York: Vintage Books, 1978.

Jencks, Christopher, and David Riesman. *The Academic Revolution.* New York: Anchor Books, 1969.

Kagonoff, Benzion C. *A Dictionary of Jewish Names and Their History.* New York: Schocken Books, 1977.

Klehr, Harvey. *The Heyday of American Communism: The Depression Decade.* New York: Basic Books, 1984.

Kohn, Stephen M. *Jailed for Peace: The History of American Draft Law Violators, 1658–1985.* New York: Praeger, 1987.

Ladd, Everett Carll, Jr. *Where Have All the Voters Gone? The Fracturing of America's Political Parties.* New York: W. W. Norton, 1978.

Lasch, Christopher. *The Agony of the American Left.* New York: Vintage Books, 1969.

———. *The Culture of Narcissism: American Life in an Age of Diminishing Expectations.* New York: Warner Books, 1979.

Leaders in Education, 1970–1971, 4th ed. New York: Jaacques Cattell Press and R. R. Bowker, 1971.

Leuchtenberg, William E. *Franklin D. Roosevelt and the New Deal, 1932–1940.* New York: Harper and Row, 1963.

Lewis, Lionel S. *Cold War on Campus: A Study of the Politics of Organizational Control.* New Brunswick, N.J.: Transaction Books, 1988.

Lichter, S. Robert, Stanley Rothman, and Linda S. Lichter. *The Media Elite: America's New Power Brokers.* Bethesda, Md.: Adler and Adler, 1986.

Lipset, Seymour Martin. *Rebellion in the University.* Boston: Little, Brown, 1972.

Lubell, Samuel. *The Hidden Crisis in American Politics.* New York: W. W. Norton, 1971.

Mansbridge, Jane J. *Why We Lost the ERA.* Chicago: University of Chicago Press, 1986.

Marchetti, Victor, and John D. Marks. *The CIA and the Cult of Intelligence*. New York: Dell, 1975.

Michener, James A. *Kent State: What Happened and Why*. New York: Ballantine Books, 1971.

Miles, Michael W. *The Odyssey of the American Right*. New York: Oxford University Press, 1980.

Miller, James. *"Democracy Is in the Streets": From Port Huron to the Siege of Chicago*. New York: Simon and Schuster, 1987.

Novak, Michael. *The Rise of the Unmeltable Ethnics: Politics and Culture in the Seventies*. New York: Macmillan, 1972.

Oppenheimer, Martin J., ed. *The American Military*. New York: Aldine, 1971.

Peck, Abe. *Uncovering the Sixties: The Life and Times of the Underground Press*. New York: Pantheon Books, 1985.

Phillips, Donald E. *Student Protest: An Analysis of the Issues and Speeches*. New York: University Press of America, 1985.

Phillips, Kevin P. *The Emerging Republican Majority*. New Rochelle, N.Y.: Arlington House, 1970.

Polenberg, Richard. *One Nation Divisible: Class, Race, and Ethnicity in the United States since 1938*. New York: Penguin Books, 1981.

Ridgeway, James. *The Closed Corporation: American Universities in Crisis*. New York: Random House, 1968.

Rorabaugh, W. J. *Berkeley at War: The 1960s*. New York: Oxford University Press, 1989.

Rothman, Stanley, and S. Robert Lichter. *Roots of Radicalism: Jews, Christians and the New Left*. New York: Oxford University Press, 1982.

Rudolph, Frederick. *The American College & University: A History*. Athens: University of Georgia Press, 1990.

Sale, Kirkpatrick. *SDS*. New York: Random House, 1973.

Schrecker, Ellen W. *No Ivory Tower: McCarthyism and the Universities*. New York: Oxford University Press, 1986.

Selcraig, James T. *The Red Scare in the Midwest, 1945–1955: A State and Local Study*. Ann Arbor: University of Michigan Press, 1982.

Sennett, Richard, and Jonathan Cobb. *The Hidden Injuries of Class*. New York: Vintage Books, 1973.

Unger, Irwin. *The Movement: A History of the American New Left, 1959–1972*. New York: Harper and Row, 1974.

Vickers, George R. *The Formation of the New Left: The Early Years*. Lexington, Mass.: D. C. Heath, 1975.

Viorst, Milton. *Fire in the Streets: America in the 1960s*. New York: Simon and Schuster, 1979.

Weed, Perry L. *The White Ethnic Movement and Ethnic Politics*. New York: Praeger, 1973.

Who's Who in America, 1932–1933, vol 17. Chicago: Marquis Who's Who, 1932.

Who's Who in America, 1952–1953, vol 27. Chicago: Marquis Who's Who, 1952.

Who's Who in America, 1966–1967, vol. 34. Chicago: Marquis Who's Who, 1966.

Who's Who in America, 1972–1973, vol. 37. Chicago: Marquis Who's Who, 1972.

Who's Who in America, 1973–1974, vol. 38. Chicago: Marquis Who's Who, 1973.

Wittner, Lawrence. *Cold War America: From Hiroshima to Watergate*. New York: Praeger, 1974.

Yarmolinsky, Adam. *The Military Establishment: Its Impact on American Society.* New York: Harper and Row, 1971.

Zaroulis, Nancy, and Gerald Sullivan. *Who Spoke Up? American Protest against the War in Vietnam, 1963–1975.* New York: Doubleday, 1984.

Articles

Draper, Theodore. "The Class Struggle: The Myth of the Communist Professors," *New Republic* 196 (26 January 1987): 29–36.

Ellis, Donna Lloyd. "The Underground Press in America: 1955–1970," *Journal of Popular Culture* 5 (Summer 1971): 102–24.

Glazer, Nathan. "The Professors and the Party," *New Republic* 195 (6 October 1986): 39–42.

"Harvard Underwater Sound Laboratory," *Noise Level* 1 (July 1981): 1–2.

Levy, Sheldon G. "Polarization in Racial Attitudes," *Public Opinion Quarterly* 36 (Summer 1972): 221–34.

Peterson, Patti McGill. "Student Organizations and the Anti-War Movement in America, 1900–1960," *American Studies Quarterly* 13 (Spring 1972): 131–48.

Ransford, H. Edward. "Blue Collar Anger: Reactions to Student and Black Protest," *American Sociological Review* 27 (June 1972): 333–46.

Ross, J. Michael, Reeve D. Vanneman, and Thomas F. Pettigrew. "Patterns of Support for George Wallace: Implications for Racial Change," *Journal of Social Issues* 36 (Spring 1976): 69–91.

Treaster, W. Lowell. "MSU's Fabulous Centennial Revisited," *MSU Alumni Magazine* 3 (Fall 1983): 13.

Films

Green, Ricki, and David Hoffman, Producers. "Making Sense of the Sixties." WETA-TV Washington, D.C., and Varied Directions International, 1990.

Index